The Media & COMMUNICATIONS IN AUSTRALIA

4TH EDITION

The Media & COMMUNICATIONS IN AUSTRALIA

Stuart Cunningham &
EDITED BY *Sue Turnbull*

ALLEN&UNWIN

Allen & Unwin
83 Alexander Street
Crows Nest NSW 2065
Australia
Phone: (61 2) 8425 0100
Email: info@allenandunwin.com
Web: www.allenandunwin.com

Cataloguing-in-Publication details are available
from the National Library of Australia
www.trove.nla.gov.au

ISBN 978 1 74331 163 9

Photographs by Mia Mala McDonald
Chapter 4 photograph by Amanda Rose
Chapter 22 photograph by Alan Lesheim Photography
Typeset in 11/14.5pt ITC Legacy Serif by Post Pre-press Group
Printed by Phoenix Print Media, Singapore

10 9 8 7 6 5 4 3 2 1

Contents

Tables and figures   vii

Abbreviations and acronyms   viii

About the authors   xiv

Preface   xx

INTRODUCTION: The media and communications today *Stuart Cunningham and Sue Turnbull*   1

PART I: APPROACHES

1   The media and communications: Theoretical traditions *John Sinclair*   15

2   Textual analysis *Alan McKee*   31

3   Representation *Kate Bowles*   43

4   Imagining the audience *Sue Turnbull*   59

5   Policy and regulation *Stuart Cunningham*   73

PART II: INDUSTRIES

6   The press *Rodney Tiffen*   95

7   Telecommunications *Jock Given*   111

8   Radio *Bridget Griffen-Foley*   133

9   Film, video, DVD and online delivery *Deb Verhoeven*   151

10   Television *Stephen Harrington*   173

11   Magazines *Frances Bonner*   193

12   Advertising and marketing *John Sinclair*   209

13   Popular music *Shane Homan*   227

14   The internet, online and mobile communication *Gerard Goggin*   247

15   Games: Mobile, locative and social *Larissa Hjorth*   269

PART III: ISSUES

16   Social media *Jean Burgess and John Banks*   285

17   Social selves *Rowan Wilken and Anthony McCosker*   291

18   'White bread' media *Tanja Dreher*   297

19   Celebrity culture *Graeme Turner*   303

20   The ethics of privacy *Kate Bowles*   309

21   Sports media *David Rowe*   315

22   Media and the environment *Libby Lester*   321

23   Public service broadcasting *Maureen Burns*   327

24   Classification and regulation *Terry Flew*   333

25   The apps industry *Ben Goldsmith*   339

26   Media ethics *Catharine Lumby*   345

27   Crisis communication *Axel Bruns*   351

References   356

Index   389

Tables and figures

TABLES

6.1 Metropolitan and national daily newspaper circulations, 1992–2011   98
7.1 Selected Asia-Pacific telcos, market capitalisation at 14 February 2013   118
7.2 Australian telecoms subscriber numbers, June 2012   123
9.1 Key industry data, 2008–12   154
9.2 Feature film industry summary   155
9.3 Two discourses of Australian film   161
9.4 Digital screens, Australia   167
9.5 Wholesale DVD sales   168
9.6 DVD rental statistics   169
9.7 Comparison of Australian online content devices and usage   169
11.1 Magazine circulations, 1 January 2012 to 30 June 2012   195
11.2 Magazine readership, June 2012   196
12.1 Top 25 advertisers   215
12.2 Top 20 advertising agencies   221
14.1 Top ten online brands, July 2012   258

FIGURES

4.1 The produser   61
4.2 Relationship between research methods and audiences   70
7.1 Australian telecoms market shares, 2003–13   116
7.2 Telstra share price, 1997–2013   117
7.3 Communication service most used, Australia, May 2012, percentage of people with a fixed-line and/or mobile phone   120
7.4 Australian telecoms market, 2001–13   121
9.1 Screen project pledges to pozible.com   160

Abbreviations and acronyms

AANA	Australian Association of National Advertisers
AAP	Australian Associated Press
AARNET	Australian Academic Research Network
ABA	Australian Broadcasting Authority
ABAF	Australian Business Arts Foundation
ABC	Audit Bureau of Circulation
ABC	Australian Broadcasting Corporation (previously Commission)
ABCB	Australian Broadcasting Control Board
ABS	Australian Bureau of Statistics
ABT	Australian Broadcasting Tribunal
ACA	Australian Consumers' Association
ACC	Australian Copyright Council
ACCAN	Australian Communications Consumer Action Network
ACCC	Australian Competition and Consumer Commission
ACMA	Australian Communications and Media Authority
ACP	Australian Consolidated Press
ACTF	Australian Children's Television Foundation
ACTU	Australian Council of Trade Unions
ADB	Anti-Discrimination Board (New South Wales)
ADSL	asymmetrical digital subscriber line
AFA	Advertising Federation of Australia
AFACT	Australian Federation Against Copyright Theft
AFC	Australian Film Commission
AFDC	Australian Film Development Corporation
AFI	Australian Film Institute
AFTRS	Australian Film, Television and Radio School

AHA	Australian Hotels Association
AI	artificial intelligence
AIIA	Australian Information Industry Association
AIM	Australian information media
AIMIA	Australian Interactive Multimedia Industry Association
AIRLA	Australian Independent Record Labels Association
AJA	Australian Journalists' Association
ALP	Australian Labor Party
ALRC	Australian Law Reform Commission
AM	amplitude modulation
AMCOS	Australasian Mechanical Copyright Owners' Society
AMPAL	Australian Music Publishers' Association Limited
AMTA	Australian Mobile Telecommunications Association
ANT	actor network theory
ANZCA	Australia and New Zealand Communication Association
AOL	America On Line
AOTC	Australian and Overseas Telecommunications Corporation
APA	American Psychological Association
APC	Australian Press Council
APEC	Asia-Pacific Economic Cooperation
APRA	Australasian Performing Right Association
ARA	Australian Recording Association
ARC	Australian Research Council
ARC CoE	Australian Research Council Centre of Excellence
ARIA	Australian Record Industry Association
ARL	Australian Rugby League
ARN	Australian Radio Network
ARPA	Advanced Research Project Agency
ARPU	average revenue and price per user
ARPANET	Advanced Research Project Agency Network
ASC	Australian Sports Commission
ASEAN	Association of South-East Asian Nations
ASTRA	Australian Subscription Television and Radio Association
ASX	Australian Stock Exchange
ATR	advanced television research
AT&T	American Telephone and Telegraph
auDa.au	Domain Administration Ltd
AUSFTA	Australia–United States Free Trade Agreement

AWA	Amalgamated Wireless Company of Australia
AWW	*Australian Women's Weekly*
BBC	British Broadcasting Corporation
BBS	bulletin board services
BMG	Bertlesmann Music Group
BRACS	Broadcasting for Remote Aboriginal Communities Scheme
BSA	*Broadcasting Services Act 1992*
BSEG	Broadband Services Expert Group
BTCE	Bureau of Transport and Communications Economics
CAD	computer-aided design
CAAMA	Central Australian Aboriginal Media Association
CBAA	Community Broadcasting Association of Australia
CBF	Community Broadcasting Foundation
CCCS	Centre for Contemporary Cultural Studies
CD	compact disc
CDMA	code division multiple access
CD-ROM	compact disc read-only memory
CE-HTML	consumer electronics hypertext markup language
CER	closer economic relations
CGI	computer-generated imagery
CLC	Communications Law Centre
CNN	Cable News Network
CRA	Commercial Radio Australia
CSE	content service enterprise
CSIRO	Commonwealth Scientific and Industrial Research Organisation
CTN	Consumers' Telecommunications Network
DAB	Digital Audio Broadcasting
DARPA	Defence Department's Advanced Research Projects Agency
DBCDE	Department of Broadband, Communications and the Digital Economy
DCITA	Department of Communications, Information Technology and the Arts
DIY	do-it-yourself
DOTAC	Department of Transport and Communications
DPP	Director of Public Prosecutions
DSB	digital sound broadcasting
DV	digital video
DVB-T	digital video broadcasting—terrestrial

DVD	digital video disc
EFTF	Experimental Film and Television Fund
EPL	England Premier League
ESA	Entertainment Software Association
EU	European Union
EULA	end-user licence agreement
FACTS	Federation of Australian Commercial Television Stations
FARB	Federation of Australian Radio Broadcasters
FCC	Federal Communications Commission (US)
FFC	Film Finance Corporation
FLICS	film licensed investment companies
FM	frequency modulation
FMCG	fast-moving consumer goods
FPC	Federal Publishing Company
FTA	free trade agreement
FTTH/FTTP	fibre to the home/premises
FTTN/FTTC	fibre to the node/curb
GATS	General Agreement on Trade in Services
GATT	General Agreement on Tariffs and Trade
GFC	Global Financial Crisis
GIS	geographic information system
GPS	Global Positioning System
GSM	global system for mobiles (European standard)
GST	goods and services tax
HbbTV	hybrid broadcast broadband TV
HBO	Home Box Office
HDTV	high-definition television
HFC	hybrid fibre-coaxial
HREOC	Human Rights and Equal Opportunity Commission
HTML	hypertext markup language
ICANN	Internet Corporation for Assigned Names and Numbers
IEAA	Interactive Entertainment Association of Australia
IFPI	International Federation of the Phonographic Industry
IGDA	International Game Developers Association
IIA	Internet Industry Association
IM	instant messaging
IRC	internet relay chat
ISOC	Internet Society of Australia

ISP   internet service provider
ITN   independent television network
ITU   International Telecommunications Union
iTV   interactive TV
LBS   location-based service
LTE   long-term evolution (services)
MCA   Media Council of Australia
MDS   multi-point distribution system
MEAA   Media Entertainment and Arts Alliance
MEAP   mobile enterprise application platform
MERCOSUR   South American group of Brazil, Argentina, Paraguay and Uruguay
MIA   Media International Australia
MMOG   massively multi-player online game
MMORPG   massively multi-player online role-playing game
MMS   multimedia messaging services
MPA   Magazine Publishers of Australia
MPDAA   Motion Pictures Distributors' Association of Australia
MTV   Music Television
MUD   multi-user dungeon
MOO   MUDs object-oriented
NAFTA   North American Free Trade Agreement
NES   Nintendo Entertainment System
NBN   National Broadband Network
NGO   non-government organisation
NIMAA   National Indigenous Media Association of Australia
NIM   newspaper-inserted magazine
NIRS   National Indigenous Radio Service
NREN   National Research and Education Network
NRP   National Radio Plan
OECD   Organization for Economic Cooperation and Development
OIPC   Office of the Australian Information Commissioner
OTC   Overseas Telecommunications Commission
p2p   peer to peer
PBL   Publishing and Broadcasting Limited
PBS   Public Broadcasting Service
PDV   post-production digital and video
POTS   plain old telephone system
PPCA   Phonographic Performance Company of Australia

PRIA	Public Relations Institute of Australia
PSA	Prices Surveillance Authority
PSP	Playstation Portable (Sony)
PSX	Playstation X
RCIADIC	Royal Commission into Aboriginal Deaths in Custody
RIAA	Recording Industry Association of America
RSS	really simple syndication
SBS	Special Broadcasting Service
SCOT	social construction of technology
SDTV	standard definition television
SLAM	Save Live Australian Music
SMS	short message service
SST	social shaping of technology
STS	science and technology studies
TCP/IP	transmission control protocol/internet protocol
TIO	Telecommunications Industry Ombudsman
TOS	terms of service
TMRC	Tech Model Railway Club
TPC	Trade Practices Commission
TPG	Total Peripherals Group
TVC	television commercial
UCC	user-created content
UHF	ultra-high frequency
UNSW	University of New South Wales
USO	universal service obligation
VCR	video cassette recorder
VCS	video computer system
VES	video entertainment system
VHA	Vodafone Hutchison Australia
VHF	very-high frequency
VIDA	Video Industry Distributors of Australia
VOIP	voice over internet protocol
VPN	virtual private network
VRF	Victoria Rock Foundation
WAP	wireless access protocol
WIPO	World Intellectual Property Organisation
WoW	World of Warcraft
WTO	World Trade Organization

About the authors

JOHN BANKS is a Senior Lecturer, Head of Postgraduate Coursework Studies and researcher in the Creative Industries Faculty, Queensland University of Technology. He researches and publishes on co-creativity, innovation and social media in the creative industries, especially video games and interactive entertainment. He has a special interest in organisational and workplace culture. His past decade of research on the topic of co-creativity in the video games industry culminated in the recently published book *Co-creating Videogames* (2013). Recent publications include *Key Concepts in Creative Industries* (with John Hartley, Jason Potts, Stuart Cunningham, Terry Flew and Michael Keane, 2013).

FRANCES BONNER is a Reader in Television and Popular Culture in the School of English, Media Studies and Art History at the University of Queensland. She is the author of *Personality Presenters: Television's Intermediaries with Viewers* (2011), *Ordinary Television* (2003) and a co-author (with Graeme Turner and P. David Marshall) of *Fame Games: The Production of Celebrity in Australia* (2000). Her research interests are in non-fiction television, its programs, presenters and formats, magazines and celebrity.

KATE BOWLES researches and teaches the social history of Australian cinema attendance and public space media practices at the University of Wollongong. She is part of a long-running ARC-funded research team investigating the history of cinema distribution and exhibition in Australia, currently led by Professor Deb Verhoeven, and co-teaches an annual online undergraduate seminar class in the US reception of Australian film and television content with Professor Janna Jones at Northern Arizona University. She is also the Head of Learning Design at the University of Wollongong.

AXEL BRUNS is an Associate Professor in the Creative Industries Faculty at Queensland University of Technology and a Chief Investigator in the ARC Centre of Excellence for Creative Industries and Innovation. He is the author of *Blogs, Wikipedia, Second Life and*

Beyond: From Production to Produsage (2008) and *Gatewatching: Collaborative Online News Production* (2005), and a co-editor of *Twitter and Society* (2013), *A Companion to New Media Dynamics* (2012) and *Uses of Blogs* (2006). Axel is an expert on the impact of user-led content creation, or produsage, and his current work focuses on the study of user participation in social media spaces such as Twitter, especially in the context of acute events. His research blog is at <http://snurb.info> and he tweets at @snurb_dot_info. See <http://mappingonlinepublics.net> for more details of his current social media research.

JEAN BURGESS is Associate Professor of Digital Media Studies and Deputy Director of the ARC Centre of Excellence for Creative Industries and Innovation at Queensland University of Technology, where her research focuses on the uses, politics and methodological implications of social and mobile media platforms. Her books are *YouTube: Online Video and Participatory Culture*; *Studying Mobile Media*; *A Companion to New Media Dynamics*; and *Twitter and Society*. She tweets at @jeanburgess.

MAUREEN BURNS is a Lecturer in Cultural and Media Studies at the University of Queensland. Her interests are in public service broadcasting in a globalised media environment and online services. Publications include *ABC Online: Becoming the ABC* (2008) and many articles on public service broadcasting.

STUART CUNNINGHAM is Distinguished Professor of Media and Communications, Queensland University of Technology and Director of the Australian Research Council Centre of Excellence for Creative Industries and Innovation. His most recent books are *Digital Disruption: Cinema Moves Online* (edited with Dina Iordanova, 2012), *Key Concepts in Creative Industries* (with John Hartley, Jason Potts, Terry Flew, John Banks and Michael Keane, 2013), *Hidden Innovation: Policy, Industry and the Creative Sector* (2013) and *Screen Distribution and the New King Kongs of the Online World* (with Jon Silver, 2013).

TANJA DREHER is a Lecturer in Media and Communications, specialising in international communications, and media and multiculturalism. Her research focuses on the politics of listening in the context of media and multiculturalism, Indigenous sovereignties and feminisms and anti-racism. She is a co-convenor of The Listening Project, exploring the practices, technologies and politics of listening as political practice. Her previous research has focused on news and cultural diversity, community media interventions, experiences of racism and the development of community anti-racism strategies after September 11, 2001.

TERRY FLEW is Professor of Media and Communication at Queensland University of Technology. He is the author of *Global Creative Industries* (2013), *The Creative Industries, Culture and Policy* (2012), *Understanding Global Media* (2007) and *New Media: An Introduction* (4th edition to be published in 2014). He is a co-author of *Key Concepts in Creative Industries* (2013) and editor of *Creative Industries and Urban Development: Creative Cities in the 21st Century* (2012). During 2011–12, he was a Lead Commissioner with the Australian Law Reform Commission, heading the National Classification Scheme Review.

JOCK GIVEN is Professor of Media and Communications at Swinburne University's Institute for Social Research. He was previously Director of the Communications Law Centre and Policy Adviser at the Australian Film Commission.

GERARD GOGGIN is Professor and Chair of the Media and Communications Department at the University of Sydney. His books include *Internationalizing Internet Studies* (with Mark McLelland, 2009), *Mobile Technologies: From Telecommunications to Media* (with Larissa Hjorth, 2009) and *Cell Phone Culture* (2006). He currently leads an ARC research project on Internet History in Australia and the Asia-Pacific, 2010–13.

BEN GOLDSMITH is Senior Research Fellow in the ARC Centre of Excellence for Creative Industries and Innovation. His current research interests include the apps development industry in Australia, the digital creative workforce, media policy and Australian film and television.

BRIDGET GRIFFEN-FOLEY is an ARC Queen Elizabeth II Fellow, Professor of Modern History and the Director of the Centre for Media History at Macquarie University. Now editing *A Companion to the Australian Media* (forthcoming 2014), she is the author of *Changing Stations: The Story of Australian Commercial Radio* (2009). Her other publications include *The House of Packer: The Making of a Media Empire* (1999; e-book 2012), *Sir Frank Packer* (2000) and *Party Games: Australian Politicians and the Media from War to Dismissal* (2003).

STEPHEN HARRINGTON is a Senior Lecturer in Journalism, Media and Communication at Queensland University of Technology. He is the author of *Australian TV News: New Forms, Functions and Futures* (2013), as well as a number of journal articles and book chapters that examine the socio-political value of entertainment and the changing nature of contemporary journalism.

LARISSA HJORTH is an artist, digital ethnographer and Associate Professor in the Games Program at RMIT University, and co-director of RMIT's Digital Ethnography Research Centre (DERC). Since 2000, Hjorth has been researching the gendered and socio-cultural dimensions of mobile, social, locative and gaming cultures in the Asia-Pacific—these studies are outlined in her books, *Mobile Media in the Asia-Pacific* (2009), *Games & Gaming* (2010), *Online@AsiaPacific: Mobile, Social and Locative in the Asia–Pacific region* (with Michael Arnold, 2013) and *Understanding Social Media* (with Sam Hinton, 2013).

SHANE HOMAN is Associate Professor and Head of Communications and Media at Monash University. His most recent books include *Sounds of Then, Sounds of Now: Popular Music in Australia* (co-edited with Tony Mitchell, 2008) and *Popular Music Industries and the State: Policy Notes* (with Martin Cloonan and Jen Cattermole, 2014). He has recently completed ARC Discovery Grant projects on music policy and popular music and cultural memory, and an Australia Council report on the needs of the recording sector in Australia.

LIBBY LESTER is Professor of Journalism, Media and Communications at the University of Tasmania. Her books include *Media and Environment: Conflict, Politics and the News* (2010), *Transnational Protests and the Media* (co-edited with Simon Cottle, 2011) and *Environmental Conflict and the Media* (co-edited with Brett Hutchins, 2013). Recent articles have appeared in *Media, Culture & Society*, the *International Journal of Communication*, *Journalism*, *Journalism Studies* and *Media International Australia*. She has been a Visiting Fellow at Oxford University's Reuters Institute for the Study of Journalism, and is an Associate Editor of the journal *Environmental Communication*. She worked as a newspaper journalist prior to joining the university.

CATHARINE LUMBY is Professor of Media in the Department of Media, Music, Communication and Cultural Studies at Macquarie University. She was the Director of the Journalism and Media Research at the University of New South Wales and the Foundation Chair of the Media and Communications Department at the University of Sydney. She is the author of seven books and numerous book chapters and journal articles. She sits on the Education and Welfare Committee and the Research Committee of the National Rugby League, advising them on gender issues. She is also a member of the Advertising Standards Board. She has been awarded five Australian Research Council grants.

ANTHONY MCCOSKER lectures in media and communications in the Faculty of Life and Social Sciences at Swinburne University. His research explores media affect, digital and visual cultures and social media practices and publics. He is author of the book *Intensive Media: Aversive Affect and Visual Culture* (2013), and has published a number of book chapters and articles in journals such as *Information, Communication and Society*, *Sexualities*, *Continuum* and *Transformations*.

ALAN MCKEE is an expert on media and healthy sexual development. He leads the Promoting Healthy Sexual Development research group at Queensland University of Technology and is Project Leader for the Queensland government-funded NIRAP grant Developing Improved Sexual Health Education Strategies.

DAVID ROWE is Professor of Cultural Research in the Institute for Culture and Society, University of Western Sydney. His books include *Sport, Culture and the Media: The Unruly Trinity* (2nd edn, 2004); *Global Media Sport: Flows, Forms and Futures* (2011); and *Sport Beyond Television: The Internet, Digital Media and the Rise of Networked Media Sport* (with Brett Hutchins, 2012). His latest edited works are *Sport, Public Broadcasting, and Cultural Citizenship: Signal Lost?* (with Jay Scherer, 2013) and *Digital Media Sport: Technology, Power and Culture in the Network Society* (with Brett Hutchins, 2013).

JOHN SINCLAIR is an Honorary Professorial Fellow in the School of Historical and Philosophical Studies at the University of Melbourne, researching the history of the advertising industry in Australia. His published work covers various aspects of the internationalisation of the media and communication industries, with a special emphasis on Asia and Latin America. His books include *Advertising, the Media and Globalisation: A World in Motion* (2012), *Latin American Television: A Global View* (1999) and the co-edited (with Anna Cristina Pertierra and Jason Antrosio) *Consumer Culture in Latin America* (2012). He has held visiting professorships at leading universities in Europe and the United States, is on the editorial advisory boards of various international journals and is active in professional organisations.

RODNEY TIFFEN is an Australian Emeritus Professor of Political Science in the Department of Government and International Relations at the University of Sydney. He is co-author (with Ross Gittins) of *How Australia Compares* (2004) and author of *Diplomatic Deceits: Government, Media and East Timor* (2001), *Scandals: Media, Politics and Corruption in Contemporary Australia* (1999), *News and Power* (1990), *The News from Southeast Asia: The Sociology of Newsmaking* (1978) and numerous articles on mass media and Australian politics.

SUE TURNBULL is Professor of Communication and Media Studies at the University of Wollongong. She has published broadly in the fields of media education, audience and television studies, with particular attention to comedy and crime. Recent publications include, The *Television Crime Drama* (2014) *Remembering Television* (2012) co-edited with Kate Darian-Smith and *Investigating Veronica Mars: Essays on the Teen Detective Series* (2011) co-edited with Rhonda Wilcox. Sue is editor of the journal *Media International Australia* and joint editor with Martin Barker of *Participations: The Journal of Audience and Reception Studies*.

GRAEME TURNER is Emeritus Professor in the Centre for Critical and Cultural Studies at the University of Queensland. The author of many works on the media and cultural studies, his most recent publications include (with Anna Cristina Pertierra) *Locating Television: Zones of Consumption* (2013), *What's Become of Cultural Studies?* (2012), *Ordinary People and the Media: The Demotic Turn* (2010) and (with Jinna Tay) *Television Studies After TV: Understanding Television in the Post-broadcast Era* (2009). His revised second edition of *Understanding Celebrity* will be published in 2013.

DEB VERHOEVEN is Professor and Chair in Media and Communication at Deakin University. She is Deputy Director of the Centre for Memory, Imagination and Invention and Director of the Humanities Network Infrastructure (HuNI) Project. Her current research project, Mapping the Movies: The Changing Nature of Australia's Cinema Circuits and Their Audiences, 1956–1984, is an ARC-funded project with Professor Richard Maltby, Professor Jill Julius Mathews, Associate Professor Colin Arrowsmith, Dr Michael Walsh and Dr Kate Bowles.

ROWAN WILKEN is a Senior Lecturer in Media and Communications at Swinburne University of Technology. He holds an ARC-funded research fellowship (an ARC DECRA) in the Swinburne Institute for Social Research. His present research interests include mobile and locative media, digital technologies and culture, theories and practices of everyday life, domestic technology consumption, and old and new media. He is the co-editor (with Gerard Goggin) of *Locative Media* (forthcoming) and *Mobile Technology and Place* (2012) and the author of *Teletechnologies, Place, and Community* (2011).

Preface

Understanding the media and the communications environment has never been simple, and it seems to get more complex every day. For a textbook covering this dynamic field, the task got a little more complex with the decision by co-editor Graeme Turner to step down from this edition. His work on this book, and in numerous other ways, has helped immeasurably in making media and communications studies in Australia what it is today. But the project loses nothing in momentum in replacing Graeme's editorial expertise with that of Sue Turnbull.

This is the fourth edition of *The Media and Communications in Australia*—although it is more accurate to call it the sixth edition of a book that began its life in the early 1990s as *The Media in Australia*. Every time we have brought out a new edition, we have endeavoured to ensure that we captured the fast-paced world of change that is the media in Australia.

In the intervening years since our last edition, the internet has increasingly taken centre stage as it has continued to develop as the major convergent communications platform of the future. Serious experiments in monetising online content—including paywalls for premium news content—are now in train, following on from the global success of Apple in establishing a reasonably secure micro-payment system that has begun to address the 'analogue dollars to digital cents' conundrum. While the pathway forward for entertainment media is marginally clearer, the challenge to secure a future funding base that supports quality journalism remains unresolved and urgent.

Reality television (cooking, home renovation, singing, dancing, personal health and so on) has become such a staple that it has generated concerns about the future of scripted drama, while being hailed as a more egalitarian and accessible media format. Digital television is now in full takeup mode after a slow start, and the stepped switch-off of the analogue TV signal is now happening across Australia. The large majority of households can now receive fifteen free-to-air stations (the 'Free TV' offer jointly promoted by the Australian Broadcasting Corporation (ABC), Special Broadcasting Service (SBS) and the three commercial networks) and a couple of dozen additional channels through monopoly pay TV provider Foxtel (or its regional resupplier, Austar). A good deal of this content can be consumed on mobile devices through apps. Meanwhile, digital radio struggles to gain traction.

Blogging, Twitter, Facebook and the use of mobile communications are, at least for the moment, firmly enmeshed in the everyday lives of many—particularly young—people. The increased capacity for interactivity with the current generation of hardware and software, and the development of platforms based almost solely around that capacity—particularly social networking—have given rise to talk of us entering the age of the so-called 'prosumer'. As traditional media such as newspapers and magazines find that the future for single-platform media enterprises is looking bleak, the media and communications industries increasingly are looking to mobile phones, computer games and related interactive multimedia as the key pathways to what the future holds. That said, television viewing is still increasing—even in the United States, where the challenge from the internet is perhaps the strongest. At the same time, the increasing popularity of the long-form drama series available worldwide via download or DVD is changing the ways in which people access and watch television.

All these current critical developments, along with many more, have been covered in this new edition.

It is fitting that we should thank the contributors to this edition for their cooperation and expertise. The quality of their work is a real testament to the strength of the field of media and communications studies in Australia. Elizabeth Weiss of Allen & Unwin has provided us with astute advice and editorial support during the preparation of this edition and Sue Jarvis has done a superb job of copy editing the book. Our most particular thanks, however, must go to Harvey May. He has worked tirelessly and expertly as project manager of what always is a large undertaking, and has made a major contribution to this book. Of course, we bear the editorial responsibility for the final form, and hope that our readers find it a valuable guide to their study and broader understanding of the media and communications in Australia.

Stuart Cunningham and Sue Turnbull

Introduction:

THE MEDIA AND COMMUNICATIONS TODAY

STUART CUNNINGHAM AND SUSAN TURNBULL

WHAT *ARE* THE MEDIA TODAY?

The aim of this book is to help students to understand the contemporary media and communications environment. It provides ways of thinking about a range of new platforms of delivery, modes of consumption and industrial structures, as well as about the structure and function of traditional print and broadcast media and communications. Its orientation reflects the fact that the changed nature of the media and communications environment in recent years has been so substantial as to provoke us to ask the question in our sub-heading above: what *are* the media today? Implicit in that question is the proposition that to continue to think of the media only through the traditional distinctions between electronic (television and radio) and print (newspapers and magazines) media, and between these and telecommunications (fixed and mobile phone) is no longer sufficient. The near-ubiquity of information-based systems of delivery, such as computers in the home, the introduction of digital technologies of production and distribution in broadcasting and the cinema, the globalisation of media and communications markets, the growing convergence of broadcasting, information services and telecommunications, and the challenges to established media posed by the explosion of Web 2.0 services and social media have all contributed to the formation of a highly volatile and greatly altered media landscape. What distinguishes the situation today from that of only a few years ago is that now every sector of the media is affected by these challenges and is responding to them. Much of what constitutes the so-called 'new' media and their influence is no longer new, while at the same time wholly new sectors—such as apps—have developed in the last few years. That said, it is also important to recognise that this situation is most pronounced in those countries with highly developed media systems, and that the majority of the world's population still does not have access to these new media platforms. Nonetheless, where they exist, the influence of the new media platforms has been profound.

Of course, there is still much for media and communications studies to understand about the traditional or 'old' media forms, and media history tells us that changes in technologies do not necessarily result in the displacement of an older media form by the new arrivals. Understanding what is currently happening in the media depends upon our nuanced understanding of what has happened in the past. In Australia, the cinema, the press and television continue to attract strong academic interest, but significant gaps remain in their history and analysis—as is revealed, for example, in the collection of essays on the coming of television to Australia, *Remembering Television* (Darian-Smith and Turnbull 2012). New comprehensive histories of commercial television (Nick Herd's *Networking: Commercial Television in Australia*, 2012) and commercial radio (Bridget Griffen-Foley's *Changing Stations: The Story of Australian Commercial Radio*, 2009) add greatly to the stock of media history, although advertising, popular music and mass-market magazines await their general historians. A major *Companion to the Australian Media* (edited by Bridget Griffen-Foley, to be published in 2014) promises to perform a significant reference function for our field.

Further progress is being made in many areas. The need to examine the role of marketing and public relations strategies in generating media content has recently been built into media studies. As a consequence of a broader view of the media and communications industries, scholars in the field have begun to recognise the telecommunications industry for what it patently is: a crucial component of the infrastructure of the information society. Where once telecommunications was left to the engineers and the business pages of the newspapers, while media studies people tuned to their favourite television programs, such a division of the field is no longer tenable. The extraordinary cultural and commercial impact of the mobile phone (discussed in Chapter 14) has been among the most dramatic provocations to such a view.

So, *what are the media today?* Importantly, central distinctions that once linked systems of delivery to their characteristic content (for example, the links between

TV programs and broadcast TV) are losing their clarity. We no longer have to turn on the radio to listen to programs produced by our favourite radio station—we can listen on our home computer and, much more often these days, to streamed content on our mobile phone or tablet. For household consumers, a pay TV subscription, internet access, landline and mobile phone services can all be bundled into one transaction with a telecommunications company and/or ISP. Even financially challenged students can usually afford a pre-paid mobile service that provides all-important access to the web, social media and texting. The co-founder of the World Wide Web, Tim Berners-Lee, regards access to the web as a human right and, whether or not regulators try to require what used to be called USOs (universal service obligations) from service providers, the vast majority of people find a way to stay connected. It *is* their contemporary human right.

As we download music or video from the net, it is not necessarily clear whether we are participating in the media industry, the music industry or the information technology industry—or perhaps committing a crime against international copyright regulations. At the level of content, the boundaries between formerly discrete media formats such as news, current affairs and entertainment have blurred as well. Reality TV has dissolved the boundaries between game shows, scripted soap operas and documentaries; television plays a disconcertingly direct role in the contestants' everyday lives as their participation in a televised game generates effects on their 'real lives' outside. Newer forms of media and communications—the blogosphere, the Twitterverse, massive multi-player online gaming (MMOG), and mobile entertainment and information apps—challenge media studies to come up with strategies of analysis that are able to understand the functions, uses and meanings of a vast array of media experiences.

Even the question of '*whose* media is it?' has become more difficult to answer, as content and audiences spread over national and geographic boundaries. In particular, the globalisation of the major international media conglomerates makes the question of what constitutes *Australian* media and communications one that must be reassessed regularly. Foreign (and cross-media) ownership of the media in Australia was deregulated in 2007, with quite dramatic effects, as Chapter 5 outlines. The Free Trade Agreement with the United States, finalised in 2005, placed an embargo on certain forms of media regulation in this country. The second biggest telecommunications business, Optus, is owned by Singtel, a company that is majority owned by the Singapore government. Foreign equity firms now play a large part in the ownership structures of the majority of commercial television networks. Major players such as Google are beginning to exert influence in the media ecology. Changes in media ownership, preferential political deals with major media proprietors and the high level of penetration of international communications content and systems into the Australian market mean that debates about what is 'Australian' about our media have changed substantially over recent years.

CONVERGENCE AND COMPETITION

One of the two most protean forces driving reassessment of the nature of media and communications today is 'convergence'. Convergence is customarily used to describe the dissolving distinctions between media systems, media content and the resulting trade between systems. Typically, it describes the activities of a communications company such as Telstra with convergent interests in pay TV (50 per cent ownership of Foxtel), fixed and mobile telephones, online video (Telstra T-Box) and internet provision (BigPond).

There are three dimensions to the idea of convergence: the convergence of technologies, of industries and of policies. *Technological convergence*, enabled by technologies of digitisation, refers to the increasing ability to carry and convert 'content'—sound, data, image or text—into multiple formats. For example, the same piece of music might be used in the form of a CD played on the home sound system, or downloaded on to the home computer or as a digital file on an MP3 player such as an iPod. Such technological capability has facilitated *industry convergence,* where formerly separate sectors of the media industries and the communications economy (such as broadcasting, telecommunications, computing, publishing and the arts) have sought to merge or form alliances.

These shifts have necessitated significant modifications to the policy regimes used to regulate the industries concerned. These might be understood better if we think of the history of media and communications regulation and policy as going through three distinct stages. The first stage, which lasted for most of the last century, was based on *scarcity,* and saw protection, universal service and public interest come to the fore. The second stage, which is now coming to an end, was based on *abundance,* and focused on liberalisation, competition, efficiency and diversity. The third stage is still emerging, but it will reflect the decentralisation of the communications infrastructure, and it is likely to begin to place the media and communications industries within the broader and more generic regulation of the services industries (see Pavlik 1996, p. 259). For those who see the media as playing a particular social, political and cultural role in society, these are far-reaching changes, the consequences of which need to be carefully considered. Chapter 5 canvasses a major 'Convergence Review' that occurred in Australia in 2011–12. It proposed the creation of a new category of 'Content Services Enterprises', which placed the big broadcasters, telcos and ISPs together for regulatory purposes. It found itself dealing with the regulation of journalism, the future of Australian content quotas on television, spectrum allocation and resale, ownership and control, matters touching on innovation and competition policy and much more. Convergence touches on virtually everything.

One of the trickier aspects of convergence is 'content convergence'. 'Content' here refers to what used to be called the media 'message'—or, within most of the industries initially concerned, programming. The distinction is between the medium or system of delivery (the technology used) and the material it is used to carry (the content). Content, as the term is used today, could refer to a television program, the information on a website, in an app or an email message. As the corporate organisation of the media and communications industries changes, and as competition between media sectors increases, there is growing pressure to gain the maximum use from the content being produced. In practice, this means exploiting the capacity to present the same content, with the necessary modifications, on as many platforms of delivery and distribution as possible. In the movie industry, a new title will carry a raft of spin-off products—from t-shirts to computer games to theme park rides. In radio, it means establishing a website that offers everything from an online version of radio programming and archived transcripts of broadcasts to fan websites, chatrooms and gig guides. The comfortable sectoral differentiations that once existed no longer hold, and competition is extraordinarily comprehensive as every medium competes with every other medium.

The fact that convergence also brings media companies into ever-wider business relations means that conflicts of interest are rife. An outstanding example in Australia is the media coverage of sport. Sport has become a driver of innovation, growth and profitability in television—especially subscription television. Media organisations—among them some of the biggest in the world—have taken up commercial interests in the sports themselves, as well as in their coverage. An example of this is the role played by News Limited as a part-owner of Rugby League in Australia since the Murdoch-sponsored SuperLeague intervention, which split the code for a short while in the late 1990s, as well as its major ownership of Super15 Rugby, shown exclusively on pay television.

As particular kinds of media services are becoming less differentiated by their content, competition is growing more pervasive and intense. Sometimes this cuts across the boundaries set by earlier conceptions of regulation, exposing the old players to what they consider unfair competition. For instance, the introduction of technologies like Skype allows internet service providers (ISPs) to provide telephone calls over the internet rather than through telephone companies. The telcos have opposed this kind of development, arguing that an access fee should be imposed on users of ISPs for this purpose. Understandably, such companies might resent what they regard as the maverick *laissez-faire* capitalism of the internet, which is not yet required by government regulation to deliver the kind of social outcomes demanded of telephone companies in addition to their commercial and technological innovations.

The commercial environment has now become more complicated, and in a way its choices have become more compressed, as the media are increasingly providing entertainment rather than information—and thus attempting to second-guess people's taste preferences before their information needs. Dealing with the tastes of audiences they never see and will never come to know personally, the media are always riding their hunches, sweating on the ratings, the charts or the circulation, and regularly looking to upgrade and refine their measurement of audiences (see Chapter 4). But this is far from being a precise science. The imprecision of mass media ratings measurement methods comes under even greater scrutiny as the relative precision of internet and mobile media metrics of use begin to attract the attention of advertisers and marketers. Hence there is intense industry interest in finding ways to 'monetise' (crudely, how to make money from) the developing usage of new media.

The performance of the media has, of course, always had a strong element of unpredictability to it, and so what must be regarded as its increased unpredictability in the current competitive framework does not mean that we should simply leave it alone. Public surveys routinely find that Australians are concerned about the quality of media performance. Issues to do with the representation of violence, intrusive methods of journalism and the quality of news and current affairs, as well as the quality and volume of advertising, are raised repeatedly in response to such surveys. The phone hacking maelstrom that engulfed UK media in 2011–12 and gave rise to the Leveson Inquiry had repercussions in Australia with the Finkelstein Independent Media Inquiry in 2012, which gave voice to much disquiet about journalistic stand-ards and the ability to talk back effectively to media. The demonstrated audience loyalty to the national broadcaster, the ABC—a loyalty that doesn't always reflect the viewing preferences picked up by the ratings system—seems to imply a commitment to maintaining a media system that is not solely commercial in nature. As a result, media performance has not been left entirely to the industry; community concerns have also required government to play a part.

THE VELOCITY OF CHANGE

The other theme that today ties more of the study of Australian media and communica-tions together than any other is the idea that we are in the middle of a rapid process of change, which is seeing established, or 'old', media being challenged for primacy in audiences' and users' attention by new modes and types of production, dissemination and display. Of course, there are commercial interests in play in public accounts of changes in the media, so it is important that the claims made for each new development be evaluated on the basis of the evidence, rather than corporate spin or the enthusiasm of the early adopters. Sorting out the credibility of such claims is one of the purposes of this book. You will discover that virtually every chapter in this book has something to say about this issue. Working out what's going on, why, how, where and with what effect are perhaps the central concerns of media and communications studies today.

To take just a few examples, we are reminded in the chapter on the press (Chapter 6) of the long-term decline in newspaper circulation, which is seemingly irreversible. But also of note is the fact that the decline is uneven. Some up-market publications have forestalled major decline by establishing a focus on hard news targeted at what are defined as the most desirable readership categories—a strategy that may work even in the dire circumstances of the contemporary print media. In Chapters 14, 16 and 27, we also encounter evidence of the rapid growth of the blogosphere, and of amateur or citizen journalism. Certainly it has been argued that this latter phenomenon is a democratising trend, but there are downsides as well. If citizen journalism were to be taken up more and more broadly, the loss of employment prospects for journalists (including rolling cuts at both major news outlets, Fairfax Media and News Limited) has as much potential for creating a democratic deficit through the loss of experienced journalists from the Australian public sphere.

The music industry has been turned upside down by the ease with which peers can download and share their favourite bands. A major new player has come into the music distribution industry—Apple iTunes—with a legal downloads business model, but it remains the case that this still represents a minority of the total download and sharing activity via the net. Significantly, it took a computer company (albeit with a remarkable record of innovation) to develop this model. As Chapter 13 points out, the recording industry remains bitterly divided about the legalities of digital consumption, with the majors continuing to claim ongoing devastation while other evidence points to judicious use of the net as a promotional medium benefiting many music entrepreneurs. As noted earlier, the debates reflect both genuine attempts to find ways to appropriately restructure the industries concerned in relation to these new developments, and corporate attempts to influence regulatory and political support for their current pattern of interests.

Film and television is finally (Australia lags behind the United States and Europe in this respect by some years) beginning to be affected significantly by digital distribution models after several years of defensive reaction as well as aggressive litigation against illegal downloading and the large aggregators such as Google (targeting its subsidiary,

YouTube). Seeing evidence of widespread illegal downloading (using platforms such as BitTorrent), numerous digital distribution initiatives are crowding into this opportunity space. The turbulence surrounding the emerging digital marketplace in film and television gave rise to the largest strike (in 2007–08) by the Writers Guild in Hollywood in 20 years. This reflected the range of ramifications to flow from these new modes of distribution: ramifications that affect not only the companies who hold copyright on the programming or movies concerned, and the new providers attempting to develop a viable business in distributing this content via the net, but also raise issues for those actors and other workers who contributed to the production of this content at a point when the prospect of cross-platform earnings was not a factor to be considered.

As we have indicated, the challenge for students of the media is that much of the debate you will encounter is polarised. There is an exaggerated opposition between enthusiastic optimism versus determined scepticism or pessimism about the potential of new technologies like the internet and Web 2.0. There are assertions of a 'fundamental crisis' in the strategies of the media and communications industries versus counter-assertions of *plus ça change, plus la même chose*—that is, that 'hegemonic capitalism' will always triumph. And, as we noted earlier, while many will claim that the situation they confront is indeed historic, few will actually turn to media history as a means to properly understand what is occurring in a more illuminating context.

The overheated nature of these debates can be confusing because the importance of the issue for so many of those concerned brings to the fore deep-seated attitudes that often result in 'glass half empty/glass half full' debates. These tend to manage the challenging complexity of trends and data by dividing them into selective portions that confirm previously established positions. But such factors do underline the importance of the issue, and show that industry figures, analysts, audiences and users are deeply aware of the stakes involved. You will also have a direct stake in this debate and its outcomes, as it is almost certain that you are both a participant in some form of social media and a consumer of traditional media.

The fact is that change is continuous, but it is less clear what we might make of it. Are we 'both witnesses to and participants in the largest, most fundamental transformation in the history of the media since the advent of typeface, the moving image, and terrestrial broadcast transmission' (Levin 2009, p. 258)? Or, alternatively, is the evidence for the wholesale supplanting of the old media by new media actually 'sparse and thin' (Miller 2010, p.10)? Such speculations ignore the lessons of history that tell us it is more likely for the new to be folded into the old, adding to what has gone before rather than killing it off.

Instead of having to decide categorically one way or the other, we need to ask a range of questions that can be researched intensively. What, for instance, are the rates of change? Are they speeding up? What are the established models of production-distribution-consumption? How and why are they changing? What are the alternative models? What have been their histories and successes/failures? What different impacts have these changes had on different sectors? Seeking to answer these questions will engage you in an exciting journey into the central aspects of media and communications studies.

THE STRUCTURE OF THIS BOOK

We have divided this book into three parts: *Approaches*, *Industries* and *Issues*. In Part I, five chapters survey the range of approaches and methodologies used within media and communications studies in Australia today. None is assumed to be sufficient by itself, and the range of disciplines covered is wide. As this introduction indicates, intellectual trade between once mutually exclusive approaches is now becoming a common occurrence in media and communications studies. Such trade may create some unstable and even threatening alliances, but it endows great explanatory power on the field. It also marks the classic location of media studies at the boundaries between the humanities and the social sciences. At its most productive, a methodologically inclusive media and communications studies maintains a dynamic relation between critical insight and empirical method, between content analysis and textual analysis, and between oppositional politics and a politics of reform and participation. As users of this book will find, it is composed of many contributing strands of theory, method and perspective. It also implies an activist relation to the field, either through the critique of media and communications policy, or through an interrogation of the performance of the media against their responsibilities to the public interest. We study the media and communications not only to find out how they work, but also to evaluate their operations as citizens, and possibly participate as aspiring professionals in their performance.

Part II deals with the media and communications industries themselves. Accounts of the established media sectors—broadcasting (radio, television), telecommunications, print media (newspapers, magazines), advertising, popular music and film—accompany chapters that respond to what we described earlier as a restructuring of the field of media and communications. The internet, online and mobile telephone cultures, and computer games and apps are included to present a thorough and comprehensive overview of the media and communications industries in Australia today. The chapters in this part provide a historical perspective that acknowledges both the industrial and the policy dimensions of the industry concerned, as well as alerting readers to key issues for the present and the future.

Part III looks at a select group of contemporary media issues. We have reshaped this section, with each of these short chapters intended as a model essay for the kinds of assessment that are often found in introductory media and communications courses. The topics have been chosen, in most cases, to cut across the industry sectors covered in Part II and to engage students across a diverse range of interests, including sports, lives 'lived' through social media and the privacy implications of the phenomenon, cultural diversity, the portrayal of celebrity culture, the environment and media use during crises. Social media is treated as an emerging industry sector in its own right, and the apps 'industry' as the newest 'new' platform to emerge. It is hoped that these short essays will act as stimuli for students, prompting them to consider how they might choose to write about these or related topics at a later date and from a different perspective.

Of course, not everyone will want to read every part of this book, so the chapters are designed to stand alone as discussions of their section of the field. The authors have been chosen for their expertise, and include many of the major scholars and experienced teachers currently working in Australia. No matter what the topic or approach, there is a common objective: a greater understanding of the media and communications, which in turn can move us towards a grounded engagement with Australian culture and society.

WHY STUDY AUSTRALIAN MEDIA AND COMMUNICATIONS?

Finally, we should ask why we want to understand the media industries, the regulatory climate within which they operate in Australia, their production processes, their products and the ways in which they are used by and contribute to Australian society. These are fair questions, and it has to be admitted that the answers we give to them throughout this book are not disinterested. Our answers proceed from a set of views about the role the media should play in our society, and about what the media are. But there can be no disinterested position on the media: their social and political function is so profound, so central, that all of us adopt attitudes towards them which reflect our own interests, our own placement within the power structures of the society and our own cultural politics.

The health of this field of study is a direct reflection of the importance of these questions. Media and communications have only been studied formally at a tertiary level in Australia since the 1970s. In that time, several surveys (Frow and Morris 1993; Turner 1993a; Wilson 2006) have pointed to a set of interrelated fields of inquiry that have emerged strongly over a generation and now occupy positions of consolidated popularity among students, maintaining the position of media and communications as the most popular specific field of study in the broad humanities for much of the last decade. It is interesting to track the consistent growth of the discipline based on two earlier comprehensive studies (Molloy and Lennie 1990; Putnis 2000). Looking at the contemporary situation based on official student enrolment data, there has been an overall growth in student numbers from 19 293 in 2002 to 22 321 in 2007 to 29 869 in 2012. While total higher education enrolments rose by 9 per cent over this period, media and communications rose by 55 per cent.

The current *Good Universities Guide* (2013) tells us that media and communications courses are now offered by 52 institutions across 102 campuses, making it the eleventh most popular field of study in Australia. Media and communications is similar in popularity to accounting or computing and IT. The *Good Universities Guide* also points out that demand for such courses (measured as the cut-off points for entry) can be very high for media and communications at some universities. Graduate satisfaction within media and communications courses is significantly higher than that of most graduates across the country in terms of assessment and workload, and more achieve full-time employment than is the norm across the broader fields of humanities or creative arts. While it was the newer universities that developed the first wave of media and communications courses, and still have more than a third of all student enrolments, the field is well represented in the older universities and in further education institutions.

What about career prospects for graduates from media and communications courses? Of course, many factors come in to play here that are quite independent of the quality and relevance of the course content and which institution provides it. But what we know about career outcomes provides a positive story.

Recognising that we don't know enough about the career pathways of our graduates, in 2012 Stuart Cunningham, with Ruth Bridgstock, conducted a survey of all alumni from the last ten years in Queensland University of Technology's media, cultural and communications studies (MCCS) degrees (for further detail, see Cunningham and Bridgstock 2012). There was a very high response rate—our graduates were happy to talk to their old university, which was very gratifying. About a quarter of the cohort had engaged in further formal study. The largest category of those who did engage in further study stayed within the discipline cluster, which indicates strong satisfaction with, and commitment to, the career trajectory opened by their initial qualification.

Although 24 per cent had been unemployed at some point since graduation, the average length of time unemployed was just two months. Only 4 per cent of the cohort had been unemployed more than once since graduation. While the expected job titles appear prominently—journalism, marketing, public relations—there was a long list of jobs undertaken by the cohort—a total of 110 different job titles for 403 graduates. The first year out is a turbulent time involving multiple job-holding, higher levels of casual work, voluntary work, work not related to MCCS and non-degree level work. This turbulence resolves itself from Year 2 onwards.

A total of 83 per cent said that graduates from MCCS courses had special skills that added value to the workplace. These special skills included written communication, the ability to apply theoretical knowledge practically, critical and analytical thinking, media-related disciplinary skills and verbal communication skills. Given the high level of volatility and disruption in the media industries into which many MCCS graduates go, no matter how vocationally oriented a course might be, the relevance of their graduating aptitudes, skills and networks will be under pressure, and the we have found that the thorough mixing of disciplinary and generic attributes and skills may situate them well.

Of course, this popularity and success have drawn criticism. Media and communications studies can be attacked by the media themselves, or by academics in other disciplines, as 'nothing more than the trivial dissection of popular movies and television shows' (Levin 2009, p. 259). Media and communications studies' influence on Australian school English curricula, for instance, has been attacked as a diversion from the core interests of the subject. However, most acknowledge that the importance of media and communications studies is actually increasing as we head into a more media-saturated society, where identity, social relationships, the future of the democratic process and what we know about the world around us are becoming increasingly dependent on media and communications industries, technologies, content and platforms. As a consequence, media and communications studies is expanding its disciplinary reach, taking on the insights offered by law, the arts, business and more.

The final word might appropriately go to an industry leader. Jordan Levin was part of the executive team that established some of US television's major youth drama programs, like *Dawson's Creek*, *Gilmore Girls*, *Buffy the Vampire Slayer* and *Smallville*. Reflecting from an industry perspective, he argues the need for establishing media studies 'as not simply a respectable interdisciplinary field of knowledge, but one that is critical to mapping our future, [which] must become a priority throughout academia, the media industry itself, and all of the constituencies it touches' (Levin 2009, p. 261).

Approaches

PART I

Chapter 1

THE MEDIA AND COMMUNICATIONS: THEORETICAL TRADITIONS

JOHN SINCLAIR

The field of Australian media and communications theory and research is in a unique position. On one hand, it is highly derivative of ideas and work generated elsewhere in the Western, and particularly the English-speaking, world—or 'Anglosphere'. This is partly due to the general globalisation of ideas today, but also to Australia's past as a British colony and, since the second half of the last century, to its involvement with the United States. On the other hand, in Australia we are able to observe and compare the influences and models emanating from the metropolitan centres of the Northern Hemisphere, and to selectively combine and modify them in accordance with our own national reality and place in the world. However, it must be acknowledged that until recent years, there has been relatively little attention given to developments in our region of Asia.

The purpose of this chapter is to identify the origins of the major paradigms or schools of thought that have arisen in European and American theory and research as they apply to media and communications; to trace the formative influence they have had on particular styles of work in Australia; and to show how they have become transformed in the process of being adapted to our experience here.

EUROPE VERSUS AMERICA

It has become conventional to contrast the main differences in theoretical orientations behind media studies and their corresponding research methodologies as 'European' or 'American' (Putnis 1986). In this characterisation, 'European' means heavily interpretive and holistic in scope—that is, taking a macro perspective, looking down on society as a whole. Its socio-political stance is critical of society as it exists and, historically, most often based upon the ideas of the major nineteenth century European social theorist Karl Marx. In its methods, it is deductive in that it applies general principles to the analysis of particular cases.

By contrast, the 'American' approach is strongly empirical and micro in its scope. At its extreme, its form of knowledge relies on the direct observation of distinct phenomena—preferably controlled and measurable occurrences, such as in a laboratory experiment. Its socio-political stance is said to be liberal, pluralistic or 'value-free'—in other words, it is not aligned with any sector of society that has an interest in producing social change, yet in that sense it is really more conservative.

This typology is a convenient way of contrasting and classifying the main differences we find within media studies, and usefully identifies the several key oppositions between critical and pragmatic approaches. For these reasons, this chapter will not break with the conventional shorthand of tagging these as 'European' and 'American' respectively. However, ideas do not belong to geographical territories, and it is important to appreciate that, even if critical theory has traditionally been weak in the United States, Europe in fact has not only produced the characteristic critical and interpretive schools of thought, but also has a strong tradition of 'positivism', which is much more aligned with 'American' empiricism and functionalism (Giddens 1974).

This contradiction was brought out in a great debate that took place during the 1970s, which was given the formidable name of *Der Positivismusstreit*, the struggle over positivism (Adorno 1976). Positivism is basically the idea that the methods of natural science can and should be applied to understand and control society and culture, including the media. This was a basic belief behind the founding of social 'sciences' such as sociology in Europe. In that enterprise, positivism had become associated with functionalism, or the theory that a society forms a complete, integrated whole in which every part exists for a purpose.

So Europe had its own traditions of empiricism and holism, which in the great debate were represented by Sir Karl Popper (1959), a philosopher of science and history. Popper was pitted against the Frankfurt School, a group of Marxists based at Frankfurt in Germany, who had developed their 'critical theory' (a necessary euphemism for Marxism) in opposition to the rise of Hitler's Nazism of the 1930s. Critical theory became a most influential form of cultural analysis and criticism, feeding into what later came to be called 'cultural Marxism' or 'Western Marxism'. The debate was fundamentally irresolvable, with Popper insisting on scientific testing as the basis of knowledge and the Frankfurt School arguing for a philosophical, transcendent approach—that is, looking above and beyond present reality by finding a better future concealed within it.

WESTERN MARXISM AND IDEOLOGICAL CRITIQUE

The debate about positivism as such need not concern us here, but in order to understand contemporary media studies it is crucial to comprehend the significance of the Frankfurt School and its tradition (Jay 1974; Slater 1977). In various works over several years, the members of this group (Theodor Adorno and Max Horkheimer in the first generation, followed by Herbert Marcuse and Walter Benjamin, among others) first set forth a critique of the rise of the mass media (mainly cinema and radio, the 'new' media of those days), which has defined one important direction for Marxist criticism ever since (Bronner and Kellner 1989). This is the ideological critique of the media—the idea that the media, taken together, form an institution within capitalism that serves to reconcile the exploited class to its domination.

To people first coming to media studies in the twenty-first century, it might seem difficult to believe that this notion was as influential as it came to be. Yet it formed the nucleus of what some labelled the 'dominant ideology thesis' that, by the 1980s, had emerged as the prevalent theoretical orientation in media studies (Abercrombie, Hill and Turner 1980). In its simplest formulation, this view argued that the media induce 'false consciousness' through diversion and misinformation, so that the working class never realises the historical destiny that Marx predicted for it—namely, to unite and overthrow capitalism. That is, media audiences were seen as 'cultural dopes' (Garfinkel 1967), who absorb the ideological messages present in all media contents; such messages induce them to believe that capitalism is both desirable and inevitable, and that they should accept their place within it.

However, there were other European theorists who made the ideological critique of the media more sociologically complex and conceptually refined, notably the Italian theorist and activist Antonio Gramsci (1891–1937), with his idea of 'hegemony'. In this conception, the bourgeoisie (or ruling class) achieved its power over the proletariat (working class) only by achieving its always resistant and unstable consent, rather than by illusion or deception. This was a significant reformulation for media studies because it has encouraged the analysis of the polysemic nature of media messages—that is, their multiple meanings, as distinct from just one, dominant ideological meaning. Through Gramsci's concept of hegemony, Western Marxism was able to incorporate other important European interpretive traditions into the study of the media, namely semiology and structuralism, discussed below.

At a later stage, the French communist philosopher Louis Althusser (1918–90) also reformulated the ideological critique tradition from Marx. For Althusser, the media were 'ideological state apparatuses', thus introducing a more mechanical and left-wing functionalist view than Gramsci's. However, Althusser made a major break with Marxist orthodoxy by arguing that the ideological (or, as we would now say, the cultural) sphere of society was 'relatively autonomous' from the economic sphere. It had always been a fundamental and defining precept of Marxism that the economic structure, which Marx saw as forming the 'base' of capitalist society, ultimately determined both its political and cultural life as well. That is, they had no development dynamic of their own. With his 'relative autonomy' formulation, Althusser was pointing the way out of the Marxist paradigm, almost by giving permission to theorists to think of media messages (and audiences, for that matter) as being amenable to interpretation without reference to their place in the economic structure of capitalism. The sheep were out of the paddock.

BRITISH CULTURAL STUDIES

So how did these European Marxist ideas, going back to at least the 1930s, ever come to be influential in Australia? To understand that, we need to take into account the influence British intellectual life continued to assert in Australia during the 1960s and 1970s. Given the keen interest in certain circles in Britain towards European Marxist ideas over that turbulent period, this meant that Britain acted as a relay station for these ideas between Europe and Australia—that is, British academics read and wrote about the European Marxists, and in turn their work was read and written about in Australia.

Britain's own major tradition of thought about media and culture—also influential in Australia—was bourgeois rather than proletarian. In that tradition, which went back to Matthew Arnold's nineteenth-century view of culture as 'the best that has been known and thought', literary figures such as F.R. and Q.D. Leavis and T.S. Eliot saw themselves as the defenders of a spiritual, aristocratic, traditional and elite 'high culture', which was under siege from the rise of working-class 'mass culture' represented by the media (Mulhern 1979). Ironically, their disdain for mass culture gave them something in common with their contemporaries in the Frankfurt School: the development of the popular press, cinema and radio in the first few decades of the twentieth century provoked both conservative and radical critiques. Indeed, it was both sides together that put the 'mass' into the debate about 'mass media' and 'mass culture' as it emerged in the 1950s (Swingewood 1977).

In Britain, Raymond Williams (1977) was particularly important in breaking down the distinction between high culture and mass culture, and at a later stage in applying the subtleties of Gramsci's concept of hegemony. It was through Williams and others, notably Stuart Hall and Richard Hoggart, that a Centre for Contemporary Cultural Studies (CCCS) was established at the University of Birmingham in the 1960s, based on an interdisciplinary combination of literary criticism and Marxist sociology. Hall, in particular, was an articulate and influential theorist who introduced much of Western Marxism to the English-speaking world (Hall et al. 1980). As well as defining the field of 'British cultural studies', the 'Birmingham School' led the way with a research agenda that linked the sociological analysis of particular social groups, such as youth subcultures, with media representation and consumption (Turner 2003).

FRENCH STRUCTURALISM AND SEMIOLOGY

One other important British influence was in the specific area of cinema studies. Just as the Birmingham School emphasised the ideological significance of media images and representations within the context of social and political conflicts, screen studies gave attention to the larger mythologies and thoughtways of Western capitalist society as represented in film. This work—much of it presented in the journal *Screen*—opened up ideological criticism of representations beyond the Marxist problematic of class to perspectives from feminism and structuralism. Laura Mulvey's (1975) concept of the 'male gaze' in cinema is the classic example.

Structuralism, largely based in France, was a broad intellectual movement that linked the psychoanalytic theory of Jacques Lacan, the anthropological theory of Claude Lévi-Strauss and the semiology of Ferdinand de Saussure, which together propelled what is sometimes called the 'linguistic turn' in cultural theory. This refers to a turn away from the more sociological and political economy modes of analysis found in the Marxist tradition, and towards the study of media representations. It was noted earlier how Althusser's theory of ideology gave some impetus to this development. In terms of media studies, the implication is that, instead of studying communication as composed of industries and technologies on one hand and audiences on the other, the emphasis comes to rest on the media messages themselves. In particular, the concern is with how meanings are produced through the codes or rules and discourses according to which images and other kinds of 'texts' are structured. These meanings are seen as ideological, but in a more universal and mythic sense than revealed by the Marxist preoccupation with class-based understandings.

POLITICAL ECONOMY

One other influential strand within the Marxist tradition that must be mentioned— even if it is engaged in a 'family dispute' with ideological analysis and the rest of the tradition—is political economy (Curran 1990, p. 139). Whereas the various European Marxists and their structuralist allies all tend to end up with the weight of their analysis—however conceived—upon the meaning of media messages, the political economy approach puts its emphasis on the production and distribution of media content, with scant regard to its meaning. At its extremes, political economy does not dispute that media content under capitalism is ideological, but rather takes it for granted as obvious, unproblematical and transparent. As well, it has tended to assume that audiences automatically fall under this ideological influence. In this regard, political economy is closer to a more orthodox, less 'cultural' Marxism, which focuses upon patterns of ownership and control of the media, strategies of corporate concentration and expansion, and the links between the media industries and capitalist structure in general.

The rise of political economy in Britain has been associated with names such as Graham Murdock and Peter Golding (1974) as well as Nicholas Garnham (1979), and in France with Armand Mattelart (Mattelart and Siegelaub 1983). However, it is not just a European tradition, as there have been important advocates in the United States—notably the late Herb Schiller (1969), the foundational theorist of 'cultural imperialism', and others elsewhere in the world. Indeed, one of political economy's leading figures has been the Canadian Dallas Smythe (1977), who trained the present generation of political economists in North America, such as Vincent Mosco and Janet Wasko. Smythe was famous for his dictum that media messages were no more than a 'free lunch' that media companies used to attract audiences, which they in turn 'sold' as a 'commodity' to advertisers (see Mosco 1996, p. 148). This is now an extreme view: much political economy in North America is seeking to reform itself of this tendency to reduce complex social processes to economic questions of ownership and control, and instead to take more account of social and cultural realities.

A corresponding approach that takes up this new direction in Britain defines the media as 'cultural industries'. This is exemplified by the work of David Hesmondhalgh (2007). He takes from political economy its emphasis on power and its normative, critical stance, but explicitly draws also on cultural studies for its capacity to provide an understanding of the significance of media content and the role of audiences—both aspects that have been notably absent in traditional political economy. Similarly, bridging the Atlantic, a collection of contemporary political economy theory and research edited by Janet Wasko, Graham Murdock and Helena Sousa (2011) provides fresh perspectives on the traditional concerns of political economy in the communications field—essentially media ownership and control, the role of the state and labour issues—as well as attention to audiences and the formation of consumer markets.

The embrace of neoliberalism—that is, free market, user-pays economic policies—by governments throughout the world, together with the rise to power of global corporations and institutions, has given stimulus to a 'cultural economy' movement in British social theory, especially since about 2000. As with structuralism and semiology, cultural economy has been greatly influenced by French thinkers such as Baudrillard, Bourdieu and Foucault, and more currently by Latour and Callon. This school of thought, which pushes out the theoretical boundaries of both political economy and cultural studies, sees the economy as a cultural construct, and hence neoliberalism as a form of ideology. Its emphasis on information and networks gives cultural economy a particular relevance for the internet age (Flew 2009; Mitchell 2008b).

Meanwhile, in the United States, political economy is still influential, and its most prominent contemporary advocate is Robert W. McChesney. A 2008 collection of his essays published over the previous two decades, during which time he was associated with like-minded figures of note such as Noam Chomsky and Edward S. Herman, provides a comprehensive guide to his concerns. McChesney (2008) has paid particular attention to the issue of media power, and how the media corporations have been able to wield their influence over governments in order to achieve and maintain extensive control over communication resources. In the tradition of Marx, McChesney is an activist as well as a theorist and researcher, and is engaged in a movement of democratic reform of the media. Unlike those of his British counterparts, McChesney's concept of media power does not recognise the extent to which the media are constrained by the cultural characteristics of the markets they seek to capture. That is, McChesney tends to see media influence as manipulation rather than hegemony. So, the kind of adaptation that political economy has made with regard to cultural studies in Britain is not apparent in the most high-profile work being done in its name in the United States.

All of these recent works in political economy, it should be noted, go beyond the traditional borders of analysis—that is, those of the nation-state—in recognition of the very considerable degree to which today's media have undergone complex processes of internationalisation. As well, they seek to provide a critical perspective on the social inequalities and the corporate power generated by new media, particularly the internet. However, it would be fair to say that understanding these two phenomena—media internationalisation and the rise of new media—continues to be one of the greatest challenges faced by contemporary media and communications theory.

AMERICAN EMPIRICISM

The empirical tradition had its origins in three historical developments in the United States in the decades after World War I. These were a preoccupation with propaganda and persuasion as a legacy of the war, a great faith in the new 'social sciences' and the benefits they could bring when harnessed to the interests of government and commerce, and the rise of the 'mass media of communication'—in those days, the popular press, cinema and radio.

In the course of maintaining its neutrality in the war, the US government and the academic establishment had become highly conscious of the use of 'propaganda'—not only as a negative force, but in the positive sense of building popular sentiment and 'public opinion'—to invoke another innovative concept from that time. The approach taken to studying propaganda was based on the then emergent 'behavioural' sciences such as psychology. Like positivism, such sciences were based on forming knowledge through direct observation, including laboratory experiments.

Harold Lasswell (1902–78) was the most representative figure from this era, with his model of communication being the question 'Who says what, in which channel, to whom, and with what effect?' This provided a research agenda that in fact concentrated mainly on the 'what', or message content, and the effect. 'Content analysis' was devised as a systematic and quantifiable method for the description and analysis of the meaning of media messages, while effects were conceived to be immediate psychological or behavioural reactions to media content, like a hypodermic needle or 'magic bullet'. In practice, this method is not so much an analysis but a quantitative description of particular media texts, which measures the frequency of certain elements or themes, such as acts of violence in a television series (Potter 1999). Whereas those in the Frankfurt School had critically interpreted the meaning of the ideology they found in media content, American social scientists were more interested in bringing to light the effect of certain kinds of media content on 'attitudes'. This was a psychological approach to the rise of the media, even though it was a social or 'mass' phenomenon (Jowett and O'Donnell 1992).

By the 1940s, a much more sociological angle was being taken, particularly since the behavioural approach—not surprisingly—had been unable to demonstrate too many effects. Paul Lazarsfeld and his colleagues at the Bureau of Applied Social Research hypothesised that 'personal influence' was at work in a 'two-step flow' process in which 'opinion leaders' mediated between the media and the wider audience. Instead of messages impacting directly upon anonymous individuals in the mass, this approach discovered that—at least in the matters of voting intentions and consumption choices that they studied in their social surveys—there were influential individuals who formed their views from newspapers and radio, and then passed them on to others (Lowery and de Fleur 1983). This shift moved the emphasis from 'mass' to 'communication', and to a less deterministic perspective.

After World War II, American empiricism was institutionalised across the social sciences and, in the absence of a social theory of its own, became allied to the conservative functionalism then dominant in sociology and anthropology. These tendencies were denounced by the American Marxist C. Wright Mills (1959) as 'abstracted empiricism' and 'grand theory' respectively. By the 1970s, a 'mass communication' approach more consistent with pluralism had consolidated itself. This basically comprised the mainstream idea that no one social group dominates society. The empirical social science tradition still continues strongly in the United States, and can be found in leading journals such as *Communication Research* and the *Journal of Communication*.

AUSTRALIAN TRADITIONS

Cultural studies

After the great expansion of university education and the wider acceptance of international influences experienced by Australia in the 1960s, as well as the beginnings of a self-conscious critique of 'the Australian way of life', fertile ground had been prepared for the seeding of British cultural studies by the beginning of the 1980s. There were already studies of popular culture, and although these tended towards cultural history (Spearritt and Walker 1979), one major collection of articles edited by Dermody, Docker and Modjeska (1982) explicitly linked Birmingham to cultural studies in Australia, and included significant pieces on Australian television production. The first BA degree in Australian Cultural Studies began in 1981 (Sinclair and Davidson 1984) and *The Australian Journal of Cultural Studies* commenced in 1983, becoming internationalised as *Cultural Studies* in 1987.

As at Birmingham, cultural studies in Australia was as interested in applying structuralist and semiological analysis to the media as it was in relating it to other dimensions of 'lived' popular culture. An 'Australian Cultural Studies' book series was inaugurated with Graeme Turner's *National Fictions* in 1986, in which Turner developed critiques of ideological discourses in Australian films from a theoretical base also informed by literary criticism and screen studies. This was followed by *Myths of Oz* (Fiske, Hodge and Turner 1987), a cultural studies approach to everyday life, tourist icons, the suburbs and the beach.

National Fictions can be taken as a useful example of how received ideas—in this case, European structuralism via British cultural studies and literary criticism—can fruitfully be hybridised, or adapted to media texts and cultural traditions in Australia (Turner 1986). It is also indicative of the way in which film analysis was congenial to cultural studies, which often found its institutional home in the literature and inter-disciplinary studies departments of universities in this country. Yet, as an approach to film, its text-based focus on narrative and representation sets it apart from the work of Dermody and Jacka published around that time. While they also were concerned with processes of national myth-making in film, Dermody and Jacka (1987, 1988a, 1988b) pursued this much more in the context of a political economy approach to the structure and development of the film industry itself.

By 1993, Australian cultural studies had seen its own eponymous reader published (Frow and Morris 1993) and formed its own professional association. The media contributions in the reader focused mostly on representation—the analysis of how meaning is produced in texts. However, there were also two notable contributions on audiences: one a critique of 'ethnographic' method as used in cultural studies audience research (Nightingale 1993); the other a polemical piece on the very idea of an audience (Hartley 1993a). Hartley's argument was that audiences were 'invisible fictions', constructed by institutions such as television networks, but also media researchers, for their own purposes. This was an influential article; notable amongst the comment it attracted was a paper from Elizabeth Jacka (1994), which argued the unfashionable case that social science method could be employed to achieve cultural studies research objectives. Jacka also contributed to another book that appeared in 1993, one that distinguished between 'Australian cultural and media studies' (though it included both), and put the question of cultural and media policy on the agenda (Turner 1993b). In the 2000s, cultural and media studies has flourished, notably in the nation-wide Cultural Research Network, funded by the Australian Research Council (ARC) from 2004 until 2009, and in centres such as the Centre for Critical and Cultural Studies at the University of Queensland, under the leadership of Graeme Turner (2012).

Social sciences

Courses in media and communications studies began to be established in Australian universities from around 1970, often in Departments of Education, Sociology and

Political Science. Because these social science disciplines were themselves being developed under the influence of US models, this was reflected in much of the early work produced. For example, Western and Hughes' *The Mass Media in Australia* (1971) was actually a sociological survey of media use, based on a national sample and broken down in terms of demographic variables and political indicators. While not behaviourist nor even empiricist in the sense discussed above, it was still limited by its purely quantitative rather than interpretive methodology, and offered much less than its title promised.

A more original example is *Children and Screen Violence* by Patricia Edgar (1977). Edgar offered the first-ever postgraduate course in media and communications in an Australian university, at La Trobe in Melbourne. Her research combined orthodox field survey methodology from sociology with personality scales from psychology in a study of adolescent responses to screen violence. She notes the relative absence of Australian studies, but in her literature review brings together a wide range of both British and US perspectives. These go far beyond conventional US behaviourism. In particular, she critically evaluates the social-psychological approach then fashionable on both sides of the Atlantic, 'uses and gratifications', and seeks to fuse social science analysis with the 'social construction of reality' philosophy put forward by Berger and Luckmann—two European theorists living in the United States. She even takes into account British political economy and Marxist ideological critique. In her actual conduct of the research, she combined the quantitative data with qualitative interview data reporting adolescents' responses to particular films and programs as texts.

All this may sound eclectic—that is, borrowing freely from here and there—but Edgar's selection of approaches is purposefully focused on her research question, and her treatment of the various influences is critical, and not at all derivative. For these reasons, *Children and Screen Violence* is an early example of how Australian media and communications researchers were able to inform themselves about relevant perspectives from elsewhere, reflect critically upon them, then adapt and fuse them together so as to research issues in our own environment. A comparable work from this same era is the late Grant Noble's *Children in Front of the Small Screen* (1975). This internationally published book also presents some original research, together with a scholarly (although idiosyncratic) critique of the literature in the field, including that stemming from psychology—the author's own discipline.

Although the US empirical tradition suffered much severe criticism during the 1970s and 1980s as the European Marxist model gained the ascendant, it was not as if the intrinsic value of methodical investigation and observation was denied. Indeed, one of the characteristics that marks off media studies from cultural studies is the former's 'real-world' orientation (as distinct from the more theoretical 'linguistic turn' in cultural studies), as well as a commitment to the rigorous collection and evalua-tion of empirical evidence, and to the development of appropriate methodologies for doing this. The critique of the US social science research model was more about its tendency to involve itself in methodological techniques for their own sake, and to so limit the scope—and even lose sight of the purpose and object—of the research. It was also a question of what was being looked at: manageable but insignificant 'micro' socio-psychological studies, or the 'macro' issues of the structure of the media and communications industries, as against political economy's 'big picture' approach.

Contemporary empirical work broadly based on the social science model in Australia can be found most often in the *Australian Journal of Communication*, which ceased production in 2013. This is a journal that published not only studies of the media, but also examined other areas in which communication theory and research have been applied, ranging over political communication, public relations, manage-ment communication and other such fields of professional practice. A similar range of interests is represented among the membership of the Australian and New Zealand Communication Association (ANZCA), though coexisting with cultural studies and political economy (Maras 2004).

Political economy: Australian media studies

The political economy tradition would be closest to the core of contemporary research on media and communications in Australia. However, the style of political economy that has flourished here is much more heterodox and supple than the traditional variety outlined in the first section of this chapter. Even when political economy in Australia has been more doctrinaire and deterministic, it has been so in an idiosyn-cratic way. Humphrey McQueen's *Australia's Media Monopolies* (1977) declared that the media companies in Australia were in fact 'not Australian', because they served 'the interests of US Imperialism' (1977, p. 6). McQueen's Maoist version of Marxism was evident in his advocacy of alternative forms of 'people's media', such as pavement chalking.

During the 1980s, a number of texts and readers appeared that helped to define an Australian political economy tradition. Bill Bonney and Helen Wilson (1983) began *Australia's Commercial Media* by distancing themselves from McQueen's reductionism: the tendency to reduce complex situations to a simple explanation. On the other hand, they reject empiricism—though not empirical investigation—in line with the distinction explained at the end of the previous section. Interestingly, they explicitly acknowledged their theoretical debts to both the Centre for Contemporary Cultural Studies at the University of Birmingham (the shrine of cultural studies/Western Marxism) and the Centre for Mass Communications Research at the University of

Leicester (the equivalent for political economy of the media) and, furthermore, sought to give them 'equal weight' (1983, p. vii).

In the United Kingdom at that time, Birmingham and Leicester were making rival claims to the relative significance of the cultural and the political economy sides of the Marxist heritage respectively, but in Australia these could be seen as complementing each other. Thus, while Bonney and Wilson drew on key political economy concepts such as class and cultural imperialism in their extensive analysis of the media in Australia and their place in the world, their treatment of advertising, for example, provided a clear exposition of the relevant structuralist and semiological concepts, and convincingly demonstrated them in practice in their analysis of particular advertisements.

Bonney and Wilson also appear among the contributors to *Communications and the Media in Australia*, a book of readings edited by Ted Wheelright and Ken Buckley (1987)—at that time the leading figures in mainstream political economy in Australia. Even here, the contributions go beyond the orthodox, descriptive ownership and control studies of media industries, which are the hallmark of the political economy of the media approach. For example, as well as essays on the ABC as a political and cultural institution, there is a critical history of the development of radio by Lesley Johnson, who at that time was building up a cultural studies group at Melbourne University. Also in that era—something of a golden age for the political economy approach—it was being diffused throughout several fields in media and communications studies, such as the analysis of news production and political influence (Tiffen 1989). In much more recent times, Terry Flew has taken up the challenge of applying political economy to the rise of new media and globalisation (2005, 2007). As for the cultural economy movement, Australian researchers have occasionally been found among contributors to the international *Journal of Cultural Economy* since its beginning in 2008.

Uniquely Australian

Just as American film critics like to describe Australian films as 'quirky' when they don't know how to fit them into their conventional categories, the term could also be applied to media and communications theory and research in Australia. The quirkiness comes from the particular fusions of international influences discussed in this chapter, but also from some of the particular individuals who have been involved, as well as certain unique features of Australia.

The single most important individual in establishing the field in Australia was Henry Mayer, Professor of Political Theory at the University of Sydney for many years, and key founder of the journal *Media Information Australia*. This was to become today's premier journal in the media studies field, *Media International Australia* (*MIA*). Mayer's own first publication was *The Press in Australia* (1964). As a critical account of the structure and performance of the press, this was closest to the political economy school in its orientation, but Mayer was fiercely sceptical and anti-doctrinaire—a 'conflict pluralist', he called himself (see Tiffen 1994a, p. xiv). Nevertheless, Mayer fostered and inspired many of the current generation of senior scholars in the field here, much as Dallas Smythe and Herb Schiller did in the United States.

One other singular individual was Eric Michaels, an American whose internationally recognised work in Australia concerned the use of television among Aboriginal people. His report, The *Aboriginal Invention of Television in Central Australia, 1982–1985* (1986), provides a highly original analysis, from several methodological perspectives, of how the Warlpiri people adapted television to their cultural values: television as 'a cultural technology' (O'Regan 1990). Michaels thus put the issues around the media and Indigenous people on the research agenda in Australia.

Other developments, also concerned in a different sense with 'cultural technologies', have been more collective. Early in the 1980s at Griffith University in Brisbane, there developed a 'critical mass' of scholars interested in the work of the French theorist Michel Foucault. Foucault's work on power and discourse was conducive to the study of the 'governmentality' of the media and other institutions. Particularly after Althusser and the collapse of Marxism, Foucault's approach seemed to provide a way of understanding social order without reference to a ruling class and its ideology. While the enthusiasm for Foucault was an international movement, in Australia it directed academic attention to the role of cultural and media policy as a key link between government and culture (Cunningham 1992; Mercer 1994). Under the leadership of Tony Bennett and Colin Mercer, the work of this influential 'Griffith School' became institutionalised in the Institute for Cultural Policy Studies, which in turn became the Australian Key Centre for Cultural and Media Policy (1995–2002). Policy and cultural industry studies have since been developed at Queensland University of Technology under the rubric of 'creative industries', while collaborative work on new media and communications technologies at several universities across the nation has been brought together under the umbrella of an ARC Centre of Excellence for Creative Industries and Innovation, established in 2005,and led by Stuart Cunningham.

The arrival of 'the policy moment' has turned out to be a durable and effective way of channelling academic theory and research into policy analysis and critique, and real-world engagement with the increasingly convergent media and communications industries. The focus on cultural and media policy has proved a useful constraint in saving cultural studies from its tendency towards abstraction and critique for its own sake, while at the same time confronting political economy with the cultural complexities with which that approach must deal. That said, there is no current consensus on the direction that media and communications theory and research should take: the creative industries initiative in particular has attracted much controversy and critique (O'Connor 2009; Turner 2012).

CONCLUSION

So this is by no means the only end-point in the story so far of the development of media and communications studies in Australia. This chapter does not pretend to be chronologically complete or comprehensive, and there are and have been other notable schools of thought, other leading figures and other centres and institutions that could have been included were this a fuller account. Suffice to say that research which fuses ('European') critical theory with ('US') attention to empirical detail is premised on an understanding of industry structure and functioning, and perhaps also maintains an eye on policy implications, representing an ideal that guides much of the best work in Australia. No centre or school of thought has a monopoly on such a fusion. Rather, this is the way in which a culturally derivative yet independent and media-intensive nation has learned to constructively adapt received ideas to deal with its own reality.

FURTHER READING

An excellent overview of British cultural studies and its theoretical roots is provided by Turner (2003), *British Cultural Studies: An Introduction*. The development of mass communication research in the United States can be further read about in Lowery and de Fleur (1983), *Milestones in Mass Communication Research*. Particular Australian examples of studying the media from a range of approaches can be found in Turner (1986), *National Fictions*; Frow and Morris (1993), *Australian Cultural Studies: A Reader*; and articles in *Media International Australia*, *Continuum* and the *Australian Journal of Communication*. Cunningham (1992), *Framing Culture: Criticism and Policy in Australia* provides an introduction to studying media from a cultural policy studies approach. For an introduction to contemporary political economy, see Wasko, Murdock and Sousa (2011), *Handbook of Political Economy of Communications*, and for a broad introduction to the whole range of relevant theory, see McQuail (2010), *McQuail's Mass Communication Theory* (6th ed.).

Chapter 2

TEXTUAL ANALYSIS

ALAN McKEE

WHAT IS TEXTUAL ANALYSIS?

Supposing you wanted to find out: is Australian culture sexist? How could you gather the data to answer that question? Some ideas spring to mind. You could do a nation-wide survey, asking people straight out whether they are sexist or (more sensibly) asking questions that are designed to reveal sexism—such as 'Do you agree with the statement: "It's fine for women to work outside the home after they have children"?' Or you could conduct interviews or focus groups with people about gender roles. But there are three key problems with this kind of data-gathering.

The first is that you only get answers to the questions that you ask. There might be forms of sexism in Australia that you don't ask questions about—for example, supposing that Australians generally think it's okay for women to be equal with men, but the one thing they wouldn't like is to take orders from a female boss. If you didn't ask a question about female bosses, you wouldn't pick that up in the survey.

Second, people aren't stupid. They know what kind of answers you are looking for and nobody wants to look bad, so they might say what they think you want to hear. The classic example of this in media research is Ellen Seiter's (1990) article 'Making Distinctions in TV Audience Research: A Case Study of a Troubling Interview'. Professor Seiter advertised in a magazine for soap opera viewers to interview. But when she started interviewing some of the people who had responded, they

> began the interview with a disclaimer about the amount of time spent viewing and insistence that they only watch soap operas occasionally . . . This was an unusual start for the interview because [he] had answered a newspaper advertisement asking to interview soap opera viewers. (1990, p. 63)

As Seiter notes, these consumers know very well that many academics are snobs who look down at 'trash' like television soap operas, and so the consumers—quite sensibly—said the kinds of things that they thought a professor would want to hear. They criticised soap operas, and asked 'what is the mentality of the people who are watching?' (Seiter 1990, pp. 64–5).

Third, there is the problem that when you ask people to think about a topic, they start to think about it. They may never have thought about the topic before, so by simply asking the question you could actually change how they think about it. When I interviewed fans of the television program *Doctor Who* to ask them whether they thought the program was political, many of them responded with comments like 'Umm... [long pause] I've never really thought about it to be honest', or 'I don't know. It's a good question' before going on to produce an answer (McKee 2004, p. 210). These interviewees were able to think of an answer for me—but it wasn't a topic that they had ever considered before. It didn't tell me anything about their everyday experience of engaging with this television program.

The big problem with answering a question like 'Is Australian culture sexist?' is this: How can you observe human beings 'in the wild' as it were? How can you gather data about how they make sense of the world in their everyday lives when there aren't any academics there asking them questions about it?

This is where textual analysis comes in—looking for the evidence that people produce in the course of their everyday lives about how they make sense of the world. Take the example of a newspaper story that says, 'In a recent court case in Cameroon, the judge ruled against a woman being allowed to inherit property, saying, "Women are property. How can property own property?"' (Abdela 2001, p. 20) This way of making sense of the world is quite different from that of most Australians. Most of us would think that female human beings should still be included in the overall category of 'people', whereas for the Cameroon judge they should more properly be put into the category of 'property'. Such differences in ways of thinking about, making sense of and representing the world around us can obviously have important impacts on how we relate to the world and to other human beings. This doesn't mean that everybody in Cameroon would agree with this judge, but we do know that it is unlikely that a judge in Australia would make a comment like this (although there have been occasions when judges have been accused of making 'sexist' comments). So we interpret texts (films, television programs, magazines, advertisements, clothes, graffiti and so on) in order to try to get a sense of the ways in which, in particular cultures at particular times, people make sense of the world around them.

When we perform textual analysis on a text, we make an informed guess at some of the most likely interpretations that might be made of that text, in order to help us understand how the people producing and consuming that text make sense of the world.

HOW TO DO TEXTUAL ANALYSIS

Write down some questions about how people make sense of the world that interest you

Textual analysis has to start with a question that you want to answer. You can't just 'do a textual analysis' of a text (film, television program, etc.), as there are an infinite number of ways in which you could 'analyse' a text. When you have a question, you can then start looking for texts.

The kinds of questions that traditionally have been addressed by textual analysis are usually about *politics* (in the widest sense of that word). For example, researchers in mass communication studies have often been interested in how the media represent traditional forms of politics. The most common texts studied to answer these questions have been non-fictional ones—newspapers, television and radio news, current affairs and documentaries. While the kinds of questions asked of those texts have usually been in terms of the ways in which they cover traditional political issues, researchers in cultural studies use the word 'politics' in a broader sense. Cultural studies research traditionally has had Marxist concerns at its base—analysing how a culture represents the wishes of the ruling classes while disempowering working-class citizens. Cultural studies has expanded this concern to look at other ways in which some cultures disenfranchise other groups, including women, queers, people with disabilities and people outside dominant racial and language groups. All aspects of culture can be analysed for answers to such questions, including news and current affairs, but also soap operas and other forms of drama, light entertainment, reality television, popular novels and so on.

If you have interests in other areas, the beauty of textual analysis is that it can be applied to any texts to answer virtually any question about sense-making. To generate your own research questions, you should consume as much culture as you can—different kinds of television, magazines, computer games, films, newspapers, novels, plays, museums and art galleries—and read lots of histories and theories of culture for new ideas, perspectives and questions. The question in which we're interested here is: Is Australian culture sexist? According to the *Oxford English Dictionary*, sexism means 'prejudice, stereotyping, or discrimination, typically against women, on the basis of sex'.

Focus your question to become more specific

'Is Australian culture sexist?' is a big question, and trying to answer it would be a massive research project. The next step is to try to make it more focused. On 24 June 2010, Julia Gillard became the first female prime minister of Australia, a position she held for just over three years. From my consumption of media in Australia over the last few years, I have noticed debates about how she has been represented. Emerging from that concern I can see a do-able question for a textual analysis project run by a single researcher: were media representations of Julia Gillard sexist? This is one way into thinking about the broader issue. Don't under-estimate the importance of focusing your question. People starting their research careers commonly try to address research questions that are too big. They want to make huge claims about the history of Western civilisation and everyone who has ever lived in it. And of course the broader question of whether Australian culture as a whole is sexist is an important one. But the point of textual analysis is to produce evidence that allows you to convince the reader about your point of view. There's no way that a single researcher could produce enough data to make a convincing claim about every aspect of Australian culture and its attitude towards men and women—it would take a huge team of people, with a lot of funding and a lot of time, to analyse texts from commercial television and men's magazines and dating internet sites, and romance novels, and government reports, and so on, to make convincing claims about 'Australian culture' as a whole. But a well-honed question can provide an insight into broader issues. Julia Gillard, as the former prime minister of Australia, held a representative role at the head of the nation. Examining the way in which she was represented in the media allows us to make some claims about sexism in Australia at the national level.

List the texts that are relevant to your question from your own experience

Having worked out your question, start to list the texts you are going to analyse. Do you want to focus on newspapers? Online news sites? Television programs or radio? If you are already familiar with Australian culture, you will be able to start listing relevant texts for analysis straight away. Use your cultural knowledge to identify the texts that are going to be most useful for you (if you don't know anything about Australian culture, your job is going to be much more difficult, as I discuss below). For this question, I will analyse newspapers, focusing on metropolitan dailies—so my question becomes even more focused (not 'the media', but 'metropolitan daily newspapers'). These form a coherent genre, which tends to work with a broadly similar 'textual system' of representation.

Find more texts by doing research—both academic and popular

Find any previous academic writing on the topic that may point you towards important texts in this area. Search the library catalogue with keywords and then do 'sideways scanning' (go to the bookshelf and look sideways at other books with the same call number). Search on the internet. Check out any other sources you can think of (go to a newsagent and browse).

Gather information about relevant intertexts

When you're doing textual analysis, you are trying to understand how these texts function in the everyday culture where they are consumed. There is no point in making clever interpretations of texts if they bear no relation to the interpretations made by their readers. When you do textual analysis, you want to use the media texts as evidence of how sense-making is going in everyday culture. As I noted above, by studying media texts we can work out how the cultures in which people live make sense of the world.

If we want to make an informed guess about the likely interpretations audiences are making of a text, we need to understand the cultural context within which they are encountering it. This includes understanding the audience—the 'demographic'—that the text is addressing. You need to have some understanding of the culture within which the text is circulating. What makes us 'informed' in our 'informed guesses about the likely interpretations of a text' is our knowledge of relevant intertexts—the same ones that audiences have on hand when they interpret that text. I would divide these into four categories—although this is only a rough guide, it's not exhaustive and they are not mutually exclusive.

- *Other texts in the series:* If you want to understand likely interpretations of a newspaper story, you must familiarise yourself with several issues of a newspaper. Don't attempt to guess at likely interpretations from your exposure to a single issue—you won't understand how the rules work and you'll probably get it wrong. Take the example of *The Drum*—an online news site that often uses humour to make its points. A sexist article published there could be a deliberate attempt to use parody to undercut sexist representations rather than to support them.
- *The genre of the text:* Genre is a powerful tool for making sense of texts. Genres work by providing conventions that allow efficient communication between producers and audiences. If somebody is hit in the face with a frying pan in a cartoon, we know that this is meant to be funny. We shouldn't worry about whether the character will survive the attack, or whether they'll be disfigured by it. By contrast, if a character is hit in the face with a frying pan in the television series *Law and Order: SVU*, we know that it's a serious assault, that it hurt and that there will be ramifications in the narrative. Knowing the genre and its rules helps us to make reasonable guesses at how a text is likely to be read by audiences. And so, for example, a newspaper attack on the policies of Julia Gillard is not necessarily sexist—because newspapers write stories attacking politicians all the time. It would only have been sexist if it drew attention to the former prime minister's gender in a way that it wouldn't do with a male prime minister.
- *Intertexts about the text itself:* You can get a sense of likely interpretations by looking at intertexts—publicly circulated texts that are explicitly linked to the text in which you're interested. These might be letters, internet posts, reviews or articles where viewers describe their own interpretations of the text, or other pieces of entertainment that reference the original text, or wider discussions about how texts in that genre function. Once again, these texts don't simply tell us the truth of how people really interpret these texts, any more than interviewing them does. And it doesn't mean that audiences simply think what they are told to think in these intertexts. But we do know that viewers draw on available ways of thinking about texts in order to make sense of them—just as academics do.
- *The 'semiosphere':* This is the wider public context in which a text is circulated and is described in detail in the next section.

Get as much sense as you can of the wider 'semiosphere'

It is important to understand as much as you can about the wider semiosphere in which a text circulates (read newspapers, magazines, watch as much television, listen to as much music as you can). The semiosphere is the 'world of meaning', or the cultural context, within which a text circulates (Hartley 1996, pp. 106-121). This is the most vague and all-inclusive category of context. We draw on all kinds of other knowledge about how the world is organised—how we make sense of it—when we make sense of a text.

By having a sense of which discourses (ways of making sense of the world) are familiar and powerful in a cultural context, you can make reasonable interpretations of texts. For example, some people have a sexual fetish for children's feet, and on a website targeted at these people there are images from the classic family film *The Sound of Music* (at one point the children in that film run around in bare feet) (Lumby 2008, p. 17). For that audience, the film might be understood as pornography. But we also know that in wider Australian culture, paedophilia is considered abhorrent—so when a commercial channel plays *The Sound of Music* at Christmas, it would be unreasonable to think that it is being interpreted by audiences in such a way. You should draw on your knowledge of the culture in which the text is circulated, and the culture of the particular audience you're talking about, when you make your interpretation.

Reading the newspapers themselves will also give you a sense of the other kinds of texts—music, films, books, television programs—in which they expect their readers to be interested. While this won't, of course, match up exactly with what every reader of the newspaper consumes, it does give you a rough idea of the kind of culture that a reader of a metropolitan newspaper might encounter. Viewing, reading and listening to some of these might be useful for getting a sense of the reading practices of their consumers.

Gather the texts

This can be often the hardest bit of the project, as so few genres of text are systematically kept by libraries or archives. The National Library is useful for finding popular, as well as academic, books. Films and television programs can be found through the national archive Screensound (<www.screensound.gov.au/index.html>).

University libraries are invaluable resources. If you're after television programs, YouTube provides a lot of material, and much is now available on DVD. For harder to find items, it is also worth contacting television production companies directly: with a little friendly persuasion, some of them can be convinced to allow researchers access to their own archives. For newspapers, it is relatively straightforward to gain access to the words of the stories—the database Factiva (accessible through many university library catalogues) includes every newspaper story from most major newspapers around the world. However, this provides only the words from the story, and excludes other important aspects of the stories—particularly photographs and layout.

Analyse as many of the texts in the genre as you can, getting some sense of the rules for how they work

As you start to read newspaper stories about politicians, you will start to see the rules by which they work. More 'quality' newspapers (those with more middle-class audiences) tend to have more stories about politicians, earlier in the paper. More 'sensationalist' (sometimes known as 'tabloid') newspapers (those with working-class audiences) tend to have fewer stories, particularly about national politics, and these tend to appear later in the paper ('soft' news stories and crime stories often have higher billing). Some newspapers (such as *The Australian*) have a strong right-wing bias, and tend to produce highly critical stories about any Labor politician (not just the prime minister of the day). Newspapers are visual media, and often lead with stories that have a strong image to accompany them (hence the reason that politicians like to cuddle babies, or put on a hard hat in a factory).

As you analyse these texts to produce interpretations that would seem reasonable to their readers, remember that this is not literary analysis. You are not trying to find a clever interpretation. You're not trying to find the 'correct' interpretation that the author intended. And it's not ideological analysis, where you are trying to find hidden political messages of which consumers aren't consciously aware. Rather, you are making an informed guess at what kinds of interpretations are actually being made of these texts in everyday use. If audiences are likely to be making the 'wrong' interpretation—one that is different from what the authors intended—then you should be more interested in the 'wrong' interpretation than the 'correct' one. For example, the authors of the stories might not be trying to be sexist—but that doesn't mean that they aren't being sexist. You might notice that they consistently talked about Julia Gillard's clothes, while they generally don't mention the clothes of male politicians. A story in the *Sydney Morning Herald* discussed Julia Gillard meeting Anders Rasmussen, the head of NATO. The story noted that the then prime minister was wearing 'a white, short jacket and dark trousers'. What was Rasmussen wearing? The story didn't mention it (Totaro 2010). In the *Daily Telegraph*, a commentator noted that, 'On what should have been one of the proudest days of Gillard's political career, she bungled it with a less than flattering haircut and a frumpy '80s tapestry print jacket' (Quigley 2006). The *Hobart Mercury* stated that, 'She recently stepped out on the town in an outfit that one fashion expert described as resembling a "cheap motel bedspread". Now, there are calls for Prime Minister Julia Gillard to be given a clothing allowance to ensure our nation's leader avoids any future fashion faux pas.' (Toohey 2010, p. 1) The next day, a follow-up story was delighted to note that, 'Gone was the "cheap motel bedspread" and in its place was a smart, dark blue pinstriped suit.' (*Daily Telegraph* 2010, p. 7). For the *Herald Sun*, 'She's been blasted for her dowdy wardrobe and greying roots, but it seems PM Julia Gillard is finally finding her fashion feet.' (Coster, McMahon and Epstein 2011, p. 37).

There are enough examples in this list (and it is easy to find others) to suggest that this is not just a coincidence or an isolated example. This is confirmed when you notice that, by contrast, senior male politicians—Prime Ministers John Howard and Kevin Rudd—were never discussed in this way. There are comments about sports wear—tracksuits (Howard) or 'budgie smugglers' (Tony Abbott)—but this is not framed in terms of their fashion sense. If 'sexism' includes 'stereotyping . . . on the basis of sex', then paying attention to the fashion sense of senior female politicians, but not senior male politicians, is sexist in that it relies on a commonsense assumption that women are (or should be) more interested in fashion than men are (see Walsh 2013; Goldsworthy 2013 for further discussion of this subject).

It's also important to notice that I'm not producing clever interpretations here. One newspaper story says that, 'She's been blasted for her dowdy wardrobe and greying roots, but it seems PM Julia Gillard is finally finding her fashion feet' (Coster, McMahon and Epstein 2011, p. 37). I maintain that this links the former prime minister with fashion. This isn't a subtle, deep or insightful interpretation—it's an obvious one. And that's what you're looking for—an interpretation that would seem obvious to the consumers of that text. The difficult part of this process is gathering the data—not the clever interpretations that you make of it.

Consider returning to texts and rethinking your interpretations of them

Bear in mind that, as you get more sense of the contexts in which these texts work, you might have to return to texts, rethink your interpretations of them and produce new guesses. You may have started off your research on newspapers asking whether their representations of Julia Gillard are sexist. As you read them, and get a sense of the wider cultural context in which they're circulating, you might start to see them differently. You might notice a number of discussions of a wider move in politics towards 'spin', including image management—and you could find that, on revisiting some of the stories that discuss Julia Gillard's clothes, you realise that they fit better into this genre of writing. A *Canberra Times* story that notes that 'Prime Minister Julia Gillard has consistently worn red this year' (*Canberra Times* 2011, p. 19) is in fact about image consultants and their increasingly important role in politics—for both men and women. Perhaps this story isn't playing into a sexist assumption that women should be more interested in fashion? Maybe it is about a more general issue in political management.

Always remember that your interpretations can only ever be informed guesses— we can never know for certain exactly what interpretation any given individual may make of any specific text. We could try to interview people to find out, but then we're back with the problems that I discussed at the start of this chapter: that just by asking the questions, you are requiring people to think about the issues in a particular way. The very act of gathering the data changes the outcome.

Write up your results in a suitable form for the purpose you want them to serve

You now have the results of your endeavours: an account of the ways in which daily metropolitan newspapers in Australia presented Julia Gillard to their readers in a way suggesting that because she is female, she should be interested in fashion. What do you then do with this information?

If you want to pass a university subject or get a higher degree, then a more scholarly form of writing is appropriate (Davis and Mackay 1996). If you want to engage in public debate, perhaps a magazine article drawing on your research would be more useful. If you want to try to get something done about an area of culture that you think needs to be changed, maybe you should write a report that you could submit to a government department. The important thing is that you write in an appropriate genre. There is no shame in 'dumbing down' research in order to reach a wider audience. The general public are not paid to spend their days reading lengthy and complicated articles. They do not have particular areas of specialism to which they devote themselves—media studies, political history, women's studies. In newspapers, every day, they are offered information about hundreds of different topics—not just Australian state and federal politics, but also the causes and effects of many different kinds of crime,; dangers to children—including swimming pools and sports; the ways in which society is changing with new technologies; and evolving gender roles and issues about the rights of people from different sexualities and different cultural backgrounds. This is in addition to the material they might read for pleasure, or that gives them information about the forms of entertainment they enjoy and the sports they follow, or perhaps data about the property market that applies directly to them, or stories from the business section that speak to their work practices. So it makes sense that when trying to reach that wider audience, you need to find a way to communicate your research findings in a way that is as simple and concise as possible, and makes them relevant to readers. 'Dumbing down'—or, as it might be put in a less elitist way, 'communicating to non-experts'—is an important skill, one that is extremely difficult to master.

One point about your results: you will not be able to quote statistics because this approach doesn't involve counting the number of stories that are sexist. Textual analysis is qualitative (expressed in words) rather than quantitative (expressed in numbers). When we use numbers to count the number of texts that work in particular ways, we call that 'content analysis'. Each approach has strengths and weaknesses. In its simplest terms, content analysis tends to have a greater *reliability* (if two researchers counted the same thing in the same newspapers, they would come up with exactly the same answer), while qualitative textual analysis tends to have a higher *validity* (it matches up better with real life). For example, one group of researchers, looking at Indigenous representation in Australian newspapers, developed a set of categories for content analysis (Jackson, Stanton and Underwood 1995). One category was 'Equivalence of Indigenous people with animals'—the researchers had noted a tendency, particularly in older representations, for Indigenous people to be equated with animals, either to celebrate their link to nature, or to condemn their lack of civilisation. One story they encountered while doing the content analysis was a celebratory interview with Indigenous film and television star Ernie Dingo—with the headline 'Ernie Dingo is top dog'. The researchers had to put this story into the category 'Equivalence of Indigenous people with animals', even though it was obviously a very different kind of story from those they had in mind when they developed this 'negative' category. If they had not counted the story in this category, then the scientific replicability of the study would have been compromised. To take account of how this text actually worked, what it was obviously trying to do and likely interpretations of it would have compromised the whole project of content analysis.

CONCLUSION

When you ask people questions, you change the way in which they think about an issue. Textual analysis is a way for researchers to gather information about how other human beings make sense of the world in their day-to-day lives, when they don't have academics watching over them. To do textual analysis, you begin by establishing a question about culture that interests you. You then gather suitable texts to analyse. In analysing them, you draw on your knowledge of relevant intertexts—in the series, genre, comments on the texts you are analysing and the wider semiosphere—in order to make an informed guess at likely interpretations of a text. In this way, you can provide evidence about the sense-making practices of a given culture at a given time—the ways of making sense of the world that are available to a community of consumers.

After going through this whole process, you have a finding: Australian newspapers have clearly been sexist in their coverage of former prime minister Julia Gillard. They have focused on the way that she dressed, her haircut and her fashion sense in a way that they never have for male prime ministers. You can expand this finding, with detailed references to the relevant texts, for an academic article that opens with a literature review of previous research on the representation of female politicians. Or you can develop it into an opinion piece for a newspaper that builds on a recent example of such sexism and draws on a small number of the most colourful examples to make your point. Importantly, however you do it, you will be able to back up your finding with empirical evidence that supports your claims. That's the joy of textual analysis.

FURTHER READING

Read further into the topic with a simple introduction such as Alan McKee (2003), *Textual Analysis: A Beginner's Guide*. Then consider more detailed examples by a good textual analyst such as John Hartley, 'Television and the power of dirt', in his *Teleology: Studies in Television*, (1992, pp. 21–44) and 'Agoraphilia: The politics of pictures', in his *The Politics of Pictures* (1993b, pp. 28–41). Round it off with more advanced writings in, for example, Robert C. Allen (1992), *Channels of Discourse Reassembled*.

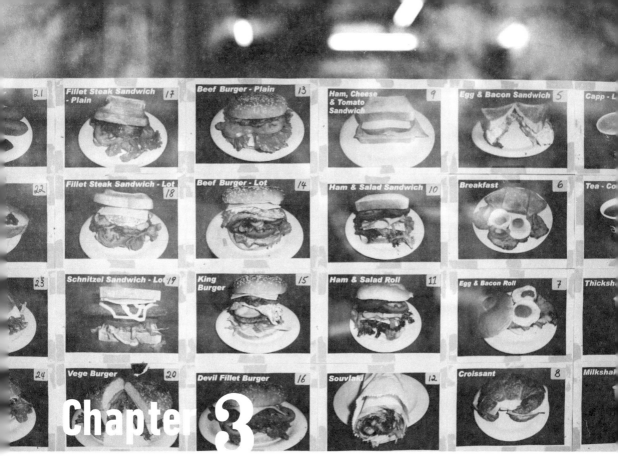

Chapter 3

REPRESENTATION

KATE BOWLES

Advertising or Marketing Communications for Food or Beverage Products shall not undermine the importance of healthy or active lifestyles nor the promotion of healthy balanced diets, or encourage what would reasonably be considered as excess consumption through the *representation of product/s or portion sizes disproportionate to the setting/s portrayed or by means otherwise regarded as contrary to Prevailing Community Standards.* (AANA Food & Beverages Advertising & Marketing Communications Code 2008, emphasis added)

One of the most obvious approaches to studying the Australian media and communications industries is to analyse how these media represent issues, ideas and things. At first sight, this seems an unproblematic and practical proposition, as the above example suggests. We need to understand representations (depictions of portion sizes, for example) in terms of their relationship to real-world 'settings' (shared community definitions of small, medium and large, for example) because of their potential impact on decision-making behaviour. This assumption extends beyond images of physical objects to the representation of more abstract beliefs, relationships and values. If we understand how the media represent these large and important concepts, we will be closer to explaining how these representations can also cause concepts—and thus behaviour and social experience—to change over time. There are many stakeholders in this discussion, including academics, television producers, advertising creatives, filmmakers, game designers and web editors. In fact, anyone whose job it is to communicate with others is constantly engaged in thinking about representation—how it works and why it matters. There are also a range of methods that have been used to try to describe the content and practice of media representation. We will look at some of these later in this chapter, but first we will consider exactly what we mean when we say 'representation':

> Tired of watching cooking shows that are nothing like the reality of your kitchen adventures? (*The Magazine* 2000, p. 115)

Representation exists in a relationship to something else we call 'reality'. Take one of the simplest and most transparent media genres: the cooking show. First, this consists of selective evidence of a real past event that occurred in front of a camera—something that really happened, on a particular day, with many unpredictable elements. The real event will have taken longer to happen than the cooking show has time to portray, so the show relies on conventions of selection and editing to explain cooking to its audience. It is important that you understand this for the show to make sense, but it is equally important that this knowledge doesn't interrupt your viewing pleasure. Second, a cooking show sets up a relationship to an imaginary but plausible future experience of cooking, in real time, in a real kitchen (perhaps yours). It is necessarily *un*realistic, but it still makes sense to you because it follows generic conventions to do with editing and time compression that you understand and accept.

But every time you encounter a representation of anything you evaluate its limitations, and then weigh up its usefulness in terms of the credibility gap between what the representation suggests and your own experience or assumptions. This is why you can be called upon to upgrade to a new type of cooking show because you've become 'tired' of something that is no longer satisfactory in terms of the 'reality' of your own adventures. This takes us to the important second dimension of representation: that it is a system of choices that are based on values that are able to be contested, enabling one representation to be judged as doing a better job than another.

JUDGING REPRESENTATION

If the form and content of any representation are the result of a series of production choices, then part of our purpose as consumers and producers of representation is to try to determine what principles governed these choices. In terms of media and communications industry practices, these choices might range from the casting in a movie, to the storyline in a TV soap, to the selection and editing of footage in news media. If you're asked to cast a character described only as a club owner, should this character be male? Could she be Chinese? If you need an image of a child to illustrate a news article, what age, shape, size or ethnicity is a typical child? The difference between representation and reality is measured by these decisions, which is why representation as a practice is loaded with implications of privilege and priority. Whose choices are these? And what motivated or restricted those choices?

Everyday media literacy means that the process of selection, composition and presentation is well understood by viewers and readers, and the results will occasionally cause some friction. Women may lobby to be portrayed more often as working in jobs considered to be typically male, for example, or parents of children with disabilities may campaign to see a broader range of children represented as ordinary. These are examples of the argument that images could—and should—do a better job of representing social reality, precisely because they have the capacity to affect the way people think and behave. Look at these two arguments about the effect of representation from two quite different sources:

Women are subjected daily to *media representations* of their gender which are very public, highly sexual and absolutely degrading. I cite specifically the Howard Showers billboards (tall, thin, naked women clenching their breasts and pouting, apparently to sell jeans), the Warner 'I love being a woman' lingerie campaigns (tall, thin, half-naked women wearing trashy underwear and too much makeup), the Pizza Hut girl (is she on the menu?). Is it any wonder that we become too easily objectified? ('A Beginner's Guide to Sexism' 2000, p 28, emphasis added)

Thus the norms of that 'television world'—chronically overpopulated as it is by professionally successful, physically fit, white, sexually attractive middle and upper class people—naturally come to define, for many people, the basic contours of how it *really* is, out there in the big wide world, beyond their immediate personal experience . . . This does produce a potentially schizophrenic situation for viewers. If their immediate (necessarily limited and often literally segregated) sphere of personal experience gives them no point of reference from which to evaluate what the media say about a given topic, they are thus rendered the more vulnerable and gullible towards (or at least bemused by) *media representations.* (Morley 1999, p 144, emphasis added)

Both of these writers are critical of representations on the grounds that they can effect real transformations of self, identity and perception of the world. The first writer—a student journalist—argues that Australian billboard advertising changes the way women feel about themselves, and encourages the habit in others of seeing women as objects. This is an argument about the effect of representation. The second writer—a media studies academic—makes essentially the same argument, in more depth. He proposes that, as our real experiences are necessarily more limited than the range of experiences presented to us in the media, we have no way of judging their accuracy and are more likely to accept them as realistic, adjusting our impression of the real world accordingly. These beliefs about the power of images to affect what we believe, and the assumptions about media users that lie behind them, have a long history. In 1937, for example, one commentator on the rise of the American motion picture industry wrote that:

> The sheer force of visual-audible representations exercises a compelling power over the individual and the mass . . . Whatever the desires or the intentions of the men who make the movies, the medium possesses *inexorable normative consequences.* (Rosten 1939, pp. 314–15, emphasis added)

USING REPRESENTATION TO FORM SOCIAL JUDGEMENTS

A useful illustration of this argument that representation affects our sense of what is normal relates to the fact that Australia is an import-dependent media culture. As a result of this, much mainstream Australian television, film, gaming and internet content has come from the United States, and a smaller but still significant proportion of the media we consume comes from Britain. Whatever impact this might have on the local production industries, or on the development of Australian cultural identity, it is also important to recognise the framework this creates for our ideas about the United States or Britain. Whenever media representations of people from other countries or cultures substitute for our direct experience of those countries or cultures, we can only test representations against other representations. Is America like *CSI* or *Grand Theft Auto IV*? Is London what we see in *The Bill*? And are American cops naturally more glamorous than British cops, or do these two different television systems represent policing differently? In the same way, we are obliged to accept or reject representations of the past by testing them against the credibility of other representations we have seen of the same historical events. In the absence of personal experience, we become highly dependent on representation to form our sense of the meaning of events, people and places in the past.

Just as our sense of what is happening in other parts of the world, or what happened in the past, is strongly inflected by media representation, so many different sections of the Australian community also know about each other primarily by means of images, often in popular media. We may therefore base very serious political, social and ethical decisions on the nature of these images. Consider the influence on your thinking of popular images of the unemployed, or private school students, or the police, or wealthy tax-evaders, or people who use illegal drugs, or suburban families, or farmers, or smokers. Now imagine that you are preparing to vote in an election in which problems relating to these social groups are being represented. If media representations have created a certain impression of any of these communities of which you happen *not* to be a member, then it is likely that your response to a political campaign focusing on one of these groups may be affected by the way those groups have been portrayed to you.

This problem does not result only from the segregation of experience from representation. Representation has its own priorities, which often have very little to do with the reality of what is being represented. Recall Morley's discussion of the representations that appear to advance the interests of a dominant class—the young, white, middle-class, healthy, able-bodied, attractive and cheerful men and women who dominate magazine covers, soap operas and billboards. The argument here is a demographic one: that in any given community, the real distribution of ethnic, gender and age diversity, health, sexuality and physical attractiveness, among many other variables, will not match the distribution of these characteristics in representations of that community. In the same way, a news journalist expresses her frustration at the way in which non-white Australians are represented in mainstream television:

> Migrant Australia is still a tribe of ghosts, fluttering along the edges of mainstream TV . . . In adland, a set of universal laws prevails. Ads for dairy products, shampoo and breakfast cereal have to be shot like a Leni Riefenstahl propaganda piece—lots of Aryan types running around in the sun, nary a non-Nordic in sight. (Verghis 2000, p. 12)

Although this situation is changing very gradually, there *are* more and different types of Australians on the streets than there are on the screen, and there *is* more real social variation among members of a particular ethnic community than representation commonly allows. The distorted demographics of mainstream television's imaginary Australia aren't there to capture reality, but rather to represent a formula that satisfies other promotional objectives. A television drama is over-populated with thoughtful, articulate, good-looking people because these telegenic actors can be promoted in associated media. Media narratives typically represent a more action-packed lifestyle (more car crashes, more kidnapping, more romance and more loss) than the one you lead because media formats are short, and the appeal of watching everyday life in real time is quite limited.

To sum up: representation attracts our critical and reformist attention because it is a value-driven practice governed by conventions and restrictions that often widen, rather than close, the gap between an image and the thing it represents. In academic analysis as much as in popular thinking, this has led to a kind of 'reverse engineering'—trying to figure out the designs that lie behind the representations we see in order to remake them, with the hope that this will lead to real-world benefits. To understand what makes representation systematic in this way, we need to move beyond a casual appreciation of how one particular portrayal works to understand the broader rules of meaning-making that govern the production and distribution of *all* representations.

THEORY: THINKING SYSTEMATICALLY ABOUT REPRESENTATION

This shifts us beyond being able to appreciate what is going on in any particular instance of representation to the use of theory to help us generalise across different examples. But first it is worth pausing to reflect on what we mean by 'theory'. As simply as possible, a theory is an attempt to understand the underlying logic that governs any system. If we can detect a pattern, we can start to think about when and why it occurs. This requires us to analyse both the individual elements in the pattern, and the way they work in combination. In the case of cultural trends, the pattern is likely to emerge over time, so we further need to understand each instance of a trend in the context of its historical development. For example, what have been the common images of women in Australian media culture, and how have these changed over the last ten years? How do we represent children differently now than we did in the 1930s, and why? What are the key features in the representation of leisure time, consumerism, paid employment or family life, and how do these contribute to real social change in any of these key areas?

When we are trying to answer these questions, cultural theory itself does not provide evidence—although the development of a theory about something may draw on empirical studies. Theory involves a certain amount of guesswork and speculation;

it is a practice of reasoning, and of constructing or reconstructing the ways in which we can think and talk about what we observe. And although critical and cultural theories can therefore seem frustratingly complex and at odds with our commonsense lived experience, our response might be more sympathetic if we remember that even the most unconvincing theoretical position is likely to be sourced in the theorist's original personal experience of perplexity, confusion or political concern—of looking at something and trying to make sense of it, or to make a difference to it.

REPRESENTATION, OBJECTIFICATION AND SEXUALISATION

As an example of this, let's start with theories that emerged during the 'second-wave' feminism movement of the early 1970s, concerned with the ways in which popular movies portrayed women. One frequently cited critical essay at the core of this thinking, Laura Mulvey's (1975) 'Visual Pleasure and Narrative Cinema', was originally written in 1973. Like many 1970s feminists, Mulvey was frustrated by the way in which women had been represented in the movies with which she had grown up. As a filmmaker herself, she was interested specifically in camera work, and in what it meant for audiences to share the viewpoint of the camera when it looked at the bodies of women in particular ways. Mulvey's argument was that popular Hollywood cinema should be taken seriously precisely because mass audiences took pleasure from it, and because this pleasure related to the psycho-sexual formation of male and female identity. Psychoanalysis lent a seemingly coherent explanation to feminism, and provided a ready-made vocabulary for the ways in which cinema was able to capitalise on a deeply seated (and perhaps even unconscious) human sexual pleasure in looking at things.

This complex theoretical position—that 'woman as representation signifies castration, inducing voyeuristic or fetishistic mechanisms to circumvent her threat'—has subsequently lost much of its specific credibility. But it left as an enduring legacy the connection between representation and an idea of 'objectification'. Literally, this means that something abstract or intangible has acquired the properties of a physical object, reducing its complexity and integrity. To an extent, all representations have this tendency, but objectification is so closely associated with claims about the representation of women that it has become commonplace to conflate objectification with 'demeaning representation', or even with 'offensive representation'. This attaches to the suggestion that the ways in which we represent people cause real effects in one of three ways:

- by harming the individual represented
- by harming the whole class of persons represented
- by harming the person who looks at the image or reads the description.

In other words, the image of a woman in an underwear advertisement that is displayed on the back of a bus can be argued to be harmful to the model who posed for the shot; it may be seen to harm all women by representing them in a particular way; and it may specifically harm the viewer of the image. We can therefore see the residue of a historically specific theoretical position on the psycho-sexual representation of women behind most legal or informal means of regulating representation generally.

In Australia, there are a very significant number of organisations and individuals involved in either setting and implementing policy standards for the things that can be portrayed, or in lobbying on behalf of community stakeholders either for those standards to change, or to stay where they are. Behind these continuing policy negotiations lie complex beliefs about the sexual dimensions involved in the practice of representing, and the associated practice of looking at representation. This has led to the emergence of the term 'sexualisation' in policy debate, often as a direct substitute for 'objectification'. One practical example of this is the 2007–08 Inquiry into the Sexualisation of Children in the Contemporary Media Environment conducted by the Australian Senate Environment, Communications and the Arts Committee, which received a large number of community and expert submissions on the question of whether or not children are harmed either by the way they are represented, or by what is represented to them (Australian Government, Senate Standing Committee 2007).

REPRESENTATION AND STEREOTYPING

The second broadly theoretical trend that we can detect behind the discussion of representation is sociological in origin: the theory of stereotyping. Imagine that you have been asked to find a typical Australian child to feature in a toy catalogue. This figure is both important and marginal, but needs to be cast within the realm of typicality. Should this child be younger or older, male or female, Indigenous or Asian? To represent a typical child in a way that enhances the wide appeal of the product to children in general, the specific features of all but one child option must be ruled out, and that remaining image must then pretend to be typical of all. However, the choice can't afford to be so random as to entirely surprise most of the audience if the cultural work of the representation has been commissioned as 'typical'. The person making the choice therefore needs to be reasonably well informed about what is accepted as typical in the target audience, and in part she or he will have to take into account what has been represented as typical before. For the reasons we have already described earlier in this chapter, certain stereotypes (white, able-bodied) will prevail as a result of this mix.

But the problem is that the typical Australian child cannot be realistically represented because there is no such singular thing *in reality*. We therefore need to be attentive to stereotypes, not because they show us how things are, but because they show us the range of beliefs that lie behind attempts to communicate by sorting the world into meaningful units. Unlike psycho-sexually derived symbols that claim to originate in universal human characteristics, social stereotypes are culturally specific and variable in terms of age, gender, race and ethnicity. Historical content analysis of Australian toy catalogues would show, for example, that the illustratively typical kid has changed quite significantly over time. The theory of stereotyping therefore enjoys one significant advantage over psychoanalytic theories of gender representation, in that it allows for (even depends upon) sensitivity to cultural and political specificity, and the prospect of social change.

REPRESENTATION AND IDEOLOGY

The question of social change attaches theories of stereotyping to a third approach, which we might call the ideological model of representation. This position, which has been strongly associated with Marxist cultural theory, argues that representation is one of the most obvious means by which cultural producers impose their preferred positions (their ideologies) on the larger populations of passive reading and viewing publics. This encourages a focus on how representation promotes, for example, certain ideals about work, lifestyle and social order in ways that sustain rather than critique the interests of a market-driven consumerist culture. In this account, what representation nurtures is a social community resigned to the inequalities of capitalism and continually persuaded by certain representational norms to aspire to things staying more or less as they are. Under these circumstances, we might see consistent positive presentations of home ownership, or the normative nuclear family, or the connection between job satisfaction and self-esteem, because each of these sustains the broad social structures that enable the global financial systems to work, more or less.

One useful Australian example of this is the gradual transformation of the representation of social drinking. Traditional Australian beer commercials, including the long-running VB series, represented beer drinking as part of the public culture of (male) mateship, in which working men drank beer at the pub at the end of a hard day's work—justifying both the experience of hard work and bonding over beer. As the ideological settings for both work and masculinity have shifted, beer commercials have kept pace, using both diversification and irony to maintain the credentials of their product. Campaigns continue to draw on the nostalgic association of masculinity, work and mateship, but there are now more women in the picture, both drinking beer with men and laughing at men who drink beer—who are now also laughing at themselves and each other. These revisions invite the viewer to share the joke about beer-drinking men who only hang out with their mates, and miss out on the more expanded sense of fun implied by drinking beer in a wider social circle. But as health policy concern about the impact of social drinking grows, particularly in terms of the risk of harm to young men and women, the settings are adjusted again, leading to the parallel genre of television commercials that advertise social drinking in mixed-gender groups as leading to harm and loss. Despite the acute contrast between these two representational trends, we can clearly see that each is motivated by the desire to use images to persuade people to behave in certain ways.

The idea that representation has something to do with a culture's ideological settings at a particular time is therefore a useful one, but it has a key weakness: like psychoanalytic accounts of gender, or sociological accounts of stereotyping, it is motivated by a belief that representation is imposed on the consumer by the producer. This is difficult to sustain. Despite the efforts of producers, the practice of making meaning consists of more than the simple transmission of an image or an idea. We now accept that meaning is not a quality that sits inside a text like a bone in a tomb waiting to be dug up by someone. This is why it is unhelpful to focus entirely on the motives of the producers of representation—if there is no bone, then no one put it there.

ONE OF THESE THINGS IS NOT LIKE THE OTHER: A WORD ABOUT SEMIOTICS

This does not mean that there is nothing to study in a text—that a text can mean anything you like—but rather that we need to approach the study of texts by thinking about the processes that structure any representation and enable it to potentially make sense. The kinds of representations we have been discussing so far (media images and products) involve the codification of meaning into systematic units of communication. It is helpful at this point to notice that our primary experience with a system of this kind is in our acquisition and use of language itself. In other words, language is a representational system, but because it is such a simple one, it is a useful illustration of a very important property of representation: that it exists in an arbitrary relationship to the real. Semiotic theories suggest that language is a collection of referential units ('signs'). These signs have both an arbitrary connection to the things they represent and a highly organised relationship to each other. So the most important thing to understand about language as a representational practice is that it is a system, in which the meaning of each individual part can only be determined by knowing how the whole system works.

The idea of language being arbitrary in its relationship to the real might initially seem confronting. However, this is precisely what makes language adaptable to different cultural and historical circumstances—and this is also what makes it obvious that meaning exists in the specific ways in which language reconstructs the physical real at any given time or for any given community, rather than in any essential characteristic embedded in the material world itself. Stuart Hall (1997, p. 21), for example, points out that there is nothing in the arrangement of letters in the word 'tree' that relates to the physical properties of a tree, and proves this point by reminding us that the French word for 'tree' is entirely different: *arbre*. As the two words are so different, and neither has anything to do with the nature or shape of trees, then each must be arbitrary in its evolution, as the word a particular language group has agreed to use to talk about a tree.

The core of this theory of language construction is that the way in which we communicate meaning has much more to do with the differences *between* signs in the same system than with any inherent properties within the individual signs themselves. So in English we use the same word 'tree' to describe many things that seem quite different from each other, but we have a separate word for a 'bush' because we think this is a distinction worth attending to. The difference between the words conveys the message that the two things they represent are also considered *by us* to be different from each other. In fact, the difference between the words *constructs* the difference between the things; in learning language, we learn which differences matter in our culture and language group, and which don't. We don't, for example, have different words for trees that are still growing and trees that have fallen down—in everyday language, we're happy to think of all of these as trees.

As Hall and many others argue, this theory of language as a practice of representation therefore helps us to appreciate the ways in which culture shapes meaning, and how depiction is based on culturally-specific systems of differentiation. This allows us to take advantage of the shift—often attributed to Italian Marxist Antonio Gramsci—away from thinking in terms of ideology as something that is dumped on the weak by the powerful—in particular, by means of representation—towards a more complicated sense of representation as a shared ideological project. This can be thought of as a powerful cultural consensus, sometimes referred to as 'hegemonic', about what things mean and why they matter. We are all continuously and collaboratively involved in maintaining this consensus, enabling it to change over time. This does not for a moment evade the question of real political power, but encourages a much broader understanding of the way power circulates around the members of a community.

This is a more sophisticated model for thinking about the representation of social complexities like gender, sexuality, age, race and ethnicity in the Australian context—perhaps the most powerful markers of identity differentiation both in critical thinking and everyday stereotyping. Just as language constructs difference as part of the meaning of the smallest everyday item (this is a rock, and that is only a stone), its larger effect can be seen in the construction and reinforcing of *social* differences and, in turn, the creation of a way of thinking about (and repoliticising) the relations of power that those differences support. So we can now see more clearly that we use terms which differentiate socially in ways that establish both the identity of the user and the immediate priority in the particular act of communication. Under what circumstances would we call someone 'Anglo', or 'Irish' or 'black'? Who might choose to say 'gay' or 'queer', and how might these terms change according to who uses them? What are the different meanings of 'freak', and how do we know which is which?

ANALYSING REPRESENTATIONS: WHAT TO LOOK (OUT) FOR

Theories of differentiation derived from semiotics help us to see that there will always be a number of different, context-specific and equally valid ways of interpreting any representation using a process of comparison with other surrounding and preceding images. Your interpretation of what is being presented to you depends on whether you have seen anything like it before, as well as how it relates to and contrasts with other things you can identify. It is only in the constant shuffling of the relationships between representations that you can start to see what positional signs like 'Indigenous' or 'young' actually signify *to you*, and why they matter—again, *to you*.

This raises an obvious problem for the nature and authority of media analysis. How can we extend our individual and perhaps idiosyncratic interpretations to speak about the content, significance or impact of a particular media text, or the tendencies across a group of texts, with a broader authority than 'this is how things look to me'? What might the practice of textual analysis look like, and how convincing will it be, once we have conceded that we are not aiming for the single, complete or correct reading of the form or content of the text? There are a number of research strategies that have been developed for the analysis of representation, originating in different disciplines that have different investments in sorting out what texts are about. Literary and film scholars, for example, have often focused on the analysis of aesthetics, form and genre, as much as thematic content. Language scholars have promoted both narrative and discourse analysis, suggesting that what is represented must be understood in terms of the cultural storyline within which it is positioned. Scholars concerned with the impact of representation on social behaviour have developed elaborate means of classifying content and counting it: content analysis of this kind is a common means of measuring the social impact of, for example, the representation of health issues such as smoking, or teen pregnancy. Media producers are very sensitive to this kind of research: you will probably have noticed that characters on teen-oriented Australian TV shows now rarely smoke, and if they drink alcohol, they do so as a sign that personal problems are imminent. The problem with content analysis is simply that it's not possible to use this method to confirm that audiences copy what they see, and the risk is that it can divert the effort to achieve social change into the reform of popular media.

Clearly, we need a less reductive approach to textual analysis—one that takes account of content *and* appreciates that form, aesthetics and narrative are part of the way in which a particular text presents itself to an audience. But we need to go beyond the features of an individual text to study how any of these features reach out inter-textually to draw on the dominant cultural discourses that surround it. First, this means that we need to decide which other texts have something in common with the text that interests us. Do we compare one TV episode with another, or a TV episode and a game that both have female lead characters, or a billboard with a popular novel because both make some reference to environmentalism? What other data do we need to put ideas like 'environmentalism' into some context? Second, we need to find out who produced the texts that interest us, and when, in order to understand a little about where they came from. It might be useful to compare an Australian war movie with a Japanese one, or a professional travel documentary with a home movie, but we need to be wary of textual analysis that overstates the cultural coherence of the production process, or the typicality of one text as representative of others like it. For example, do we search for consistency in the way the Australian media represent things, and make an argument from these about Australianness? What would make this credible? And why would this be useful?

Finally, we need to accept that the arguments we make about the importance of representation cannot be incontrovertibly demonstrated by textual evidence on its own. Texts are like maps: they are suggestive, interesting documents that encourage us in the practice of curiosity. They help us to trace some of the priorities of some parts of the cultures within which we operate. To return to the example above, this means that if we find thematic consistency in the way the Australian media represent something—children, for example—then this will tell us very little about the naturally occurring qualities of children in this (or any other) culture, but it will expand our understanding of some of the investments this culture makes in the idea of the child. Media representations can both augment and challenge the assumptions embedded in the law and everyday life—this is why, in Australia, we don't commonly represent children as workers, soldiers or car drivers, whatever their physical capacity to do these things may be.

But we will also be able to find contradictory representations, and plenty of evidence that cultural settings are changing, and we need to deal with this. There is no ideal number of texts that we need to analyse to achieve some objectively determined standard of research rigour: we simply need to accept the limitations of what we can do, on the basis of the choices that we make—after all, textual analysis is itself a practice of representation, and works like all the others we have been discussing. In other words, textual analysis is a method that helps us gain important clues about Australia's cultural settings, and to this extent can be a really useful beginning to our inquiry into the significance of the media and communications industries. However, it shouldn't be its end.

CONCLUSION

This chapter has argued that representation is of interest to media analysts because it gives us an opportunity to investigate a series of deliberate choices made in the pursuit of effective communication. Because representation is considered to have important real effects in the social world, many theories have been developed to consider its effects, and some (but not all) of these have been considered here. However, this chapter has suggested that the most valuable insight comes from semiotic theories of communication. These explain that meaning has an arbitrary but systematic relationship to the real: it is made in the ways in which individuals process the differences between things.

FURTHER READING

A comprehensive analysis of the structure and political impact of representational practice is given in Stuart Hall's (1997b) edited collection *Representation*, which includes Hall's important essay 'The Work of Representation' (Hall 1997a). Like Hall, cinema scholar Richard Dyer has looked closely at the conventions and techniques of representing race, focusing on the representation of whiteness, in *White* (1997). In the Australian context, studies of representation include Catharine Lumby's *Bad Girls* (1997), a significant rethink of conventional analysis of media images of women and sex as offensive, and Fiona Nicoll's *From Diggers to Drag Queens* (2001), a study of the way in which representations of masculinity form part of the construction of Australian national identity.

Most book-length studies of the Australian film and television industries have included some discussion of the ways in which movies and TV shows made in Australia have represented (and contributed to) the public discussion of Australian nationalism, including Felicity Collins and Therese Davis's study, *Australian Cinema After Mabo* (2005). Good introductory books for studying textual analysis include

John Hartley's *Tele-ology: Studies in Television* (1992) and Alan McKee's *Textual Analysis: A Beginner's Guide* (2003).

One very useful summary of the reason why we might move beyond our focus on the media text as the key object for analysis can be found in Nick Couldry's article 'Theorising Media as Practice' (2004). Nevertheless, the text continues to have practical, political valency, and we need to remember why it is that texts remain the focus of regulatory effort. A recent Australian article that considers the process by which controversial texts are used to anchor the public discussion of ideas and values is Anna Munster's 'The Henson photographs and the "network condition"' (2009). Munster also draws attention to role of the internet in changing the way digitised images can be distributed among users, which has had such a significant impact on traditional means of regulating who has access to those images.

Chapter 4
IMAGINING THE AUDIENCE

SUE TURNBULL

In 2006, American journalist Jay Rosen published a statement on behalf of 'The People Formerly Known as The Audience', directed to media producers everywhere. In it, the 'former' audience was described as those who were once:

> on the receiving end of a media system that ran one way, in a broadcasting pattern, with high entry fees and a few firms competing to speak very loudly while the rest of the population listened in isolation from one another—and who *today* are not in a situation like that *at all*. (Rosen 2006)

Rosen goes on to suggest that people today are using the technology that is at hand to connect with each other and to produce their own media, including blogs and podcasts. While Rosen's conception of the formerly 'atomised' audience might be something of an over-statement, his reimaging of people's 'new' relationship with the media signals the ways in which the internet and related media technologies have enabled people to participate in the media in new and unprecedented ways.

The concept of the media audience has therefore become increasingly problematic, since most people now use various forms of media technology and many different media platforms all day and every day, not only to 'receive' but also to create and 'send' various mediated content of all kinds. In the process, the once-clear distinctions between the spaces of leisure and work have become increasingly blurred.

For example, equipped with a wireless connection on public transport, a student on their way to class might be writing a blog post as part of an assignment on their laptop, while also keeping their Facebook page open in order to coordinate with friends where they will meet that evening. At the same time, they may be listening to their own 'library' of music on their smartphone, which is simultaneously updating them via Tumblr or Twitter on a breaking news story that they may re-send to their own 'followers'. Having spotted something unusual at a railway station, they may use their phone to capture the image and send it to their local newspaper, where they are working as an intern. In this instance, the student is hardly a member of a media audience, but is engaged in a range of simultaneous media practices for a number of different purposes.

While the concept of 'the media audience' might therefore be outdated, it is still important to understand how media audiences have been imagined and constructed in the past. What this history reveals is that most media audiences have never existed—at least not in the way that the highly visible (and audible) audience for a tennis match or a rock concert exists in a specific time and place. Even though we might reliably assume that a lot of people are reading the same magazines, listening to the same radio stations and accessing the same websites, it is unlikely that they will be doing so in the same place or necessarily at the same time.

Consider the audience for the extremely popular American television series *Game of Thrones*. Produced and written by David Benioff and D.B. Weiss for the niche American cable station Home Box Office (HBO), according to the file-sharing website Torrentfreak, *Game of Thrones* was the most 'pirated' TV series of 2012 (Ernesto 2012). Given that the show was only 'officially' available in the United States and elsewhere on subscription-based television services, this piracy rate was hardly surprising given the critical and word-of-mouth success that the show had enjoyed in the press. What was surprising was the fact that this rampant piracy appeared to have little effect on the DVD sales of the show, with the box set of the first and second series breaking all of HBO's previous records for DVD sales (Hibberd 2013). The key point to be made here is that people all over the world were finding ways to watch this television show via a variety of platforms and means. Whether their viewing was scheduled by a television network or completely at their own convenience, there is little doubt that those who watched *Game of Thrones* were also aware that they were part of a global audience for the show.

People would know that they were part of the *Game of Thrones* audience for a number of reasons. For a start, reports on ratings, illegal downloads and DVD sales provide ongoing evidence that other people are watching the same show (more about ratings later). Viewers would also know they were not alone because of references to the show on other TV shows, or references to it in other media such as newspapers and magazines. They may also know they were part of the *Game of Thrones* audience because they had 'googled' the show on the internet and found either the official program site or unofficial fan sites where people are invited to post their thoughts about the characters and the story-lines. They may even feel impelled to write and publish their own *Game of Thrones* storyline (this kind of writing is called fan-fiction), or to create their own *Game of Thrones* images and media. All of these possibilities suggest that people who watch *Game of Thrones* do not have to be in the presence of others in order to know that they are part of a global media audience for the show, with which they have a connection by reason of their shared media preference.

What this account also suggests is that members of the audience for *Game of Thrones* may not only be *consumers* of the media text, but also *producers* of their own media forms about that text. In bringing together these two ideas, Axel Bruns has coined the term 'produser' to identify the role of the media audience member in this new configuration:

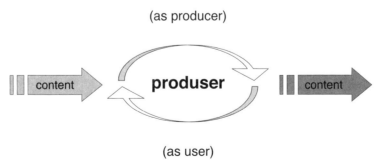

Figure 4.1 The produser
Source: Bruns (2008, p. 21).

The shift from thinking about media audiences in terms of their reception and consumption of specific media to thinking about that audience in terms of what they do with the media is by no means recent. The idea that people might use the media for their own purposes became current in the 1940s, and was described in terms of the 'uses and gratifications' that the media made available (Ruddock 2001, p. 68). However, the uses to which the media can be put have taken many new directions since the arrival of the internet and the kinds of social software associated with Web 2.0. The internet as a converged medium of communication has made it very easy for people to make and distribute their own media products, whether this be a Facebook page or a video clip that they have uploaded to YouTube.

American academic Henry Jenkins has written enthusiastically about what he describes as the new 'convergence culture' enabled by the internet, arguing that it heralds a new era of social and civil participation (Jenkins 2006b). As evidence of this (possibly) coming to pass, in early 2009 the US administration under President Barack Obama, who made skilled use of the internet during his presidential campaign, redesigned the White House home page to include a blog, a photo stream and a video upload entitled 'Your Weekly Address'. The home page also included the word 'Participate' in a box. Clicking on the box brought the user to the Office of Public Liaison, described as 'the front door' through which people may 'pass' in order to engage directly with government (Salomon 2009).

Being able to participate in the social and political life of a culture via what is often described to as 'the public sphere' now requires access to the kinds of media that enable one to do so. Regrettably, at the start of the twenty-first century there is still a technological divide between the rich and poor, both within and across nations. This means that some people in some parts of the world will be more able to participate in the relevant, and increasingly mediated, public sphere than others.

The concept of the public sphere, what it is and who participates in it has been the topic of great debate over the years. Within what is described as a 'modernist' version of the public sphere (often associated with the work of Jürgen Habermas), the role of the mass media—particularly journalism—is considered vital because it provides the information that enables citizens to make decisions about how to act within a democratic society (Dahlgren and Sparks 1991, p. 1). This version of the public sphere has been challenged for being too narrow, masculine and elitist. The focus on 'serious' journalism excludes more popular and tabloid forms of media—especially those favoured by young people and women, as well as those without political power. Indeed, there are many who would argue that there is not one public sphere, but many (Hartley 1996; McKee 2005). As Catharine Lumby (1999) suggests, it is in the messy proliferation of the 'postmodern' public spheres that circulate around such popular media as the tabloid newspaper or the television talk show that the majority of people form their moral judgements about how to be and how to participate in society.

Media audiences have been able to participate in their social world via the media since the media first came upon the scene, as Bridget Griffen-Foley makes clear in her article 'From *Tit-Bits* to *Big Brother*: A Century of Audience Participation in the Media'. This essay discusses the ways in which readers of periodicals in the 1880s and mass market magazines in the 1920s participated in discussions about issues that concerned them via the medium of print (Griffen-Foley 2004). As Bridget Griffen-Foley also points out, since the invention of the 'beeper-phone' in the 1960s, radio listeners have often been invited to call into a station with a request or a comment (Griffen-Foley 2004), and the same has also been true of television, with its 'vox-pop' segments and studio audiences. However, each of these examples also demonstrates that in the past it has been the media themselves that have largely controlled the terms of the audience's social participation. While this is still true for the most part, since the advent of the internet and related developments in mobile phone and tablet technologies, audiences not only have more control over what they consume, but also the capacity to interact directly with the producers of the media product, thereby having much greater influence on the direction that interaction might take.

BOX 4.1: *BIG BROTHER* AND TELE-PARTICIPATION

Consider the globally syndicated popular television show *Big Brother*, which was pro-grammed in Australia from 2001–08 on Channel 10 and subsequently revived by Channel 9 in 2012, as an example of tele-participation (Ross 2008). *Big Brother* has been described as a 'watershed' in media audience research because it involved the audience in a range of dif-ferent practices across a number of different media platforms (Ross and Nightingale 2003, p. 1). Viewers of the show were not only invited to watch half-hour programs every week-night, which provided a daily digest of the main events in the *Big Brother* House, but also late-night editions such as *Big Brother Uncut* (which included scenes deemed too explicit before the 9.30 p.m. cut-off point intended to ensure younger viewers were not watching). There were also special events in some seasons of the show, including the *Sunday Night Live Evictions* and the *Monday Live Nominations*, watched by thousands at home but also attended by thousands of fans at the *Big Brother* House in the Dreamworld theme park on Queensland's Gold Coast. Channel 10 also encouraged fans to visit the official website of the show, where they could subscribe and eventually have 24-hour video access to the house via digital streaming, as well as participate in a diary section and discussion forums. Fans set up their own websites (such *as Big Brother Underground*), where they could exchange views about the show. Telephones—especially mobile phones—were incorporated into the viewing experience, as viewers sent text messages voting for or against housemates, thereby partici-pating in decisions about the direction the show would take. *Big Brother* and its housemates also regularly featured on the radio and in the print media. When the show was not on air, visitors to Dreamworld were invited to visit the house in order to go 'behind the scenes'.

The case of *Big Brother* (along with other such 'reality' shows such as *MasterChef*, *The Block* and *The Voice*) illustrates how difficult it is to track the many ways in which a media audience might be involved in a show like this, especially since it involves so many media platforms and technologies. But why should we bother? Who is interested and why?

WHO WANTS TO KNOW ABOUT MEDIA AUDIENCES?

In the case of the television show *Big Brother*, discussed above, a lot of people wanted to know about the audience for the show. Those with a particular interest included media producers, members of the public, the government and academics from a wide range of disciplines, including education, sociology and psychology, as well as media and communications.

Industry interests in media audiences

Channel 10, the television network that originally bought the format for *Big Brother* from the Dutch production company Endemol for a considerable amount of money, wanted to know about the audience for the show because it hoped to make a profit on its financial outlay. Depending on the ratings for the show and its share of the television audience, Channel 10 could charge larger amounts of money for advertising or sponsorship.

BOX 4.2: RATINGS

The term *ratings* in this context refers to the statistical information that is gathered from a relatively small number of media users known as a *sample*, selected on the basis that this sample is a reflection of the population of users as a whole. The argument for the value of the ratings figures thus produced is that larger patterns of consumption can be inferred from a relatively small number of cases. Ratings are thus very important to media producers because they constitute the basis for charging commercial companies for advertising space. They are a therefore a kind of currency in which the television networks trade. For an industry perspective revealing how the television ratings are arrived at in Australia, visit the OzTAM website (<www.oztam.com.au>).

While the ratings for *Big Brother* in its first few seasons were high, these began to drop in subsequent seasons, prompting Channel 10 to invent increasingly bizarre twists and gimmicks, including in the final season the introduction of such American personalities as Pamela Anderson and Carson Kressley—the first to direct a glamour shoot featuring the housemates, and the second to suggest a makeover wardrobe based on his role as a style guru in another Channel 10 import, *Queer Eye for the Straight Guy*. Despite the producers' best efforts, in 2008 during a season that involved new presenters (Kyle Sandilands and Jackie O, who replaced Gretel Killeen) and a more diverse range of housemates (including a grandmother in her fifties who went on to win after being evicted on the first night), Channel 10 announced that it was no longer going to produce the show. The audience—or rather, the ratings—had spoken.

For the commercial media, the ratings—and therefore the audience—mean money. For some media, this is obtained at the point of sale. Newspapers, magazines and other print media are able to track their circulation figures in this way, although they may also include an estimate of the number of people who might be presumed to read the product when it has been purchased (in a doctor's waiting room, the same magazine might be read by a large number of people). However, most commercial media—including print, radio, television and the internet—derive the greater part of their income from advertising. As is often somewhat cynically suggested, the function of the commercial media is to deliver audiences to advertisers (Ang 1991, p. ix). It then follows that the commercial media have a great deal of interest in knowing who their audience is, and exactly what will attract and hold people's attention. Armed with this knowledge, they can then sell that audience to advertisers willing to pay to reach their target consumers. In this transaction, it is the audience that is for sale—although to imagine the audience simply as a commodity is to misconstrue the nature of the audience's engagement in the exchange. Most people don't access the commercial media with the primary intention of making themselves available to advertisers. As a result, the media industries have to know what will attract and hold audience attention long enough for the advertiser to reach them.

Media industry research is therefore not just concerned with measuring the audience using *quantitative* measures such as statistics, but is also in finding out as much as possible about how audiences relates to the product, what they think of it and what it means to them. This last interest may involve more *qualitative* methods such as focus groups and interviews, which cannot easily be reduced to a statistical measure. In this way, the knowledge that a media producer might seek about a media audience may be similar to the kind of knowledge a social scientist working for the government or an independent cultural critic might find of value, although it is unlikely to be published. Media industries don't always want their competitors to know what they know about their audiences.

Public and government interests in media audiences

In the case of *Big Brother*, there was considerable public interest in the show, stimulated by a tsunami of media attention when it was first broadcast. The media are often responsible for drawing attention to themselves in ways that may be critical or narcissistic. Newspapers, magazines, radio and other television networks, including the public service network the ABC, regularly interrogated the motives of the *Big Brother*'s producers and its audience, while Channel 10 cross-promoted the show ad nauseam at every opportunity. In July 2001, the ABC devoted a *Four Corners* program to the phenomenon of 'reality TV', revealing that, far from being simply a matter of concern in Australia, *Big Brother* was a matter for public debate in every territory where it was being produced (<www.abc.net.au/stories/s335957.htm>). Other national versions included the United Kingdom, the United States and France, where demonstrators clashed with the police in protests motivated by what was described as '*telly poubelle*'s' (trash television's) exploitation of the contestants and its abuses of human rights. Everyone, it seemed, wanted to talk about *Big Brother* and what it might mean to be watching it. Frequent concerns were raised about the perceived 'effects' of the show on young people.

This concern reached something of a climax in the 2006 season after two male housemates 'allegedly' sexually assaulted a female housemate. The police did not press charges. Although this incident was not broadcast on television, but streamed via the internet for an audience willing to pay for such 24-hour access, the public outcry was tremendous, as registered by the media. At this point, the then prime minister, John Howard, voiced his opinion that this was an excellent opportunity for Channel 10 'to do a bit of self-regulation and get this stupid program off the air'.

The relationship between media concern, public interest, and government attention is a familiar one. Governments are usually called upon to act in relation to a media audience when that audience is perceived to be at risk from some kind of harm as a result of exposure to the media. While the Coalition government of the day did not act in the case of *Big Brother*, the subsequent Labor government under the leadership of Kevin Rudd was responsive to a related expression of public concern about the effects of the media on a particular audience group.

In 2006, the independent research body know as the Australia Institute published two discussion papers about the sexualisation of children. The first of these, *Corporate Paedophilia* (Rush and La Nauze 2006), denounced what was described as the 'sexualisation' of children in the media. The report received considerable media attention, not least because the David Jones department store chain objected to being named in a press release as one of the companies in Australia that practised 'corporate paedophilia' because of its advertising to and for children. Newspapers, magazines, radio and television revisited the topic, and various lobby groups pressured the government to act. In March 2008, the Australian Senate referred the matter to the Senate Standing Committee on Environment, Communication and the Arts, and this committee commissioned a report to be delivered by June 2008.

BOX 4.3: THE SEXUALISATION OF CHILDREN IN CONTEMPORARY MEDIA

One of the terms of reference for this inquiry was that it should 'review the evidence on the short- and long-term effects of viewing or buying sexualising and objectifying images and products' in order to determine 'their influence on cognitive functioning, physical and mental health, sexuality, attitude and beliefs'. The inquiry received over 167 submissions and held two public hearings in Sydney and Melbourne. Given the short timeframe, the inquiry was not able to conduct any original empirical research involving children. However, many of those who made submissions to the Senate inquiry cited a report published by the American Psychological Association (2007) on the sexualisation of girls. This report was based on research conducted with women of university age and older, provoking a debate about how relevant this US report might be to children in a very different cultural and social context. The committee thus concluded that in reviewing the available research, there was 'a lack of definitive evidence concerning the media and the effect of premature sexualisation'. In its long list of recommendations, the inquiry called for further research, including a major longitudinal study into the effects of premature and inappropriate sexualisation of children. The case was far from closed. (Senate Standing Committee 2007)

The recommendation of the Senate Standing Committee that further research be conducted in Australia points to the ways in which governments can become involved in commissioning audience research into areas of public concern about the media and audiences.

In Australia, as in the rest of the world, public and hence government concern tends to be similar in nature, involving specific audience groups (especially children, youth and those otherwise deemed vulnerable in some way), specific content (violence and the representation of sexuality are perennial bugbears) and particular media forms (every new media form or platform is greeted with a contradictory mix of deep suspicion and/or celebration). However, despite the continuity of concern about the effects of the media on their audiences, and the considerable body of government-sponsored and independently produced research, the quest for definitive answers about the audiences and the media appears to be an elusive one. This is hardly surprising, given that the media continue to evolve in terms of technology, delivery and content, at the same time as the social and cultural world in which they are experienced is also always changing. To make matters even more complicated, the media themselves are a major force in the production of social change, as in the case of 'globalisation'.

Despite the vagaries and uncertainties, almost a century of academic audience research has produced some revealing insights into the ways in which audiences relate to the media.

Academic interest in media audiences

It would be wrong to assume that academic audience research is removed from the interests of the media industries, the public or the government of the day, although it may be in disagreement with all or any of these groups by virtue of the independence of academic work. In their daily lives, academics are themselves members of media audiences and participate in the public life of a culture. In this way, academic audience research is generally responsive to public concern about the media. Furthermore, it is usually academics and/or people who have been trained in university settings, who are employed by governments and their agencies to undertake commissioned audience research on their behalf. For example, the Australian Communications and Media Authority (ACMA), which is the government agency currently responsible for the regulation of broadcasting, the internet, radio communications and telecommunications, regularly commissions audience research involving academics. In 2007, ACMA released a major report entitled *Media and Communications in Australian Families*, which was written with the involvement of many academics and clearly informed by the history of academic research and theory relating to media and audiences.

In the case of *Big Brother*, academic research was conducted in many different countries where the program was shown. In the United Kingdom, Annette Hill's research was funded not only by the government, but also by the Independent Television Commission and Channel 4 (Hill 2005). In Australia, as part of a major ARC-funded study of how young women related to the media, Catharine Lumby and Elspeth Probyn conducted focus group interviews with over 200 teenage girls between the ages of 12 and 18, asking them what they thought about the show and the contestants. Their thoughtful responses led Lumby to conclude that *Big Brother* 'was a text that allowed young women to reflect on the ethical dilemmas of life in a mediated and highly self-conscious world' (Lumby 2003, p. 18).

Theory and method in media audience research

For the most part, it is academics working in academic settings who have done most to develop theoretical and methodological approaches to media audience research. However, there have been many different ways of thinking (or theories) about the audience for a media product or text, and many different ways of going about the business of trying to find out what this audience might be (using different research methods). As Andy Ruddock (2001) makes clear in an excellent overview of the field, critical to any research study is the way in which the audience is imagined and the perspective of the researcher.

To make a very broad generalisation, within what has been described as 'the effects tradition', the audience is usually imagined as passive and attempts to measure the negative impact of the media have usually involved a scientific approach involving quantitative measures. Often cited in this regard is the work of Albert Bandura and his infamous Bobo doll studies, involving a large inflatable doll, a mallet and adults acting very strangely in front of small children in order to prove that exposure to violent images teaches children to act aggressively (Ruddock 2001, p. 61). More recently, the work of George Gerbner—who is associated with 'cultivation theory'—has sought to demonstrate how prolonged exposure to images of violence and conflict in the media may 'cultivate' an attitude in the audience that the world is a violent and mean place (Shanahan and Morgan 1999).

Approached from another theoretical perspective, the audience is imagined as 'active', and the research methods employed are more likely to be qualitative, involving interviews and focus groups. The work of John Fiske in particular has been associated with this approach, inspiring many audience researchers—especially in the field of fan studies—to examine the ways in which media audiences might appropriate the media for their own subversive ends, although it might be noted that Fiske himself engaged in very little empirical research with audiences (Fiske 1989). It is Henry Jenkins' (1992) study of the audience for the TV series *Star Trek* that is the 'key' (most referenced) text in this regard, especially since as a *Star Trek* fan himself, Jenkins was able to describe the fan culture from the position of an insider. Through this endeavour, Jenkins described himself as an 'aca-fan' (a combination of academic and fan), and subsequently established a highly influential and popular weblog on the topic of media audience research in a converged media environment (<http://henryjenkins.org>).

It is, however, quite usual in the pursuit of obtaining better and more complete data to combine both quantitative and qualitative methodologies in what is often described as a multi-method approach. For example, a questionnaire can ask questions that can be quantified, or it may ask questions that require people to respond in longer comments that have to be analysed using qualitative methods of language or discourse analysis.

Figure 4.2 represents the relationship between how audiences have been constructed in theory and the types of research used to study them in a schematic way, although it should be noted that there have always been exceptions.

While it might be convenient to imagine that there has been a steady progression in thinking about media audiences from the bad old days when audiences were imagined as passive to a more enlightened present when they are imagined as active, this is clearly not the case. The 2008 Senate Inquiry into the Sexualisation of Children was instigated by people who for the most part imagined children as passive consumers of the commercial media and particularly vulnerable to negative effects of certain kinds of media images (see Chapter 3). Some audiences are regarded as more passive than

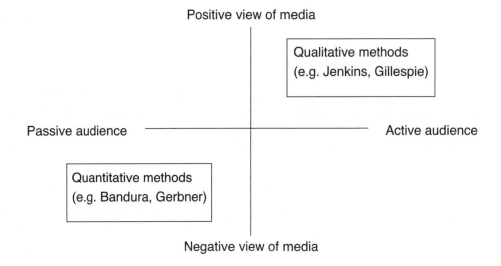

Figure 4.2 Relationship between research methods and audiences

others. This particular conception of causal media effects, variously described as the 'hypodermic needle' or 'bullet theory', still has currency. Old theories die hard. However, the final report of the Senate inquiry included the following comment, which suggests an awareness on the part of the authors of other possibilities and perspectives:

> Many young people make sense of the media in very different and diverse ways. Many young people access existing media in ways which may assist the formation of healthy sexual identities, including factual information on sex and relationships. (Senate Standing Committee 2007)

This conception of children as active users of the media, which they mine in order to produce their own sexual identity, echoes the 'uses and gratifications' theory of media functions noted earlier.

The idea that people come to the media for specific purposes and take from it what they require or need has been current since the 1940s (Blumler and Katz 1974). In 1941, Herta Herzog conducted research into the effects of listening to radio serials on daytime audiences in the United States, using both a survey and personal interviews with 100 women, thereby employing a mixed-method approach involving a combination of quantitative and qualitative methods. Herzog argued that the women derived 'three main types of gratification' from these serials: 'emotional release', a 'wishful remodelling' of their own domestic 'drudgery' and 'recipes' for adjusting to their daily lives (Herzog 1941, p. 69).

In pointing to the ways in which the women interpreted these daytime serials in the context of their own experience, Herzog's conclusions foreshadow a subsequent major development in media audience research concerned with matters of interpretation. This approach received considerable impetus after the publication of an essay by British sociologist Stuart Hall in 1973, entitled 'Encoding and Decoding in the Television Discourse'. It argued that before any media message might have an effect, satisfy a need or be put to use, it must first be interpreted by the receiver of the message whose individual 'frameworks of knowledge' would determine how the message would be understood. In suggesting this approach to 'decoding' a text, Hall was much influenced in his thinking by the foundational work of American structural linguist Charles Peirce, as well as by the French thinker Roland Barthes, whose book on semiotics, or the science of signs, was also influential in rethinking matters of media interpretation (Barthes 1968).

Hall's theories subsequently were put to the test by David Morley in a landmark study entitled *The Nationwide Audience* (1980). This research project endeavoured to verify the 'encoding/decoding' model by exploring how different audience groups drawn from different sectors of society might interpret the same television news broadcast differently, depending on their different frames of knowledge and ideological persuasion. One of the primary criticisms made of this study—and one of which Morley (1992) himself was well aware—was that in creating a number of 'artificial' viewing groups, Morley was not really finding out how people might make meaning from the media in the context of their own everyday lives, but rather constructing a series of audience groups for his own research purposes.

This lack of attention to the everyday and ordinary experience of the media lies behind the turn towards what has been described as an 'ethnographic' approach to media audience research (Moores 1993). The term 'ethnographic' should be treated with some caution, however, as it has been employed to describe projects that have simply used methods common to ethnography, such as interviews and observation (Nightingale 1993). With this in mind, the research of Marie Gillespie into the role of the media in the lives of young Punjabi people living in Southall, London, where she herself lived and taught for five years, is an example of media audience research that can more properly be described as 'ethnographic', since Gillespie was an active participant in the life of the community that she was also studying (Gillespie 1995).

Gillespie's research is of particular interest not only because she points to the critical role of the media in young people's lives, but also because she examines the ways in which specific media may function within diasporic communities in a globalised media environment. For example, the Australian television serial *Neighbours* was found to have particular value in the lives of these young Indian people living in London, who identified with the experience of a close community sustained by constant 'talk'. Gillespie's endeavours to understand how and why this should be the case illustrate both the promise and the challenge of media audience research.

CONCLUSION: WHY AUDIENCE RESEARCH STILL MATTERS

Although there may be individuals or groups who have little or no access to the media, for most people their sense of self and the social and cultural context in which they live may be dependent on their access to, and use of, various media technologies. Indeed, full participation in an increasingly mediated public sphere is now largely conditional on access to the media that enables one to be involved. Interest in and concern about media audiences are therefore unlikely to diminish as media technologies and media industries continue to evolve. However, what must also evolve are the ways in which media audiences are imagined, and the ways in which information about them is collected and interpreted. Knowing how this has been done in the past, and being aware of the various theoretical and methodological approaches that have been employed, along with their the advantages and disadvantages, are therefore vital for working out how best to understand the many different ways in which the media now matter in people's lives.

FURTHER READING

Understanding Audiences by Andy Ruddock (2001) provides a useful recent overview of media audience research, while *Investigating Audiences*, also by Ruddock (2007), discusses methodological issues with references to specific cases. Nightingale and Ross's (2003) collection of critical readings about media and audiences includes a number of essays by theorists mentioned in this chapter, including Blumler, Hall, Gillespie and Jenkins. A themed issue of the academic journal *Media International Australia* (no. 145, 2012) on the topic of 'Digital Ethnography' includes some interesting examples of recent research on new media use in different cultural settings. On the topic of convergence cultures and new forms of audience participation, see Henry Jenkins (2006b), *Convergence Culture* and Axel Bruns (2006), *Blogs, Wikipedia and Second Life*. For an overview of the ratings in Australia, see Mark Balnaves and Tom O'Regan (2002), 'The ratings in transition'. For more on the concept of the public sphere, see Alan McKee (2005), *The Public Sphere: An Introduction*. On the topic of media violence, see Martin Barker and Julian Petley (2001), *Ill Effects*, and for a comprehensive overview of the kinds of audience research undertaken in this regard, see Glenn Sparks (2002), *Media Effects Research*. *Beyond the Box*, by Sharon Ross (2008), provides an excellent account of 'tele-participation', based on the author's own empirical research with the audience for *American Idol*.

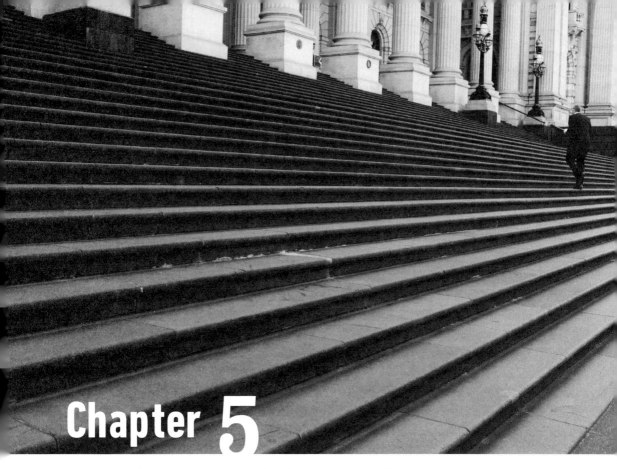

Chapter 5

POLICY AND REGULATION

STUART CUNNINGHAM

WHERE DOES THE POLICY APPROACH SIT WITHIN MEDIA AND COMMUNICATION STUDIES?

Policy issues are central to the study of media and communications, and may involve a discussion of political economy, public administration, politics and government. In order to come to grips with these issues, you may therefore find yourself studying everything from technical policy handbooks (e.g. Althaus, Bridgman and Davis 2012) through to racy critiques of unbridled deal-making, the power of media tycoons and spectacular corruption—such as the News International phone hacking scandal of 2011–12 (<http://en.wikipedia.org/wiki/News_International_phone_hacking_scandal>).

Discussion of policy issues are also often grounded in normative assumptions about how media should perform. Such assumptions typically include the independence of media outlets, broad community access to media, diversity of media content, objectivity of media content (especially in the area of news), promotion of social solidarity and cohesion, cultural pluralism and the promotion of quality media (see McQuail 2010). Such concerns are often grounded in a political economy approach, which has for the most part explored these questions in order to demonstrate the complicity of governments and regulatory agencies with the dominant economic interests in the media, as part of a larger project of establishing the functional (if at times contradictory) role of the state in the management of Australia's society and economy.

In Australia, this approach undergirds the 'media mates' approach to policy studies, which focuses on human agency and the contingencies of the policy process. It stresses the ways in which normative goals of media policy have been subverted by close patterns of interaction between Australia's powerful media proprietors, most notably the Packer and Murdoch families, and leading figures in both the Liberal and Labor Parties (e.g. Chadwick 1989; Griffen-Foley 2003, 2009; Masters 2006). To understand the underlying logic of 'media mates', it must always be borne in mind that often the most effective and powerful influencers of government policy (and therefore the generators of much policy themselves) remain those whose commercial interests are most directly impacted by such policy. Owen and Wildman (1992, pp. 24–5) state this with bluntness about another country:

> In the United States, as in other democratic societies, the process by which government makes and implements policy can be influenced by individual firms, acting alone or through associations. In the past, firms and industries made effective strategic use of their potential to shape government policy. Those who did not succeed in influencing policy became the victims of those who did.

Some would argue that the 'media mates' era came to an end in 2005 when Kerry Packer died, after which his son James Packer moved rapidly out of major holdings in media in favour of casinos and gambling. But that, if anything, has placed an even stronger spotlight on the influence exerted by Rupert Murdoch's News Limited. And in 2011–12 mining tycoon and Australia's wealthiest person, Gina Rinehart, acquired large stakes in Ten Network Holdings and, for a time, Fairfax Media, in what many saw as an attempt to exert influence.

Cultural policy studies represents a left-of-centre, reformist position that attempts to connect political economy with achievable change. Against the traditions of the Marxist left, cultural policy studies argues that real political and social change *is* possible in liberal-capitalist societies, and that one condition that enables advocates to more effectively achieve such goals is the capacity to learn the 'language' of decision-making agents and to participate in policy formation. Policy advocates (Bennett 1992; Cunningham 1992) contest the Marxist *cipher image* of public policy (Dunleavy and O'Leary 1987), where policy is seen largely as the reflection of outcomes achieved through elite bargaining among powerful agents outside of the policy process. By contrast, they believe that an ability to influence both the principles or governing 'discourses' and the more 'mundane' technical, administrative and organisational aspects of policy formation can make a significant political difference.

It is vital to recognise that reformist inspiration does not emerge full-blown from desk-bound theorising. Public-interest advocacy groups, consumer associations (like CHOICE), youth media groups (such as the Australian Children's Television Foundation (ACTF), and sector unions (such as the Media Entertainment and Arts Alliance (MEAA), play important roles in maintaining public participation in media policy, combining a commitment to public-interest goals with attention to the nuts and bolts of engagement with legislation and with bureaucratic systems and structures (Beattie and Beal 2007). This is a politics of bureaucratic reform that borrows more from American elite theory than from European neo-Marxist theories for its theoretical support. (The former posits that policy change is driven by struggles *between* elites rather than the assumption, seen in the latter theories, that elites *reinforce* each other's power and influence.)

The critical tradition of media and communication studies, which sees questions of policy as largely subordinate to understanding the main game of how economic and political forms of power interact in capitalist societies, has been under challenge from the centre-left of the political spectrum. Variations on the political tradition of social democracy—once dubbed 'third-way' political thought—argue that such third-way variation should no longer be seen as an inadequate halfway house between market capitalism and socialism, but rather as the best way to reconcile the core principles of the political left—such as a belief in equality, participatory democracy and social justice—with the challenges of globalisation, cultural pluralism and an increased assertion of the rights of the individual (Giddens 2001, 2002).

Applied to media, this approach can criticise leftist radicalism for its tendency to promote 'paternalist corporatism' (state-funded media are always better for you than commercial media) and become nostalgic over past golden ages at a time when technological change, industry competition and the development of new products more tailored to individual consumer requirements point to a need to seek new forms of synthesis between the promotion of dynamic competition and elevation of the principles of social and economic justice. Indeed, it is arguable that communications is one of the prime policy fields in which the balance between increased competition and social principles of access, equity and communication 'rights' needs to be found. Former Labor ministers Lindsay Tanner (1999) and Craig Emerson (2006) have promoted this approach to policy generally. Trevor Barr has sought to outline such an approach to Australian communications policy (Barr 2000, pp. 189ff).

Highly normative approaches to policy assessment are not, of course, the sole preserve of the political left. At the other end of the spectrum, think-tanks promoting libertarian, small-government approaches (such as the Centre for Independent Studies or the Institute of Public Affairs) publish critiques of the 'over-regulation' of Australian media (e.g. Berg 2012). (It should be noted, though, that libertarian approaches can be found on the left as well as the right of the political spectrum—for example, Lumby (1999, 2008)). Such studies adopt a pure neo-classical economic position on the pitfalls of state intervention and the virtues of markets that, if applied, would place at considerable risk the viability of Australia's media industries in a highly competitive global economy by programmatically limiting the role of government (with only minimum social regulation allowed). According to these approaches, public-sector commitments to cultural and industry development are held to be market distorting, inefficient and unsustainable in budgetary terms. Such advocacy also often positions itself as speaking for the concerns of mainstream citizenry against so-called 'cultural elites'.

Contemporary approaches to policy and regulation have attempted to take some of the ideological heat out of these debates. They emphasise the necessarily cooperative nature of regulation (the regulated must participate with the regulator in the outcomes of regulation), and the notion of regulatory design (state intervention must be fit for purpose, and constructed with the impact carefully thought through). In general, we can observe a principle of limiting regulation, eliminating outdated regulation and using regulation to protect and promote competition. These have been recurrent themes of Australian public policy since the mid-1980s, and they are enshrined in the goals and principles of the National Reform Agenda, adopted in 2006. The pro-competitive agenda—particularly in highly commercial areas such as telecommunications—sees fair degrees of agreement across the political spectrum (e.g. Ergas 2008). The 2011–12 Convergence Review (Australian Government Department of Broadband, Communications and the Digital Economy 2011) provides an excellent case study of a contemporary approach to policy and regulation.

MEDIA AND COMMUNICATIONS POLICY IN AUSTRALIA

The next part of the chapter provides a brief overview of the principles and actual public policy-making practice in media and communications in Australia. The components of such policy consist of *laws* (around competition, ownership and control, defamation, copyright, contempt, *sub judice*, vilification, obscenity, blasphemy, sedition), *regulations* (for example, for Australian content on commercial broadcasting) and *policies* (of a political party or of a government, which may be enacted into laws or regulations).

Media and communications policy is the province of the relevant federal minister, supported by the associated bureaucracy. Section 51(v) of the Australian Constitution gives the Commonwealth powers over 'postal, telegraphic, telephonic and other like services', which is interpreted as giving federal government responsibility over broadcast media and the internet. The relevant department is currently the Department of Broadband, Communications and the Digital Economy (DBCDE), but it has been called many things in the past (which you may come across in your reading): Postmaster-General (to 1972); Media (1972–75): Communications (1976–86); Transport and Communications (1987–93); Communications and the Arts (1994–96); and Communication, Information Technology and the Arts (1996–2007). This portfolio area leads the development of national policy, and implementation through laws and regulation (but should interact effectively with other portfolio areas). The name change to DBCDE has become progressively more relevant, particularly with the rollout of the National Broadband Network (NBN) and the government's Digital Economy Goals in areas of access, health, education, employment and government services.

In undertaking a policy approach to media and communication issues, you will also encounter different types of government action. There are 'carrots' (incentives that encourage certain behaviours such as the production of children's or other Australian drama and documentary production) and 'sticks' (prohibitions on certain behaviour, such as racial vilification). There is *direct regulation* (rules for minimum levels of Australian content) and *self-regulation* (in the form of industry codes, including those of print media, commercial television and radio, pay TV, advertising and community broadcasting). We have already encountered the notion of *co-regulation* (cooperation between the regulator and the regulated.) *Deregulation* refers to attempts to reduce the amount and costs of regulation by shifting away from 'specialist' to 'generalist' regulation.

The main principle we will follow here is the distinction between government action directed at '*input*' (subsidisation of production) or '*output*' (regulation to encourage and manage the distribution and exhibition of product) activity. The levels of output regulation are based on the perceived nature of the specific media. Traditionally, the 'arts' have been considered artisanal or non-industrial in nature, and have attracted a subsidy or input approach from government. The 'media' have been considered industrial in nature, and have attracted a regulatory or output approach. This latter approach varies along an axis ranging from a highly regulated broadcasting industry to the virtual open market (subject to generic laws of defamation, libel, obscenity, racial vilification and so on, based on community standards) in print, video and film distribution and exhibition.

Print

The print media (in the absence of an independent regulatory authority) are subject to general laws regarding trade practices, competition and monopoly, as well as the laws of defamation and contempt. The general provisions of the *Trade Practices Act* prohibit mergers that would result in one company being in a position to 'dominate a market'. The *Trade Practices Act* is 'general' law, and typically does not operate with precision and pertinence in the area of the media. As we shall see in the next section, print media ownership is highly concentrated, but it needs to be said that there are powerful inhibitors to the operation of principled competition policy in Australia, given its small market, high barriers to entry because of infrastructure costs, and a rapid loss of the sector's profitability due to declining readership and loss of classified advertising revenue.

The only medium-specific form of regulation is through the Australian Press Council, a self-regulatory body established in 1976. The council is funded by press proprietors, and voluntary membership includes public representatives as well as representatives from the major publishers. Although freelance journalists sit on the council, the industry union, the Media, Entertainment and Arts Alliance (MEAA), is not represented. The Press Council's rulings in response to complaints about media practice have historically offered an example of feather-like, rather than even light-touch, regulation. In 2012, following the release of an Independent Media Inquiry report that raised the prospect of a statutory regulator for the industry in the light of heightened concerns about press performance, the Press Council's resource base and membership were substantially strengthened (see Box 5.1).

Broadcasting

Broadcasting is very different. Two principles have traditionally grounded higher levels of regulation in this sphere. Broadcasters use the airwaves (the electromagnetic or radio spectrum) to transmit to their audiences. The spectrum is a public resource, and its capacity to carry broadcasting signals is not unlimited, thus its ownership, leasing and licensing are regulated. Second, it has been held that the media of sound and image have greater power to influence their audiences by virtue of their pervasive presence in contemporary society, and because they are consumed *en bloc* to a greater degree than media of 'choice' (like print, or film and video). *Television* is watched and *radio* is listened to as generic technologies. Their consumption is said to be less by direct selection of specific, separable items than is the case with media that depend on payment for the delivery of each service. This, of course, is why so much advertising is inserted into the 'flow' of television and radio programs. Structural regulation to underpin diversity (with three categories of broadcaster—commercial, community, and national or public) is also considered as a desirable policy outcome.

The broadcasting system was established under the *Broadcasting Act* 1942, which defined service areas, determined the appropriate number of licensees within a service area and set out criteria for who could hold a broadcasting licence and for the conduct of those licensees. These provisions applied to the commercial sector and the community sector, though not to the public service (or national) broadcasters, the ABC and SBS, whose legislation is the *Australian Broadcasting Corporation Act* 1983 and the *Special Broadcasting Service Act* 1991.

The *Broadcasting Services Act* 1992, the legislation that currently governs this area of the media, marked a major philosophical as well as regulatory change in broadcasting policy, and replaced the old legislation—described by the chief regulator of the time, Peter Westaway, as 'a poor, wretched animal, designed for reasons which are less and less relevant and made grotesque by years of patchwork amendment'. Premised upon the idea of a transition from media scarcity to media abundance with the development of cable and other new technologies and services, it was intended to apply light-touch regulation in order to facilitate the entry of new competitors and technological developments. It also marked a move from over-arching regulation by government bodies towards a greater degree of self- and co-regulation.

But that was a generation ago. Broadcasting regulation is due for another big shake-up, and its possible shape has been sketched by a wide-ranging Convergence Review, which we will consider at the end of the chapter.

Film and video

The film and video production, distribution and exhibition industries largely have followed the press model of regulation. There have been various attempts to regulate the distribution and exhibition sectors of the industry in the form of quotas for Australian material, and even anti-trust style divestment recommendations in the early 1970s. However, it has remained a structurally unregulated market characterised by oligopoly and significant levels of foreign ownership in distribution. Rather than regulation, government intervention in film is characterised by subsidy and support along the lines of arts patronage. The major approach of government policy has been to subsidise the production, rather than intervene through structural regulation in the distribution or exhibition, of film in Australia (although there are also subsidies for alternative distribution and exhibition, including some support for new forms of exhibition such as digital cinema). The video industry is even less the object of regulatory intervention or of government subvention than film. Classification and issues regarding the censorship of objectionable material constitute the main forms of regulation, although general competition regulation applies. As more and more film and video are consumed online, this sector is being caught up in issues of convergence of technologies.

Arts

The governance of the traditional arts is the purest form of input intervention. Consistent with its comparatively long history, this governance also exhibits a highly coordinated approach, with one major federal body, the Australia Council, interacting with the various state arts bodies (through the mechanism of the Cultural Ministers Council) to provide subsidies to a wide field of arts activities, which range from elite 'flagship' national companies in the areas of opera, ballet and theatre to community arts in far-flung regions of the nation. Government has intervened also by providing tax incentives (one could argue with their extent and effectiveness) to encourage corporate support and by setting up the Australian Business Arts Foundation (ABAF), a body now folded into the Australia Council.

Internet and telecommunications

By contrast, the internet, as a highly decentralised global network, has not been amenable to such nationally based policy approaches. Attempts by the Gillard Labor government, for example, to introduce compulsory filters for objectionable internet content were met with considerable industry and community concern, as they would catch much more than is intended and slow down broadband speeds. Ultimately, the proposed filter proved to be untenable and the idea was abandoned in 2012.

Telecommunications has seen dramatic shifts in policy and regulatory arrangements. Since the early 1990s, telecommunications policy has moved from a system based around a highly regulated public monopoly and universal provision of basic services to a system based on much more open competition between multiple carriers, regulated generically by the Australian Competition and Consumer Commission (ACCC). Having said this, the market is still dominated by the major incumbent, Telstra, from which most of the other telecommunications providers have to purchase access to basic network infrastructure. Since 1997, there has been no limit on new service providers, with strong growth particularly in the area of mobile telephony. There is competitive tendering among carriers for provision of services that need subsidising because they may never be profitable, such as connections to rural and regional areas, pay phone services and services for those on low incomes or with disabilities.

Such moves have been part of an international trend towards liberalising access to telecommunications markets, privatising former public monopoly telecommunications carriers, and implementing the principles of national competition policy. Underpinning changing telecommunications policy is a move from *conduct regulation*, where restrictions on market entry constitute a condition for ensuring that incumbent providers meet social policy objectives, to *structural regulation*, where a more competitive environment is promoted as a condition for generating a more efficient and innovative industry that is more responsive to consumers and other end-users. It is incorrect to see this as deregulation, as competition has required a more active role for the general regulator, the ACCC, in the industry—particularly to ensure that competitive safeguards exist for new service providers in accessing the infrastructure of the incumbent providers such as Telstra.

But the most dramatic shift occurred in 2009 with the announcement of the NBN—the largest infrastructure project in Australian history. Carried out by a wholly owned state enterprise, NBN Co, using an estimated $36 billion of public money, this provision of fast broadband infrastructure throughout the nation signifies a massive reintroduction of the state in the wake of the privatisation of Telstra. The broader significance of this policy, which has seen an eight-plus-year rollout planned and is partly implemented, is that NBN infrastructure will be the portal for very ambitious digital economy goals (<www.nbn.gov.au/the-vision/digital-economy-goals>). It is also, understandably, a very contentious policy that may be much modified with a change of government.

BOX 5.1: MEDIA POLICY PLAYERS
Government

- **Australian Communications and Media Authority (ACMA) (<www.acma.gov.au>):** ACMA has a number of responsibilities in the media and communications environment. Its brief is to:
  - promote self-regulation and competition in the communications industry, while protecting consumers and other users
  - foster an environment in which electronic media respect community standards and respond to audience and user needs
  - manage access to the radio-frequency spectrum, and
  - represent Australia's communications interests internationally.
  ACMA is also responsible for monitoring online content, including internet and mobile

phone content, and enforcing Australia's anti-spam laws. It also informs the community about internet safety issues, particularly those relating to children.

- **Australian Competition and Consumer Commission (ACCC) (<www.accc.gov.au>):** The ACCC is an independent statutory authority, which was formed in 1995 to oversee the *Trade Practices Act* 1974 (renamed the *Competition and Consumer Act* 2010 on 1 January 2011) and other Acts. The ACCC defines its primary roles as:
  - promoting competition and fair trade in the marketplace to benefit consumers, business and the community
  - regulating national infrastructure industries
  - ensuring that individuals and businesses comply with the Commonwealth's competition, fair trading and consumer protection laws
  - complementing the state and territory consumer affairs agencies, which administer the mirror legislation of their jurisdictions, and the Competition and Consumer Policy Division of the Commonwealth Treasury.

  The ACCC is the only national agency dealing generally with competition matters and the only agency with responsibility for enforcing the *Trade Practices Act* and the state/territory application legislation. The ACCC deals with such matters as access and pricing, and looking into anti-competitive conduct in the communications industry.

- **Telecommunications Industry Ombudsman (TIO) (<www.tio.com.au>):** The TIO provides a free and independent alternative dispute-resolution scheme for small business and residential consumers with unresolved complaints about their telephone or internet service in Australia. Established in 1993 and provided for under a federal Act of Parliament, the TIO is operated by Telecommunications Industry Ombudsman Ltd and is independent of industry, the government and consumer organisations. The TIO is governed by a Council and a Board of Directors, and is managed by an independent Ombudsman appointed by the board on the recommendation of council.

- **Screen Australia (<www.screenaustralia.gov.au>):** Screen Australia is the key federal government direct funding body for the Australian screen production industry. Its functions are to support and promote the development of a highly creative, innovative and commercially sustainable Australian screen production industry. Screen Australia supports the development, production, promotion and distribution of Australian screen content by:
  - supporting production of a range of content
  - supporting the growth of screen businesses
  - supporting marketing and screen culture initiatives
  - developing high-quality scripts and proposals
  - facilitating innovation and audience-engaging online content, and
  - supporting Indigenous talent and distinctive stories.

  Screen Australia administers the Government's Producer Offset and International Co-production Program to increase the commercial sustainability of production in Australia.

Industry self-regulation

- **Australian Press Council (APC) (<www.presscouncil.org.au>):** The ACP is a self-regulatory body of the Australian print media. Along with promoting standards of media practice, enabling community access to information of public interest and protecting press freedom, it is responsible for adjudicating on complaints about Australian newspapers, magazines and associated digital outlets. Prior to 2012, the APC had minimal powers of regulation, and was economically dependent on the subsidisation of voluntary member organisations, which retained the option of withdrawing from the Council at any time.

Changes to the Australian Press Council following the 2012 release of the Independent Media Inquiry substantially addressed key concerns raised about its independence and effectiveness. The ACP's vulnerability to funding withdrawal has been greatly reduced, and APC members have agreed to specific funding commitments for the next three years. The council has also strengthened conditions regarding membership. Members' obligations to provide funding and comply with Council processes will now become legally binding. Members will be required to give four years' notice of withdrawal from the Council, and remain part of the Council throughout that period; they also remain subject to the council's jurisdiction to adjudicate on complaints about their publications. Publishers' obligations to comply with the Council's complaints processes will become legally binding, including requirements to publish adjudications with due prominence.

- **Communications Alliance (<www.commsalliance.com.au>):** The Communications Alliance was formed to provide a unified voice for the Australian communications industry, and offers a forum for the industry to make coherent and constructive contributions to policy development and debate. It presents a unified role on behalf of the industry and its members—particularly in areas of competition, innovation and industry development. Its prime mission is to promote the growth of the Australian communications industry and the protection of consumer interests by fostering high standards of business ethics and behaviour through industry self-governance.

- **Advertising Standards Bureau (ASB) (<www.adstandards.com.au>):** The ASB administers a national system of advertising self-regulation through the Advertising Standards Board and the Advertising Claims Board. The self-regulation system recognises that advertisers share a common interest in promoting consumer confidence in, and respect for, general standards of advertising. The Board provides a free public service of complaint resolution in relation to issues including:
  - the use of language
  - the discriminatory portrayal of people
  - concern for children
  - portrayals of violence, sex, sexuality and nudity
  - health and safety, and
  - marketing of food and beverages to children.

Industry associations

- **Internet Industry Association (IIA) (<www.iia.net.au>):** The IIA is Australia's national internet industry organisation. Members include telecommunications carriers, content creators and publishers, web developers, e-commerce traders and solutions providers, hardware vendors, systems integrators and ISPs. The IIA provides policy input to government and advocacy on a range of business and regulatory issues regarding internet laws and initiatives within Australia.

- **Free TV Australia (<www.freetv.com.au>):** Free TV Australia began life as the Federation of Commercial Television Stations (or FACTS) in 1960. It now represents all of Australia's commercial free-to-air television licensees, and is one of the few industry bodies in Australia to represent every organisation in its sector. Free TV Australia formulates advice and recommendations in relation to policy and regulatory issues, engineering and technical issues.

    The content of free-to-air commercial television is regulated under the 2010 Commercial Television Industry Code of Practice, which was developed by Free TV Australia and registered with the Australian Communications and Media Authority (ACMA). The Commercial Television Code of Practice covers matters prescribed in section 123 of the *Broadcasting Services Act* and other matters relating to program content that are of concern to the community, including program classifications, accuracy, fairness and respect for privacy in news and current affairs, advertising time on television, placement of commercials and programs promotions, and complaints handling.

- **Australian Subscription Television and Radio Association (ASTRA) (<www.astra.org. au>):** ASTRA is the peak body representing the subscription television industry in Australia on regulatory and policy matters. ASTRA is responsible for the development of the codes of practice for the subscription television industry in consultation with the ACMA.

- **Community Broadcasting Association of Australia (CBAA) (<www.cbaa.org.au>):** The CBAA is the national peak body for community radio stations. CBAA members include fully licensed stations as well as groups aspiring to hold a permanent broadcast licence. At present, the CBAA has over 270 member stations, which are actively broadcasting nationwide. The CBAA aims to promote the values of the community broadcasting sector, advance the interests of the sector through policy leadership, advocacy and public campaigns, and raise awareness and knowledge of the sector.

- **Australian Mobile Telecommunications Association (AMTA) (<www.amta.org.au>):** The AMTA is the peak industry body representing Australia's mobile telecommunications industry. AMTA members include mobile Carriage Service Providers (CSPs), handset manufacturers, retail outlets, network equipment suppliers and other suppliers to the industry. AMTA aims to promote both the mobile telecommunications industry in Australia and its contribution to the Australian community.

Other media policy players

- Australian Association of National Advertisers (AANA) (<www.aana.com.au>)
- Advertising Federation of Australia (AFA) (<www.afa.org.au>)
- Commercial Radio Australia (<www.commercialradio.com.au>)
- Public Relations Institute of Australia (PRIA) (<www.pria.com.au>)
- Media Entertainment and Arts Alliance (MEAA) (<www.alliance.org.au>)
- Australian Children's Television Foundation (ACTF) (<www.actf.com.au>)
- Consumers' Telecommunications Network (CTN) (<www.ctn.org.au>)

SELECT POLICY ISSUES

Open virtually any newspaper or news magazine, or go to any major online information service, and you will find grist for the mill of media and communications policy.
Policy issues often dominate the business press, and sometimes the news and opinion
pages as well. As examples, we will consider the enduringly public and contentious
issue of ownership and control policies, as well as a recent forward-thinking and
wide-ranging review of convergence that may continue to have reverberations into
the future.

Ownership and control

Ownership and control are perennial issues in the media garden. This is unavoidable
when Australia has one of the most oligopolistic media sectors in the world. Box 5.2
provides details of the effects of major relaxation of the ownership and control laws
governing all established media in Australia in 2007.

What is at stake in media ownership deregulation? The arguments in favour of
relaxation of the rules include the need, in a small market like Australia, for increased
private-sector investment in the burgeoning field of media and communications.
Foreign investment will find Australia an easier and more attractive proposition, and
the huge 'institutional' investors (insurance and superannuation funds managers)
inside the country will want to invest more if the companies become larger and more
profitable through consolidation. The large companies regularly argue that they need
to be bigger if they are to compete in a globalised world.

Those who argue against change, or for more restrictive ownership and control
rules, insist that Australia already has one of the most concentrated media sectors,
and that further concentration would mean even less diversity of views in sensitive
areas such as news, current affairs and opinion. They point to the way the diversity of
outlets has been reduced as media companies deliver value to shareholders in advance
of their public service obligations, and argue that this would only increase under
relaxed rules.

One of the highly contested issues between protagonists and antagonists in the
ownership and control debate is the principle of diversity. Traditionally, it has been
held that diversity of ownership leads to diversity of content and perspective. No one
disagrees with the desirability of diversity of content and perspective, but the idea
that it can only be guaranteed through diversity of ownership is coming under attack.
The claim can be made that the proliferation of media content on the internet makes
assertions of untoward control over perspective outdated and redundant. This is
surely a major over-statement of the internet as a reliable alternative source. A more

elegant economic theoretical argument is that a major player may be in a better position to seek to address several readerships or audiences through diversifying content and editorial into niche markets than several smaller players tending to compete in the middle ground, driven to maximise their audience.

The rules under which media ownership operates were last amended in 2007. Box 5.2 summarises the changes that have occurred since 2007, and the state of play as of late 2012. Look out for further changes, particularly as a result of recommendations from the 2011–12 *Convergence Review*.

BOX 5.2: MEDIA OWNERSHIP AND CONTROL 2007–

The *Broadcasting Services Amendment (Media Ownership) Act* 2006 brought in new media ownership laws in 2007. The new laws remove broadcasting-specific restrictions on foreign investment in Australia's media sector. The media remain a 'sensitive sector' under foreign investment policy, meaning direct media investment must be approved by the Treasurer. The previous law restricted foreign ownership of broadcasting licences, such as preventing a foreign person controlling a company interest greater than 15 per cent, or more than 20 per cent of directors of a commercial television licensee being foreign persons.

New cross-media ownership restrictions apply to commercial television and radio broadcasters and major newspapers (called 'regulated platforms'). They prohibit transactions that will result either in a person controlling more than two out of three regulated platforms in a licence area or in an 'unacceptable media diversity situation'. An 'unacceptable media diversity situation' is judged by counting points based on the number of independent regulated platforms and media groups operating in a licence area. The law prohibits transactions leading to there being fewer than five points in metropolitan licence areas or fewer than four points in regional licence areas.

The dramatic and largely unanticipated impact of removing foreign ownership restrictions was a major refinancing of free-to-air television by private equity firms, effectively taking much of the network ownership offshore into private institutional ownership. At the same time, liberalisation of the cross-media rules allowed consolidation by existing players; the ownership of print, radio and television has been concentrated into fewer hands.

The number of controllers of commercial radio went from 34 in 2007 to 32 in 2010, and the number of controllers of commercial TV went from eight in 2007 to seven in 2010, despite the release of new licences.

Television

Two commercial free-to-air TV networks, Seven and Nine, sold 50 per cent of their media assets into private equity arrangements (first Nine with CVC Asia Pacific and then Seven with Kravis Kohlberg Roberts), using the cash from the sales to position themselves for expansion into other media and non-media assets.

Nine Entertainment Co is majority owned by CVC Asia Pacific Limited. Nine's television assets include the Nine Network (Sydney, Melbourne, Brisbane and Darwin), GO!, GEM, eXtra, NBN (broadcasting to the Central Coast of New South Wales and Gold Coast in Queensland). Nine also holds assets in pay television through Sky News (a joint venture with Seven and British Sky Broadcasting) and shares joint ownership of the online venture ninemsn (50 per cent) with Microsoft.

The assets of *Seven West Media*—controlled by Kerry Stokes—include Channel 7 (Sydney, Melbourne, Adelaide, Brisbane, Perth and regional Queensland), 7Two, 7mate and TV4ME. Seven also holds assets in pay television through its stake in Consolidated Media Holdings, which owns 25 per cent of Foxtel and Fox Sports, and Sky News Australia (33 per cent stake). Seven West Media's interests extend to radio (Redwave Media); newspapers (*The West Australian*—the sole metropolitan daily not owned by News Limited or Fairfax) and various West Australian regional newspapers; and magazines (Pacific Magazines, which publishes *Home Beautiful*, *Who* and *New Idea*); and a 50 per cent stake in Yahoo!7

Australia's other commercial television network, the Ten Network, is a consolidated entity held by a variety of multinational banking, financial and investment services companies. High-profile board members include chairman Lachlan Murdoch and director Gina Rinehart; the Australian mining magnate was appointed to the board after purchasing a 10 per cent stake in the company in 2010. Ten's television assets are the Ten Network; ONE; ELEVENCo (co-owned 66.6/33.3 per cent with US broadcaster CBC), TVSN and WIN Corporation.

Newspapers

The cashed-up Seven Network initially bought 14.9 per cent of West Australian Newspapers (WAN). This has since risen to about 22 per cent, well over the defined controlling position of 15 per cent under the pre-2007 laws. The highest rating free-to-air TV network in Western Australia now has indirect control of the highest circulation daily newspaper and the second most popular online news site (<www.thewest.com.au>).

When share prices were still buoyant, Fairfax initiated a pre-emptive defensive move, merging with the Rural Press group bringing nine more newspapers and seven commercial radio licences under the control of Fairfax Media. This created Australia's highest net value media group. The deal was valued at around $9 billion (including $2.3 billion in debt). At the time of the merger, the group held more than 240 regional, rural and community publications, nine radio stations and the leading New Zealand internet site, TradeMe, as well as 20 agricultural titles in the United States. Since then, Fairfax has had to sell down substantial holdings to manage its high debt levels.

As of 2012, Fairfax Media controls 21 per cent of the metropolitan daily news market via the *Sydney Morning Herald*, *The Age*, the *Australian Financial Review*, the *Canberra Times* and regional newspapers in important cities such as Newcastle and Wollongong. Fairfax holds other print media interests, including *Business Review Weekly* and *Personal Investor* magazines. In addition to its print interests, Fairfax is involved in radio, holding various metropolitan and regional radio licences via its takeover of Southern Cross Radio. Fairfax's online interests include Fairfax Digital (*Brisbane Times*, *WA Today*). Fairfax newspapers also dominate in New Zealand, and the company's interests in that country also extend to magazines, the digital newspaper portal <www.stuff.co.nz> and the online auction site <www.TradeMe.co.nz>.

News Australia Holdings' parent company, News Corporation—controlled by the Murdoch Family—added to its existing dominance of the metropolitan, regional and community newspaper markets (around 70 per cent of newspapers in Australia) by acquiring the Federal Publishing Company's magazine and community newspaper interests (thirteen community newspapers, two commuter papers, 25 magazines and six online properties). The competition policy regulator, the ACCC, approved the deal despite the unprecedented concentration.

News controls 70 per cent of the metropolitan daily news market through masthead titles *The Australian,* the *Daily Telegraph,* the *Herald Sun,* the *Courier-Mail, The Advertiser, The Mercury* and the *Northern Territory News,* alongside addition regional papers including *The Cairns Post,* the *Gold Coast Bulletin,* the *Townsville Bulletin* and the *Geelong Advertiser).* News also publishes a stable of free suburban weekly community publications (NewsLocal, Quest, Leader, Messenger, Community Newspapers) and free daily metropolitan commuter newspapers (*mX*).

Radio

Southern Cross Media Group (formerly Macquarie Media Group), a subsidiary of Macquarie Bank, the investment bank that specialises in Infrastructure projects, owns Australia's largest radio network. It took a strategic 14.9 per cent $170 million positioning stake in Southern Cross Broadcasting (a networked radio and TV operation).

Shortly after the Fairfax/Rural Press merger, a three-way deal involving Fairfax Media, Macquarie Media and Southern Cross Broadcasting was launched. This merger was the first major cross-media transaction under the new rules. The Fairfax/Macquarie Media Group/ Southern Cross deal was a complex deal requiring approval from both ACMA and the ACCC. Under the deal, Macquarie Media Group will then on-sell metropolitan radio stations to Fairfax Media.

Southern Cross Austereo was formed following the July 2011 merger of Southern Cross Media Group and Austereo Group. Its assets include 68 commercial radio stations across (mostly) regional Australia, including the Today FM network and the Triple M network.

Sources: Dwyer (2008); Harding (2010).

The October 2012 buyout of Consolidated Media by News Corp offers an illustration of the ACCC, the competition regulator, in action. Prior to the buyout, Seven Group Holdings owned just over 25 per cent of Consolidated Media, and sought clearance from the regulator on the basis that it was actively considering a takeover bid for Consolidated. The bid was rejected because it would lead to the Seven Group owning substantial interests in both a major free-to-air network and the largest subscription television company in Australia. The ACCC also had concerns about Seven Group holding a 50 per cent stake in Fox Sports, which may have given it an unfair advantage over other commercial networks in bidding for sports broadcast rights. Following the decision, Seven voted in favour of News Corp's takeover of Consolidated. This deal increased News Corp's share in Foxtel to 50 per cent, and gave it full ownership of sports channel Fox Sports. Telstra continues to hold the other 50 per cent of Foxtel.

THE POLICY CHALLENGE OF CONVERGENCE

As suggested in the Introduction, convergence has also been a hardy perennial in the media policy garden. In 2011, an independent inquiry into convergence was commissioned in recognition that increased access to high-speed broadband networks, the digitisation of media products and services, convergent media platforms and services, the rise of user-created content (UCC) and the globalisation of media platforms, content and services have significantly altered the media landscape over the past few decades.

In terms of policy and regulation, the key issue arising from convergence is the manner in which it breaks the link between media content and delivery platforms. Convergence points towards a shift from *vertically integrated industry 'silos'* (print, broadcast, telephony, etc.) and the associated need for sector-specific regulation to a series of *horizontal layers* of infrastructure, access devices, applications/content services and content itself.

In an overview of Australian broadcasting and telecommunications regulations undertaken for the Convergence Review, ACMA (2011) identified 55 'broken concepts' in current legislation, including the concept of 'influence' in broadcasting, the concept of a 'program' in broadcasting and the distinction between a 'content service provider' and a 'carriage service provider' in relation to the internet. The Convergence Review concluded that not only were policies on new media required, but a new approach to media policy overall was also needed.

With a broadly deregulatory thrust, the Convergence Review identified three enduring areas that justified ongoing regulation of media and communications: media ownership; media content standards across all platforms; and the production and distribution of Australian and local content (Convergence Review 2012: viii). In determining 'who' or 'what' should be regulated in a converged media environment, the review proposed a regulatory framework based on size and scope, departing from the tradition of regulating around particular delivery platforms. Significant media enterprises—defined as 'content service enterprises' (CSE)—that had control over 'professional content' (television- and radio-like services, newspaper content, etc.) would be subject to regulation once they had reached a certain threshold. This approach would replace the current system of Australian content quotas that commercial broadcasting has to meet.

As of 2013, the current Labor government has only succeeded in implementing a tiny fraction of the Convergence Review's recommendations, and it remains to be seen whether another government will be able to deal effectively with the now well-identified challenges of convergence. One thing is sure, though: the industry, technological and social changes that give rise to the expectation of policy response will continue to increase.

CONCLUSION

This chapter has shown that the policy approach is an integral element of media and communications studies. It connects your academic studies directly to matters of public interest and social concerns about the media—whether 'progressive' or 'conservative'—and gives you a window into many practical applications of media and communications studies. But, by its very nature, the field is constantly changing— what might have worked only some years ago in regulation or policy may not work now or in the near future. So getting to grips with media and communications policy requires you to stay alert to the changing landscape while being prepared to consult policy papers, and even regulatory and legislative documentation. But all this welter of information won't mean much if you haven't really tried to understand where policy sits within the debates about power, change, representation and identity that undergird our discipline. Perhaps most interestingly, though, it may challenge you to form views about how media and communications in Australia can be changed for the better, and how you might contribute to making those changes.

ACKNOWLEDGEMENTS

Thanks to Adam Swift and Christina Spurgeon for helpful suggestions.

FURTHER READING

An alternative perspective on approaches in Australian policy studies is found in Pearce (2000), 'Perspectives of Australian broadcasting policy'. Errington and Miragliotta (2012), *Media & Politics: An Introduction* outlines the effect that Australia's liberal democratic tradition has on the operation and structure of the media, and in turn the effect of the media on politics. Freedman (2008), *The Politics of Media Policy* is an approach to US and UK media policy that structures its argument around the historical shift from 'pluralism' to 'neo-liberalism'; it provides a useful background reference. Lunt and Livingstone (2012), *Media Regulation: Governance and the Interests of Citizens and Consumers* examines how global media regulation affects the relations between government, the media and communications market, civil society, citizens and consumers.

Extended policy approaches to Australian media and communications include Barr (2000), *newmedia.com.au*, Given (2003), *Turning Off the Television: Broadcasting's Uncertain Future* and Kenyon (2007), *TV Futures: Digital Television Policy in Australia*. The challenge of the policy approach for cultural and media theory is covered in Cunningham (1992), *Framing Culture*. Sandra Braman's extensive work on public interest communications policy advocacy in the United States in *Communication Researchers and Policy-making* (2003) and *Change of State* (2006) provides an excellent comparison with Australia. The websites of the policy players are always worth checking for up-to-date information and valuable perspectives, as is the leading journal *Media International Australia* (<www.uq.edu.au/mia>).

Industries

PART **II**

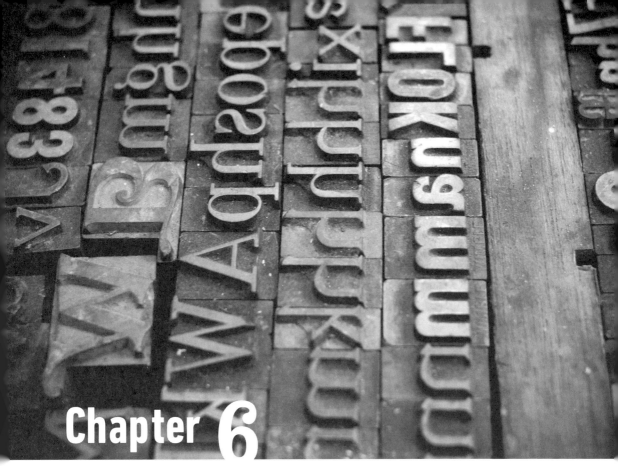

Chapter 6

THE PRESS

RODNEY TIFFEN

On 18 June 2012, the CEO of the Fairfax company, Greg Hywood, announced the closure of two printing plants, the change of its most prestigious titles from broadsheet to tabloid formats commencing in 2013 and the shedding of 1900 jobs over the next three years. This announcement of unprecedented cutbacks was followed within days by the resignations of three of the organisation's most senior newspaper editors, signalling a shift in the company's internal hierarchy from newspaper to digital products.

A few days later, it was expected that the Australian CEO of News Limited, Kim Williams, would announce similar cutbacks. Instead he announced two expansion plans: one to acquire an internet business journalism website, *Business Spectator*; the other to bid for James Packer's one-quarter-share of Foxtel and half-share of Fox

Sports. He also made some seemingly anodyne announcements about restructuring newspaper divisions, but with only the vaguest of references to unspecified future job losses. Nevertheless, News soon began making cutbacks in its newspapers. The announcements 'made it clear that the future for Australian news media organisations is smaller, and less profitable—with fewer journalists employed' (Simons 2012, p. 9).

Such adverse developments have not been confined to Australian newspapers, and the decline in newspapers has actually been even more pronounced in some other developed democracies. Indeed, looking only at the limited period 2007–09, Australian newspapers fared among the best in an OECD study (2010), with revenue declining by only 2 per cent, while the most severe declines were in the United Kingdom (down 21 per cent) and the United States (down 30 per cent). The prognoses for US newspapers have become progressively more dire. The first influential prediction of their demise was offered by prominent journalism scholar Philip Meyer, who predicted in 2004 (p. 16)—with tongue-in-cheek precision—that the last reader of a printed newspaper would disappear in the first quarter of 2043. The CEO of Microsoft, Steve Ballmer, told the editorial board of the *Washington Post* in 2008 that 'there will be no newspapers, no magazines, that are delivered in paper form' by 2020 (Fallows 2010). Jeffrey Cole, the director of the University of Southern California's Annenberg Center for the Digital Future, has most recently predicted that most print newspapers would disappear in five years:

> Circulation of print newspapers continues to plummet, and we believe that the only print newspapers that will survive will be at the extremes of the medium—the largest and the smallest . . . It's likely that only the four major daily newspapers will continue in print form: *The New York Times*, *USA Today*, the *Washington Post* and the *Wall Street Journal*. At the other extreme, local weekly newspapers may still survive. (Cole 2011)

In some ways, the declining trend has been a long-term one. Examining the United States, which has the most systematic data, paid circulation per capita is half what it was in the 1960s, and in real terms newspaper advertising revenue is where it was in 1982 (Varian 2010). But it was only from around 2005, later hastened by the Global Financial Crisis (GFC), that revenue started trending sharply down. Alan Mutter (2011) notes that in 2005 newspapers achieved a record $49.4 billion in advertising revenue, but in 2011 it came in at less than half that figure, at around $24 billion. 'Between 2006 and 2009, daily newspapers cut their annual editorial spending by $1.6 billion per year, or more than a quarter', and staff was reduced by a similar proportion (Waldman 2011). The total number of journalists employed in the United States in

2009, in a country with a population of over 300 million, was at about the same level as it was in the early 1970s, when the country's population was 200 million. That figure is now around 40 000, while in 1992 it was as high as 60 000. These cuts impact directly on how much independent reporting is done. For example, 'the number of newspaper reporters covering state capitals full-time fell from 524 in 2003 to 355 at the beginning of 2009' (Downie and Schudson 2009, pp. 17–18). In a recent survey of Australian journalists, 50 per cent felt the quality of news reporting and journalism was worse than it had been five years earlier, and only 15 per cent thought it had improved (O'Donnell, McKnight and Este 2012, p. 9).

Nevertheless, while the sense of crisis has gathered ever-increasing momentum in recent years, in reality what was once newspapers' central place among the media had already steadily eroded over several generations. At the beginning of the twentieth century, the press was the most important of the mass media. Before the arrival of radio and television, 'the newspaper enjoyed the same kind of social monopoly as the railroad did before the coming of the automobile and the airplane . . . It dominated the sphere of information as the train dominated that of transportation.' (Smith 1980, p. 318) Even in the middle of the twentieth century, one could plausibly argue for the pre-eminence of the press in the sphere of information. The major companies that owned newspapers had considerable financial strength, and their products occupied a seemingly impregnable place in the public's consumption routines. Newspaper reading seemed to be among the most habitual of behaviours, with people reading the same paper at the same time each day. Indeed, a British panel study in the 1960s—and remember that the British market has always been much more competitive and dynamic than the Australian one—found that 'newspaper reading was the most stable variable apart from sex and date of birth' (Tunstall 1971, p 18). In the late 1940s, when a strike stopped the delivery of New York newspapers, a sociological study found that many felt a strong sense of loss at having this valued part of their daily routine denied them (Berelson 1949).

However, even in the 1950s and 1960s, to say that the press was the most important of the mass media would no longer have been a very sensible proposition, given the greatly varying roles played by movies, radio and the infant television industry. At the beginning of the twenty-first century, by all the most tangible measures, newspapers are in relative, and increasingly in absolute, decline.

Their circulation has not kept pace with population growth, and now is in absolute decline as well. The number of daily newspapers sold in relation to population almost halved in Australia between 1980 and 2007—a more dramatic decrease than in most other advanced democracies (Tiffen and Gittins 2009, p. 180). The primary reason for Australia's more precipitate fall was the reduction in the number of titles.

In particular, all Australia's afternoon newspapers closed in the five years between 1988 and 1993 (Tiffen 1994a). However, the surviving newspapers have not only failed to fill that gap in lost readership, but in some cases have also failed to retain the readers they had. As Table 6.1 shows, all except the two national titles have a lower circulation than they did nineteen years earlier. When considered in the light of continuing population growth, the decline in newspaper circulation in relation to population is dramatic. In 1947, metropolitan and national newspapers sold 38.6 copies per 100 people. This declined slowly but surely over the next three decades, down to 28.8 in 1977, but in recent times more sharply, to 13.0 in 2000 and 9.7 in 2011 (Finkelstein 2012, p. 69).

Table 6.1 Metropolitan and national daily newspaper circulations, 1992–2011 (000s)

Title	1992	2002	2011
Herald Sun	584	546	488
Daily Telegraph	459	398	350
Sydney Morning Herald	269	249	224
West Australian	263	233	216
Courier-Mail	258	238	212
Age	240	212	210
Advertiser	220	216	185
Australian	150	157	157
Australian Financial Review	75	89	75

Source: Audit Bureau of Circulation.

Another piece of evidence that points to the change is that, for the last decade or so, the Audit Bureau of Circulation—the commercial organisation that monitors newspaper sales—has been publishing separate figures for Monday to Friday and for Saturday circulations. This differentiation has been necessitated by the growing disparity between the two: Saturday is when most papers substantially increase their circulation, with the biggest increases being enjoyed by the general quality papers. But the disparity is itself an indicator that reading newspapers during the working week now occupies less of an established place in many people's routines than was the case a generation ago. In the United States over just the decade from 2002 to 2012, the proportion of people who said they had read a newspaper yesterday dropped from 41 per cent to 23 per cent (Pew Research Center 2012).

Just as important for the press's commercial survival is the fact that advertising is migrating elsewhere. According to the World Association of Newspapers (*The Local* 2008), Australian newspapers generate 65 per cent of their revenue from advertising, but their share of national advertising has declined. In 2001, they commanded 43.4 per cent, but by 2010 it was down to 31.1 per cent (Finkelstein 2012, p. 76).

Newspapers' role in public appreciation has also declined. Surveys consistently find that more people say they rely on broadcasting than newspapers for news, that they accord television a higher credibility (and the ABC by far the highest credibility) and that television is the medium they would be most reluctant to do without. In addition, surveys just as consistently show general scepticism about all journalists. A Roy Morgan survey in 2006 found three-quarters of the public endorsing the idea that 'media organisations are more interested in making money than in informing society'; however, while 53 per cent of people say they don't trust TV journalists to tell the truth, 63 per cent don't trust newspaper journalists (Roy Morgan Research 2006). There are substantial differences among newspapers, however. The highest ranking paper among its readers is The *Age*, with 79 per cent having a lot or some trust in the paper, while with regard to the lowest, the *Daily Telegraph*, only 52 per cent of its readers say this (Finkelstein 2012, p. 380).

It is difficult to definitively pinpoint the changes in lifestyle and public taste that have contributed to newspapers' increasingly marginal role, and to identify the factors that seem to have made ours an increasingly time-poor society, even as material wealth has increased. One very pertinent change is the decline in public transport. When people travel by car, they listen to the radio or a CD rather than read a newspaper.

Central to any explanation, however, must be the way that broadcasting and the internet have supplanted many of the traditional functions associated with the newspaper. As late as the 1950s, newspapers would bring out a special edition to notify the public of some late-breaking major news event. Today, with the superiority of radio and television, and the immediacy of the internet—and consequently their capacity for instantaneous broadcasting of news—the press typically lags well behind in the disclosure of major news events. The production of newspapers has undergone many improvements in efficiency and quality in recent decades, especially with increasing computerisation. The widespread introduction of colour is the most obvious. However, the speed of their distribution has not increased at all, and this slowness is the press's Achilles heel in its competition with other media.

Despite these disadvantages, arguably newspapers had adapted relatively profitably and professionally fruitfully to the challenges of being second to broadcasting; however, the twenty-first century has brought an even bigger challenge in the form of the internet, and this threatens to cut far more drastically into the financial viability of newspapers.

OWNERSHIP AND CONTROL

Partly as a result of these changes, and partly contributing to them, Australia has the most concentrated press ownership among established democracies (Tiffen and Gittins 2009, p. 180), and of 26 countries on which the international media concentration research project had data, Australia had by far the highest concentration (Finkelstein 2012, p. 60). Two proprietors account for more than 90 per cent of daily metropolitan circulation. Now there are only eleven metropolitan daily newspapers, six of them owned by News Limited and four by Fairfax, plus the *West Australian*. They include two nationally circulating papers, available across the country but accounting for only a small percentage of the circulation in any particular metropolitan market. Outside Melbourne and Sydney, all the other cities have local monopolies.

In contrast, in 1903 Australia had 21 capital city dailies with seventeen independent owners (Mayer 1964, p. 31). The zenith in the number of newspaper titles and owners came in 1923, when there were 26 capital city dailies and 21 independent owners. The general trend since then has been towards a contraction of titles and a concentration of owners. The Depression, which started earlier in Australia than in most other developed countries (Tiffen and Gittins 2009, p. 44), brought with it the demise of many newspapers. At the same time, ownership went from being of single titles to a spread of titles around the country. During the interwar period, the most aggressive of the acquisitors was the Herald and Weekly Times company, headed by Keith Murdoch. After World War II, the trend towards concentrated ownership continued. By 1950, the number of metropolitan daily newspapers had fallen to fifteen, although still with ten different owners. Keith Murdoch's Herald and Weekly Times group of titles accounted for 38 per cent of circulation, while the second largest, the Fairfax company, accounted for 10 per cent, with the remainder split between a variety of others (Goot 1979, p. 214).

By 1972, when Rupert Murdoch bought the *Daily Telegraph* from Frank Packer, the number of independent owners had been reduced to three (although the number of titles was up to eighteen). In broad terms, the Herald and Weekly Times newspapers accounted for just over half of daily metropolitan circulation. The company was not represented in Sydney, but was the largest publisher in each of the other state capitals. In turn, the Fairfax newspapers—including most of Australia's quality press, and the relative newcomer Rupert Murdoch, with his four titles (the *Adelaide News*, the *Daily Mirror*, the *Daily Telegraph* and *The Australian*)—split the rest almost equally, with just under a quarter each.

The next fifteen years were largely stable in market terms, until the federal Labor government's changes to television ownership policies in 1986–87 brought about huge convulsions in media ownership. After a long period of internal division and indecision, the Hawke government brought in rules that allowed TV ownership to be extended to stations covering 60 per cent of the population, but at the same time introduced a ban on cross-media ownership in any particular market (Chadwick 1989; Bowman 1988; Tiffen 1994b). This was seen by many in the media industry as the last chance to own a TV station, and led to frenzied buying and selling.

As a result of the ownership convulsions, twelve of the nineteen metropolitan daily newspapers changed owners in less than a year—three of them twice—while one closed. Over the next several years, the impact of debt and other financial considerations continued to shake out the industry. Between March 1988 and April 1992, all the nation's evening newspapers disappeared, although in Melbourne and Sydney they were (initially) replaced by '24-hour newspapers'. There had been a long-term declining trend in the circulation of afternoon newspapers and, even more importantly, they were becoming a less attractive vehicle for advertisers.

So Australia's metropolitan daily newspaper titles were reduced from nineteen in 1987 to eleven five years later. Newspapers with a total circulation of 1.22 million had closed. Treasurer Paul Keating, the architect of the policy that triggered the frenzy, thought the outcome was 'a beautiful position compared with what we did have' (Bowman and Grattan 1989, p. 154). In contrast, the Australian Journalists' Association (AJA) calculated that, in the three years leading to 1991, 1200 journalism jobs had disappeared (AJA 1991).

Not only had the number of newspapers radically declined, but the concentration in the ownership of the survivors had radically increased. By far the largest group was Murdoch's News Limited, now owning papers accounting for around two-thirds of Australian metropolitan daily press circulation. After the washout of all the closures and ownership changes, the Fairfax group (disastrously debt-ridden as a result of a family split and privatisation) emerged with its new share almost unchanged at around a quarter. In addition, there were two 'stand-alone' titles: the *West Australian* and the *Canberra Times*.

STRUCTURE OF THE AUSTRALIAN PRESS

While the spectacle of the ownership changes—the machinations of the media moguls and the political implications of such concentration of commercial power—commands our attention, it is important also to appreciate how the mix of geography and history created the context within which they could occur. The consolidation of titles within each city—particularly the shrinking of directly competing titles—and the extension of ownership between states was built upon Australia's original press structure of city-based newspapers. To a considerable extent, demography was destiny. The most important newspapers circulated in the state capital cities, and penetrated to varying degrees into their provincial and rural hinterlands. The technology did not exist to allow national distribution, but reader interests and advertising markets were over-whelmingly local anyway.

Australia's structure of newspaper development is similar to that of the United States, Canada, New Zealand and South Africa. It is in contrast to the pattern of media that occurs in countries with one dominant city, the population of which dwarfs all others, and that is also the financial, political and cultural capital. In the United Kingdom, France and Japan, for instance, although there are strong regional news-papers, the major titles are those emanating from the national capital. In London, there are eleven competing morning newspapers, all striving to increase market share, all fighting to get the news first, to make the biggest 'splash' and often to expose each other's failures. Whatever their individual diligence or competence, their combined force leads to much greater pressure for disclosure.

It also means that each individual newspaper is a much bigger and more complex organisation, with a much larger potential readership. For most of the 1980s, Rupert Murdoch's *Sun* had a circulation of over four million, while the circulation of its main competitor, the *Daily Mirror*, was over three million (Seymour-Ure 1991, p. 29). Both are now radically reduced, but they are still much greater than for any Australian newspaper.

The relative degree of competition has both pros and cons as far as the quality of journalism is concerned. There are more extremes among British than Australian newspapers. Most of them, for example, are very solidly partisan. The *Daily Mail* can be counted upon to savage Labour in its editorial columns, to have an overwhelming imbalance towards Conservative columnists, to dig more fiercely for anti-Labour than anti-Conservative stories, to find the most anti-Labour headlines and slant to put on the news, even sometimes to the point of major distortion (Toynbee 2005).

Similarly, Britain enjoys a much bigger range of journalistic styles. The journalistic distance between *The Guardian* and *The Sun* is as great as the comic distance between Monty Python and Benny Hill. That distance has increased, with most analysts arguing that the crucial period was the 1970s after Rupert Murdoch took over the *Sun*, and created an attractive, down-market alternative to the *Mirror*. It was most famous 'for the relentless use of sex', including the introduction of the topless page-three girl (Greenslade 2003, p. 250). It also emphasised sport, television and crime news; cheeky, sensational and opinionated story presentations; and a range of circulation-boosting moves, such as *Bingo*: 'Murdoch was always as lavish on promotion as he was tight on editorial expenditure.' (Shawcross 1992, p. 154) In the lead-up to the 1979 election, the *Sun* swung from its traditional pro-Labour support to an avidly pro-Conservative Party editorial stance, which it retained until the lead-up to Blair's 1997 victory. On election day in 1992, for example, its full front-page headline read: 'IF KINNOCK WINS TODAY WILL THE LAST PERSON TO LEAVE BRITAIN PLEASE TURN OUT THE LIGHTS' (Shawcross 1992, p. 542), and afterwards it boasted about its role in Labour's defeat—'It's the *Sun* wot won it' (Greenslade 2003, p. 606).

In contrast to their British counterparts, Australian newspapers tend to be more centrist—both journalistically and politically. Australian tabloids are less sensational, while the best 'quality' newspapers in Britain have a standard of writing and a depth of reporting that Australia's best newspapers rarely match. However, the two have very different market shares. The *Sydney Morning Herald* and Melbourne's *The Age* both have around 40 per cent of the circulation in their respective cities, whereas the total circulation of the five upmarket British dailies combined is only 20 per cent (Tunstall 1996, p. 10).

The danger for most Australian newspapers is not so much competitive excess as monopoly complacency and arrogance. Where there is a single newspaper in a city, the market logic is towards appealing to everyone. It would not make commercial sense for Brisbane's *Courier-Mail* to be as partisan as the British *Sun*, as this would risk alienating half its potential readers. On the other hand, the monopoly position also insulates it somewhat against such market logic. The only alternative for a discontented reader is to stop reading a local printed newspaper at all. Although active partisanship in the absence of a range of outputs is not conducive to stronger democracy, the greater danger of monopoly newspapers is that they are less vigilant in digging out information, and this danger of journalistic passivity is by its very nature less visible to the public than partisan distortion.

So the different structures of the press in Britain and Australia have led to very different ranges of newspaper journalism. While a country's population and socio-economic structures are crucial to the shape of its press, absolute size is also important. The United States and Australia share somewhat similar press structures—a decentralised national press with few competing local outlets—but one difference is that the much greater number of newspapers in America led to the growth of news agencies. At its peak, the United States had more than 2000 daily newspapers, mostly with small circulations—the great majority less than 100 000, and many less than 10 000. To cover the world beyond their local area, they principally relied on subscribing to a news agency. As a result of the strong domestic market that then resulted, the two American news agencies—the Associated Press and United Press International—became two of the world's four largest agencies, which dominated international news flow (the others being Reuters and Agence France-Presse).

News agencies grew with the spread of the telegraph in the nineteenth century. They supplied stories to a diverse array of clients, and have been credited with a strong influence on the development of news style. In maximising their value to their clients, the emphasis was on speed and offering a comprehensive array of available news. In ensuring ease of use and processing, their reports emphasised brevity, and had an inverted pyramid style of presentation, with a strong lead sentence encapsulating the most newsworthy point to immediately command attention. To protect their clients against publishing inaccurate accounts, there was an emphasis on 'strong' sourcing, where all important claims were attributed to a named source—preferably an officially certified one, such as government officials and political leaders. These conventions came to be associated with ideals of 'objective' reporting (Schudson 1978).

News agencies never prospered in Australia. The major proprietors were more likely to rely on cooperative news-sharing alliances in their respective cities. In international news, they banded together to form Australian Associated Press (AAP), which was aligned with the British news agency Reuters. Because AAP was owned by the major proprietors, they used membership of it and access to its news service to restrict competition. As early as 1905, for example, the president of Sydney's *Daily Telegraph* company assured shareholders that 'excessive competition' had been avoided, and that 'substantial security' against the establishment of competing newspapers had been achieved because they controlled access to international news through AAP, and for a new venture to mount its own service would be a prohibitive expense (Mayer 1964, p. 28).

The difference in total market size allowed news agencies to emerge as an independent force in US journalism while AAP remained for decades as a weak organisation in its own right, the creature of its owners. The difference in market size is also important in the ability to support minority publications. An American niche publication such as the *New York Review of Books* can attract a circulation of about 100 000; when combined with its specialist advertising appeal, this is sufficient to establish its viability. On a comparative population ratio, however, a similar circulation in Australia would only be around 7000, insufficient to maintain a professional organisation or reach a threshold of commercial viability.

THE BUSINESS OF NEWSPAPERS

So far, we have examined the circulation side of the viability of the press. At least as important is advertising revenue. In 1957, when Melbourne's third morning newspaper, the *Argus*, closed, its circulation was around 170 000—40 000 more than the *Age* (Mayer 1964, p. 30; Goot 1979, p. 215), but the latter had a sounder advertising base, built especially on its dominance in classified advertising. There has been a tendency for more popular papers to rely on display advertising, and for the quality ones to rely on classified advertising. The latter means that it is less likely that any individual advertiser will be able to exercise much leverage with the paper. In contrast, in the 1960s, it used to be said that the Melbourne *Herald* was printed on the back of Myer ads—and in this case at least, the paper seemed more faithful to its main advertiser than to its readers. One of Bob Hawke's important victories as head of the Australian Council of Trade Unions (ACTU) was to break down 'resale price mainte-nance' (D'Alpuget 1982), a device that had allowed major retailers like Myer to inflate their profits. Hawke's campaign was of great benefit to consumers, but never a cause championed by the *Herald*.

Advertising is another force encouraging concentration of titles. Sometimes a publication has a market niche, where an advertising market fits its readership's interests well, but in advertising to a general market the tendency is to advertise in the market leader, so that a paper lagging in readership often suffers a disproportionate loss in advertising revenue.

The lack of appeal to general advertisers is just one of a battery of reasons why it is extremely unlikely that any new daily newspapers will be launched in Australia. (Specialist and general readership online titles such as the *Brisbane Times*, *Business Spectator*, *Crikey*, *The Punch*, *Online Opinion* and *New Matilda* either struggle to attract advertising as well or do not even attempt to do so.) Of current titles, *The Australian* (begun in 1964) is the youngest. The *Canberra Times* and the *Australian Financial Review* both developed from weeklies, becoming daily newspapers in the early 1960s. Apart from these comparative infants—two of them born from the technological possibility of distributing a newspaper on a national scale, the other from the growth of the national capital—the youngest of the other surviving capital city dailies is the Melbourne *Sun*, which was established as Australia's first tabloid newspaper in 1922 (Mayer 1964, p. 30). All the others were established in the nineteenth century. There have been some other attempts to establish new daily newspapers since World War II (e.g. *Newsday* in Melbourne, the *Sun* in Brisbane and *Business Daily*), but none of them survived.

The nature of newspapers is that there are huge start-up costs, while consumer takeup tends to be very slow. This also means that the advertising markets remain skewed very much to the incumbents. Apart from any new challenger needing to have an improbable amount of initial capitalisation, it would face very lopsided compe-tition against the full panoply of advantages enjoyed by an incumbent in terms of economies of scale, consumer habits, marketing prowess and pricing strategies.

But possibly the most telling commercial argument against any new (printed) newspaper is that it is a product that is declining in public consumption. Quite apart from all the closures of Australian papers that we have seen, even among surviving newspapers the trend in relation to population is downwards. So it is unlikely that any corporation will launch any new newspapers. Nor is there any likelihood of government support for such a move in the near future. First, it would be roundly denounced by the other newspaper proprietors, and second, no government is likely to think it is in its political interest to bring more critical scrutiny on itself.

Nor, at the moment, is there any policy rationale for them to do so. There are directly contrasting traditions about state involvement in broadcasting and the press—as we saw in Chapter 5. In broadcasting, state involvement was always seen as a necessity. In most countries, including Australia, there was a public service broadcaster, and in many broadcasting began as a state monopoly. Even in the United States, with its marginal public service broadcasting presence, there was always extensive regulation. Television, for example, was regulated not only to secure wavelength usage, but very extensively regarding its content. In contrast, in most democratic societies there is a strong tradition of press independence from government. The licensing of newspapers is overwhelmingly seen as an infringement on the freedom of the press. Indeed, the independence of the press from government—its role as a fourth estate (Schultz 1998)—was a central strand in the rise of liberal democracy.

The core rationales for state involvement in broadcasting included that the broadcasting spectrum was a public resource, the cultural (and perhaps political) power of broadcasting and the scarcity of wavelengths. The argument was that, as broadcasters had privileged access to a scarce public resource—the spectrum—then certain obligations followed. Similarly, because there was no prospect of market forces working in a normal way in broadcasting, there was to be state involvement and support.

Ironically, there are now already far more television channels than newspapers in any particular market—typically now twelve free-to-air channels, controlled by five different organisations, but only one locally produced daily newspaper. The scarcity argument now applies far more to newspapers than to television.

The oligopolistic structure of the media is not a commercial problem for their owners—rather the opposite. Nevertheless, what is good for the commercial fortunes of the media proprietors is not necessarily good for the media's democratic role. Apart from the threat to democracy posed by the concentrated press ownership, a more subtle, but potentially damaging change in the political economy of press journalism—one facilitated by the trend towards comfortable oligopoly—has also occurred. There is a stronger emphasis in internal operations on profit maximisation. It is impossible to quantify such a change in attitude—and it is certainly impossible to try to rectify it through any legislation—and journalists have always moaned that the 'bean counters' have taken control. However, now organisational structures have changed to integrate advertising and editorial considerations, especially in the content of special supplements and sections, so that what in quality newspapers used to be called the separation of church and state, of editorial and business factors, has disappeared. There is much more use of market research than there once was, and at least anecdotal evidence that it forms a larger part of editorial decision-making. This means that newspapers are less likely to invest in unprofitable areas like foreign correspondents and less willing to endanger the profit flow by investing in and publishing investigative journalism. Most pervasively, the emphasis on journalistic productivity means that there is less time for digging, for going beyond the obvious. Kohler (2008) comments that the Australian media have failed 'to invest in journalism at the same rate as the manipulators of journalism have invested in the means of manipulation'.

THE PRESS, THE INTERNET AND DEMOCRACY

The optimistic view is that as printed newspapers decline, their role will simply migrate to the internet, along with the revenue streams they have lost—that the decline, even the death, of newspapers is a change in the means of production and delivery, but not in the essential functions of newspaper journalism. Alan Kohler (2008) puts it most succinctly: 'Fearing for the death of newspapers is a bit like fearing for the death of vinyl records ... Newspapers are just vehicles to disseminate journalism and the advertising needed to pay for that journalism, they are not the journalism itself.' This is also the view put forward by Rupert Murdoch, who said that 'the internet won't destroy newspapers', but followed this by saying that 'too many newspaper executives thought the business was only about print ... Our real business isn't printing on dead trees. It's giving our readers great journalism and great judgement' (Luft 2008). Murdoch's thoughts were echoed by News Limited editorial director Campbell Reid, who told a conference on the future of journalism that he couldn't wait for the end of the tyranny of the printing press, the day when 'this great weight of doom slips off our shoulders and we go and compete on whatever platform the audience wants' (Este 2008). The shared theme in these accounts is one of opportunity: the idea that the internet disposes of many of the overhead costs of production and distribution, and promises in many ways greater immediacy and flexibility to the consumer of news.

However, to equate the migration from print to the internet simply with the increase in production efficiency and consumer convenience analogous to the move from vinyl records to CDs or VHS to DVD is fundamentally misleading. The unstated, but far from self-evident, assumption is that the product will be the same, simply delivered better.

There is no evidence that an equivalent amount of revenue that is lost from newspapers will flow to the internet. One American study concluded that while advertising revenue for the print newspapers would plunge from $42 billion in 2007 to $19 billion in 2015, advertising revenue for internet newspapers would rise from $3.2 billion to $6.9 billion (Simons 2008)—a loss of $22 billion against a gain of only $4 billion. In many ways, the ethos of the internet is that editorial content should be free. While there are premium services to which dedicated consumers subscribe, casual and passing consumption is confined to sites that are free to view. This suggests that any internet newspapers will have to be much leaner operations than is currently the case with print newspapers.

While each of the media plays a distinctive role in the total mix of news that becomes public, television and radio (and internet blogs) feed off the information made available by the press. Although in the interplay of initiative and reaction it is frequently misleading to isolate a single source, most often newspapers play the pivotal role in setting the agenda that the other media follow. In the news mix, newspapers do the heavy lifting: 'Newspapers form the living heart of the news cycle.' They have the biggest news rooms with the most specialist reporters (O'Donnell, McKnight and Este 2012, p. 4).

The internet has rightly been welcomed as ushering in an era of diversity, but this relates mainly to the expression of opinion and of analysis. Overwhelmingly, the informational content of the internet is supplied by official and commercial sources, and in a news sense is an adjunct activity to the existing major news media. Some news websites have become staples of news consumption—the *New York Times* website (*Economist* 2008) on the day that Obama was first elected had 61.6 million unique page views—but their content is still overwhelmingly subsidised by the print editions of the papers. Another aspect of internet newspapers, with their universality of access, is that consumption is disproportionately of leading brands. The *New York Times* and *Guardian* are now accessed by people around the world. It is the internet editions of the middle-sized and 'medium quality' papers that seem to attract less patronage.

CONCLUSION

The editor/publisher of the Manchester *Guardian*, C.P. Scott, once proclaimed that comment is free but facts are sacred. In the age of the internet, a variation might be that opinion is free (and plentiful), but facts are expensive to produce. One of the most successful of the new internet newspapers in America is the *Huffington Post*, but in comparison with the *New York Times*, whose newsroom has 1200 employees, it has only one-fiftieth that number. While there have been many excellent bloggers commenting on the Iraq war, the *New York Times* maintained a Baghdad bureau at the cost of $3 million a year (Alterman 2008).

At their best, newspapers make governments publicly accountable. Although all the media play their different roles in political reporting, newspapers are still the biggest diggers for news among the mix of media organisations. Bloggers are no substitute for journalists. Issues of quality control are crucial, and perhaps even more basic than the ventilation of opinions is newspapers' role in disclosure. At their best, newspapers provide systematic critical scrutiny of authorities; their reports are disseminated in a timely and credible way to large, politically relevant constituencies. Obviously they do not always perform at their best, but no other media institution is equipped to play their crucial democratic role.

FURTHER READING

A good Australian account of the daily production of news in both broadcasting and newspapers is given by Conley (2002), *The Daily Miracle* (2nd ed.). Bennett's (2005) American textbook, *News: The Politics of Illusion* (6th ed.) offers many succinct analyses of central issues. The reader edited by Bob Franklin (2008), *Pulling Newspapers Apart: Analysing Print Journalism*, has many interesting contributions, while Michael Schudson (2008), *Why Democracies Need an Unlovable Press* is an accessible and eloquent introduction to central issues. Penny O'Donnell, David McKnight and Jonathan Este's (2012) *Journalism at the Speed of Bytes* and Margaret Simons' (2012) *Journalism at the Crossroads* are two recent Australian publications on the crisis facing news and newspapers.

Chapter 17

TELECOMMUNICATIONS

JOCK GIVEN

Telecommunications has always been important in Australia. The availability, quality and price of services are often hot political issues. Big communications projects like the Overland Telegraph Line in 1872, direct overseas wireless telegraph and telephone services in the 1920s and 1930s, coaxial telephone cables and satellites in the 1960s and optical fibre links in the 1990s and 2000s were all celebrated as great national achievements, bridging vast distances across the continent, the region and the world.

The 'information age' of the late twentieth and early twenty-first centuries shifted communications closer to the centre of economic policy. Although 'information, media and telecommunications' still contribute a much smaller share of the value added in the Australian economy (2.8 per cent in 2011/12) than mining (9.7 per cent), financial and insurance services (9.5 per cent) or manufacturing (7.3 per cent), it has grown rapidly over recent decades. Manufacturing's share of the national economy has halved since 1975; information, media and telecommunications' share has increased more than two and a half times (ABS 2012b).

The growth of communications has been an international trend, and has been even more striking in developing countries. Mobile telephony brought two-way electronic communications for the first time to many people never reached by fixed-line telephone networks; the decline of the fixed-line business and infrastructure has not been as significant for telcos (telecommunications companies) in developing countries as it has been for their developed country counterparts. In 1993, 85 per cent of the world's mobile telephone subscribers were in the mainly rich, developed Organization for Economic Cooperation and Development (OECD) countries. By 2005, these countries accounted for just 43 per cent of global mobile subscribers. In March 2012, the top five mobile operators in Asia each had more than 150 million subscribers (Evans 2012).

Beyond its raw size, the communications sector is a vital input to other industries. New services and applications can raise productivity by improving the information available about products and prices, and making it more timely and easier to find. Supply chains can be more efficient. Banking, travel, government and other services can be delivered more cheaply or with extra features. Work can be reorganised so employees and contractors can work from home or on the road. Across the whole economy, some of the innovation that drives productivity growth comes from decentralised users linked by high-quality communications services, rather than centralised institutions.

FROM STATE MONOPOLY TO PRIVATE COMPETITION

One of the first things the new Australian parliament did in 1901 was pass legislation creating and funding a state-owned national post and telecommunications monopoly. Exercising the power given in the Constitution to make laws about 'postal, telegraphic, telephonic, and other like services' (section 51(v)), the separate post and telegraph administrations of the six colonies were merged into a single public enterprise, the form and functions of which changed little until post and telecommunications were split into Australia Post and Telecom Australia in 1975.

International telecommunications was handled differently. There were private and public enterprises and periods of competition as well as monopoly. Soon after Federation, the governments of Australia, New Zealand, Canada and Britain established a new enterprise to build and operate a Pacific telegraph cable. Connecting Australia and New Zealand to Britain and Europe via Canadian landlines and trans-Atlantic submarine cables, the Pacific Cable provided state-owned competition to the privately owned cables that reached Australia via India, Singapore and Java to the north and the Indian Ocean to the west. Further state-supported competition started in 1927, when a direct wireless telegraph service with Britain was opened by a Sydney-based company, Amalgamated Wireless (Australasia) (AWA) and the British Post Office. The Commonwealth government had taken a half-share in AWA in 1922, recapitalising it to support the risky new infrastructure. A second wireless service linking Australia with Canada opened in 1928.

Wireless took market share from cable so quickly that the British government, needing the cables for secure defence communications, supported a merger in Britain between the cable company and the Marconi wireless company. The new enterprise, Cable and Wireless, also took over the state-owned Pacific Cable. Australia did not merge its international cable and wireless services until after World War II, when the governments of the Commonwealth again cooperated to reorganise British international communications as a network of nationally based, state-owned corporations coordinated by a central authority in London. Cable and Wireless was nationalised in Britain; in Australia, AWA's international wireless services and Cable and Wireless's local operations were acquired by a new, public Overseas Telecommunications Commission (OTC). Submarine telephone cables were built across the Pacific and through Southeast Asia in the 1960s under these Commonwealth arrangements. OTC became Australia's participant in the global satellite system INTELSAT, whose first spacecraft was launched in 1965 (Harcourt 1987).

In the 1980s, the Thatcher government's privatisation of Cable and Wireless and British Telecom in Britain and the court-endorsed break-up of American Telegraph and Telephone (AT&T) in the United States were the first steps in the processes of liberalisation and privatisation copied around the world. In Australia at first, both the Liberal/National and Labor governments in the early 1980s rejected competition for Australia. But less than a decade later, Labor's hand was forced by the parlous financial state of AUSSAT, the state-owned domestic satellite system launched in the mid-1980s. Competition was introduced in infrastructure as well as services. It started with one new fixed line carrier (Optus, the new name of the privatised AUSSAT) and two new mobile operators (Optus and Vodafone) in the early 1990s, moving to open competition from 1997. Seeking a 'world-class telecommunications company that has the ability and ethos to compete vigorously in what will be a key industry in a very competitive global environment' (Beazley 1991), Telecom Australia was merged with OTC in 1992. The new 'Megacom' changed its name to Telstra in 1995 and was privatised over ten years from 1997.

PUBLIC AND PRIVATE PARTNERS

Even during the long era of state-owned domestic telecommunications, private manufacturers had a big role to play in supplying and installing the cables, switching and other equipment used by providers and the telephone handsets, telex and fax machines used by customers. This role expanded as competitors were allowed to build networks of their own and to interconnect with those of the incumbent, and as customers connected an expanding range of equipment to these networks, like mobile phones and desktop and laptop computers. Networks came to be used to distribute more kinds of content—still and moving images as well as Morse Code and voice—and to handle an increasingly sophisticated array of data applications, making telecommunications converge with the media and information technology industries. This convergence motivated the creation of a single regulator in 2005, the Australian Communications and Media Authority (ACMA), merging the broadcasting regulator that had existed in various forms since 1949 and the telecommunications regulator created in 1989 as one of the first steps in opening the market to competition.

Introducing competition into telecommunications required a new form of regulation. Where the monopoly era required the boundaries of the incumbent's exclusive rights to be policed, the competitive era required vigilance to ensure all players, especially a powerful incumbent, did not engage in anti-competitive conduct. Particularly important was an 'access regime' that could be used by entrants to gain access at fair prices to those parts of networks that it was uneconomic for them to build for themselves. In practice, this created a space of high controversy, where service providers and their economists battled each other to define which parts of networks should be made subject to the access regime, and the true cost of providing access to them. Opening the market to full competition in 1997, Australia gave the job of overseeing telecommunications competition to the general competition regulator, the Australian Competition and Consumer Commission (ACCC) rather than the specialist communications regulator.

SERVICE PROVIDERS

Australia's telecommunications services are provided by three major and many smaller or 'second-tier' companies. The major three are still the first three: Telstra, Optus and Vodafone. The younger players are smaller, although some have grown considerably as the industry has consolidated, especially in 2011 and 2012. iiNet, the largest of the second-tier players, bought Internode and Transact in 2011, Netspace in 2010, Westnet in 2008, Ozemail in 2005, Froggy in 2004, iHug in 2003 and many other smaller operators. TPG, the next largest, bought Pipe Networks in 2009; M2 bought Primus in 2012 and People Telecom in 2009 (CIMB 2012; ACMA 2012, pp. 27–9).

Consolidation was not restricted to the second-tier players. In 2012, Telstra announced it was buying Adam Internet (the competition regulator, the ACCC, was still investigating the proposed transaction in February 2013); its 50 per cent-owned pay TV operation, Foxtel, bought Austar; and Optus bought Vivid Wireless. Despite the overall trend towards consolidation, there has been some unwinding of the trans-Tasman ownership of telecoms interests. Telstra sold its New Zealand subsidiary, TelstraClear, to Vodafone NZ in 2012, and in 2010 Telecom New Zealand sold the consumer division of AAPT, one of the pioneers of the early competitive era in Australia, to iiNet.

Telstra

Australia's biggest telco is also one of the country's largest companies. Telstra's market capitalisation of A$56 billion in early March 2013 (the total value of publicly listed shares in the company) made it the seventh largest by this measure—around half the value of BHP Billiton and the Commonwealth Bank, but bigger than Wesfarmers and Woolworths ('Top 150 Companies' 2013). Different measures like total assets, annual revenues or profit would give different rankings, and changes in share prices alter the rankings by market capitalisation—sometimes sharply. The company's $25.2 billion revenue in 2011–12 was around twice the size of the total main media advertising market in Australia, and more than six times the size of the television advertising market (ACMA 2012, p. 54, citing CEASA data). Telstra has by far the largest share of the total Australian telecommunications market, although its share of different market segments varies. Its $25.2 billion in revenue in 2011–12 represented a little under 60 per cent of total industry revenue; it accounted for an estimated 64 per cent of the industry's capital spending; and its $3.4 billion after-tax profits comprised an estimated 72 per cent of the industry's profits (Martin 2013).

Diversifying into new businesses and markets has been an important part of Telstra's transformation in the era of liberalisation and privatisation. In Australia, it expanded on its own and in partnerships beyond traditional telecommunications into media services. It jointly owns the pay TV company Foxtel in a 50/50 partnership with News Corporation, profiting from this business as a shareholder, through dividends, as well as through fees paid for carriage of the service to cable customers over the hybrid fibre-coaxial (HFC) network it built in the mid-1990s and bundling pay TV with other services in discounted offers. Telstra also operates the online video service BigPond Movies, the subscription music-streaming service MOG and

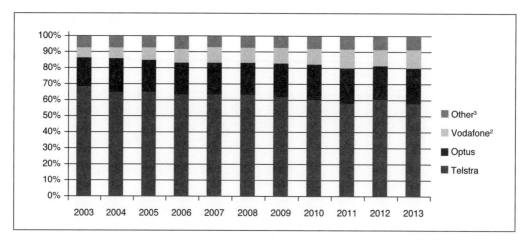

Figure 7.1 Australian telecoms market shares, 2003–13[1]
Notes
[1]Generally financial years ending 30 June, but these vary for different providers.
[2]Vodafone and Hutchison/3 are combined before 2009.
[3]Budde.com estimates.
Source: Budde and McNamara (2012, pp. 27–8).

acquires rights to content like live football broadcasts for delivery to its own mobile customers. Its Sensis directories and advertising business, built from its White and Yellow Pages directories, have struggled, with declining revenue every year since 2009. Internationally, Telstra owns CSL, one of the largest mobile operators in Hong Kong, and Autohome, which provides digital marketing services for the auto industry in China.

BOX 7.1: A SHARE OF TELSTRA

Privatisation of Telstra was one of the main issues that divided the major parties at the 1996 election and for the next decade. The incoming Howard Liberal/National Coalition government did not control the Senate, but gained the support of enough independent senators—including two former Labor Party members—to narrowly pass the legislation needed to sell a third of Telstra. In the initial public offering, public shareholders paid a total of $3.30 in two instalments in 1997 and 1998 for each share in the company. A further sixth of the company was sold in 1999. The share price soared around this time during the telecommunications and 'dot.com' boom (Fransman 2002; Askew 2011) when, according to CIMB Securities senior telecoms equity analyst Ian Martin, 'everyone thought telcos were growth stocks' (Martin 2013).

In the early 2000s, the government faced considerable resistance to further privatisation, even from within its own ranks—especially from country members who feared a fully privatised Telstra would reduce services and service quality in the bush but raise prices. Eventually, most of the rest of the company was offered to the public in November 2006. The remaining Commonwealth shareholding was transferred to the Future Fund early in 2007, the year the Howard government lost office, and progressively sold.

Martin says Telstra 'held up well as a defensive stock until it got thrown out of the bidding process for NBN Mark I (see below) in late 2008' at the height of the GFC—Lehman Brothers collapsed in September 2008. For the next two years, as the government launched NBN Mark II and Telstra's role in it remained highly uncertain, the share price was battered. Once a deal was struck with NBN Co and the government in June 2010, under which large payments would be made to Telstra for the use of some of its infrastructure, the migration of its fixed-line traffic to the NBN and new universal service arrangements, the share price rose steadily. In the post-GFC era, when more conservative sharemarket investors were seeking solid yields rather than dramatic capital growth, Telstra's strong, regular dividends brought it back into favour—although at a share price still well below the 1999 peaks.

Figure 7.2 Telstra share price, 1997–2013, weekly $A
Source: Iress, CIMB Securities.

Optus

Australia's other two major telcos are foreign owned. While their share of the Australian market is much smaller than Telstra's, their international operations are much larger. Optus, the No. 2 operator, is owned by the SingTel group, a state-controlled enterprise based in Singapore. It also wholly owns the major local telco, Singtel, and has shareholdings of between 20 and just under 50 per cent in six mobile operators in Asia and Africa: AIS (Thailand), Globe (the Philippines), PBTL

(Bangladesh), Telkomsel (Indonesia), Warid (Pakistan) and Bharti Airtel (India, Africa and South Asia). The Group's subsidiaries and associates had 445 million mobile customers in March 2012.

Optus won the second fixed line and mobile licences when Australia introduced competition in the early 1990s. Initially created by privatising the state-owned satellite company AUSSAT, Optus was owned by British and US telcos Cable and Wireless and Bell South and Australian investors. Cable and Wireless bought out the Americans after a few years, and floated part of Optus on the Australia Stock Exchange (ASX) in 1998. Three years later, it sold its stake to Singtel, which succeeded in a full takeover: investors interested in exposure to Optus now need to buy shares in SingTel. Optus built a hybrid fibre coaxial (HFC) cable network in the mid-1990s to offer cable TV, telephony and internet services, and invested in a pay TV operation of its own, Optus Vision, that was effectively merged into Foxtel's and wound down. It wholly owns the Virgin Mobile brand in Australia, still owns and operates satellites, and has launched several new spacecraft since the company was founded.

Table 7.1 Selected Asia-Pacific telcos, market capitalisation at 14 February 2013

Company	Country where based	Bloomberg Ticker	Market capitalisation at 14 February 2013 (US$billion)
Telstra Corporation	Australia	TLS AU	59.7
iiNet	Australia	IIN AU	0.8
TPG Telecom	Australia	TPM AU	2.2
M2 Telecommunications	Australia	MTU AU	0.7
Telecom Corporation	New Zealand	TEL NZ	3.4
Chorus	New Zealand	CNU NZ	1.0
Singtel [owner of Optus]	Singapore	ST SP	46.3
Advanced Info Service [AIS]	Thailand	ADVANC TB	20.1
Axiata Group	Malaysia	AXIATA MK	17.3
Telekomunikasi Indonesia	Indonesia	TLKM IJ	20.1
Bharti Airtel	India	BHARTI IN	23.0
China Mobile Limited	China	941 HK	221.5
China Telecom	China	728 HK	42.7
China Unicom	China	762 HK	35.5

Source: CIMB Securities (2013).

Vodafone

Primarily a mobile provider, Vodafone has the third largest share of Australia's telecommunications market. It won the third mobile licence issued in the early 1990s and operated independently until 2009, when it created a 50/50 joint venture with Hutchison 3G, Vodafone Hutchison Australia (VHA). Customers of Hutchison's '3' brand have been progressively migrated to Vodafone's, along with Crazy John's, which Vodafone acquired in 2006. Hutchison is majority owned by the Hong Kong-based Hutchison Whampoa group: it has interests in ports, property, hotels, retail, energy and infrastructure, as well as its Hong Kong telecommunications business.

Much younger than Telstra and Singtel but more global, Vodafone began as a mobile communications company in the United Kingdom in the 1980s. It expanded through mergers, acquisitions, joint ventures and partnerships, and in 2011/12 had over 400 million customers. Listed on the London and NASDAQ stock exchanges, Vodafone's most lucrative subsidiaries and majority-owned companies are in Germany, Italy, Spain, the United Kingdom, South Africa (Vodacom), India, the Netherlands and Egypt. It also controls 45 per cent of Verizon Wireless, one of the two largest mobile operators in the United States, and has partnership agreements in over 40 countries with local operators who pay Vodafone for the right to use its brand (Vodafone Group 2012).

Although the idea of the VHA joint venture was to create a stronger third force in the Australian market, major network congestion problems have resulted in a loss of around a million customers since 2009. The company has since invested heavily to improve access speeds, reliability and coverage (Bartholomeusz 2013). Vodafone's 50 per cent share of the VHA joint venture in Australia contributed 3 per cent of the company's global revenue and 1 per cent of its earnings (profits) in 2011–12. In New Zealand, Vodafone's wholly owned subsidiary is the leading mobile operator. The acquisition of TelstraClear from Telstra in 2012 further demonstrates Vodafone's intention to strengthen its presence in fixed line services.

SERVICES

The telecommunications services most used by Australians vary greatly depending on the age of the user. In May 2012, among people aged 18–24, texting from a mobile phone was the most popular service, followed by mobile phone voice calls. Just 3 per cent said email and 2 per cent said a fixed line telephone at home was their most popular communications service. Among people aged 65 and over, the situation was completely reversed. Texting was the least popular and mobile calls the second-least popular. Nearly 60 per cent said the home phone was their favourite service and 19 per cent said email. Other services such as social networking, instant messaging and VOIP were most popular among people aged 18–24—although even in this age group, more people said texting and mobile phone calls were their most used communications services (ACMA 2012, p. 31).

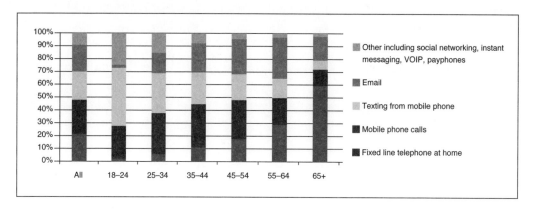

Figure 7.3 Communication service most used, Australia, May 2012, percentage of people with a fixed-line and/or mobile phone
Source: ACMA Communications Report 2011/12, p. 31—amended.

The popularity of different services highlights the commercial challenge for 'full-service' operators who need to offer and promote different services and service packages to different market segments (consumers, businesses, governments) while managing big long-term structural shifts in demand. Over the last decade, revenue from fixed-line telephony has fallen; revenue from mobile telephony and data has risen sharply but then plateaued; mobile revenue has shifted from voice to data. A particular challenge has been the rise of 'over-the-top' providers, offering services that compete with those supplied by telcos, but employing business models that deliver lower revenues to the network operators, or draw users to communicate and transact in new ways from which the telcos find it hard to profit (OECD 2011, pp. 31–3). The term 'over the top' is used widely (and inconsistently!) to refer to applications as diverse as telephone calls (Skype), social media (Facebook and Twitter), search (Google) and online video (YouTube, Quickflix, catch-up TV) (Budde and McNamara 2012, p. 56). Network operators have worked to create new applications and services businesses—for example, building data centres and offering cloud storage services, or deploying and managing the hardware and software needed for networked vending machines.

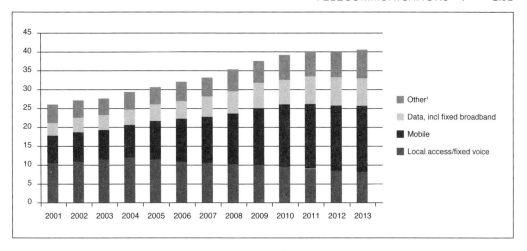

Figure 7.4 Australian telecoms market, 2001–13, $ billion

[1]Includes specialised data and IP access, business services and applications, online advertising and directories, pay TV, overseas activities and other minor items.

Source: Budde and McNamara (2012, p. 39), financial years ending 30 June.

Mobile

Mobile is the largest sector of the Australian telecoms market. The number of mobile voice services overtook fixed line telephony services in 2001 (Australian Communications Authority 2001, p. 78) and mobile revenue (including SMS) passed fixed voice revenue in 2006–07. In 2012–13, Buddecom estimates mobile share was at 44 per cent of total industry revenue, up from 29 per cent in 2000 (Budde and McNamara 2012, p. 39). Growth has plateaued, however. The number of 'mobile handset services' actually fell slightly to 24.3 million over the year to June 2012, although this still represents an average of more than one service per person in Australia. The time spent on calls originated on mobiles continued to increase, and it exceeded fixed line call minutes for the first time in 2011–12 (41 billion minutes from mobiles, 31 billion from fixed lines), but average revenue and price per user (ARPU) fell. Buddecom estimated annual mobile revenue growth of just 2 per cent in 2011–12 and 2012–13 after a decade of double-digit growth (Budde and McNamara 2012, p. 39; ACCC 2013, pp. 11–13).

Australia's first mobile telephone services were provided by Telecom in 1987, using its analogue 'AMPS' network. Telecom, Optus and Vodafone built second-generation (2G) networks from 1993 using the European Global System for Mobiles (GSM) standard. The AMPS network was closed in 2000 after Telstra built a second digital network using CDMA technology that offered better country coverage than GSM. Hutchison, using the '3' brand, was the first operator to offer 3G services in Australia in 2003 and one of the first in the world. Telstra, Optus and Vodafone launched their own 3G services in late 2005. The following year, Telstra built and launched a second 3G network, NextG, claiming 99 per cent coverage of the Australian population in mid-2008. Commercial 4G/Long Term Evolution (LTE) services were launched by Telstra in 2011 and Optus in 2012, to help cope with demand for fast access speeds and larger volumes of data.

During most of the long era when telephone services were fixed line and supplied by a domestic monopoly, standard handsets were provided as part of the service and manufactured mainly by the same companies that made other telecommunications equipment. Mobile telephony developed in the competitive era, and handsets are a crucial part of the battle for consumers. In 2008, the biggest, Finland's Nokia, made 40 per cent of the 1.25 billion units sold around the world. Korean manufacturers Samsung and LG had 17 per cent and 9 per cent respectively; Sony Ericsson, a joint venture between the Swedish equipment manufacturer and the Japanese consumer electronics firm, had 8 per cent.

Since then, the handset and mobile market has been transformed by 'smart-phones', allowing users to browse the web more easily and to download extra applications (apps), and by companies new to the mobile market. Apple's touch-screen iPhone was launched in 2007; a year later, search and advertising giant Google released Android, a mobile operating system based on Linux, adopted by many handset manufacturers—most notably Samsung. In 2012, around nine in ten smartphones sold around the world were Apples or Samsung/Androids. Their popularity enabled Apple and Samsung to strike tough deals with mobile operators who wanted to offer these smartphones to their customers, and the apps and content sold and given away through Apple's App Store and iTunes and Google Play drew the revenue and customer loyalty that mobile operators had hoped to secure for themselves through portals with exclusive features and content. Early in 2013, a group of the world's mobile operators announced they were supporting a new mobile operating system intended to attack Apple's and Google's position (Thomas and McCarthy 2013).

Internet

Australia had 12.0 million internet subscribers in June 2012, an increase of more than a million on the previous year. A little over nine million of these were household subscribers; just under three million were business and government subscribers. In addition, 16.2 million 'mobile handset subscribers'—a sub-set of the 24.3 million mobile voice subscribers noted above—could access the internet via their mobile phones.

Table 7.2 Australian telecoms subscriber numbers, June 2012

Sector	Number of subscribers at 30 June 2012 (millions)
Mobile voice[1]	24.3
Internet	
Dial-up	0.4
DSL	4.6
Cable	0.9
Fibre	0.1 [52 000]
Satellite, fixed wireless, other	0.1
Mobile wireless—datacard, dongle, USB modem or tablet SIM card[1]	5.9
Sub-total	*12.0*
Mobile handset[1]	16.2
Fixed-line voice	**10.4**

[1]The total number of mobile voice and data services was 30.2 million, the sum of 'mobile voice' and 'mobile wireless services'. 'Mobile handset internet services'—'smartphones' that allow the user to make voice calls and access the internet—are a sub-set of 'mobile voice services'.

Source: ABS (2012a); ACMA (2012b).

Virtually all the 12.0 million internet subscribers now have broadband connections, defined as providing an access speed of at least 256 kbits/sec. Just 439 000—less than 4 per cent—were still on dial-up. Nearly half used mobile wireless broadband connections like datacards, dongles, USB modems or tablet SIM cards, the fastest-growing form of dedicated internet access in recent years. Just under 40 per cent used DSL, previously the most popular form of internet access. Access speeds have been increasing: 46 per cent of subscribers have connections advertising access speeds of at least 8 Mbps.

The rapidly growing volume of data downloaded by subscribers has presented the telecoms industry with 'both an opportunity and a challenge', according to the (ACCC 2013, p. 1). It increased by 76 per cent in the year to June 2011 and a further 51 per cent the following year (ABS 2012a). This growth was due to increased streaming and downloading of bandwidth-hungry video, increased time spent online using more easily accessible smartphones and tablets, and some growth in subscriber numbers. The industry has responded by investing in improved and new fixed, mobile, backhaul and international networks, establishing priorities for traffic carried over them, modifying some voice and data caps and increasing some prices (ACCC 2013, pp. 23–4). The federal government's main response is the National Broadband Network (NBN)—see below.

The second-tier telcos have done well in fixed internet access, mainly DSL. Over the three years 2010–12, they achieved a market share of 41–43 per cent; Telstra had 41–42 per cent and Optus 16–17 per cent. Within the second tier, iiNet (14 per cent in 2011–12) and TPG (11 per cent) increased their shares through the acquisitions noted earlier (ACCC 2013, p. 24). Consistent with the general industry trend towards consolidation, the number of ISPs with more than 1000 subscribers fell from 97 to 81 over the two years to June 2012, and the number of very large ISPs—those with more than 100 000 subscribers—fell from ten to eight (ABS 2012a).

When competition was introduced in the early 1990s, some thought the network of copper lines linking houses and businesses to telephone exchanges would quickly be superseded by more modern technologies deployed by new entrants. Optus built a hybrid fibre-coaxial cable (HFC) network in parts of Brisbane, Sydney and Melbourne to supply pay TV and internet access as well as fixed-line telephony. Telstra built a similar network passing more households in more cities, but continued to operate its copper network. Like other telcos around the world, it deployed DSL over the copper lines, allowing broadband services to be carried. This reinvigorated the commercial potential of the almost ubiquitous copper network.

Other telcos also sought to install equipment in Telstra's exchanges, enabling them to offer DSL broadband and voice telephony to customers without using Telstra's wholesale services. The ACCC 'declared' certain services needed by other telcos to ensure they could do this. Declaration compelled Telstra, if requested, to supply these services without discrimination at prices fixed by the regulator. By the end of 2008, competitors had installed equipment in just over a tenth of Telstra's more than 5000 exchanges. In around 5 per cent of them—generally covering the most heavily populated areas—five or more competitors had done so, enabling vigorous broadband competition (ACCC 2009). This drove faster access speeds, bigger data caps and lower prices in metropolitan areas, but was less effective in regional and rural areas, where only about one in eight Telstra exchanges had competing infrastructure installed in June 2012 (ACCC 2013, p. 20).

Fixed line voice telephony

Australia's first five million telephone lines took a century to connect. The second five million took 20 years (Standard Telephone Service Review Group 1997, p. 29).

Since the mid-2000s, the number of fixed line telephone services has declined: it fell by more than half a million in the four years to June 2012. Roy Morgan estimates the number of people with a mobile phone but no fixed line telephone trebled between 2008 and 2012 to more than three million (ACMA 2012, pp. 29–30). Revenue from fixed line services has also declined, as customers substituted mobile calls, email, instant messaging, social networking and other forms of communication. Higher monthly access charges partly offset lower call charges and fixed telephony was still estimated to contribute nearly 20 per cent of total industry revenue in 2013—half the share in 2000.

Telstra dominates this sector of the market. Managing its decline has been a vital part of the company's overall strategy. Of the 10.4 million fixed-line voice services in mid-2012, 66 per cent were Telstra retail or business customers and a further 11 per cent were wholesale services, supplied to customers by Telstra's competitors but using its facilities. The remaining 23 per cent were provided by competitors who had installed some facilities of their own (ACMA 2012, pp. 29–30). One factor contributing to the decline in fixed-line voice services and revenue is the takeup of 'voice-Over-Internet-Protocol' (VOIP) services like Skype, using internet-connected computers and tablets and, to a lesser extent, internet or mobile phones. In June 2012, Australia had 4.3 million VOIP users, up 21 per cent over the year (ACCC 2013, p. 14).

International connectivity

Australia's major and second-tier telcos all contract with global cable and satellite providers to bring international data and voice traffic to and from their customers. Several of them wholly or partly own submarine cables. Originally laid to carry Morse Code telegraph messages in the nineteenth century, then telephone calls from the 1950s and 1960s, most new submarine cables have been made of optical fibre since the late 1980s. They now carry the vast amounts of data exchanged over the internet and other networks. SingTel (40 per cent) and Telecom New Zealand (50 per cent) own the Southern Cross cables that link Sydney to the West Coast of the United States via New Zealand, Fiji and Hawaii. Telstra owns the Endeavour cable between Sydney and Hawaii and TPG took over Pipe's Pacific Cable (PPC-1) between Sydney and Guam: both link into other trans-Pacific systems. Telstra also has a stake in the Australia–Japan cable system. Vodafone acquired Cable and Wireless's global networks business in 2012.

POLICY

BOX 7.2: SPECTRUM: A 'DIGITAL DIVIDEND'

A crucial issue for wireless operators is getting access to the spectrum they need to transmit their services. Radio-frequency spectrum is the part of the range of electromagnetic radiation that is used for communicating. Services that use this spectrum include mobile telephony and broadband, TV and radio, air traffic control, emergency and defence services. In Australia, the ACMA regulates the use of radio-frequency spectrum. Legislation makes it generally unlawful to operate a radio-communications device unless it is authorised by an ACMA licence.

The tremendous growth of mobile communications services has made the parts of the spectrum best suited to transmitting them extremely valuable. Large blocks of spectrum for wireless telecommunications services were allocated by auction in the 1990s and early 2000s for fifteen-year terms. In 2012, the Minister for Broadband, Communications and the Digital Economy determined that it would be in the public interest to reissue these licences to the incumbents, Telstra, Optus, Vodafone and vividwireless (subsequently acquired by Optus) and set fees to be levied. This began a process that is likely to ensure mobile voice and data services continue to be offered using this spectrum as the licences expire between 2013 and 2017 (Conroy 2012).

A further large block of spectrum is being made available for wireless services by shutting down analogue TV services by the end of 2013. This complex transition is being undertaken all around the world. In Australia, it began in 2001, when free-to-air TV services started simulcasting in digital alongside their analogue transmissions (see Chapter 10). Digital transmission of TV signals allows the use of additional frequencies that were previously kept vacant to prevent unacceptable interference to the analogue transmissions. By reorganising the frequencies that will be used for digital TV transmissions once 'analogue shutdown' or 'digital switchover' has occurred, a substantial 'digital dividend' is being realised. This spectrum is likely to be acquired at auction by mobile network operators, including Telstra and Optus, to help satisfy the growing appetite for mobile broadband.

A National Broadband Network and 'structural separation'

The Australian Labor Party's plan for a National Broadband Network responded to the perception that the country had become a 'broadband backwater'. In June 2002, Australia had just 1.3 broadband subscribers per 100 inhabitants—about a third of the OECD average and well behind market leaders Korea (20.3) and Canada (10.3). Increasing DSL competition made fixed broadband more widely available, but average speeds remained slow and prices were comparatively high. In June 2008, Australia's 23.5 broadband subscribers per 100 inhabitants still placed it sixteenth out of 30 OECD countries, well behind the leader, Denmark, at 36.7. On download speed, measured as the average advertised speed of plans surveyed in October 2007, Australia ranked ninth, but scored only one-quarter of France's and Korea's average speeds. The combination of moderate speeds and data caps made broadband in Australia around seven times as costly as Japan's, measured by average monthly price per advertised Mbit/sec (OECD Broadband Portal).

The plan promised by the then Labor opposition promised at the 2007 election involved committing $4.7 billion in debt or equity to a Fibre-to-the-Node or Curb FTTN/FTTC) or Fibre–to-the-home/premises (FTTH/FTTP) network, delivering 12 Mbits/sec to 98 per cent of the population within five years. The operator would have to allow open access to the network at a uniform national price (ALP 2007). This plan drew heavily on a proposal presented by Telstra to the previous government in 2005. Some form of public–private partnership allowed Labor to acknowledge the reality of Telstra's privatisation, which it had consistently opposed, while incorporating a measure of state participation in a critical part of its network.

After the election, the new Rudd Labor government requested proposals for the proposed network. Telstra's was rejected for failing to comply with one of the bidding criteria. In April 2009, the government announced a new and more ambitious plan for a National Broadband Network (NBN), delivering download speeds of 100 Mbits/sec to 90 per cent (later increased to 93 per cent) of Australian homes and workplaces within eight years. This FTTP network would deploy optical fibre to wholly replicate and perhaps replace the copper lines that connected Australia's roughly 5000 exchanges to its eleven million households and business premises. The remaining 7 per cent of households would also get much faster broadband via fixed wireless or satellite connections. The NBN would be built and operated by a company in which the Commonwealth would be the majority shareholder, and run as an open-access wholesale business, with no retail customers (Conroy 2009).

The NBN highlighted sharp divisions in the debate about Australian telecommunications policy. After two decades of liberalisation and privatisation, many agreed that the prevailing structures and regulation were failing, but they disagreed violently about why. Paul Fletcher, a former Optus executive and now Liberal member for the federal seat of Bradfield, argued it was because Telstra was 'far too big and dominant'. Its vertical integration in retail and network/wholesale businesses, and control of most of the fixed line customer access and back-haul networks, produced a 'horribly lop-sided industry structure in fixed line telecommunications'. Regulatory arrangements were 'too weak to control Telstra'. Slow broadband take up could be explained simply: 'Telstra kept prices sky high. Once they fell, take up rocketed.' Fletcher argued that the key to broadband policy was tackling the problem of Telstra and correcting the structure of the telecommunications market. He favoured 'structural separation', with a new national fixed line network owned and operated by a company selling wholesale services, separate from the companies that sell retail services (Fletcher 2009, pp. 209–33).

Telstra and its supporters argued that the heart of the problem was the access regime administered by the ACCC. By regulating too much of Telstra's network and setting third-party access prices too low, it 'severely distorted' price signals and discouraged investment. This had made Telstra reluctant to undertake the 'new wave of telecommunications investment now required to complete the task begun in 1986 by restructuring and renewing the customer access network'. Its rivals 'prefer to "cheap ride" on Telstra's network rather than upgrade, much less further deploy, networks of their own,' according to Henry Ergas, an economist and regular Telstra consultant. He thought 'a radically new approach was needed—one that was more modest about what regulation could achieve, provides investors with a more certain and consistent environment, and then allows market forces to do the heavy lifting'. He thought structural separation 'would likely impose very substantial costs', particularly by increasing inefficiencies in planning, building and migrating customers to new networks (Ergas 2008, pp. viii, 2–3, 8, 28, 164–70, 192).

As the idea of the NBN was refined, important elements were modified. Private investors were unlikely to find the modest forecast rate of return attractive, so the corporation established in 2011 to build and operate the network, NBN Co, has stayed a wholly state-owned enterprise. The possibility that service providers—particularly Telstra—would continue to use their own copper and HFC networks to compete aggressively with the NBN made some sort of accommodation vital to the economics of the new network: agreements were reached with Telstra and Optus, and approved by the ACCC. The core idea remained: a new fixed-line network extending fibre all the way to most premises, operated as a wholesale-only, open-access network, aimed at maximising competition in the provision of services using the network. A similar policy was adopted in New Zealand, although there the state is investing alongside private operators in a series of regional fibre partnerships, and the incumbent, Telecom New Zealand, has 'structurally separated' formally, creating a new listed network enterprise, Chorus, distinct from the service provider, Telecom.

The NBN was a critical factor that convinced country independents to support Labor after the 2010 election, allowing it to form a minority government (Given 2010). The Liberal–National opposition repeatedly criticised the cost and pace of the rollout and released its own 'Plan for Fast Broadband and an Affordable NBN' in April 2013. This plan proposed less dramatic improvements in download data rates than Labor's NBN but promised to deliver them sooner and more cheaply (Liberal–National Coalition 2013).

Consumer regulation and support

Competition is intended to be the primary force ensuring consumers get the telecommunications services they want at the best possible prices. There is, however, a lot of regulation in areas where governments believe an unfettered market might not produce satisfactory outcomes. These include the availability and quality of services, prices, advertising and contracts. ACMA and the ACCC are responsible for administering different parts of this regulation. A specialist Telecommunications Industry Ombudsman (TIO) is funded by the industry to resolve disputes about telephone and internet services between small business or residential consumers and service providers. A peak body, the Australian Communications Consumer Action Network (ACCAN) is funded by the federal government to represent and advocate for residential consumers and small businesses, including not-for-profit organisations.

Levels of basic service are guaranteed under a universal service obligation. This includes requirements about service and handset features for people with disabilities. All telephony services must offer access to emergency ('000'), operator and directory services. A Customer Service Guarantee financially compensates customers where service providers fail to connect or repair services within prescribed time limits. Telstra is still subject to price caps on some of its services, and all providers of standard voice telephone services are required to charge untimed rates for local calls. A particularly contentious pricing issue in recent years has been the cost of international 'mobile roaming'. In early 2013, Australian and New Zealand regulators released a report recommending new powers enabling them to act to reduce trans-Tasman roaming charges (NZ Ministry 2013).

BOX 7.3: MISLEADING ADVERTISING: WHAT IS IT? WHO DOES IT? WHO IS RESPONSIBLE?

In its role as the national consumer protection regulator, the ACCC acts against misleading advertising in the often aggressively competitive telecommunications industry. It has criticised providers of mobile phone and broadband plans, phone cards and mobile premium services for failing to properly disclose the true costs and contractual terms before customers sign up. 'Free' inclusions, 'unlimited' offers and claims about broadband speeds and the impact of data caps are favourite targets.

During 2011–12, the ACCC undertook nineteen major investigations in the telecommunications sector under the Australian Consumer Law (ACCC 2013, pp. 33–4). These included action in the Federal Court against:

- TPG Internet, alleging consumers had been misled by advertisements representing that they could buy unlimited ADSL2+ broadband services for $29.99 per month, when in fact these services were only available when purchased together with home phone line rental from TPG at an additional cost of $30 per month. The court ordered TPG to pay $2 million in penalties.

- Apple, alleging misleading promotion of the 'new iPad with WiFi+ 4G'. The ACCC argued that Apple had represented that the new iPad could connect to networks promoted in Australia as '4G' networks, when it could not. The iPad could operate in frequency bands being used for 4G in other parts of the world at the time, but not the bands being used in Australia. The court ordered Apple to pay $2.25 million in penalties and $300 000 in costs.

In 2008, the ACCC won a court action against Telstra, successfully arguing that the slogan initially used for its NextG mobile network, 'Coverage Everywhere You Need It', overstated the real reach. The slogan was changed to 'Telstra NextG Network Works Better in More Places' (ACCC 2008).

In 2013, the ACCC lost an appeal in the High Court in an action against Google, alleging internet users were misled when advertisers used the names of their competitors as keywords to attract visitors to 'sponsored links' via Google's AdWords. The court agreed consumers could be misled, but disagreed that the misleading representations were made by Google. It accepted Google's arguments that the advertisers created the sponsored links, so any representations were made by them and not Google (*Google Inc v ACCC* 2013).

CONCLUSION

In the 1990s and early 2000s, Australian telecommunications was transformed from an industry dominated by a small number of state-owned monopolies to a competitive market with many private service providers. For a time, during the telecommunications and internet boom of the late 1990s, financial markets came to see the newly liberalised industry as a growth business rather than the utility it had been treated as for a century. Investors were prepared to pay nearly three times the initial public offer price for a share in Telstra just two years after it floated. After the telecommunications market crash, a perception that the structures set for the industry and Telstra were constraining the development of fixed line broadband services in the 2000s motivated a policy rethink.

The liberalisation of Australia's telecommunications market was bipartisan policy, but the privatisation of Telstra was not, and nor was the approach to building and operating a National Broadband Network. Labor established a new state-owned enterprise and committed billions of dollars to build an all-fibre network to most households and businesses, and to operate it as an open-access, wholesale business. The Liberal/National opposition complained that the plan was too expensive, would take too long to fix the most urgent problems and returned the government to a role in choosing telecommunications technologies and investment strategies that it was ill-equipped to play. But it stressed that it agreed with the government's goal of faster, cheaper broadband, and eventually seemed to accept the structural separation of Telstra.

Telstra's success in the mobile market, where it has invested heavily in the quality of its networks, and Vodafone's mobile network crisis have shown the continuing commercial attraction of vertical integration through networks and services—a telecommunications business model that is effectively no longer available for fixed line services under the NBN. This mobile market experience might be as influential in evaluating the performance of the industry over the next few years as the Telstra/ Optus dual HFC cable rollout was to assessing the strengths and weaknesses of the 1990s industry and regulatory structure. But while politicians debate the future of the NBN, and telcos and others reconsider the merits of traditional network/service integration, other applications, service and device providers will be working to maintain and create 'smart' business models that leave the 'telecommunications industry' tending 'dumb' infrastructure and declining product lines.

FURTHER READING

A good regular source of articles and interviews about telecommunications in Australia and overseas is the quarterly *Telecommunications Journal of Australia*. Industry and policy developments in other countries are analysed in the monthly *Telecommunications Policy* and bi-monthly *Info: The Journal of Policy, Regulation and Strategy for Telecommunications, Information and Media*. The acrimonious policy debate about telecommunications regulation and broadband in Australia is the subject of books by Ergas (2008), *Wrong Number: Resolving Australia's Telecommunications Impasse*, and Fletcher (2009), *Wired Brown Land? The Battle for Broadband*. Fransman (2002), *Telecoms in the Internet Age: From Boom to Bust to . . .?* covers the rise and fall of the telecommunications industry around the turn of the century and Barry (2003), *Rich Kids: How the Murdochs and Packers lost $950 million in One.Tel* charts one of its corporate casualties in Australia, One.Tel. Grant and Howarth (2011), *Australian Telecommunications Regulation* (4th ed.) is the most detailed account of recent Australian telecommunications law, regulation, policy and history, and includes chapters on the United States, United Kingdom, European Union and New Zealand. Moyal (1984), *Clear Across Australia: A History of Telecommunications* and Harcourt (1987), *Taming the Tyrant: The First Hundred Years of Australia's International Communication Services* are the most comprehensive histories of Australia's domestic and international communications.

Chapter 8

RADIO

BRIDGET GRIFFEN-FOLEY

Immediate, intimate, portable and inexpensive, radio is the most pervasive medium in Australia. The average Australian spends sixteen hours each week listening to radio. There are 37 million radios in Australia—in the bedroom, bathroom, kitchen, office, shop, gym and car. Radio regulates and punctuates our day, promotes and shapes music consumption, and helps to set the political agenda.

However, until recently, radio—despite its ubiquity—was arguably the most neglected medium in the academic (particularly historical) literature on Australian media and communications. Over the last few years, fine scholarship on the main public broadcaster, the Australian Broadcasting Corporation (ABC), has been augmented by work on the Special Broadcasting Service (SBS), community radio, commercial radio and talkback.

This chapter first outlines the historical development of Australian radio from the 1920s to the 2000s. The second part examines the contemporary industry's constituent parts—commercial, public and community. The chapter concludes by addressing new digital platforms for the delivery of radio.

HISTORY

A dual system (1923–36)

The Wireless Telegraphy Act 1905 granted the infant Commonwealth government control of the developing field of radio-communications. Amateur experimenters and professional engineers interested in the two-way, point-to-point possibilities of radio telegraphy competed with, and were gradually vanquished by, retailing, manufacturing and other business interests, which saw greater commercial possibilities in providing regular content on a point-to-multipoint basis. Although Australian broadcasting officially commenced in 1923, various schemes, conferences and a Royal Commission were to pass in a quest for the basis of a sound regulatory regime and a genuinely national system that would, in the words of *Wireless Weekly*, penetrate this 'land of magnificent distances' (Griffen-Foley 2009, pp. 2–7).

A conference in 1924 agreed to a bifurcated system, with 'A' class stations to be maintained by revenue from listeners' licence fees and some advertising, and 'B' class stations continuing to broadcast radio concerts (Counihan 1982, pp. 122–3). In 1928, the government announced its intention to nationalise the 'A' stations; in 1932, these twelve stations formed the basis of the Australian Broadcasting Commission (ABC). Closely modelled on the British Broadcasting Corporation (BBC), it was an imperial artefact, designed as an independent corporation, governed by a board of commissioners and financed solely by licence fees (Inglis 1983, p. 19). 'B' (or 'commercial', as they preferred to be known) stations—many of which had passed into the hands of newspaper, religious and political interests—were allowed to continue and some new licences were granted. In 1930 they formed what became the Federation of Australian Radio Broadcasters (FARB), which throughout its history has been anxious to ward off government regulation. By 1935, Australia had over 60 commercial stations.

Rather than attempt to define the 'public interest', or select news from a national standpoint, the ABC focused on its mission to culturally uplift all sections of the community. Commercial stations relied largely on the importation of American transcription discs containing music and dramas. These stations sometimes arranged 'prestige' broadcasts of such things as 'synthetic' cricket Tests, the Sydney Harbour Bridge opening and parliamentary sittings in a direct challenge to the ABC's claim to be the national broadcaster.

World War II and local content (1937–55)

By 1937, two out of every three Australian homes had a radio set. A year later, the most enduring commercial network, Macquarie, was formed to appeal to advertisers wanting a national reach. World War II ushered in an even more prosperous period for Australian radio, and resulted in profound changes to the industry's regulation, content and infrastructure.

In December 1939, the new Department of Information began supplying material for the ABC's shortwave service, originally designed for listeners in outback Australia. Now the service began countering broadcasts from Germany directed at Asia, and by the middle of the war most broadcasts were in Asian, rather than European, languages. With its eclectic mix of talks, English lessons, cricket, music and a listeners' mailbag, Radio Australia—as it became known—returned to ABC control in 1950 (Inglis 1983, pp. 78–9; Lucas 1964).

During the war, the ABC decreased its reliance on BBC news and increased its Australian news service. In 1942, a single Act was passed regulating the commercial sector and guaranteeing the ABC's independence. The *Broadcasting Act* stipulated that at least 2.5 per cent of radio time be devoted to the work of Australian composers; it was a curious provision, for there had been no sustained agitation for a quota (Counihan 1992, p. 12). In the short term, wartime economies had the greatest protectionist impact: newsprint rationing and restrictions on the importation of American transcriptions heightened radio's appeal to advertisers and encouraged a local production industry. Steering the shape and prosperity of commercial radio in the 1940s were two major advertising agencies: the Australian arm of the American behemoth J. Walter Thompson, and George Patterson, which established the Colgate Palmolive radio production unit (Potts 1989).

In 1949, the Australian Broadcasting Control Board (ABCB) was created as a statutory authority to regulate the industry. However, the Postmaster-General retained powers to award and revoke licences and to make appointments to the board. The ABCB survived by endeavouring not to offend the government or powerful interests, and rejected thousands of applications for new commercial licences, citing a shortage of available frequencies (Armstrong 1982, p. 39).

Television, talkback and rock'n'roll (1956–71)

The *Broadcasting and Television Act* 1956 legislated for a dual television system, as with radio, and doubled the local music quota. The advent of television meant that radio lost its place as the sole medium of electronic entertainment in the home, and introduced a new competitor for advertising revenue. Several commercial radio stations hedged their bets by buying into the new medium. There were some consolations for the radio industry. The decision to allow television transmission in parts of the VHF band usually designated for FM radio effectively insulated AM stations from a major new threat (Marcato 2004, pp. 14–15). The ABCB's program duties were diluted and the 1958 Broadcasting Program Standards were premised on self-regulation.

In 1956–57, the radio industry's profits fell, but they resumed a sharp upward spiral the following year: by 1960–61, only three of the 110 commercial stations were making a loss. Radio drama was the biggest casualty, as writers, producers and audiences turned to television.

In a 1956 memo entitled 'Television Counter Measures', a Macquarie executive wrote of the need to intensify local advertising and an active interest in community affairs, promote microphone 'personalities' and encourage the sale of car and transistor radios (Griffen-Foley 2009, p. 55). Radio changed from a family to a highly individualised medium, with one radio for each person over the age of 16 by 1962. Broadcasters began targeting separate audiences, such as teenagers, instead of the whole family. In 1958, the first Australian 'Top 40' music program was introduced to 2UE by Bob Rogers, and many other stations followed (Griffen-Foley 2009, pp. 264–5).

Weather and traffic reports improved, and reporters used telephones for on-the-spot news and interviews. The success of 'conversation' programs in the United States demonstrated to Australian radio executives that the telephone had other uses, and in 1967 the Broadcasting Program Standards were amended to allow the recording and rebroadcasting of telephone calls. Established radio presenters like Norman Banks and Ormsby Wilkins moved into talkback, along with younger hosts such as John Laws (Gould 2012).

Expansion (1972–86)

Between 1947 and 1971, Australia's population nearly doubled, but only thirteen new commercial stations—principally in the regions—were licensed. The Whitlam government of 1972–75 spearheaded important, if at times controversial and muddled, media reforms: the licensing of FM and new AM stations was approved; experimental licences for non-profit community access stations were awarded under the *Wireless Telegraphy Act*, bypassing the *Broadcasting and Television Act*; and listeners' licence fees were abolished.

Fine music buffs, educational institutions and ethnic groups seized the opportunity to move into community radio. After a patchy post-war history of foreign-language programming on some commercial stations (Griffen-Foley 2009, p. 80), 2EA Sydney and 3EA Melbourne were granted experimental licences for foreign-language broadcasting in 1975. Three years later, they were incorporated in the new, publicly funded Special Broadcasting Service (SBS).

By the 1970s, Aboriginal languages were being heard on a small number of commercial stations in Western Australia and the Northern Territory. The Central Australian Aboriginal Media Association (CAAMA), formed in 1980, broadcast in several Aboriginal languages on ABC, commercial and community stations, and secured its own licence for a community station. The Broadcasting for Remote Aboriginal Communities Scheme (BRACS),, announced in 1987, delivered ABC and commercial radio by satellite, and gave remote communities basic equipment to make their own programs (Meadows 1992, pp. 5–6, 35–7).

The ABC developed a more national focus during this period. In 1975 it opened a youth AM station, 2JJ, to encourage new Australian rock music; it became Triple J on the FM band in 1980. In 1976 the ABC also launched a classical music FM network from Adelaide. From the 1960s, current affairs had assumed an increasing role on ABC radio. The daily current affairs programs *AM* and *PM* were established in 1968–69, and in the mid-1980s the once all-powerful News Division was split between radio and television and integrated with current affairs (Petersen 1999, pp. 13, 19, 41, 60). *Australia All Over*, which had begun life under different names as a session for country listeners, began being heard in the cities. By 1991 Ian McNamara's 'carefully uncultivated' voice was being heard by 1.2 million people (Inglis 2006, pp. 93, 205).

While the Fraser government meddled in the ABC's affairs, cut its budget and inspired the formation of the 'Friends of the ABC' (Inglis 1983, pp. 373–4, 390), it was also responsible for significant shifts in the size and scale of Australia's broadcasting operations. In 1976 it initiated an overdue inquiry into the entire industry and replaced the Australian Broadcasting Control Board (ABCB) with the Australian Broadcasting Tribunal (ABT). The ABT prepared a report on self-regulation, which it did not view as synonymous with 'no regulation'. To FARB's chagrin, the local content requirement—which had recently been increased to 10 per cent—was maintained.

In 1978, community broadcasting licences became a legal entity. The community sector consolidated and expanded due to delays in the awarding of commercial FM licences, for which FARB's lobbying was partly responsible. When commercial FM finally debuted in 1980, playlists were more varied than the Top 40 format, the rate of rotation was low and the number of advertisements was restricted (Turner 1993a, p. 151).

With its superior sound quality and appeal to younger audiences, FM radio came to be associated with music and comedy, and AM radio with news and talk. AM stations increasingly vied for success by signing up opinionated talkback hosts. In 1985, the beleaguered 2GB, which had adopted 'Newstalk' as its slogan, lured John Laws from 2UE to host the morning session for a salary rumoured to be over $1 million per year.

As Mark Armstrong noted in 1986 (p. 49), changing community values and a move towards deregulation saw the 1958 program standards cut from 34 to four pages and the removal of the advertising time limit (eighteen minutes per hour) in competitive markets. But he was also buoyed by the opening of the frequency spectrum to more stations; by 1986, Australia had 139 commercial and 58 community stations. Observing that 'nearly all radio stations are programmed separately and independently', Armstrong predicted it was unlikely that big media or entertainment groups would have anything like the national audience shares available to television networks.

Development (1986–92)

Legislative changes in 1986–87 imposed restrictions on cross-media ownership and allowed the limited growth of commercial radio networks. The legislation, strengthened in 1992, contained the expansion of major press and television empires into radio. However, other factors were at work that would massively transform and consolidate the pattern of radio ownership in Australia.

By 1988, the Australian Broadcasting Corporation, as it was now known, was using satellite to feed news to studios around the country, and three commercial networks had also embraced satellite. The Macquarie Network formed MACSAT to transmit program content—various combinations of news bulletins, music, a midnight-to-dawn program and John Laws—to 32 stations. Time calls and local weather and advertising were operated by pulses sent individually to stations to create a 'local' feel ('Do YOU need satellite radio programming?' 1988).

In 1988, the Hawke government announced the National Radio Plan for metropolitan services. It involved the conversion of two AM stations to FM in each mainland capital city and the staggered introduction of new commercial FM stations in these cities. New licences would be awarded by tender, with the licence going to the highest bidder rather than on the basis of commercial viability. The two relinquished AM frequencies would be used to provide in each city a Radio for the Print Handicapped station, and a separate ABC network was established to broadcast parliament (which the ABC had been required to do since 1946) (Clark 1988).

These regulatory developments, combined with the 1987 stock market crash and a frenzy of interest in the media sector, saw more than half of Australia's metropolitan commercial stations change hands between 1986 and 1989. Record prices were paid, meaning that for the first time in 50 years the radio industry was collectively in debt in 1990–91 (Brown 1990, Preface; Miller 1995, p. 90). The Macquarie Network was sold off in pieces, but some newer players expanded quickly: licence auctions in 1989 allowed Austereo to form the first national FM network.

Expectations and pressures of a different sort affected Triple J (Turner 1993a, p 149). The prospect of export sales encouraged the government to expand Triple J's broadcast area to include all metropolitan cities in 1989 (Miller 1995, p. 91). But Triple J's counter-cultural, and frequently controversial, comedy and documentary broadcasts unnerved ABC management. In 1990 a new general manager was recruited from Triple M, senior staff were sacked and the station set out to target a youth audience aged 15–24 (Turner 1993a, p. 153; Austin 2005).

BOX 8.1: THE TYPES OF RADIO SERVICES

Broadcasting services in Australia are regulated primarily through the *Broadcasting Services Act* (BSA) 1992. The Act defines six categories of radio broadcasting services:

- *National, publicly owned broadcasting services*: The Australian Broadcasting Corporation and the Special Broadcasting Service:
  - The ABC has four national radio networks (Radio National, Triple J, ABC Classic FM, and ABC NewsRadio on the Parliamentary and News Network); ABC Local Radio, consisting of 60 metropolitan and regional stations throughout Australia; and Radio Australia, an international radio service broadcasting by shortwave and digital satellite to Asia and the Pacific.
  - SBS Radio, which can be heard in all capital cities and some regional centres, broadcasts in 68 languages.
- *Community broadcasting services:* non-profit, free-to-air services provided for community purposes. By 2012 there were 362 community radio licences on issue.
- *Commercial broadcasting services:* free-to-air services operated for profit and funded by advertising revenue. By 2012 there were 273 commercial radio licences on issue.
- *Subscription broadcasting services:* services with general appeal to the public and funded by customer subscriptions.
- *Subscription narrowcasting services:* services with limited appeal to the public and funded by customer subscriptions.
- *Open narrowcasting services:* services providing programs targeted to special-interest groups (for example, foreign language and horse racing), or of limited appeal due to content or location, and not funded by subscriptions.

A national survey commissioned by the Australian Broadcasting Authority in 2003 found that 70 per cent of respondents regularly listened to commercial radio, 51 per cent listened to the ABC or the SBS and 18 per cent listened to community radio.

Sources: Butler and Rodrick (2007, pp. 490–6); ABA (2003); ABC (2012); ACMA (2012).

Deregulation (1992–)

The *Broadcasting Services Act* 1992 liberalised access to capital and reflected a deliberate shift to a market-oriented approach to broadcasting (Butler and Rodrick 2007,

p. 579). The cap on the number of stations a company could own and restrictions on foreign ownership were removed. Ownership of Australian radio consolidated rapidly, and in the mid- to late 1990s there was considerable overseas investment: Ireland's Australian Provincial Newspapers and the American radio behemoth, Clear Channel International, bought the Australian Radio Network (ARN) and Britain's Daily Mail Group formed DMG Radio Australia.

The Act also ushered in a new industry-based self-regulatory regime, the limitations of which were amply demonstrated by 'Cash for Comment' (see Box 8.2). A new regulator, the Australian Broadcasting Authority (ABA), invited commercial, community and subscription radio industry groups to work with it to develop and register codes of practice concerning key areas of content that took into account prevailing community standards (*Halsbury's Law of Australia* 2004).

Commercial and community stations were to retain Australian music quotas as high as 25 per cent for formats such as contemporary rock and pop, but could reduce them to 5 per cent for niche programs such as 'nostalgia'. These quotas did not induce commercial stations to program *new* Australian artists or to broaden the mainstream musical base (Whiteoak and Scott-Maxwell 2003, p. 560). Top 40, middle-of-the-road and easy listening formats dominated metropolitan music stations on the AM band, with country music having some representation on regional stations. Commercial FM was dominated by album-oriented rock. Callout audience research privileged music that was already known. 'Teen radio' was abandoned as FM aged with its audience. Those aged 25 to 39 came to be seen as the safest source of advertising revenue, and managements competed for this audience through on-air personalities rather than on the basis of music content (Jonker 1992, p. 29; Turner 1993a).

Temporary community licences are available for up to 12 months to encourage people to trial their services, allow the ABA—or the Australian Media and Communications Authority (ACMA) since 2005—to monitor the licensee's performance and make full use of the broadcasting services band. At least one such station demonstrated the commercial potential of niche programming and spooked the established players. In 1993–94, HITZ-FM conducted a 90-day test broadcast in Melbourne, presenting an alternative to mainstream FM formats. Its dance pop formula was outstandingly successful with teenagers and young adults, provoking a campaign of opposition from Melbourne's stations and FARB (Counihan 1996).

BOX 8.2: 'CASH FOR COMMENT'

In 1999, ABC TV's *Media Watch* revealed that 2UE's John Laws had made a lucrative deal with the Australian Bankers' Association to cease criticising banks on air and to present a segment called 'The Whole Story'. The ABA launched an investigation into whether the commercial agreements of Laws or his then stablemate, Alan Jones, had affected the content of their programs, and whether 2UE had failed to comply with the BSA or the code of practice of Commercial Radio Australia (CRA, FARB's successor). The terms of reference were subsequently expanded to include allegations involving stations in Melbourne, Adelaide and Perth (ABA 2000, pp. 51–4). The ABA was moved to ask whether it was 'appropriate in a democracy for a corporation to seek to purchase covert rather than overt dissemination of its opinions'. The inquiry found that Laws' and Jones' failure to disclose their commercial agreements had led to numerous breaches of the code, and that 2UE had failed to comply with the code and the conditions of its licence; the other stations were also found to have committed breaches. New conditions on 2UE's licence required the disclosure of interests and the differentiation of advertising from program material. The systemic failure to ensure the effective operation of self-regulatory codes of practice that the episode revealed resulted in the ABA imposing three standards on commercial radio licences (ABA 2001, pp. 30–1, 41–3).

Laws turned the disclosure of the sponsorships he was 'proud' to have into something of an advertisement, replete with cowbell sound effects. Then, in 2002, he was accused of failing to disclose an agreement with NRMA Insurance. Finding that 2UE had repeatedly breached its licence conditions, the ABA referred the matter to the Commonwealth Director of Public Prosecutions (DPP). The DPP decided not to proceed as it would be too difficult to prove that the station had engaged in conduct with requisite criminal intent. By 2002 Telstra, which had been nervous about paying talkback hosts for support in 1999, was also prepared to pay $1.2 million to sponsor Jones' show on 2GB. An ABA investigation found that there had been no breach by Jones or 2GB, as Telstra had entered into the arrangement with the Macquarie Network rather than with Jones (ABA 2004, pp. ix–xii). These episodes exposed significant flaws in the regulatory framework and an urgent need to expand the range of civil law sanctions available to the ABA, given its reluctance to suspend or cancel commercial radio licences. Questions about the transparency of other agreements continue to surface on *Media Watch*.

STRUCTURE

Since the 1970s, Australia's dual (ABC and commercial) radio system has expanded considerably. But, while it is easy to view the Australian system as consisting of discrete sectors, it is worth noting that there have been significant overlaps between the constituent parts: the ABC was formed out of private-sector interests; the ABC provided a 'community access' station, 3ZZ, between 1975 and 1977; and Australia had some 'ethnic radio' before the SBS was established. In 1999, dozens of community radio stations began broadcasting via satellite *Theatre of the Mind*, featuring classics from Australian radio's pre-television 'golden era'; in 2006, the program was replaced by *From the Archive*, produced by the National Film and Sound Archive.

Commercial radio

By 2004, CRA could classify only 10 per cent of commercial stations on air as independent. Until recently, there were three major metropolitan owners: Austereo, ARN and DMG. Austereo had two FM stations in each capital city; its Triple M network concentrates on music for 25–54-year-olds and 2Day targets the 18–44-year-olds. ARN has twelve stations; the Mix FM network is a contemporary format aimed at 25–44-year-olds, while the 'classic hits' brand aims at 35–54-year-olds. Also concentrating on FM is DMG, which came under full control of Lachlan Murdoch's Illyria Pty Ltd in 2012; DMG runs the Nova network for the under-40s and the Smooth FM easy listening network. The regional market is dominated by the Southern Cross Media Group—owned by Macquarie Bank and unrelated to the Macquarie Network—with 68 stations. Strong regional networks can provide a launching pad into metropolitan markets. In 2004, DMG opted to sell 57 of its regional stations—with three programming 'hubs' in Albury, Townsville and Bunbury—to Southern Cross Media in order to concentrate on its new metropolitan FM licences. In 2011, Southern Cross Media purchased a majority of Austereo.

In response to music industry demands, the ABA worked with CRA in 1999 to produce a revised code of practice, introducing a minimum percentage for 'new' (released within the last twelve months) Australian music (Whiteoak and Scott-Maxwell 2003, p. 560). Although the quotas were generally met, by 2000 Triple M was playing only four to six new songs a week, and it was apparent that the young rock fan was drifting away from the bigger FM stations. Ironically, Kasey Chambers' break-through success came in 2002 with *Not Pretty Enough*, a song about the reluctance of commercial stations to play her music; as an established performer in 2004, she saw her new single become the most added track to radio playlists.

Commercial stations also syndicate music programs and formats. Since 1984, the radio production house MCM Entertainment has been producing *Take 40*, a count-down of the country's most popular songs, from 2Day. On his retirement as host in 2004, Barry Bissell was being heard on around 90 stations. Nor has the syndication process slowed in the news and talk markets. Collingwood (1997, p. 26) estimates that the number of journalists employed in commercial radio fell by a third between 1986 and 1996. Turner's (1996a) study of broadcast news in Brisbane showed that the ABC's 4QR was the sole provider of locally produced news and current affairs, and offered a much more comprehensive service than its six commercial counterparts. By 2003, Southern Cross Media was sending its metropolitan news bulletins to 177 commercial stations (Javes 2003, p. 5).

The provision of news and current affairs has effectively been abandoned in favour of talkback. By 2000, half of all metropolitan stations and 38 per cent of all large regional stations carried talkback. The mobile telephone increased the genre's popularity. On Southern Cross Media's acquisition of 2UE in 2001, a newspaper observed that the station's value vested largely with its two stars: John Laws, who was networked to over 60 stations, and Alan Jones (Ward 2002, p. 22). When Jones, untarnished by the 'Cash for Comment' scandal, defected from 2UE to 2GB in a multi-million dollar deal in 2002, he heralded a new development in Australian commercial radio by securing sizeable equity in the station (Masters 2006, p. 419).

Politicians see the advantages of a medium that allows them to talk directly with voters. Prime Minister John Howard intuitively understood that talkback radio had emerged as a 'new' news medium with a very different logic from the 'old' news media driven by journalistic values (Ward 2002, pp. 23, 27). In the lead-up to the 2007 election, his Labor opponent, Kevin Rudd, periodically subjected himself to humorous turns in FM studios in a bid to connect with younger voters.

In 2002, the ABC news/talk stations in the mainland capitals averaged over two million listeners a week for the first time. Some industry observers speculated about whether FM talk—'hip, pacey, satirical, a bit blue'—might be the next big thing on Australian commercial radio (Day 2002, p. 5). Networks such as Triple M have moved towards talk-oriented programming, with more news, sport, entertainment and gossip, and personality-driven shows around ensembles such as Kyle and Jackie O, Merrick and Rosso, and Hamish and Andy. Still, in 2008 Nova and 2Day responded to research showing that listeners are overwhelmed by the amount of new music posted on the internet and want radio to act as a filter by introducing late-night programs featuring new releases and artists (Javes 2008, p. 5).

In 2009, Kyle Sandilands, the morning co-host on 2DayFM, was suspended by Austereo for an on-air interview that involved an alleged teenage rape victim. There were to be other controversies involving the host known for his ego and for pushing the boundaries of acceptable on-air behaviour. An inquiry into his abusive comments about a television journalist in 2011 led ACMA to impose an additional condition on the licence of 2Day, prohibiting the broadcast of any content that 'offends generally accepted standards of decency' for five years (ACMA 2011–12, p. 12).

In 2011, ACMA also conducted a review of the three commercial radio program standards that were determined following 'Cash for Comment'. ACMA decided to continue to regulate advertising on commercial radio through a standard that more effectively promoted community standards until the industry has in place an appropriate code of practice dealing with advertising; to continue to regulate commercial influence on commercial radio through a program standard based on a disclosure model; and to introduce two new standards relating to advertising and current affairs disclosure.

The next controversy engulfing Alan Jones resulted in a fascinating clash between the old and the new media. In September 2012, a newspaper revealed that Jones had remarked, during an address to a Young Liberals dinner, that the father of Labor Prime Minister Julia Gillard had recently 'died of shame'. Lobby groups, including change. org and Destroy the Joint, launched a massive social media campaign calling for advertisers to boycott Jones' program. To try to contain the backlash, 2GB suspended advertising from the program for a week, while Jones claimed to be a victim of 'cyber bullying'. Although ACMA had no role in the affair as the broadcaster's comments were made off-air, at around the same time it found that Jones had breached the code of practice by airing inaccurate material about climate change, and entered into an agreement whereby 2GB would ensure that Jones' program undertook fact-checking, he would undertake training, and the station would make greater efforts to ensure it presented a range of viewpoints on controversial issues.

With the exception of major controversies such as this, radio and its 'celebrities' now tend to be reported on in newspaper social pages. In recent years, the press has largely vacated the arena of serious radio commentary, with the *Age*'s Green Guide and the Media section of *The Australian* notable exceptions. Industry news and commentary has largely moved online, with one of the earliest sites, radioinfo, established on a subscription basis by Steve Ahern in 1996.

The ABC

Under its charter, the ABC is expected to offer an innovative and diversified service that contributes to a sense of national identity and provides information, entertainment, education and cultural enrichment for the Australian people, as well as encouraging awareness of Australia overseas (*Halsbury's Laws of Australia* 2004, pp. 275–310). It now has four national networks. Radio National ('radio to think by') presents in-depth information and analysis of national and international issues, along with music and the annual Boyer Lectures. Since 1994, when parliament has not been sitting, ABC NewsRadio has operated as Australia's only around-the-clock news and current affairs radio service. Its coverage is being expanded to 70 regional centres with populations of 10 000 and above, making NewsRadio available to 95 per cent of Australians. ABC Classic FM is devoted to classical music, jazz and acoustic art. Triple J, the national youth network, extended into regional areas in 1995 (Jonker 1992, p. 30; Turner 1993a, p. 153).

There is also ABC Local Radio, with nine metropolitan (in capital cities and Newcastle) and 51 regional stations. They are designed to cater to their local communities and to have broad popular appeal, and often obtain exclusive non-commercial Australian radio rights to major sporting events like the Olympic Games. The ABC's final component is its international service, Radio Australia.

The ABC has always been vulnerable to government review, and significant shifts in news policy since the 1970s have been viewed with considerable suspicion by political forces (Petersen 1999, p. 59). The ABC endured sustained attack for a lack of balance throughout the 1990s, along with increasingly political appointments to its board. On gaining office in 1996, the Coalition announced an immediate budget cut and set up the Mansfield Review. The review reaffirmed the non-commercial nature of the ABC, and the dismantling of Radio National and ABC news and current affairs did not eventuate. However, severe budget cuts were implemented and hundreds of jobs were lost. With Mansfield declaring that the ABC's 'core business' was domestic free-to-air broadcasting, the government shut down Radio Australia's shortwave transmitters. The folly of Radio Australia falling silent in much of Asia became apparent during the East Timor referendum crisis, and in 2000 some funding was restored for shortwave and satellite transmission into Asia (Dempster 2000, p. 251).

During his volatile term as managing director in 2000–01, Jonathan Shier at least managed to extract additional government funding, some of which was allocated to three new regional radio stations. This, along with several other initiatives focused on the regions, suggests the involvement of the Coalition's National Party. In 1997 the government established an ABC Science Development project, which facilitated ABC Science Week. A year later, the ABC joined with the Department of Regional Services to launch *Heywire*, designed to produce and broadcast the stories of regional youth. On 31 December 1999, Radio National presented a highly acclaimed marathon radio history of the second millennium, *A Thousand Years in a Day*. In 2001, the ABC's Radio Regional Production Fund was established as a National Interest Initiative to commission original content. Additional government funding in 2001–02 allowed ABC radio to recruit and train an extra 50 broadcasters who were assigned to 32 regional stations around the country. However, DMG's fledgling Nova stations in Sydney and Melbourne attracted listeners with a format somewhat similar to that of Triple J and intensified traditional conflicts about how distinctive Triple J should sound (Inglis 2006, p. 538).

Mark Scott, formerly editorial director at John Fairfax, was appointed ABC managing director in 2006, ushering in a period of greater stability. In 2008, ABC Radio recorded its highest ever audience share, with stellar performances by 702 ABC Sydney and 891 ABC Adelaide. However, at least one attempt at reform was poorly handled. Radio National's specialist programming makes it particularly vulnerable to accusations of elitism, along with cuts to programs and funding. In

2008, Stephen Crittenden announced that his program, *The Religion Report*, was to be cancelled, along with six other specialist programs, mostly heard in the flagship 8.30 a.m. spot. Crittenden was suspended for his outburst, and the head of ABC Radio, Sue Howard, was dismissed in 2009 (Bodey 2008; Meade 2008). Eventually, in 2012, *The Religion Report* and *The Media Report* were reinstated.

Soon there was another controversy, with Radio National announcing plans to cut a number of programs from its 2013 schedule in an attempt to rein in its budget. The performance program *Airplay* was to be cut, along with *The Book Reading*, with declining audiences cited as the reason. Several other arts programs also faced the axe, although Radio National announced plans to create a new Creative Audio Unit ('Radio National plans program cuts to save money' 2012). If *Airplay* is axed, there will be very few remaining outlets for drama on Australian radio, with *The Castlereagh Line* serial on 2CH and the *How Green was My Cactus* political comedy on community stations rare exceptions.

SBS

SBS, established to provide multicultural radio and television services to Australia, has always been programmed along language rather than community lines. Now a national network, SBS Radio has as its main audience the 3.1 million Australians who speak a language other than English at home. Since 1991, public funding of SBS has been supplemented by advertising revenue.

In 2003, for the first time in nearly a decade, SBS Radio launched new program schedules. On the basis of nationwide consultations and Census figures, SBS ceased broadcasting in Gaelic, Welsh and Belarusian in order to free up space for new programs in Malay, Somali, Amharic and Nepalese. Each of the 68 language programs starts with news—Australian, international and homeland. News bulletins are compiled in part from the SBS national radio newsroom and from international news agencies. The programs contain a mixture of current affairs, social welfare issues, talk, sport, community information and music. With close ties to their local communities, they cover the myriad issues that affect their listeners, report on health issues, support cultural festivals and disaster appeals, stage outside broadcasts and often feature talkback (Ang, Hawkins and Dabboussy 2008, Ch. 3).

The SBS Radio network has moved from a predominantly homeland news service to what it calls an 'Australian Information Network—providing balanced and impartial Australian and international news and information'. In 2011–12, there was another review of the SBS Radio analogue schedule. A multi-platform Indigenous Content Unit also produces *Living Black* on radio.

Community radio

In 2012, there were 362 community radio licences. Although metropolitan stations have the longest history in the sector, around 70 per cent are now located in the regions. By 2002 there were 37 areas of Australia in which community radio provided the only service. In Bordertown, South Australia, for instance, 5TCB served a population of about 4000 people and played a critical role in disseminating local news, current affairs and information about cultural events (Forde, Meadows and Foxwell 2002, p. 36). The somewhat controversial Community Radio National Listener Survey (2008) found that 57 per cent of people aged 15 years and over listened to community radio in an average month.

Community stations may have specific or broad constituencies. Into the latter category falls FBi, established in Sydney in 2003 as an alternative music station; 50 per cent of the music played is Australian, and a proportion is by unsigned bands. But the research of Forde, Meadows and Foxwell (2002, pp. 1, 14, 63) demonstrates that, while community radio participants see themselves as offering alternatives to the mainstream media, what is equally important is the community created within the station. Community stations encourage their listeners to participate in station operations and program content, and the sector has over 20 000 volunteers.

The Community Broadcasting Association of Australia (CBAA) provides a point of articulation for the industry, and there are other examples of centralisation, due in part to resource constraints. In 1991, fine music stations—which traditionally have supported Australian composers and live recordings of new classical music—formed the Australian Fine Music Network for marketing and logistical purposes (Forde, Meadows and Foxwell 2002, pp. 11, 41). The *Australian Country Music Showcase*, presented by Smoky and Dot Dawson on 2NSB on Sydney's North Shore, could be heard on community stations in Birdsville, Lightning Ridge and Kangaroo Island until shortly before 94-year-old Smoky's death in 2008.

While 80 per cent of community radio stations broadcast some form of news service, two-thirds of these used a syndicated service for their national or state news by 2002. The sector produces National Radio News, which is taken for a fee by half of the stations broadcasting syndicated news. Many other community stations take commercial news services (Forde, Meadows and Foxwell 2002, p. 84).

Indigenous and ethnic voices are key features of Australian community radio. With Aboriginal people having little opportunity to control their own representation in the commercial media, the National Indigenous Radio Service (NIRS) was set up in Brisbane in 1996. Aiming to link all Indigenous broadcasting services, NIRS has Indigenous music at its core. Around this, it programs its own national news service; national programming dealing with health, education and other relevant issues;

coverage of sporting events and festivals; contemporary Australian music; and local programming. In 2002, the National Ethnic and Multicultural Broadcasters' Council reported broadcasting in languages other than English on more than 100 community stations around Australia (Forde, Meadows and Foxwell 2002, pp. 11, 50–1).

As the number of community stations has grown, federal government funding has fallen to barely 10 per cent of the sector's income. The rest is provided by fund-raising and sponsorship from local business, although stations must ensure that their funding efforts do not impact adversely on their commercial counterparts. Community stations can apply for grants through additional government and arts agencies, but this can be a time-consuming and lengthy process (Forde, Meadows and Foxwell 2002, pp. 98, 105). The Productivity Commission's Inquiry into Broadcasting in 2000 viewed the community sector's social and cultural benefits as secondary to the need to justify radio in economic terms. The sector, the report concluded, receives free access to scarce frequency spectrum. Decreased government funding and the pressure to increase audience figures to attract sponsors have the potential to compromise the very aims on which the community sector was established (Forde, Meadows and Foxwell 2002, pp. 15, 117).

NEW DIGITAL PLATFORMS

Subscription broadcasting and open and subscription narrowcasting services were broadcasting categories introduced by the *Broadcasting Services Act* 1992, and since 1997 they have been represented by the Australian Subscription Television and Radio Association (ASTRA). By 2011, 253 open narrowcasting transmitter licences—mostly FM—had been allocated by the ACMA. There are many more low-power narrowcasting services around Australia. The Vision Radio Network, operated by United Christian Broadcasters (UCB), obtained about 300 transmitter licences for an estimated cost of just $300 000 in an effort to make Christian radio available across the nation (MacLean 2005).

In the online environment, radio can be a point-to-point as well as a broadcast medium. Since 1999, several internet stations—with the potential to reach a global audience—have been established in Australia. As these stations do not require a licence, the biggest cost is bandwidth, and the principal challenge is finding sufficient advertising support (Macleay 2000).

Australian radio stations face the challenge of remaining attractive to audiences and advertisers as portable audio devices such as MP3 players grow in popularity. The ABC riches were swiftly adapted to the online environment, hosts forums, audio streams of its programs, and podcast programs and print transcripts. Triple J Unearthed had been launched in 1995 to discover and share independent and unsigned artists; it was followed by a digital radio station devoted to new Australian music in 2011. On the ABC's 70th birthday in 2002, an online music station, DiG, targeted at 30- to 50-year-olds, was launched; DiG Jazz and DiG Country followed (Inglis 2006, pp. 539, 558). In 2008, Radio National established Pool, a new online social networking and media sharing site inviting audiences to collaborate and share content and offering ABC archival material for mash-up. Meanwhile, 'ABC Local' provides 54 areas with local coverage through ABC Local Radio and ABC Online.

In 2008, the Australian Music Radio Airplay Project (Amrap) was established to distribute and promote new Australian music to community radio stations. In 2012, commercial radio, in partnership with the Mushroom Group, launched First Break for unsigned artists who have not charted in the top 100 Australian national airplay chart.

Many commercial stations, networks and presenters now also live-stream their programs and use their websites to provide program and personality information, conduct promotions and interact with listeners. Networks such as Austereo are seeking to extend their brands and position themselves as 'content' rather than simply 'radio' providers. A web presence allows music radio to begin to reclaim its role in young people's lives, more through cutting-edge technology than through the provision of new music; the capacity to create new revenue streams by selling music downloads is limited by copyright. In 2010, SBS launched Chill, a world music digital radio channel, and PopAsia, offering mainstream Asian pop music for younger Chinese Australians; they were followed by PopDesi and PopAraby in 2012.

The digital transmission of radio signals in terrestrial broadcasting had the potential to provide services by satellite to remote and regional areas, dramatically improve reception and supply additional services and content, such as information, pictures, niche programs and time-shifting. But, while Britain has had digital radio since 1995, the introduction of digital radio to Australia was protracted, with concern and debates about the most appropriate technology, the cost of the requisite infrastructure and receivers, and the role of incumbent commercial licensees (Given 2003b, pp. 100–1, 111–14). The ABA announced a five-year moratorium on the issue of new commercial digital licences in order to protect the incumbents and signalled that digital radio may never fully replace analogue services (DCITA 2004, p. 2). In 2006, the government unveiled plans for a staged roll-out of digital ABC, SBS and commercial services, which commenced in the major capitals in 2009; trials began in Canberra and Darwin the following year. 'Designated' community broadcasters (those with the same licence area as a commercial radio service) in these metropolitan licence areas were also eligible to begin digital broadcasting, and some services commenced in 2011. Work continues to be undertaken on the planning of, and costing for, the digital roll-out to regional Australia. With special DAB+ receivers necessary for listening in all settings, including vehicles, digital proponents face a significant challenge from internet radio, which can be listened to on multiple electronic devices, and which enables Australians to hear overseas as well as domestic broadcasters.

CONCLUSION

The Australian radio industry has survived challenges and threats due to constant adaptations. Governments have also played a role in protecting established players from new technological developments and, in doing so, have limited the choices available to Australian listeners. Over the last 25 years or so, commercial radio has been weakened by successive waves of deregulation, the lack of any effective enforcement of standards and ethical practice, and the dilution of ownership restrictions. The ABC, SBS and the community radio sector may be precious cultural resources, but they have proved vulnerable to government review and financial pressures, including the expectation that they deliver content in new ways While the commercial sector is characterised by large, sometimes foreign-owned, networks, SBS Radio and some community radio stations and narrowcasters have also succumbed to networking, reducing radio's claim to be a 'local' medium. Those early champions of radio who thought that it could annihilate Australia's vast distances could not have envisaged a time when a radio host would broadcast his Sydney morning show from Perth, nor would they have condoned a station, WS-FM, failing to interrupt its classic hits playlist to broadcast information about the bushfires that threatened Sydney on Christmas Day 2001.

FURTHER READING

The ABC has attracted historical scholarship by Inglis (1983), *This is the ABC* and (2006), *Whose ABC?* and Petersen (1993), *News Not Views* and (1999), 'Whose news?' Thornley (1995), 'Debunking the "Whitlam" myth' and (1999), 'Broadcasting policy in Australia' examines the evolution of community radio, and Forde, Meadows and Foxwell (2002), *Culture, Commitment, Community* provides a recent overview of the sector. Since the 1990s, commercial radio has been attracting serious scholarly interest, culminating in Griffen-Foley's (2009) *Changing Stations*. A special issue of *Media International Australia* on Radio (no. 91, May 1999) was followed by an issue on talkback (no. 122, February 2007). Given's (2003b) *Turning Off the Television* addresses digital broadcasting. The websites of the ACMA, ABC, SBS, CRA and CBAA provide up-to-date information about the industry.

Chapter 9

FILM, VIDEO, DVD AND ONLINE DELIVERY

DEB VERHOEVEN

The road to writing about the contemporary cinema in Australia is pitted with deep, hollow ruts formed from industrial and critical conventions, training and preconception. Take for example the title of this chapter. It describes a well-worn but now largely by-passed film distribution itinerary, from large public screens to smaller domestic ones through a series of consecutive release 'windows'. However, the path from production to the audience is no longer so well signposted. 'Film' is now, categorically, an anachronistic term that has become completely stripped of the value it may have once held as a material description of industry practice. So very little celluloid is now used in production or exhibition that supply companies once considered the stalwarts of global cinema enterprise and infrastructure, such as Kodak, are financially bankrupt or obsolete. Similarly both 'video' and 'DVD' are no longer dominant or even prominent methods for delivering content to audiences. And so we are left with 'online delivery', a description of content distribution as a form of commercial exchange that does not distinguish cinema from any other type of business.

The history of critical assessments of the Australian film industry has tended to dwell on how the 'Australian' in 'Australian cinema' can or should be *distinguished*, both in the sense of how it can be differentiated from other national cinemas and how it contributes to abiding discourses of Australian excellence and 'goodness'. Given widespread technological disruptions, we may now need to examine how the 'cinema' itself is distinguishable as both an industry and as a social experience. In this context, perhaps the greatest challenge for writing about the contemporary Australian cinema is to understand it as an embedded (rather than distinct) industry, involved in or supplementary to other (national) cinemas, other industrial practices and other commercial exchanges.

GOVERNMENT AND CINEMA FROM THE 1970s TO THE 2000s

Many of the arguments for a production industry in Australia were founded on a reaction to the perception that Australian exhibition outlets were dominated by foreign, and particularly American, product. So when cultural policies for the film industry were eventually realised, they were careful to emphasise the role a local film production industry would play in promoting a national cultural vision. Films funded by the government would be required to demonstrate 'significant Australian content', evident in crew composition, subject-matter and setting.

Crucially, it was also decided that film funding should be managed by government as a special domain of policy. This decision was the product of a 1968 report by the Interim Film Committee of the Australia Council for the Arts. The report recommended the establishment of government support in three key areas: the creation of a film development funding agency; the establishment of an experimental film fund; and the formation of a national film school.

As a direct result of these recommendations, the modern era of film bureaucracy began with the busy establishment of a wide array of institutions (and an equally dizzying proliferation of acronyms) to broker the relationship between industry and government. The first 'corp' off the rank in 1970 was the Australian Film Development Corporation (AFDC—later reconstituted as the Australian Film Commission in 1975), set up with $1 million at its disposal. Honouring the Australia Council's advice, the government also established an Experimental Film and Television Fund

(EFTF) the same year. And the final arm of the council's recommendations, a national film school, was realised in 1973 with the advent of the Australian Film and Television School (now, with the addition of radio production to its curriculum, known as AFTRS).

By the 1980s, the idea of government-supported film production was popularly assumed to the extent that the very idea of the film industry was synonymous with the production of films. Films funded by government seemed to have developed a 'house style'—referred to by Dermody and Jacka (1987), for instance, as the 'AFC genre'. The government, however, decided to experiment with the level of its support by increasing tax subsidies for investors willing to back film-production activity. This initiative became known as '10BA' after the section of the *Taxation Act* that outlined the extent of the investment benefits. The results were immediate and extraordinary in their scale.

More than 400 feature films and documentaries were made in the eight years to 1988 (the comparative boom of the silent period, between 1906 and 1928, produced 150 films). Many of these films were never intended to be seen by an audience and were simply produced for the benefit of accountants. Wages in the industry inflated rapidly as film productions tied themselves to the financial year and competed for cast and crew. On the upside, many films that might have struggled to find financial backers were supported by investors with little concern for the outcome. And, somewhat surprisingly, those films that were released during this period achieved successful box-office statistics for Australian cinema that have not been repeated since.

Recognising the difficulty in regulating the output of films financed under the 10BA tax concessions, the government proposed that another funding agency be established: the Film Finance Corporation (FFC), which would invest in commercial films with guaranteed distribution (pre-sales) and then recoup profits for later disbursement to new projects. From its inception in 1988 to its closure 20 years later in 2008, the FFC invested more than $2.58 billion into more than 1000 films. However, the FFC's success at supporting profitable films was questionable, with only a handful of funded films returning significant monies despite the FFC's practice of ensuring itself a position of 'privileged recoupment' in which its own investment was returned ahead of those of other financiers. The evident disappointments in the FFC's performance led to a comprehensive overhaul of government support to the sector in 2008. From this reconsideration, a new government entity, Screen Australia, was formed from the merger of the Australian Film Commission, the Film Finance Corporation and the documentary production entity Film Australia. Like its predecessors, Screen Australia was expected to fulfil twin aspirations for the Australian film industry—balancing demands for better commercial performance against expectations for quality and culturally significant content.

Table 9.1 Key industry data 2008–12

	2008	2009	2010	2011	2012
Cinema admissions	84.6 m	90.7 m	92 m	85 m	85.9 m
Cinema screens	1980	1989	1996	1991	1995
Average ticket price	$11.17	$11.99	$12.26	$12.87	$13.10
Gross box office	$945.4 m	$108.7 m	$1132.8 m	$1093.8 m	$1125.5 m
Domestic share box office	3.8% ($35.5 m)	5% ($54.8 m)	4.5% ($50.6 m)	3.9% ($42.9 m)	4.3% ($47.9m)
Total films released theatrically (new releases)	301	347	326 (US releases under 50%. First time in 27 years)	342 (US still under 50%)	421 (42% from US)
Australian films released theatrically	32 (11%)	44	29	36 (11%)	43 (7.8%)
Top Australian film at box office	Australia ($26.9 m)	Mao's Last Dancer ($14.9 m)	Tomorrow, When the War Began ($13.4 m)	Red Dog ($21.3 m)	The Sapphires ($14.4 m)

Source: MPDAA.

GOVERNMENT AND CINEMA, 2000s–2010s

At the beginning of the 1970s, it was the perception of foreign dominance of Australia's audio-visual industries that prompted calls for greater government involvement in local film production activities. At the end of the 1990s, it would be fair to say that international interests remained influential in the Australian film industry, but that international involvement was considered to be neither wholly negative nor antithetical to government support. By the beginning of the 2010s, government policy rested on the idea that the fortunes of major Australian productions are largely reliant on international participation in the industry. Foreign production (a project originated, developed and controlled by non-Australians) and international co-production (in which creative control is shared between Australian and foreign partners) are increasingly occurring in Australia and are responsible for substantial employment of support personnel and the dramatic expansion of the post-production industries.

To date, pressure for internationalisation of the domestic industry has come about as a direct result of trade agreements, federal and state policy initiatives offering substantial incentives to producers and the relative value of the Australian dollar. For example, the Australia–United States Free Trade Agreement (AUSFTA), signed in 2004, includes a range of provisions restricting Australia's capacity to regulate local audio-visual content. At an even more local level, state film agencies in New South Wales, Queensland and Victoria have pursued foreign or 'runaway' film productions with a vengeance, and have enthusiastically subsidised studio facilities specifically designed to attract big-budget foreign film and TV projects such as *I, Frankenstein* (Victoria, 2013), *The Great Gatsby* (New South Wales, 2013) and *Sanctum* (Queensland, 2011). Queensland, New South Wales and South Australia also offer payroll tax exemptions, while Victoria and Western Australia offer grants and project funding to foreign producers. Their efforts have been underlined by federally regulated refundable tax offsets geared specifically to supporting to attracting foreign (offshore) productions to Australia. The principal policy mechanism for delivering this outcome is the location offset. In order to qualify, productions are required to spend a minimum of $15

Table 9.2 Feature film industry summary

	2007–08	2008–09	2009–10	2010–11	2011–12
Australian feature films produced	39	38	42	21	28
Australian films budget spent in Australia	$172 m	$368 m	$273 m	$89 m	$296 m
Co-productions	3	2	5	4	4
Co-production budget spent in Australia	$37 m	$25 m	$53 m	$67 m	$44 m
Foreign features made in Australia	22	13	11	14	20
Foreign features budget spent in Australia	$118 m	$21 m	$180 m	$31 m	$41 m
No. of offset features	19	24	30	15	28

Source: Screen Australia.

million in Australia in return for a 16.5 per cent tax rebate. A further extension of the location offset was announced in 2013 to accommodate the continued high value of the Australian dollar and as an effect of a one-off payment to *Wolverine* which lifted the rebate for that film to something more in the order of a 30 per cent rebate. Of equal interest is the post-production digital and video (PDV) offset, which has enticed foreign films such as *Ted* (2012), *The Hunger Games* (2012) and *The Avengers* (2012) to use Australian companies for their post-production work.

Adding to the value of Australian production, several prominent Australian producers and directors have brought international finance to Australia by basing their films here, including George Miller (*Happy Feet Two*, 2011, Warner Bros), Baz Luhrmann (*The Great Gatsby*, 2013, Warner Bros) and Hugh Jackman (*Wolverine*, 2013, Fox). From the mid-2000s, a range of internationally successful 'marquee name' actors also began signing up with Australian projects in what was hoped would be a boon for domestic and international box office. Recent examples of this trend include Robert Pattinson (*The Rover*, 2013), Ethan Hawke (*Daybreakers*, 2010), Willem Dafoe (*Daybreakers* and *The Hunter*, 2011) Chris O'Dowd (*The Sapphires*, 2012), Charlotte Rampling (*The Eye of the Storm*, 2011) and Robert de Niro and Clive Owen (*Killer Elite*, 2011). Major internationally recognised Australian stars continue to return home to work: Nicole Kidman (*The Railway Man, 2013*), Guy Pearce (*The Rover*), Ryan Kwanten (*Not Suitable for Children*, 2012), Toni Collette (*Mental*, 2012 and *Defiant*, 2013), and Mia Wasikowska (*Tracks*, 2013). The picture is one of a fluid industry joining a global film economy at a structural level rather than simply in terms of narrative or thematic choices.

BOX 9.1: STRUCTURAL ISSUES IN THE EARLY 2010s

- Eligibility eased for the Producer Offset in 2011–12, meaning all feature films in that year were offset titles
- Average increase in feature film budgets over the past five years, with more features made in the over-$6 million category
- Increasing concessions and incentives to filmmakers by all levels of government
- Increased confidence in private finance as the impact of the GFC eases
- Industry revenue has marginally declined on average in recent years but is expected to rise
- Impact of multi-channel digital free-to-air and pay TV is raising demand for local product
- Australian industry continues to be a key beneficiary of Hollywood cost-cutting. During the 2000s, Australia received an estimated 5–6 per cent of the value of Hollywood's offshore film production spend. About 33 per cent of all Hollywood film production now occurs overseas.

- Cinema screens have moved from city centres (73, 'a historic low') to the suburbs (1111, 56 per cent of screens), which contributed 62 per cent of the gross box office.

Summary of international shifts in the 2010s

- Revenues earned by US studios are in free-fall. Pre-tax profits of the five studios controlled by large media conglomerates (Disney, Universal, Paramount, Twentieth Century Fox and Warner Bros) fell by around 40 per cent between 2007 and 2011.
- Many films intended for wide international release are adopting plus-sized budgets, increasing the risk of catastrophic failure. In 2009 there were five films budgeted at more than $200 million. In 2010, there were six and in 2012, there were eight.
- Rapidly declining popularity of DVD sales (down 36 per cent since they peaked in 2004) but compensated for by online video.
- Increasing popularity of prestige television, with some episodes now costing US$5–6 million an hour
- Decreasing output. Between 2006 and 2012, the six big studios cut the number of films they made by 14–54 per cent.
- Intensified demand for film product from new digital services such as Netflix and Amazon's Prime (streaming movie rental services). Netflix now accounts for one-third of all internet traffic in the United States.
- Proliferation of consumer devices. Americans own around 560 million internet-connected devices, such as games consoles, tablets, smartphones and laptops (approximately 2.7 per person).
- Development of cloud-based rights management (such as 'UltraViolet') rather than ownership as a retail model.
- Emergence of China as the second largest film market after the United States (taking over from Japan). The number of cinema screens in China doubled in the five years to 2012.

The role of the government in promoting national film production occurs in a variety of ways. The foremost methods, and the easiest to track, are direct production subsidies and tax incentives. The most significant organisation in this regard is the federal agency Screen Australia, which usually works in conjunction with various state film offices. The proportion of film finance tied to federal and state government funding has averaged 13 per cent since the introduction of the producer offset in 2007, with 8 per cent coming from private investors over this period (*Red Dog*, for example, was substantially financed by the mining industry), 28 per cent from the producer offset itself, 9 per cent from the film and TV industry (from distributors for example) and 42 per cent from foreign investors.

Certainly, the introduction of the offset incentives in July 2007 has generated an immediate fillip to private investment levels in Australian film, as well as attracting offshore projects. The producer offset is available to producers of projects with 'significant Australian content' or official co-productions. Replacing the 10BA tax concessions, the scheme was adjusted in 2011 after initial success and significant pressure from film industry lobbyists for its expansion. In 2012, all eligible Australian feature films relied on the producer offset to structure their finances. Rebates are accessed via the production company's tax return once a film is completed, and are worth 40 per cent of the Australian film's expenditure. The long lead time for feature films means that we are really only just beginning to see the impact of the offset on the performance of Australian film (for example, in terms of box office).

The second principal form of government intervention is content regulation, which is applied to television broadcasting in Australia either in terms of hours of broadcast (free-to-air TV) or minimum expenditure (subscription or pay TV). The AUSFTA restricts the government's flexibility in adjusting these amounts in the future or changing the mode of regulation for pay TV. As we move rapidly towards a more technologically convergent and globalised dissemination of content, traditional cultural measures such as the regulation of content standards will become increasingly difficult to control. Furthermore, the FTA exempts new media from local content rules altogether. It will be at this point that the government-funded television networks the ABC and SBS will stand to take a more influential role in the fortunes of the domestic industry. This is particularly true given that direct government funding to film agencies has stagnated for some time, failing to keep pace with rising industry costs. Instead, government has increasingly sought to find strategies to promote private investment in the industry.

NON-GOVERNMENT PRODUCTION: CROWDSOURCE FUNDING

The emergence of small-scale private funding platforms such as Kickstarter (founded in 2009), IndieGoGo (2008) and the Australian-based Pozible (2010) has been a major development for independent and low-budget filmmakers who do not meet the minimum budget threshold for the producer offset. These sites offer opportunities for members of the public to financially support creative projects. The objective is to raise a nominated funding target within a self-stipulated time limit. This is an all-or-nothing opportunity (if the target isn't realised within the timeframe, then the pledged funds are not released to the filmmakers). In addition to providing an unprecedented funding opportunity, these sites also provide useful ways for creating audiences for unrealised works during the development and production process as well as providing a new platform for film promotion (a deeper form of 'onset' marketing).

The Australian-based crowdsource funding website Pozible.com has had a significant impact on screen content funding since it started in 2010. In the first eighteen months, around $2.47 million has been pledged to screen projects, with $2.21 million collected across 330 projects. More than 21 000 individual donors have backed screen projects via the site. Screen content on Pozible mainly takes the form of short films and web-based videos, which represent the largest funding category of Pozible ahead of music. But bigger projects are beginning to emerge as contenders for crowdsource funding. Perhaps the best-known Australian feature to use crowd funding is *Iron Sky* (2012), with an Australian company a co-production partner. David Barker's new feature, *The Second Coming*, raised $76 585 in six weeks and used incentives to entice donors included signed film posters, digital downloads of the completed film, DVDs and making of books, an acknowledgement in the credits and, for a particularly significant ($15 000) donation, an associate producer credit.

Crowdsource funding opportunities are important to producers because they help to fill budget holes, although they rarely cover the entire cost of production. Very few projects relying on crowdsource funding achieve targets higher than $100 000. In 2012, the government agency ScreenWest undertook a $250 000 matched funding program with Pozible in which the agency committed to provide funding at a 3:1 ratio (for every dollar raised the government would provide three dollars capped at $50 000). Within a couple of days, ScreenWest had expended its entire budget on the first six projects to meet the target. Projects funded included a digital documentary (*Punjab to Perth*), fiction shorts (*Tango Underpants*), stop-motion animation (*Edison: Adventures in Power*) and an iPad app (for *The Golden Triangles*).

DISCOURSES OF AUSTRALIAN CINEMA

Boom and bust in early Australian cinema

Generally speaking, both Australian policy-makers and film historians have focused on the production context as the defining feature of the national cinema, relying on a narrative that prefers the surety of the quantifiable. As a result, Australian film history is typically divided into periods defined by numerical standards in terms of film production —periods of boom and bust. Despite vividly capturing the sense of impermanence and fragility, there are many issues raised by the 'boom and bust' story of Australian cinema. First, when considered in an international context, the conventional version of booming and busted years misconstrues a type of global significance to the Australian cinema where perhaps none is deserved. So, although by Australian standards a large number of films were made in the early years of the cinema, or in the early 1980s, the influence of these films—especially outside Australia—is negligible. On the other hand, the period after World War II—typically described as one of drought or bust—was a time during which international interest in the Australian

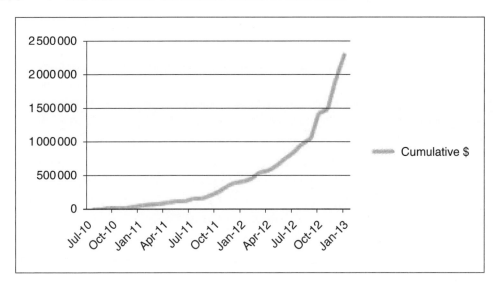

Figure 9.1 Screen project pledges to pozible.com
Source: Pozible.com.

cinema was high (Molloy 1990). The English Ealing Studios were particularly active in the late 1940s and early 1950s, producing some five feature films in Australia over thirteen years, including the popular epic *The Overlanders* (Harry Watt, 1946). The US studios Warner Bros and Twentieth Century Fox produced *The Sundowners* (Fred Zinneman, 1960) and *Kangaroo* (Lewis Milestone, 1952) respectively, with Hollywood stars (Robert Mitchum, Deborah Kerr and Maureen O'Hara, among others) taking the roles of intrepid Australians.

This period was also a time of intense activity for those with a passion for watching cinema. The film society and festival movement prospered in the immediate post-war years, importing non-Hollywood films and publishing reviews and debates around their exhibition. By 1958, the screen culture movement had expanded to include a new national body, the Australian Film Institute (AFI). This organisation, which operates Australia's annual film industry awards, participated in the successful campaign for greater government support for film production.

The two industries, 1975–90

Dermody and Jacka (1987) argue that the history of Australian cinema production between the mid-1970s and the mid-1980s was marked by patterns of tension between the dual roles of art and commerce and by the ways in which the changing interaction between these two antithetical aspirations for a local cinema affected the nature of the films funded. For Dermody and Jacka, these competing understandings of what the industry should or could be were best described as Industry 1 and Industry 2, which referred to 'discourses of nationalism' and 'discourses of commercialism' respectively (Dermody and Jacka 1987, p. 197). Table 9.3 sets out the main features of each of the two discourses.

Table 9.3 Two discourses of Australian film

Industry 1	Industry 2
Socially concerned	Social concern is not the business of film; entertainment is
Search for an Australian identity	Australia is part of the international scene; national identity is equivalent to xenophobia
Leftish Labor	No pointed political affiliation but could be Liberal voters
Modestly budgeted films for local audiences	Big-budget films for an international audience
Didactic films, films with social purpose	Anti-message films; they are 'audience downers' or 'social engineering'
Interested in other arts, literate, middle-class	Anti-snobbery, anti-art, middlebrow
Film literate or film buffery	Anti-art film
Anti-monopolistic values; champions of independence	Pro-Hollywood: 'they do it bigger and better—we can learn from them'
In favour of government regulation of the industry	For the 'free market'
Against cultural imperialism	'Cultural imperialism? Never heard of it!'
Cultural and political benefits for film not necessarily quantifiable	'Bums on seats' and box-office dollars are all that count

In Dermody and Jacka's schema, Industry 1 incorporates 'AFC genre' films such as *My Brilliant Career* or *Breaker Morant*, as well as more subversive or experimental films like *Palm Beach* or *Pure Shit*. Although the AFC has long been superseded as a production force in the Australian cinema, it is possible to identify recent exemplars of Industry 1—films such as *The Eye of the Storm* (2011) and *Tracks* (2013), films focused on identifiably local themes and delivered to Australian art-house audiences.

In contradistinction, Dermody and Jacka's Industry 2 describes filmmakers who wanted a profitable local industry modelled on Hollywood—in other words, film producers who opted for a more scalable, industrialised and streamlined approach to filmmaking. An exemplary producer identified by Dermody and Jacka within this group is Anthony Ginnane, producer of thrillers such as *Patrick* (1977) and science fiction films such as *The Time Guardians* (1986) (Dermody and Jacka 1988b, pp. 30–6). These filmmakers were seen as explicitly seeking audiences beyond the geographical bounds of Australia. Increasingly, it is possible to identify many contemporary examples of internationally and commercially oriented genre production in Australia. Similarly, there is an increasing trend for some very large Australian companies to finance wholly offshore production with no evident connection to an Australian 'national agenda'. The international output of Village Roadshow Pictures (for example, *Gangster Squad* or the Will Smith vehicle *I am Legend*) and the global television slate of Beyond Productions (*Mythbusters*) are notable examples, as is the international investment activity of Omnilab, a major Sydney-based post-production company that also produces films and co-finances productions both in Australia and abroad, including *Killer Elite* (2013).

Industry 3

By the end of the 1990s, it might just have been possible to point to a third industry in addition to Dermody and Jacka's two-industry model. Industry 3 is actually hinted at by Jacka (1997, p. 88), and comprises films and filmmakers happily embedded in *both* the local and global, where niche does not simply mean domestic or art-house and where global does not simply mean overseas or commercial. Industry 3 typically comprises films initiated by Australians wanting to work with large budgets, international resources, high-profile actors, and local content or personnel, and shooting either in Australia or offshore, or combining the two. Good examples of these productions would be Jane Campion's festival screening/premium TV drama *Top of the Lake* (2013) (an Australian/UK co-production), Baz Luhrmann's *The Great Gatsby* (Warner Bros, 2013), Alex Proyas' *Knowing* and George Miller's *Happy Feet* series (Warner Bros). They might also include 'smaller' films such as Cate Shortland's *Lore* (funded by European and Australian investors) or Pauline Chan's pioneering Australian-Chinese co-production *33 Postcards*. The influence of these 'Australian-international' productions can also be seen in a film like *Mad Max: Fury Road* (2013), an Australian-produced drama shot almost entirely in Africa.

Jane Campion and Baz Luhrmann have been exemplary figures for this emergent international-Australian industry—transnational filmmakers capable of working anywhere, sourcing finance globally but unwilling to compromise their artistic independence and interest in pursuing an antipodean perspective. Campion has been an especially important figure in the development of these 'crossover' films. Her highly successful film *The Piano* was perhaps the first of the 'artbusters' (an art-house blockbuster). Using big-name Hollywood stars to widen her audience (cleverly reducing one of them to muteness in order to escape accusations of lack of authenticity), Campion reconceived conventional art film production, distribution and exhibition practices.

The new raft of government offsets has further cemented the presence of this third industry in Australia. These incentives, specifically designed to increase the amount of private and international finance in the sector and lift budget levels, combined with an increase in official co-production treaties, point to a shift in the organisation of the contemporary industry away from previously intractable distinctions between government-supported national cinema and internationally oriented commercial film production.

Industry 4

As we enter a period of significant industrial disruption, a fourth industry model seems to be emerging. Industry 4 is characterised by the adoption of new methodologies for producing and distributing content afforded by the digitisation of the screen industries. If we think of screen producers as being located somewhere along an axis drawn between a strategic approach to producing work at one end and a tactical one at the other, then Industry 4 lines up more with a tactical approach. The distinction is adapted from Michel de Certeau's *The Practice of Everyday Life*. De Certeau aligned 'strategies' with powerful institutions that set norms and conventions (which he called 'producers') and 'tactics' with individuals ('consumers') who creatively negotiate these strategically defined environments looking for opportunities in the gaps and slips of conventional practices. Developing de Certeau's thinking for a contemporary, converged media ecology, it is now possible to argue that 'producers' can also work tactically (and conversely consumers might 'define' environments). A traditionally strategic approach to screen content production would typically involve working from a fixed location and within limited time-zones, paying local overheads and relying on existing funding structures such as government grants. A tactical approach would use data mining to identify audiences, rely on outsourcing labour, adopt a 24-hour work cycle and use an opportunistic approach to finance. A good example of a more tactical approach to film production in Australia is *The Tunnel* (2011). This film was simultaneously released in a limited number of cinemas in Australia, on pay TV and DVD in Australia and New Zealand, and legally online via <www.bittorrent.com> (a popular peer-to-peer exchange site). Within four days, the film had been downloaded by over 40 000 users and by the end of the first week nearly 100 000. By way of comparison, another Australian horror film released more traditionally in cinemas at around the same time, *The Reef*, was viewed by only 3800 patrons on its opening weekend. *The Tunnel* was financed in piecemeal fashion. Upfront, the producers offered single frames from the movie at one dollar apiece for sale to the public. On this basis, they raised around $40 000. Later, small donations were made by visitors to the bit-torrent site (mostly in the $12–15 range). Since its initial release, the movie has also been seen on ABC iView (a catch-up TV website) and is also available as an iTunes 'app' for $1.99 which gives purchasers a full-length version of the film plus extra features such as 'behind the scenes' video, a photo gallery and so on.

BOX 9.2: INDUSTRY 3 AND 4 CHARACTERISTICS

Industry 3

- Both international and national success
- Transnational actors and crew
- **Films:** Generically knowing and playful digital production technologies integrated with audiovisual industries
- **Audience:** Global niche audiences
- **Filmmakers:** Use both national and international locations; use both government and non-government funding

Industry 4

- **Content:**
  - Realised with the support of 'communities of interest' ('onset' marketing and crowd-sourcing) rather than defining audiences as external to the development process.
  - Realised via 'tactical' (under-the-radar) rather than 'strategic' approaches.
  - Sensitive and therefore scalable to audience interest.
  - Continue to realise funds through concurrent long-tail marketing strategies with a variety of pathways to audiences rather than a sequential series of exclusive release 'windows'.
- **Audiences:**
  - Participatory and invested as projects develop.
  - Defined by interest rather than geo-political allegiance.
- **Filmmakers**
  - 'Embedded creatives' in which content production skills are seen as transferable to other industries.
  - No particular interest in or concern about 'Australianness' or any nationality as a defining feature of on-screen content or production methodology.

DISTRIBUTION AND EXHIBITION

Each year, around a thousand films are submitted for classification in Australia. Of these, more than 300 films (over 400 in 2012) are released for the first time each year. These appear on almost 2000 screens dominated by four major exhibition chains, which deliver more than 70 per cent of the national box office and control over half of all cinema screens: Greater Union (479 screens) (incorporating Birch, Carroll and Coyle in Queensland); Hoyts (369 screens); Village (506 screens) and the US company Reading (160 screens). Mid-size cinema chains account for around 18 per cent of cinema screens and independent cinemas for more than 30 per cent. The vast majority of films (around 95 per cent) are handled by a small number of major international distributors that are in turn linked to local companies (for example, Orion, Twentieth Century Fox and Columbia Tri Star are linked to Hoyts and Warner Bros Entertainment is allied to Village Roadshow). There are many much smaller Australian distributors (more than 40) that compete for films on a one-by-one basis (Palace, Dendy and Icon, to name a few). Of these, Palace Films also operates some 85 screens. Some major players also operate venues overseas (with mixed results). Amalgamated Holdings, for example, operates cinemas in Germany and New Zealand, and Village Roadshow has cinemas in Singapore.

Films are now largely distributed and screened in digital format, which represents significant savings for distributors in terms of print, freight and storage costs. The change from film-based formats to digital formats has had an impact across the entire cinema industry value chain. Stock suppliers and film-processing entities all face a dim future, with mainstream 35mm projection projected to cease entirely in the US and other major markets by the end of 2014 and global cut-off likely soon afterwards. At its peak, global film distribution used approximately four billion metres of film a year. That amount began to decline sharply in 2010, and is now closer to 1.2 billion metres.

For the production studios, digital distribution offers the promise of easy access to global markets, irrespective of geographic distance. For the cinemas, there is the tantalising prospect of pristine Hollywood titles direct to a screen near you at the touch of a button and a fraction of the cost (no projectionist, minimal equipment maintenance). And, while this improved screen experience is mostly true, it is not entirely unknown for incorrect titles to be screened because the digital files provided to cinemas are unable to be unlocked until immediately prior to the scheduled session and can't be tested in the same way that film reels once were.

Cinemas are also responding to digitisation by lowering costs through staff reductions (most cinema chains now employ a very small number of roving projectionists where once there might have been several per cinema). Costs have also come down with the introduction of touch screen ticket machines and online booking systems. The use of online information systems has reduced the amount of advertising in local newspapers. Aside from this cost-cutting, digital distribution also offers opportunities for multi-trailer campaigns, more direct marketing, ease of subtitling and tailoring for the hearing impaired, and the possibility of content customisation such as multiple endings for films. Film releases are more easily scalable so that 'breakout' hits can quickly and easily be extended to additional screens. On the downside, there are enormous implications for the archiving of content, since there is no digital format that has yet matched the effectiveness of film as a preservation medium.

The prospect of a National Broadband Network (NBN) in Australia has raised industry expectations for the delivery of content over higher-speed terrestrial networks, although the global outlook continues to be based on the likelihood of satellite delivery. In March 2013, the US-based Digital Cinema Distribution Coalition (formed by AMC Theatres, Regal Entertainment Group, Cinemark Theatres, Universal Pictures and Warner Bros) reached agreements with most of the major studios to establish a cross-industry distribution service that will provide each chain with direct theatrical digital-delivery services across North America based on satellite technologies.

But not all the factors affecting film exhibition and distribution in Australia can be attributed to the impact of digitisation. Annual domestic box-office figures in Australia are greatly influenced by one big hit (*The Sapphires, Happy Feet, Australia* and so on—anything that can realise more than $10 million). Without the money generated by *Australia*, the 3.8 per cent local share of box-office in 2007–08 would have sunk to less than 1 per cent. Between 2003 and 2005, there was not even the one big hit—painfully pointing to the vulnerability of the local box office. In fact it would take a nostalgic return to 1996 to remember the halcyon days of Australian cinema returns.

A succession of significant changes to the distribution of films occurred in the sixteen or so years after 1996—changes that continue to run apace. In the comparable sixteen years prior to 1996, Australian films realised more than 8 per cent of the total Australian box office nine times. Since 1996, this has not occurred once (Jericho 2013). These statistics tell us a great deal about the significance of change in the Australian film market. So in 2001, when a record $63.4 million was earned by local features (*Moulin Rouge, Lantana, The Man Who Sued God* and *Crocodile Dundee in LA*), this amounted to only 7.8 per cent of the Australian box-office. One explanation for these anomalies lies in the number of screens and seats available to audiences. In 1986, when the first *Crocodile Dundee* was unleashed on the Australian public (taking more than 21 per cent of the local box-office alone), there were 626 screens (for a total of 295 000 seats). By the time *Crocodile Dundee in LA* was released, there were nearly three times that number—1855 screens (463 000 seats). By 2012, this had risen again to 1995 screens. If *Crocodile Dundee* were to take as much money at the box office (even adjusted for 2012 ticket prices), it would only total around 9 per cent of the Australian box office (Jericho 2013). So today's success stories face a far loftier bar than previous high performers. This is because, even though Australia's total box office has been increasing, the actual number of tickets sold (admissions) has flatlined since the early 2000s. Furthermore, the average number of cinema attendances per film-goer has also declined (11.3 in 1996 compared with 6.8 in 2011) despite a big increase in the number of films released (280 in 1996, 342 in 2011). Between 2011 and 2012 the number of films obtaining a release climbed by 23 per cent (548 films reported box office, of which 421 screened for the first time in Australian cinema), a rate that was significantly out of proportion to the overall box office growth. Yet the number of local films getting a first release in 2012 slipped from 36 in 2011 to 27, the lowest figure in five years. All this makes for an unprecedented 'crowded market' in which all films—including Australian productions—struggle for attention.

Table 9.4 Digital screens, Australia

2006	2007	2008	2009	2010	2011	2012
27	30	54	311	452	704	1436 (72%)

Source: Screen Australia; MPDAA.

DVD

The vast majority of films seldom make a profit solely on their theatrical release. In the current environment, a film takes about 2.5 years to exploit the full range of possible distribution channels; however, as this chapter is being written, release windows are collapsing, distribution platforms are converging and devices for accessing films are fragmenting. In general, around 20 per cent of industry revenue is now derived from gross box-office receipts received from cinemas. In the past, the role of DVDs (and, before them, videos) in creating audiences for film titles could not be under-estimated, even if they relied on a successful theatrical season to create a 'cascade' of returns. The DVD industry was a critical component of the ways in which films were made, marketed and watched in Australia. In 2003, DVD and video sales in Australia outstripped cinema box office for the first time. In 2008, DVD retail sales exceeded $1.4 billion, easily eclipsing the year's cinema box office ($946 million). On the other hand—and to put this success in context—sales revenue from video games (hardware and software) well exceeded these figures ($1.96 billion in 2008). However, DVD rentals and sales began to decline in Australia from 2008 (despite the introduction of the relatively new higher definition Blu-ray format) before plummeting from 2009 onwards. This steep decline was not stemmed by lower prices, nor the emergence of self-serve rental kiosks in shopping centres and diminishing window between cinema and DVD release.

Table 9.5 Wholesale DVD sales

	2007	**2008**	**2009**	**2010**	**2011**
DVD wholesale revenue	1334 m	1385 m	1295 m	1176 m	1029 m
Blu-ray wholesale revenue	9.24 m	38.4 m	81.7 m	111.5 m	183.5 m
Combined DVD/Blu-ray and other retail revenue	1135 m	1166 m	1189 m	1142 m	1094 m

Source: The Australian Home Entertainment Distributors Association.

Rental kiosks (such as Hoyts Kiosks, formerly Oovie) are seen as a very small market player at the moment. Kiosks are based on a 'rent anywhere, return anywhere' ethos, and currently there are around 300 machines located in shopping centres across four states and with around 500 000 customers. The ageing start-up, Quickflix, has only secured 0.9 per cent of market share, with around 120 000 subscribers at the start of 2013 using both their postal and streaming services. Despite Quickflix reporting 68 per cent growth in online streaming (pay-per-view) and bundled users (unlimited access subscriptions) over the six months to December 2012, the company has struggled to realise profit and in 2012 it shed a third of its workforce, scaled back advertising and closed five of six of its DVD fulfilment centres. Quickflix offered new-release films for the first time in late 2012, but faces fierce competition from both major distributors such as Hoyts, which has announced its intention to provide movie streaming (with rewards for customers who return to cinemas) and catch-up TV services such as Foxtel, which has an exclusive contract with HBO for the right to broadcast its new dramas in Australia just hours after they have aired in the United States. Other competing online services include Sony Entertainment Network, FetchTV and Big-Pond Video, to name a few. In terms of content streaming, Quickflix and the Sony Entertainment Network are of particular interest because they are compatible with so many media devices such as new Sony televisions and Blu-ray players, as well as the PlayStation 3, computer browsers and some Android devices.

Table 9.6 DVD rental statistics

	2007	2008	2009	2010	2011
Rental wholesale	211.3 m	230.3 m	187.8 m	146.0 m	119.1 m
Rental wholesale units	13.1 m	11.8 m	11.1 m	7.5 m	6.4 m

Source: Australian Home Entertainment Distributors Association.

Despite less than ideal network speeds and access conditions, Australians are avid consumers of online content and the Australian video and music streaming market was valued at just under $200 million in 2012. According to the Australian Communications and Media Authority (ACMA), on average Australian internet subscribers watched an estimated 86 hours of catch-up TV viewing or 132 hours of YouTube videos in the 12 months to June 2011. During June 2011, online Australians viewed 19.2 billion pages of web content, compared with 18.5 billion in June 2010. Many international companies (such as Apple iTunes and the popular online movie site Hulu) attempt to restrict access to and/or charge higher prices for the same content in the Australian market. Many Australian consumers have become adept at using secure virtual private networks (VPNs) in order to access international online content provider services.

Table 9.7 Comparison of Australian online content devices and usage

	June 2010	June 2011
Household consumers with a mobile phone	14.9 m	15.8 m
Mobile wireless broadband subscribers	3.45 m	4.79 m
Mobile phone handset internet subscribers	6.78 m	9.68 m
Pay TV subscribers (households)	2.38 m	2.41 m
Australians with broadband at home	11.8 m	12.7 m
Australians streaming TV online	0.6 m	1.1 m
Australians downloading TV programs	0.8m	1.0 m

Source: ACMA.

CONCLUSION

In the late 1960s and early 1970s, the boom-or-bust narrative of Australian film history was used as the basis for arguments for a revitalised, government-sponsored Australian film production industry. The idea that a film production industry had once thrived but then been left to lapse gathered momentum. The history of Australian cinema, it was believed, was one of local initiative defeated by powerful commercial—especially American—interests and government disinterest. The legacy of these arguments is the still-constant sense of threat in the Australian film industry—as if government support for local film production, and with it the entire Australian cinema, could disappear without notice. And, in emphasising the production sector at the expense of other ways of approaching the national cinema (via the exhibition and distribution sectors—for example, in which Australian films constitute usually much less than 10 per cent of the annual box office)—policy-makers and academics have repeatedly defined the Australian cinema defensively, as a moment of cultural resistance against a dominant Hollywood 'other'. This has in large part created a disproportionate emphasis on cultural autonomy in the way we speak about the Australian cinema. By failing to understand how the Australian film industry is actively engaging and exchanging with international industries, we diminish the historical and economic importance of our relationship with American cinema, and we limit our ability to see our similarity to many other national cinemas in which American cinema also plays a key role.

However, recent changes to the expectations of government involvement in the sector, combined with the decreasing proportion of federal and state funding in film finance, indicate a national industry that is finally embracing its global and commercial possibilities. With this in mind, we can re-address the basic questions that have pestered Australian policy-makers since the advent of a government-subsidised film sector in the mid-1970s. Film industry policy-makers once invested in the idea of a national cinema simply so that we might 'tell our own stories', but Australian audiences have repeatedly shown that they are unwilling to 'hear' these stories despite an evident ardour for cinema consumption. However, new research by Screen Australia into contemporary Australian audience behaviour strongly suggests that Australian films enjoy far wider success on the myriad small screens that are now available to audiences for viewing screen content. Amidst spiralling industry disruptions, we need to address the very real impact of practices of disintermediation (the cutting out of the 'middleman'), and the remediation of titles to new formats and devices (the way content now flows to consumers in a variety of rapidly proliferating formats and the challenges for preserving legacy media in this context) on how we describe the Australian cinema. In particular, these developments draw attention to the historical influence, and new shape, of distribution as an industry practice that has frequently been overlooked in the focus on production as the sole measure of national endeavour.

FURTHER READING

Useful histories of the Australian film industry can be found in Shirley and Adams (1987), *Australian Cinema: The First Eighty Years*, or Pike and Cooper (1998), *Australian Film 1900–1977*. Scott Murray's (1995) *Australian Film 1978–1994* picks up where Pike and Cooper finish. Also useful for its thematic discussion and general information is Bertrand, McFarlane and Mayer (1999), *The Oxford Companion to Australian Film*. Detailed and current industry statistics are provided by the Australian Film Commission in its annual publication *Get the Picture*, which is regularly updated online (<www.afc.gov.au/gtp>). One of the most profound considerations of the cinema can be found in Tom O'Regan's (1996) ambitious *Australian National Cinema*, which adopts a variety of perspectives to give a sense of the cultural, economic and theoretical nuances of the local film industry.

Chapter 10

TELEVISION

STEPHEN HARRINGTON

In spite of predictions about its demise, television is, and will continue to remain for some time, the most popular media form in Australia. Even with the growing use of online communication, time spent viewing television remains extremely high for a broad cross-section of the community (Screen Australia 2012). It is, as Sonia Livingstone (2004, p. 76) notes, a medium that 'has achieved a comprehensiveness of appeal and reach never before surpassed nor likely to be in the future'.

Television's power and influence can be assessed via a number of indicators. The sheer volume of time that TV viewing occupies in people's lives points to its importance, as it has become the principal source of news, information and entertainment for the majority of the world's population. Social critics such as Robert Putnam (2000) worry, however, that this pervasiveness of television has caused a decline in social capital, promoting the privatisation of leisure time and a reduced commitment to join public cultural institutions. By contrast, media theorists such as Catharine Lumby (1999) and John Hartley (1999) propose that television has actually been associated with a democratisation of public life, as 'the contemporary media sphere constitutes a highly diverse and inclusive forum in which a host of important issues once deemed apolitical, trivial and personal are now being aired' (Lumby 1999, p. xii).

Television studies is now a burgeoning and multidimensional field of research (see Gray and Lotz 2012; Bignell 2008; Miller 2010), and there is a growing academic literature on Australian television. One question that therefore arises concerns how Australian television should be studied. McKee (2001) draws attention to the extent to which much academic work on Australian television has paid less attention to programs than it has to industries, policies and regulatory mechanisms. Bonner (2003) similarly points to the need for television studies to focus upon those programs—particularly in non-fiction genres—that are broadcast on a regular basis, and hence appear to be 'ordinary'. Bonner argues that an analysis of such programs—which, in the Australian context, range from gardening and home renovation programs to daytime chat programs—draws attention to 'the ways in which the content of television draws upon ordinary, everyday concerns . . . as guides to style, appearance, and behaviour' (2003, p. 32).

This chapter addresses the historical development of Australian television from the 1950s to the present. In doing so, it adapts Cunningham's (2000, pp. 14–15) division of the history of Australian television into four 'phases', combining the first two of those phases (innovation/diffusion and establishment) and adding a fifth, which is the present 'multi-channel' era in which Australia—like many other TV systems across the Western world—now finds itself. It connects four elements of television's development: industry and technological trends; policy developments; the programs that were broadcast during these periods; and shifts in audience demographics and viewing trends. It aims to give an appropriate weighting to developments in commercial free-to-air television, public broadcasting (the ABC and SBS) and pay television. The chapter concludes by outlining a number of technological, financial and viewership challenges faced by the Australian television industry, and examining how it is attempting to address those challenges.

PRE-1975: ESTABLISHMENT

The first television broadcast in Australia was by TCN 9 in Sydney on 16 September 1956, and within six months there were two commercial stations in Sydney (TCN 9 and ATN 7) and two in Melbourne (GTV 9 and HSV 7). The ABC commenced broadcasting in Sydney and Melbourne in November 1956, and its coverage of the 1956 Melbourne Olympics gave an immense stimulus to the demand for television. Broadcasting commenced in Brisbane, Adelaide and Perth in 1959. Ownership of commercial broadcast licences was dominated by print media interests, with the Packer family's Consolidated Press controlling the Nine stations by 1960, the John Fairfax newspaper group controlling ATN 7 in Sydney and the Herald and Weekly Times newspaper group controlling HSV 7. A pattern of high-level political allegiances between the commercial broadcasters and Liberal-Country Party Coalition governments emerged early in the history of Australian television (Curthoys 1986). As a consequence, the Australian Broadcasting Control Board (ABCB), the principal broadcasting regulator, was left very weak and uncertain of its capacity to control broadcaster conduct, and exhibited strong symptoms of *regulatory capture*, or over-identification with the industry it regulated.

In the 1950s and early 1960s, programs from the United States, and to a lesser extent the United Kingdom, were dominant on Australian television. The Senate Select Committee on the Encouragement of Australian Productions for Television (also known as the Vincent Committee) found that 97 per cent of drama screened on Australian TV between 1956 and 1963 was imported. This dominance of imported programming was contrary to the requirement of section 114(1) of the *Broadcasting and Television Act* 1953 that 'licensees shall, as far as possible, use the services of Australians in the production and presentation of radio and television programs'. The demand for local content regulations for commercial television licensees would become a rallying cry for production interests and cultural nationalists from the mid-1960s, leading to the gradual development of Australian content quotas for commercial television (Flew 1995; Papandrea 1997).

In the early years of Australian television, the major forms of local content were low-cost variety and quiz shows. A number of factors led to a significant increase in local production from the mid-1960s, including the establishment of a third capital city network (the 0-Ten Network) during 1963–65; the introduction of videotape and other developments that made smaller production companies more financially viable; the requirement from 1960 that advertisements screened on Australian television be produced in Australia; a ratings drift away from American programs over the 1960s; and a major increase in the ABC's commitment to TV drama production (Moran 1985). The ratings success of *Homicide*, an Australian police drama produced by Crawford Productions and screened on Channel 7 from 1964, was a major stimulus to local TV drama production. *Homicide*'s success would lead to other Crawford productions in the police/crime genre in the 1960s and 1970s. For the local production industry as well as cultural nationalists, this success of local programming was indicative of what Gil Appleton (1988) terms the 'shock of self-recognition', when Australian TV audiences were confronted by culturally familiar locales and modes of behaviour.

This was the period in which the Australian Broadcasting Commission (ABC) established itself as the national leader in news and current affairs with *Four Corners* and *This Day Tonight*, as well as in drama with programs such as *Bellbird, Rush* and *Certain Women* and as the pre-eminent source of locally produced children's TV with *Play School* and *Mr Squiggle* (Inglis 1983). Jacka (1990) refers to the period from 1968 to 1975 as the 'golden age' of ABC drama, and Turner (2005) argues that *This Day Tonight* established itself between 1967 and 1973 as the 'gold standard' of Australian current affairs television.

1975–86: A MATURING MEDIUM

Colour television was introduced to Australia in 1975. It was an immediate hit with viewers, and made the medium even more attractive to advertisers (Herd 2012, p. 153). This contributed to the consistent financial success of broadcasting in the 1970s and early 1980s, with profit margins for commercial broadcasters in the range of 15–20 per cent for much of this period. At the same time, Australian television was also acquiring what Tom O'Regan (1994) describes as the localising dynamics of a mature broadcasting industry, leading to a boom in local program production. The combination of growing audience ratings for Australian programs, policy and regulatory activism to require commercial networks to broadcast a greater level of Australian content, and spin-offs from the growth of the Australian film industry led to significant increases in the amount of local content—particularly local drama—screened on Australian television.

The boom in television drama production saw the emergence of distinctive local production houses. Crawford Productions had followed its success with *Homicide* and other police/crime dramas with *The Sullivans*, a family drama set in the World War II period, which consistently topped the ratings for Channel 9 from 1976 to 1982. The Grundy Organisation also branched out from its success in producing quiz shows to become a leading producer of serial dramas (or 'soaps'), with its successes including *Class of '74/'75*, *The Young Doctors*, *The Restless Years* and *Prisoner*. The Ten Network experienced ratings success for the first time since its establishment in 1963–65 with the adult soap *Number 96*, which broke many taboos around television content concerning sex, nudity and homosexuality. Indeed, as McKee (2001) observes, programs such as *Number 96*, *Prisoner* and *The Box*—all broadcast on Ten during the 1970s—were vitally important in framing debates both about sexuality and personal relations more generally in Australian public culture.

The 1970s and 1980s were turbulent years for the Australian Broadcasting Corporation (ABC), which until 1983 was the Australian Broadcasting Commission. The decision of the Whitlam Labor government in 1973 to abolish the television and radio licence fees that had been used to finance the ABC (based on the BBC model that continues to operate to this day) was popular with voters at the time, but it left the ABC very much exposed to the annual budgetary process of federal governments, which could in turn challenge its independence. The mid-1970s saw the beginnings of cuts to ABC funding as economic times became more difficult, and the first murmurings of what would become a roar from the conservative side of politics that left-wing bias was inherent within the ABC as an organisation. The Dix Report into the ABC, commissioned by the Fraser Liberal government, found that the ABC had faltered in meeting its goals over the course of the 1970s, becoming 'slow moving, overgrown, complacent, and uncertain of the direction in which it is heading' (quoted in Inglis 1983, p. 430). By the end of the 1980s, with David Hill as managing director, the ABC had been substantially overhauled, and had significantly increased the amount of Australian content on air, through serial dramas such as *GP*, comedies such as *Mother and Son* and live shows such as *Live and Sweaty*, *The Big Gig* and Andrew Denton's *The Money or the Gun*.

Over the 1970s and 1980s, there was a renewed focus in broadcasting regulation on the considerable reach of commercial broadcasting, and its role in social and cultural policy areas such as local content and children's programming. The Australian Broadcasting Tribunal (ABT) was established in 1977, and sought to bring direct public accountability to commercial broadcasting through annual licence-renewal hearings (Hawke 1995; Flew 2001). While licence-renewal processes bogged down in legalism and were quietly abandoned during the 1980s, a more successful policy process was conducted by the ABT around Australian content regulations in the 1980s, which led to the introduction of Australian content quotas for commercial broadcasters; today these require that at least 55 per cent of material shown between 6.00 a.m. and midnight be primarily Australian-made, or New Zealand-made with some Australian creative input. Additional local content sub-quotas also exist to help stimulate the areas of drama, children's programming and documentary.

Perhaps the most genuinely innovative development in Australian television during this period was the establishment of the Special Broadcasting Service (SBS), which commenced television broadcasting in 1980. SBS grew out of the government policy of multiculturalism, and addressed what was seen as the lack of responsiveness among Australia's media institutions to an increasingly culturally diverse society. Importantly, SBS was not exclusively conceived of as an ethnic broadcasting service. Its first managing director, Bruce Gyngell, was one of the most senior people in Australian television, and he understood SBS as a television service with a multicultural remit, rather than as an outlet designed primarily for self-expression on the part of Australia's ethnic communities. While SBS has been criticised for the preponderance of Anglo-Australians in its upper management (e.g. Jakubowicz et al. 1994), the approach to broadcasting developed by SBS from its early days has been one that has emphasised the importance of reflecting cultural diversity back to the whole Australian population, as was seen in its first slogan, 'Bringing the World Back Home'. The commitment to subtitling all non-English language programming, undertaken at some cost to a broadcaster that has always received limited government funding, has been one way of ensuring that all Australians can access the cultural diversity offered through SBS Television.

1987–2005: SPECIALISING

The late 1980s and early 1990s saw the Australian commercial television industry fall into its deepest slump since broadcasting began. Changes to media ownership laws in 1986–87 (which effectively paved the way for the formalisation of nation-wide networks, as opposed to stations acting semi-autonomously) saw a number of stations frantically snapped up by a new breed of entrepreneurs who had expectations that their investments would be cash cows in the long term. Christopher Skase, Alan Bond and Frank Lowy bought the Seven, Nine and Ten Networks respectively at over-inflated prices. However, a combination of the new owners' relative inexperience in the industry and the economic downturn that followed the 1987 stock market crash meant that by the end of the decade the Seven and Ten Networks were in receivership, while Kerry Packer bought back Nine from a bankrupted Alan Bond for one-fifth of the $1.05 billion that Bond had paid for the network in 1987. Following this dramatic shakeout and subsequent restructuring of the various businesses involved, Australian television did enter a long period of stability and financial prosperity, which Herd (2012, p. 207) argues shows that the 'entrepreneurs' instincts were probably right'.

Australian programs continued to be popular with local audiences during the 1990s, but there were some major shifts in the types of program that were popular, and a significant split in audience demographics. The most dramatic changes were at the Ten Network, which came out of near-bankruptcy in the early 1990s through a counter-programming strategy that placed less emphasis on maximising overall audience share, and instead targeted the lucrative 16–39-year-old market (Green 2001). The network initially focused on imported programs such as *The Simpsons*, *Seinfeld*, *The Nanny*, *Beverly Hills 90210*, *Melrose Place* and *The X-Files*. These shows were complemented in the late 1990s by local programs such as *Good News Week* (purchased directly from the ABC) and *The Panel*.

The program format that most defined Australian television in the 1990s was the lifestyle program. The first successful lifestyle program was *Burke's Backyard*, which was broadcast on Channel 9 from 1987 to 2004. While the ABC was a major innovator in lifestyle programming, screening *Holiday*, *The Home Show* and *Everybody* from 1987 to 1994, lifestyle programming was most strongly associated with the commercial networks, particularly as it allowed close tie-ins between programs, program sponsors, associated magazines and the broadcaster's website. The leader was the Nine Network, partly because lifestyle programming fitted well with its emphasis on mainstream suburban audiences and personality-based programming, but it was also taken up by the Seven and Ten Networks, as it provided a low-cost way of meeting local content requirements as budgets for new local drama production were increasingly stretched. Popular Australian lifestyle programs have included *Our House*, *Backyard Blitz*, *Getaway*, *Good Medicine*, *Changing Rooms*, *Money* and *Renovation Rescue* (Nine); *The Great Outdoors*, *Harry's Practice*, *Better Homes and Gardens*, *Hot Property* and *Ground Force* (Seven); and *Healthy, Wealthy and Wise* (Ten).

The development of lifestyle programs was accompanied by a renewed commitment to series and serial drama by the commercial networks in the second half of the 1990s. The Nine Network developed successful dramas such as *Water Rats* and *Stingers*, as well as high-rating occasional series such as *Halifax F.P.*, while the Seven Network—which had been the traditional leader in this area—developed strong weekly local programming with *Blue Heelers* and *All Saints*. Ten had a brief period of success in 2001–03 with *The Secret Life of Us*, which was a product of Sue Masters' move from being Head of Drama at the ABC to Ten. With its open depiction of gay and lesbian relationships and its culturally diverse cast—including Aboriginal actress Deborah Mailman in a lead role—it recalled the earlier success of Ten in the 1970s (particularly *Number 96*) with local drama that diverted from the mainstream.

If lifestyle shows defined the 1990s, then the 2000s were certainly the decade of reality TV for Australian commercial broadcasters, as has been the case in many parts of the world. Australia's first real dose of the genre came as early as 1992 in the form of *Sylvania Waters*, a 'fly-on-the-wall' insight into the daily lives of *nouveau riche* couple Noelene and Laurie Donaher, residents of the titular waterfront suburb in southern Sydney. Throughout the 1990s, programs featuring 'ordinary people'—such as *Weddings* (Nine)—and competition/talent show programs—like *Popstars* (Seven)—became more common. But the watershed came in 2001 when Ten first broadcast *Big Brother*, which was arguably the defining program of the modern era. With its capacity for multi-format distribution and audience participation (through the *Big Brother* website, voting off contestants by phone or attending the eviction nights held at Dreamworld on the Gold Coast), the many opportunities for product tie-ins associated with the show and its 'must-see' nature, the commercial pay-offs for Ten and Endemol-Southern Star (the program's producers) were immediate and considerable. Although *Big Brother* was expensive to produce (Roscoe 2001), the attraction for Ten lay in the show's specific popularity among its target demographic, and also in the amount of (locally produced) content that could be extracted from that initial investment. At one point, Ten was able to screen over 15 hours of *Big Brother* material per week (across a number of different versions of the show), which is significantly greater than the hour or less that is gleaned from a high-end local drama production.

The success of *Big Brother* inevitably led to a proliferation across the sector, and by 2004 local or imported reality TV was taking up almost 40 per cent of total prime-time hours (Dale 2004). Aside from *Big Brother*, two programs that were particularly successful were *The Block* (Nine) and *Australian Idol* (Ten). *The Block* was a locally developed hybrid format, where four couples would renovate a block of beachside apartments, and the winner would be the couple whose apartment realised the highest price at the end-of-series public auction. *The Block* combined lifestyle and reality TV staples such as home improvement, competition among the contestants, public auctions, viewer voting, dramatic tension among the participants and a quite breathtaking amount of product placement. *Australian Idol* was also an enormous ratings success for Ten, with the 'Final Verdict' show being the second top-rating program in 2003 and the top-rating program in 2004 (Screen Australia 2009). *Big Brother* was cancelled in late 2008 after a series of high-profile scandals and falling ratings (although it recommenced on Nine in 2012), and it could be argued that *Idol*, and the spate of other shows that followed it (*MasterChef, So You Think You Can Dance, Australia's Got Talent* and so on) reflected a significant turn in the genre away from the fairly shallow pursuit of fame and celebrity towards more substantial career aspirations and merit-based rewards.

BOX 10.1: PAY TV IN AUSTRALIA

By the time pay television (or subscription television) commenced in Australia in the mid-1990s, it was already well established in many parts of the world (Westfield 2000). Close ties between the incumbent Australian free-to-air broadcasters and successive governments had seen the stifling of efforts going back to the early 1980s to introduce subscription television services, and it was not until the deregulation of the telecommunications industry in the early 1990s that the impetus was sufficient to sway the government's hand. As a result, pay television in Australia has always been closely tied to the telecommunications industry, with the major providers Telstra and Optus using pay TV services to lure customers to their much more profitable telephony services.

The first subscription television services, Australis/Galaxy, Foxtel—owned by Telstra (50 per cent), Consolidated Media Holdings (originally under PBL, 25 per cent) and News Limited (25 per cent)—and Optus Vision (now Optus Television)—owned by Singapore Telecommunications—commenced operations in 1995; these were closely followed by regional and rural provider Austar in 1996. These services used a combination of cable, satellite (DBS) and Microwave (MDS) technologies. Australis ceased operations in 1998 under mounting debts, while the two metropolitan carriers, Foxtel and Optus, waged a damaging war of attrition, refusing to share programming, channels and infrastructure, with the result that subscription rates for consumers in Australia were almost five times the international average (Shand 2002). After strong initial demand, growth for pay TV was relatively sluggish in the early 2000s, and by 2002 the industry was facing debts of $4 billion and an uncertain future due to static subscriber numbers and high programming costs.

A dramatic restructuring of the Australian pay television sector in 2002, however, allowed the industry to adopt a more profitable business model. The so-called 'Point Piper Accord' (Shand 2002)—known officially as the 'Content Sharing Agreement' (CSA)—which was signed between Optus and Telstra and approved by the ACCC in November 2002, saw a significant regression of the existing content rivalry between the two providers. Under the new agreement, Foxtel would be the major content provider for all subscription services in Australia, with Optus Television acting essentially as a re-seller of the Foxtel service. In 2012, Foxtel merged with Austar to effectively become the sole provider of pay TV services in the country.

While takeup rates for pay TV stagnated badly between 2001 and 2003, subscriber numbers grew steady after the CSA came into effect. As of mid-2011, there were just over 2.4 million subscribers to pay television services in Australia, which represented approximately 29 per cent of all households (Screen Australia 2011). Despite this, because the pay television audience is dispersed across so many channels and is much more 'niche' oriented, it remains less attractive to advertisers than commercial free-to-air television.

A significant obstacle faced by pay television operators in Australia is the problem of anti-siphoning legislation, which is one of several policies that have sought to protect the incumbency of free-to-air channels (McCutcheon 2006), and therefore affected pay TV's ability to drive subscriptions. ACMA's anti-siphoning rules are designed to help protect major public events from appearing exclusively on subscription television, thus providing the free-to-air networks with first bidding option (not necessarily a requirement for broadcast) on a list of major sporting events considered to be of 'national importance' or 'cultural significance'. Although this anti-siphoning legislation is among the most stringent in the world, it has been thwarted in part by rights-sharing deals between free-to-air and pay TV (as with the National Rugby League, Australian Football League and A League deals), and the creation of a number of pay television-only sporting events, such as the Super Rugby competition and Big Bash League cricket.

THE ABC SINCE 1990

The Australian Broadcasting Corporation in the 1990s and 2000s experienced what Craig (2000) has described as a sense of 'perpetual crisis'. The crisis of this period had two ostensible causes. The first was the decision of the Howard Coalition government upon its election in 1996 to cut 10 per cent of the budgets of the ABC and SBS over 1996–98. For the ABC in particular, this had a severe impact on its capacity to commission local production, only partly alleviated by the move towards outsourcing program-making to independent producers that was also a dominant change during this period.

The review of the ABC undertaken by Bob Mansfield (the Mansfield Review), which was completed in 1997, posed a question being asked all over the world about public service broadcasters, which is whether they should aim to provide all forms of programming for all potential audiences—that is, be a *comprehensive* broadcaster—or focus upon providing programs and catering for audiences neglected by the commercial media—that is, be a *complementary* broadcaster? The Mansfield Review, and the vast bulk of the 10 615 public submissions it received, took the view that the ABC could and should do both, whether through more public funding (which most public submissions favoured) or through outsourcing program production to independent producers, selling surplus real estate and withdrawing from non-core activities such as international satellite TV broadcasting (as the Mansfield Review favoured).

Another recurring issue was the Liberal-National Party Coalition's perception that the ABC exhibited a left-wing political bias, and that there was a need for root-and-branch reform of its organisational culture. Graham Morris, a senior adviser to then prime minister, John Howard, characterised the ABC as 'our enemy talking to our friends' (quoted in Inglis 2006, p. 372), and a large raft of conservative commentators had long complained of ABC bias. The issue of political bias bubbled away throughout this period, particularly during the periods of Brian Johns (1996–2000) and Jonathan Shier (2000–03) as managing directors. These issues are amply covered in Inglis (2006) and elsewhere, and won't be dwelt upon here, except to note that there were recurring debates throughout the period from the late 1990s to 2007 about whether there was evidence of bias in news and current affairs programs such as *The 7.30 Report*, *Lateline*, *Four Corners*, *Media Watch* and *Insiders*, as well as in documentaries such as *The Howard Years* (about the Howard government).

In 2000, the then-director of television, Gail Jarvis, expressed concern that the ABC prime-time schedule looked like it was 'designed by middle-aged men for middle-aged men' (quoted in Inglis 2006, p. 476). This echoed Jacka's (2006) observation that the ABC TV audience was skewed notably towards the over-55s and middle- to higher-income professionals. She argued that the ABC 'wears its ageing AB demographic on its sleeve', and wondered whether 'the rubric [of] "quality" . . . is really a pre-text for a privileging of middle-class cultural values' (Jacka 2006, pp. 350–1). Many of the ABC's most notable successes over the 1990s and 2000s were those programs that broke out of the mould of 'worthy', middle-class, public-sphere television. *Sea Change*, in which Sigrid Thornton played a divorced 40-something lawyer moving to a coastal town with her children, was a significant ratings hit when it ran from 1998 to 2000, tapping into a desire among affluent professionals to move from capital cities towards small coastal towns that were seen to be more community-minded (Burnley and Murphy 2004). Satirical comedy continued to be a strength of the ABC, with programs such as *The Games* (based on the planning of the 2000 Sydney Olympics), *Backberner* and *The Glass House*, while the ABC comedy *Frontline*, which ran from 1994 to 1997, satirised the increasingly absurd conventions of commercial current affairs television.

Several stand-out ABC programs from the 2000s broke from normative expectations about satire and its appeals to a middle-class audience, and were major ratings successes. *Kath and Kim* debuted in 2002, and immediately drew an audience of one million-plus from across the demographic spectrum. Set in the newly developed outer Melbourne suburb of Fountain Lakes, *Kath and Kim* plays with the aspiration, lavish consumerism and dubious taste of outer suburban dwellers. *Summer Heights High*, which ran in 2007, provided an even darker take on suburban Australia. It also attracted audiences of over one million, and—like *Kath and Kim*—has proved to be very successful on the DVD market. One of the ABC's biggest successes after 2000, however, was *The Chaser's War on Everything* (2006–07, 2009), which heavily satirised the various foibles of modern politics and the media. Generally popular among younger audiences—with which the ABC has traditionally struggled—viewership reached its peak in late 2007 after several members of the show's cast and crew were arrested (and made news internationally) for performing a stunt involving a 'fake' motorcade at the 2007 Asia-Pacific Economic Cooperation (APEC) meeting in Sydney. That highly anticipated episode was watched by 2.24 million people, making it the public broadcaster's third most-watched program since the introduction of the current TV ratings system in 1991.

One of the most substantial changes to the ABC's structure in recent years has been the expansion and re-branding of its television services. Following the BBC model, ABC became ABC1, mirroring the name of its existing digital sister channel ABC2. This was then joined by ABC3, which is solely targeted towards children and young adults. Finally, the introduction of the rolling HD news service ABC News 24 in 2010 was met with some controversy, as a number of high-profile commentators criticised the broadcaster (and its ambitious managing director, Mark Scott) for over-stepping what they saw as its purely complementary remit, in that it began competing head on with Sky News Australia, which was an existing commercial entity jointly owned by Nine, Seven and BSkyB. The same issues were raised when ABC Online began running opinion pieces (under their 'Unleashed' and 'The Drum' banners), as this was perceived to be in direct competition with the email-based subscription news service *Crikey!* Despite these criticisms, the ABC has remained the almost-undisputed leader in news and current affairs, with the 2011 *Four Corners* exposé of live cattle exports to Indonesia a particularly good example of the enduring political and social power of the medium.

SBS SINCE 1990

The passing of the *Special Broadcasting Services Act* 1991, ensuring that the SBS would remain independent of the ABC—a recurring controversy in the 1980s—established that the principal function of the SBS was to 'provide multilingual and multicultural radio and television services that inform, educate and entertain all Australians and, in doing so, reflect Australia's multicultural society'. In their history of SBS, Ang, Hawkins and Dabboussy (2008) argue that, as a public service broadcaster with a multicultural remit, SBS 'situates specific community interests, ethnic or otherwise, in the wider framework of a public media institution . . . that takes diversity as its starting point . . . [and] facilitates cross-cultural communication'. This enables SBS to be 'a force for *integration* rather than separateness, bringing together various viewpoints and experiences within a common public sphere' (Ang, Hawkins and Dabboussy 2008, pp. 6–7). Ang, Hawkins and Dabboussy argue that SBS Television has developed its programming around three discourses of multiculturalism that have coexisted within the organisation:

- *ethno-multiculturalism*, focused on the special needs and interests of migrants and ethnic communities
- *cosmopolitan multiculturalism*, encouraging all Australians to embrace global cultural diversity
- *popular multiculturalism*, where cultural diversity is taken as a given element of Australian everyday life.

It has been argued that the 1990s saw SBS TV move more decisively towards a more cosmopolitan understanding of multiculturalism, linked in part to the decision in 1990 that SBS could carry limited advertising and sponsorship of programs, hence becoming a hybrid service rather than one purely funded by government (Lawe Davies 1998). This was criticised at the time as a retreat from its commitment to ethnic communities (Jakubowicz and Newell 1995). The SBS theme from 1993 was 'The World is an Amazing Place'. As Hawkins (1996) argues, it pointed to cultural diversity as something that could be consumed pleasurably by all Australians as cosmopolitan would-be global citizens. Two programming areas that have been central to this are documentaries and movies. SBS screens more documentaries than any other Australian television channel. While most of these are not about Australian multiculturalism, they 'have been central to positioning SBS Television as a channel with an expansive outlook on the world and its complexities' (Ang, Hawkins and Dabboussy 2008, p. 112). Movies have also been central to SBS scheduling, and the 1990s saw a concerted effort to address a historical bifurcation within SBS towards screening, on the one hand, movies with appeal to a particular language group or ethnic community but with little appeal to others and, on the other, 'art-house' films of the sort selected and introduced by David Stratton.

By the end of the 1990s, SBS had distinctiveness and strength in the areas of news, documentaries, movies and specific sports (particularly soccer), and was clearly an alternative PBS to the ABC that could nonetheless credibly claim to compete with it as a quality broadcaster. The danger with such a positioning—aside from the question of whether SBS TV continued to adequately serve ethnic communities—was that both SBS and ABC could be seen as serving primarily the 'quality' demographic of older, highly educated and middle-class Australians, and lacking engagement with the majority of Australian society.

The breakout from this 'ethnics and eggheads' image of SBS came from a rather surprising source, the then little-known American animated comedy *South Park*, which SBS began broadcasting in 1998. *South Park* brought to SBS an under-40 audience, and particularly males aged 18–24, which it had been seeking for some time. Programs such as *Mythbusters* and *Pizza* have also appealed to this younger SBS audience, but it is notable that none of the programs *South Park*, *Mythbusters* or *Top Gear* (which commenced on SBS in 2006) could make claims to be multicultural or to meet SBS's charter obligations in terms of programming (Ang, Hawkins and Dabboussy 2008). These programs build audience share for SBS among demographics which otherwise largely watch commercial or pay TV, and the challenge for SBS is how to attract them to other programs that are closer to its charter mandate. The recent success of *Go Back to Where You Came From* (a documentary series addressing the refugee crisis) suggests that there is some movement in that direction.

2006–PRESENT: THE MULTI-CHANNEL ERA

After a long period of sustained calm, during which no change was the *status quo*, Australian television has again undergone a series of significant upheavals since 2006. One of the most important has been the gradual shift towards digital broadcasting. DVB-T (which stands for digital video broadcasting–terrestrial) was first used to transmit Australian television (initially simulcast with the analogue signal) in 2001, but the uptake of the technology was painfully slow in the first five years. This can be explained by the fact that digital TV offered no new services (even ABC2, which commenced in 2005, mainly offered time-shifted versions of the material already screened on the main channel—then still known only as ABC), and most consumers did not have the television equipment to make the most of the improved picture quality and wider aspect ratio. Indeed, the analogue switch-off date had to be pushed back to the end of 2013 for capital cities, due to a lack of movement with the technology up until 2006. From that point, however, as the cost of flat-screen TVs (plasmas, LCDs) dropped significantly (coming down to around one-tenth of their typical list price of $20 000 at the start of the decade), digital television began to represent a worthwhile investment, and finally started being taken up in greater numbers. Then, after free-to-air television re-branded itself 'Freeview' in 2008, and the restrictions surrounding multi-channelling were lifted—after a great deal of industry consternation regarding the issue—networks began to make the most of the digital spectrum that they had, until then, used rather inefficiently.

For Nine, its 'golden age' came to an end—perhaps only symbolically—with the death of influential media tycoon Kerry Packer on Boxing Day 2005. His son, James, who then took full control of PBL, quickly shifted the company's focus away from media holdings, and turned instead to its casino interests in Australia, Macau and Las Vegas. The company subsequently split its media and gambling concerns, and sold half of Consolidated Media Holdings (which housed Channel 9) to the private equity fund CVC Asia Pacific in late 2006. The sale was made possible by new legislation that relaxed the previous restrictions on foreign and cross-media ownership, which was readily passed by the Howard government, which had control of both houses of parliament at the time. A program of severe cost-cutting under the short but eventful stewardship of Eddie McGuire in 2006 and 2007 resulted in a number of high-profile PR disasters, staff defections and an undermining of the Nine Network's flagship news services.

At the same time, Seven, which had nearly run third to Ten in the overall ratings for 2004, began to invest wisely in a series of ratings hits, such as a local version of *Dancing with the Stars* and foreign imports like *Lost* and *Desperate Housewives*. Breakfast television became a new battleground too, as Seven's *Sunrise* began to overtake Nine's *Today*, which had enjoyed ratings comfort for many years. Not surprisingly, in 2007 the Seven Network unseated Nine's place at the top of the ratings, thereby forcing Nine to unceremoniously drop its 'Still the One' slogan, which it had used proudly for over two decades.

Although Seven continues as the most popular network in Australia (at the time of writing), Nine has enjoyed a number of programming successes in recent years. Most notable was the 2008 hit *Underbelly*, a true-crime gangster program loosely based on the life of Melbourne underworld figure Carl Williams and others involved in the Melbourne 'gangland wars' of the late 1990s and 2000s. This has been followed by a new series every year since, and a greater interest across the sector in crime dramas based on real-life events (for example, Ten's mini-series *Bikie Wars: Brothers in Arms*). In fact, after going through something of a lull in the mid-2000s, local drama made a minor comeback in the late 2000s, with a small number of locally produced shows becoming ratings standouts, such as *Packed to the Rafters*, *Winners and Losers* (Seven); *House Husbands* (Nine); *Offspring* (Ten); *The Slap* and *Rake* (ABC1), along with mini-series like *Howzat! Kerry Packer's War* (Nine), *Paper Giants* (ABC) and *Underground: The Julian Assange Story* (Ten). This follows a global resurgence of high-quality scripted drama, as evidenced by the critical and commercial success of shows such as *The Wire*, *Downton Abbey*, *Homeland* and *Mad Men*.

Whereas recent years have been highly prosperous for Seven, the current era has been a particularly disastrous one for the Ten Network. The primary explanation for this downturn is that the strategy of counter-programming has been rendered largely ineffective in the new multi-channelling environment. For example, Go!, one of Nine's new digital channels, has essentially emulated Ten's approach of the 1990s by relying on cheap imported programs such as *Wipeout*, re-runs of *Two and a Half Men* and *The Big Bang Theory*, all of which hold some appeal for Generation Y viewers. Ten's fortunes have become heavily reliant on the fortunes of some big-ticket investments. The colossal hit *MasterChef* (2009–), itself a replacement for *Big Brother*, was a stroke of very good luck for the network, but a string of high-profile failures, such as *6:30 with George Negus* (which filled the slot left vacant after *Neighbours* was moved to the new Channel 11), *Breakfast* and *The Renovators*, alongside a failure to secure the rights to shows that would be 'at home' on the network (in particular, *The Voice*), have seen it struggle badly. As a result, the network laid off a large number of staff in 2012, which followed the resignation of its chief programmer, David Mott, earlier that year. Ten was the first commercial TV network to launch a second channel, One, in 2009. Initially positioning it as an all-sport offering, this expensive and poor-performing strategy was unsustainable (particularly given that its highest-profile sports were

Formula One and the Indian Premier League cricket), and it shifted towards a more general male-oriented schedule in 2011. *MasterChef* and *Offspring* aside, one of the only true success stories at Network Ten in recent years has been *The Project*, a relatively informal, often humorous news and discussion format, which followed very much in the footsteps of *Good News Week* and *The Glass House*. Starting out as *The 7pm Project* in 2009, it has managed to sustain a consistent daily audience, and attracted admiration from politicians and journalists at the same time.

Ten's financial woes (dramatically highlighted by a share price drop of nearly 90 per cent over the period 2007–12) are indicative of the precarious position in which a number of TV networks and other media companies (e.g. Fairfax) now find themselves. In 2012, the Nine Network was able to stave off potential bankruptcy with some ease, but the fact that a network that was seen as almost untouchable a decade earlier faced such a prospect highlights the volatile nature of the industry in the early 2010s. That also leaves open the question of the long-term viability of the free-to-air networks in the current economic and technological environment.

CONCLUSION: THE FUTURE OF TELEVISION

Given the deepening penetration of broadband internet for personal use since the turn of the century, alongside the introduction of internet-enabled mobile devices, 'smart' TVs, and the dramatic rise in popularity of social media, it would be very easy to suggest that television's glory days are behind it, and that the internet will eventually take its place at the centre of our culture. However, the evolving relationship between digital media and television is considerably more complex than that.

One reason why the internet has often been viewed in competitive or antagonistic terms is the issue of peer-to-peer online piracy. It is very difficult to gauge the true impact of this practice on the television industry, as many of the claims that abound in the industry have tended to rely on very rough estimates (if not outright fabrications), and on the flawed premise that any viewing of pirated material supplants viewing of actual broadcast content. In a visible attempt to partially circumvent the issue, some networks (particularly TV) dramatically shortened the once-vast gap between a program screening overseas and it screening in Australia. They have made much of their 'fast-tracked' episodes of particular series—for example, *Lost*, *Top Gear* and, more recently, *Homeland*—which appeal to younger and more tech-savvy demographics. The ABC has moved to screen episodes of *Doctor Who* just hours after their initial broadcast in the United Kingdom.

BOX 10.2: THE POWER OF 'LIVE': SPORT AND SOCIAL MEDIA

While the audience may have fragmented, the mass audience still exists for those events that bind us together in space and time. Exploiting the continuing power of this immediacy will be the future of commercial television. (Herd 2012, p. 313)

Given the tendency for new media technologies to fragment existing audiences, a lot of attention in recent times in the television industry has focussed on those kinds of television programming which instead have the power to unite viewers together around a single cultural event. This attention is generally being directed in two different ways.

First, broadcasters are quickly beginning to see the potential of social media (especially Twitter, or mobile applications such as Fango, Zeebox or Cricket LIVE Australia) to add value to live television as a 'second screen', rather than as a straight replacement of the existing technology. *Twitter* has become an informal back-channel for live discussions of content, and most networks now actively push their viewers to join the social media conversation by setting up Twitter accounts, and promoting formal hashtags via on-screen prompts. In some cases, such as *Q&A* (ABC1) or *Can of Worms* (Ten), tweets from viewers actually become a significant part of the show itself. And, given that the full benefits of this social dimension are only available to those who are watching the program live, then this technology potentially is reducing the possibility that people might time-shift or download it, thereby giving renewed emphasis to networks' scheduling power (see Harrington, Highfield and Bruns 2012). There have also been moves internationally to start 'measuring' engagement more formally via social media, such as with the 'Nielsen Twitter TV Rating', which was first announced in late 2012.

The other type of programming that remains incredibly popular is, of course, sport. By virtue of its emphasis on immediacy (that is, the difficulty of audiences 'hiding' from results), and the insatiable enthusiasm of its fans, sport has become a key site of investment for the Australian television industry. Three of the four major football codes in this country (AFL, NRL and the A League) have all negotiated highly lucrative new television rights deals in recent times, with those of the AFL and NRL exceeding $1 billion in value over five years.

Both of these trends speak to the growing importance of 'live-ness' to the future of the industry, which is borne out by the fact that live sport (such as the AFL and NRL grand finals, the State of Origin and the Melbourne Cup) and live (or nearly-live) reality TV grand finales now dominate the annual lists of most-watched TV programs in Australia. This trend is reflected overseas as well. In the United States, for instance, the annual NFL Superbowl has grown in popularity, and now attracts a domestic television audience in excess of 100 million people.

At the same time, all of the main free-to-air channels have launched 'catch up' TV services—not too far away from the example set by Hulu in the United States, or the BBC's iPlayer—in which content remains available for local consumption online, for some time (typically two weeks) after its initial broadcast. In Australia, the ABC has effectively been at the forefront of this push, in the form of its iView service, which first launched in 2008. iView is now available on mobile devices such as iPads and smartphones, and through any web browser. In a way, such services are probably a more accurate reflection of the future of television than BitTorrent or YouTube, in that they are a digital platform provided by a major media organisation. Although such platforms do allow certain freedoms and new points of access, they are still reliant on the same content, and to a large extent the same genres and formats, and remain subject to some of the same old forms of top-down control.

Either way, the new platforms for TV viewing (delivered via data, rather than a broadcast signal) turn television into an increasingly asynchronous, multi-sited activity, and further complicate traditional understandings of television itself, and what Kompare (2006, p. 336) identifies as its 'established theoretical paradigms'. With these many different ways in which TV content is now accessible to the average consumer, it is becoming even more difficult to articulate what television content *is* when it exists outside of the medium that has defined it historically (Green 2008). Indeed, the myriad ways in which viewers can now access content raise several problems for the ongoing academic study of television, given that many of the discipline's most important works are premised on a particular historical form of television that may no longer be applicable to the new media environment. This is why a number of academics are increasingly referring to this as a 'post-broadcast' era (e.g. see Turner and Tay 2009).

While it is undeniable that television itself has been forced to undergo some significant changes as a result of digital media, the pressing question for the industry in the coming years will be how these may best enhance the existing television experience, and whether sufficient income can be generated via these technologies. It is also fair to say that those technologies will continue to drive further innovations in a sector that has progressively evolved and adapted to a large number of changes over more than five decades.

FURTHER READING

The following books provide very detailed insight into some of the arguments briefly outlined in this chapter. They cover how we can (or indeed, should) approach television as a field or object of study—see Gray and Lotz (2012), *Television Studies*; Turner and Cunningham (2000) *The Australian TV Book*; incredibly detailed histories of the Australian context, both commercial and public service providers—Herd (2012), *Networking: Commercial Television in Australia*; Inglis (2006) *Whose ABC? The Australian Broadcasting Corporation 1983–2006*; Ang, Hawkins and Dabboussy, (2008), *The SBS Story: The Challenge of Cultural Diversity*; a focused industry analysis—Stone (2007), *Who*

Killed Channel Nine?; an examination of culturally significant Australian television shows—McKee (2001), *Australian Television: A Genealogy of Great Moments*; and a collection that reconsiders television's role in the contemporary context—Turner and Tay (2009), *Television Studies After TV: Understanding Post-broadcast Television*.

Chapter 11

MAGAZINES

FRANCES BONNER

As with television, it is all too easy to paint a gloomy picture of decline from the available data about consumption of magazines. Television ratings show far fewer viewers for individual shows than was the case 20 years ago and magazine circulations have similarly fallen. The top-selling magazine, the *Australian Women's Weekly* (AWW), has a current circulation that is less than half its 1991 peak. The twice-yearly release of data from the Audit Bureau of Circulation (ABC) identifies some categories that have risen or held steady, but the trend overall is down. Despite this, the picture is certainly not one in which the medium is unimportant in the contemporary, highly diversified mass media world.

Data from 2009–10 still support the claim that 80 per cent of people over the age of 14 read at least one magazine a year, and if that sounds rather scant, 2012 data for audited magazine sales reveal 172 million magazines sold annually, meaning that Australians buy 5.5 magazines per second (like much of the data on which this chapter is based, this information comes from the Magazine Publishers of Australia (MPA) website, <www.magazines.org.au>). The MPA continues to assert that we are among the biggest consumers of magazines in the world. The ABC figures certainly under-estimate the number of magazines we buy, since they and the circulation figures relate to audited magazines, not the majority of titles. The number of magazines being audited has diminished substantially in recent years—only 129 were counted in mid-2012. Auditing is costly, and this decline in the number of titles finding it worthwhile has also been seen in the United States. This results in a misleading picture for scholars for several reasons. First, there are many unaudited magazines, and while they have comparatively small circulations, their presence dominates most newsagents. Second, readership data reveal that some magazines that are available only via subscription, and thus not needing to be audited because their owners already know how many magazines are consumed, rank very highly. These include the magazines of the state automobile associations and the one that provides details of Foxtel's schedule. Finally, ABC auditing applies only to Australian magazines, while many available magazines are imported.

Magazines are audited so that advertisers can buy space on the assumption that data on the number of magazines sold are defensible. Reading the MPA site brings home how very much the purpose of magazines is to carry advertising. The stories there are not about the features or even the covers, but about how to persuade advertisers to include magazines in the mix of media purchased.

Until recently, magazines were regarded as a necessary component of the largest media companies. Nine Entertainment Company (ACP Magazines), Seven Media Group (Pacific Magazines) and News Corporation (NewsLifeMedia) all included magazines in their Australian media empires. In September 2012, however, ACP Magazines—owners of the largest number of high-circulation magazines, including the *AW* and *TV Week*—was sold, for a reported $500 million, to the German media company Bauer Media Group as part of the restructuring of NEC necessary to manage its debt-load. The new company announced that it would retain the name ACP, replacing it with Bauer only for high-level managerial purposes, so I have followed that practice here. It was certainly not the first time that Australian magazines had been acquired by foreign companies: British company EMAP had previously owned a number of titles, but had itself been bought by Bauer in 2008 (Jackson 2012).

CIRCULATION AND READERSHIP

Individual circulations of all of the older magazines, whatever their type or target audience, have fallen (especially on a per capita basis). The *AWW's* circulation was 600 000 in 1945 (Bonney and Wilson 1983, p. 222), when Australia's population was around 7.5 million. Circulation figures for 1991 show the *AWW* selling 1 167 567 copies and *New Idea* 1 048 356 (Cunningham and Turner 1993, p. 368). Table 11.1 indicates a very substantial decline in 21 years—the *AWW* by 60 per cent and *New Idea* by over 70 per cent. The decline is steep and continuing: 51 million fewer audited magazines are being sold in 2012 compared to 2007.

Table 11.1 Magazine circulations, 1 January 2012 to 30 June 2012

Position	Publication	Circulation	Company
1	*Australian Women's Weekly*	465 477	ACP
2	*Better Homes and Gardens*	362 085	Pacific
3	*Woman's Day*	360 409	ACP
4	*New Idea*	303 264	Pacific
5	*That's Life*	233 118	Pacific
6	*Reader's Digest*	205 400	Reader's Digest
7	*Super Food Ideas*	197 794	NewsLifeMedia
8	*Take 5*	191 848	ACP
9	*TV Week*	163 085	ACP
10	*Who*	131 853	Pacific
11	*Cosmopolitan*	119 108	ACP
12	*Recipes+*	117 482	ACP
13	*Australian House and Garden*	116 094	ACP
14	*Delicious*	110 084	NewsLifeMedia
15	*NW*	102 251	ACP
16	*Australian Good Taste*	101 175	NewsLifeMedia
17	*Marie Claire*	97 702	Pacific
18	*OK! Magazine*	97 411	ACP
19	*Donna Hay*	94 691	NewsLifeMedia
20	*Famous*	93 534	Pacific

Source: Media week.com.

Competing titles are often owned by the same company, but the magazine market is one area where there is space for new operators—especially for special-interest publications with circulations below 30 000. New magazines appear all the time, but the failure rate is high, making it impossible to know how many actually exist. Imported magazines complicate the picture further, especially with simultaneously available air-freighted and cheaper older issues. Those that are successful may be licensed for Australian versions: Fairfax began an Australian edition of *Cosmopolitan* in 1973 (ACP immediately launched *Cleo* as direct local competition, but now owns both titles); *Time Australia* began in 1986; *Marie Claire* in 1995; *FHM* in 1997 (it ceased publication in 2012); *OK!* in 2004; *Zoo Weekly* in 2006; and *Grazia* in 2008. An Australian *Elle* was launched in 2013.

Readership is perhaps a more significant indicator than the number of magazines sold, but they are often elided or confused. Audited circulation figures are based on sales, and are thus more definite than readership, which must be ascertained by surveys that are dependent on the sample, and the knowledge and truthfulness of the people involved. Yet readership gives a more accurate impression of the actual consumption of magazines, most of which have multiple readers. Circulation gives a minimum figure and links to production, while readership figures allow for the pleasure they give, for the sharing of magazines in households, and for the chains of kinship and friendship along which magazines are passed.

Roy Morgan conducts regular readership surveys and, while circulation is down, readership is up. Whether as a result of a changed methodology in the compilation of readership figures or changed consumer behaviour—perhaps linked to great economic anxieties post-GFC—the number of reported readers per copy of most of the magazines considered has increased significantly (see Table 11.2). Where once magazines averaged two or three readers per copy, the figure is now more often five. In the year to September 2012, the (comparatively expensive) 'Women's Fashion' category had increased its readership by 6.7 per cent over the previous year (Roy Morgan website).

Table 11.2 Magazine readership, June 2012

Position	Magazine	Readership	Company
1	*Australian Women's Weekly*	2 411 000	ACP
2	*Better Homes and Gardens*	1 863 000	Pacific
3	*Woman's Day*	1 762 000	ACP
4	*New Idea*	1 193 000	Pacific
5	*National Geographic*	915 000	National Geographic
6	*Open Road* (NSW)	912 000	NTMA Publishing

Position	Magazine	Readership	Company
7	*That's Life*	910 000	Pacific
8	*Super Food Ideas*	886 000	NewsLifeMedia
9	*Australian House and Garden*	755 000	ACP
10	*Take 5*	711 000	ACP
11	*Royal Auto* (Vic)	669 000	RACV
12	*TV Week*	659 000	ACP
13	*Reader's Digest*	648 000	Reader's Digest
14	*Australian Good Taste*	604 000	NewsLifeMedia
15	*Road Ahead* (Qld)	577 000	RACQ
16	*Cosmopolitan*	530 000	ACP
17	*Foxtel Magazine*	527 000	ACP
18	*Australian Geographic*	513 000	ACP
19	*Who*	503 000	Pacific
20	*MasterChef Magazine*	480 000	NewsLifeMedia

Source: Media week.com.

ECONOMICS

The print media have two sources of income: advertising and cover price. The relationship between them and the proportion they contribute to costs and profits vary from title to title. A higher cover price does not necessarily mean fewer ads. *Shop til You Drop*, with a cover price of $7.80 a month is 35 per cent display advertising, but since virtually its entire 'editorial' content is direct product presentation with availability and cost details, it could easily be assessed at 98 per cent ads. Magazines with high production values paid for by high cover prices rather than much advertising have not survived the last three years. The cheapest mass circulation weekly magazine, *That's Life* (currently priced at $3), has about 23 per cent advertising content, a significant increase on its initial proportion twelve years ago. If those contests that comprise a significant proportion of the magazine and offer proprietary prizes are included in the category, then advertising increases to 38 per cent, but this is not formally paid-for space. *That's Life* depends primarily on a large circulation (over 230 000), and controls one of the major costs for magazines by avoiding expensive glossy paper. *TV Week*, which carries few ads, needs none to be profitable—its provision of detailed TV program information means it pays little for content.

This should indicate that attracting readers is more important than pleasing advertisers. Yet one of the most notable events in the history of magazines in Australia indicates otherwise. In 1982, the *AWW*—then, as now, the country's highest-circulation magazine—shifted from weekly publication, which had persisted from its establishment in 1932, to monthly. Circulation was not falling; it was recording what was then its highest circulation ever (selling well over 800 000 copies per issue and occasionally tipping the one million mark). The shift followed increased advertising charges intended to cover a glossier format. Advertisers were reluctant to pay more than was being charged by the competition—*Woman's Day* and *New Idea*—so advertising volume dropped (Windschuttle 1988, pp. 46–7). The change of frequency to monthly was thus based on advertisers' behaviour, not readers' wishes.

Despite Australia's high level of magazine consumption, only 5.2 per cent of total 2010 advertising expenditure is spent on magazines. Advertisers much prefer television, where combining free-to-air and pay accounted for 32.77 per cent. The very significant recent shift is shown by 26.3 per cent now being devoted to online advertising (these figures—the most recent available at the time of writing—are derived from Sinclair).

MAGAZINES' LINKS TO OTHER MEDIA

Yet magazines, television and the online world are quite intricately involved with each other—especially those magazines published by the major media corporations, which are prime sites for the promotion of other company products. Celebrity features—notable in virtually all large-circulation magazines—promote the current products of television and film personalities far more often than they gossip about royal personages. Celebrity coverage is not restricted to women's magazines: televised sport is regularly promoted through stories about sports personalities in magazines targeted at men. Television celebrities feature in teenage and lads' magazines, and several magazines—such as *TV Week* and *TV Soap*—are entirely about television.

Co-productions between conventional television production houses and magazine companies have flourished. The second-highest circulation magazine, *Better Homes and Gardens,* pre-dated the high rating Channel Seven television show, but the combination is very highly integrated. *Money Magazine* and *Burke's Backyard* were both established after the success of the respective television shows. The former ran from 2004–12 without the television tie-in; the latter continues even though the show ceased in 2002. Most ABC magazines are produced by NewsLifeMedia: *Gardening Australia* is a direct spin-off from the television program, but *Delicious* is more general, with links to various ABC food shows. ACP's joint venture with BBC Magazines led to the production of the *Top Gear Australia* magazine following the success of the BBC show on SBS before SBS and then Nine's Australian versions; unlike the latter, it continues, as does its MPA award-winning website. *Grand Designs Australia* shows that pay TV programs have magazine spin-offs too, though it is produced by Universal Magazines, a Sydney-based company that manages 50 (unaudited) magazines and thirteen websites.

Newspaper-inserted magazines (NIMs) are a feature of almost all major newspapers' weekend editions, in another blurring of media distinctiveness. News Limited's *Australian Magazine* and Fairfax's *Good Weekend* resemble generalist titles, and are much favoured by up-market advertisers. Both companies have additional monthly glossy inserts for their leading titles, and the *Australian Financial Review*'s two monthly magazines are even more up-market. NIMs are audited separately from either newspapers or magazines, and in the January–June 2012 period all lost circulation, with Fairfax titles losing considerably more than News Limited ones.

DISTRIBUTION AND SUPERMARKET SALES

A further significant part of the industry is the distributor, the intermediary between publisher and point of sale. There are now two main distribution companies, each linked with a larger media company: long-time market leader Gordon and Gotch (Seven Media Group) and Network Services (ACP). Distributors are especially important in Australia because subscriptions are comparatively unimportant here. Most magazines sell about 90 per cent of their copies through newsagents or supermarkets.

Supermarkets place the highest circulation magazines—significantly, women's (including gossip) and home magazines—at checkouts, with a comparatively limited range of others available elsewhere in store. Details on what proportion of magazine sales has shifted to the supermarket are unavailable, but estimates go as high as 30 per cent for some titles. The main impact on these magazines has been in terms of attracting the 'floating' purchaser. The weekly women's titles in particular compete fiercely for uncommitted buyers, and the increase in sensational stories trumpeted on the cover is attributed to this. Gossip magazines like *Who* and *NW* are designed for supermarket checkouts, with 'teaser' statements on the cover to intrigue consumers waiting to be served.

SEGMENTING THE MAGAZINE MARKET

The magazine market is a highly segmented one, divided demographically and in terms of interests. Gender forms the basis of the greatest division, with the majority of all individual audited magazines sold being women's weeklies and monthlies. Of the top 20 circulating magazines, eleven are women's titles and the remainder non-gender specific. Not all of the latter appeal equally—the five food titles and the two house and garden magazines are targeted primarily at women, but do have male buyers as well as readers. The two other titles are *Reader's Digest* and *TV Week*, although the latter is categorised by the ABC as 'mass women's'. *Club Marine* (85 598) and *Men's Health* (73 111) are the highest selling magazines targeting men rather than women.

The term 'men's magazines' is problematic. It can be used to refer to magazines that appeal primarily to male purchasers—including not only sports and motor vehicle magazines, but also *Business Review Weekly* and *New Scientist*, both of which have about 30 per cent female readers—or it can be used for sex magazines, the central content of which is photographs of naked and near-naked women. The distinction, based on displayed female genitalia, is clear, but in recent years a complicating factor has developed. One of the magazine success stories of the last twelve or so years has been 'lads' mags'—men's lifestyle magazines like *FHM* and *Zoo Weekly* that, while (just) clothing their pin-ups, carry sex-based stories alongside more general male-oriented articles. While these experienced about a decade of reasonable Australian sales, the last few years have seen a collapse in circulation. *FHM* ceased publication early in 2012; *Zoo Weekly* had the second greatest 2012 fall of circulation—over 22 per cent to 63 276. In 2010, it had been the highest circulating men's magazine. Indeed, from being a category with ten or more ABC counted titles, there are now only *Zoo Weekly*, *Men's Health* and *Australian Men's Fitness*, in a category called Men's Lifestyle. As far as the audited magazines are concerned, men have returned to their specialised interests—especially motor vehicles.

The ABC divides the 129 audited magazines into sixteen categories, though the General Interest category combines genuine general interest (*Reader's Digest*) with single examples of specialised titles like *Dance Australia*. The largest number of titles (24) are in the Motoring category, followed by Home and Garden (14), Women's Lifestyle and Fashion (13), General Interest (12), Food and Entertainment (11), Mass Women's (10), Sports (9), Computing, Games and Info Tech, Buying and Selling, and Health and Family (6 each); Business and Finance, and Children's (4 each); and Men's Lifestyle, Women's Youth and Music, and Movies (3 each). The remaining category, Craft, comprises the two remaining titles. Newsagent magazine racks indicate a much larger number and range of unaudited magazines. Indeed, what appear to be very marginal interests can be covered by a substantial number of titles: my local newsagent stocks at least sixteen different titles under the category Aviation and Defence.

Generally speaking, women's interests are seen to be more homogeneous across the field of gender-specific magazines than men's are. The *AWW* is both the highest-circulation Australian magazine and one of the oldest. Its concerns have from the beginning delineated women's interests. The chapter titles in Susan Sheridan et al.'s (2002) study of the magazine since 1946 list these as: the housewife as consumer; sex, romance and marriage; motherhood; women's work; house and garden; food and cooking; health; and fashion and beauty (2002, p. iii). This underplays the role of celebrities throughout the period, but otherwise still describes women's magazine content across the field. Because 'women's work' describes domestic rather than paid employment, with the partial exception of the celebrity stories, all these concerns are with the self and the private, personal world.

An Australian version of the US magazine *Cosmopolitan* and the all-Australian *Cleo* launched in 1972/3. They combined aspects of the (less radical) feminist ideas then circulating about equal rights in the workplace and greater sexual freedom for women with beauty and fashion sections into very marketable products. *Cleo* differentiated itself by a male centrefold designed as a riposte to the pervasive use of the female nude in men's magazines and workplace calendars.

What magazines reveal women as having in common is in stark contrast to what men are shown to share—sex, sport, motor vehicles and, if news and business magazines are included as men's, the public world. This distinction can easily be demonstrated by contrasting baby knitting patterns from *New Idea* or hints on pleasing your man sexually from *Cleo* with interviews with the federal treasurer in *AFR Smart Investor* or comments on the Australian cricket team's morale in *Zoo Weekly*. To do this alone, though, is to ignore some signs of change, which can be seen in the prevalence of male fashion features (in both NIMs and *Business Review Weekly*) as well as the success of *Men's Health,* or stories of international campaigns against sexual violence in *Marie Claire*.

There are four audited children's magazines, targeted either at preschoolers or 'tweens' (children aged 6–12 years). Gendering is evident in both groups, and most visible in those titles aimed at girls: *Total Girl* and *Little Angel*. The previously ungendered *K-Zone* now primarily targets boys, as does *Mania*, while the earlier boys title *Dmag* is no longer explicitly age-based, being categorised as Computing, Games and Info Tech. Gendering continues for teenagers, with girls having moved on completely by the time they are 12 to *Girlfriend* or *Girl Power*, followed by *Dolly,* although data indicate a strong readership of gossip magazines among this age group (Jackson 2008). Boys still have a number of years of presumed non-interest in magazines before *Two Wheels* and *Tracks* cut in, unless they continue a specialised interest in computer games, which the category shift of *Dmag* reflects.

While gender-specificity in address is inappropriate for magazines like *Reader's Digest*, *Australian Geographic* or most travel magazines, no other single demographic factor operates as strongly for magazines as gender. More complex segmentation can be described as 'gender plus', with the additional factor differing according to gender. Women's magazines are further segmented demographically, especially on the basis of age and to a lesser extent socio-economic factors (see below), but magazines targeting men far more regularly base their segmentation on interest. Many magazines are targeted solely on the basis of interest, but these are frequently characterised as targeted more at one gender than another: fishing, computers, chess—male; home decorating, art—female. Gardening probably stands as the major non-gender-specific interest area for which magazines cater well.

WOMEN'S MAGAZINES

Women's magazines represent the dominant segment of the magazine market, and are by far the most studied, so I want now to examine their further segmentation. The trajectory through which the magazine-reading woman passes is well mapped out, determined by the three characteristics of gender, age and income—although as yet none of the main companies has titles in each age group. The ideal Pacific Magazines consumer moves from *Total Girl* to *Girlfriend* through a small flirtation with ACP's *Cosmo* or *Cleo* before returning to *Marie Claire* and then to *Vogue Australia*, ending up with *New Idea*. The ACP ideal reader starts with the Pacific 'tween' titles, moves to *Cosmo* and *Cleo*, then takes *New Weekly* for gossip, or perhaps if wealthier has an interlude with *Harper's Bazaar*, before coming to rest with *Woman's Day* and the *AWW*. There are many additional magazines that can supplement this—bridal ones, for example—but the important aspect is that at each stage in the progress from a child to a mature woman an appropriate title is available to give advice, principally on matters of consumption. *Cosmopolitan* developed a personalised version of a segment of this with the launch of *Cosmo Bride* in 2003, followed by *Cosmo Pregnancy*.

It is worth considering *Cosmopolitan* a little further, because it has been the subject of a major study on globalisation that examined 44 different versions of the magazine. David Machin and Theo van Leeuwen (2003, 2007) discuss the 'global branding' involved, and the extent to which—even though national variation inflects individual versions—the discourse of the '*Cosmo* girl' persistently shows her as someone oriented to remarkably similarly framed social interaction, both sexually and at work. She signifies her allegiance to the *Cosmo* 'community' through her individualised consumer behaviour, rather than any more collective or cultural belonging.

The ABC differentiates women's magazines into 'mass women's' and 'women's lifestyle and fashion'. The latter has more titles and the more desirable reader profile, but it is a very homogenising grouping paying little attention to age or publication frequency and allocating some gossip magazines to each category. Desirable readers are 25–39-year-old ABCs—the marketing world describes socio-economic groups from A (the highest) to E (the lowest, a group virtually never mentioned in the trade papers)—attractive to the cosmetic, clothing and accessory advertisers whose patronage is a necessity for a magazine like this to survive.

In the discussion of market gaps and niches that has accompanied the launches of new women's magazines over the last 35 years, almost all the focus is on women under 39. Mass-circulation titles like the gossip sheets *OK!, NW, Who Weekly* and *Famous* were pitched at this younger readership, as were the more sexual *Cosmopolitan* and *Cleo* and those seeking a largely fashion-defined market, like *Madison. Grazia*, launched in 2008, pitched a little higher, though only to 44, but differentiated itself, as its cover line says, as 'Australia's only fashion weekly'. Such claims are aimed at advertisers rather than resulting from analysis of actual purchasers.

The 2012 MPA Magazine of the Year and Women's Fashion Magazine of the Year targets the same under-39 group, but looks very different from the rest. *Frankie* hit its 50th issue in November/December 2012, has a circulation of 58 631, and is published by the small Queensland company Morrison Media. It started very much as an independent production, and has worked to retain signs of this—matt paper, a very self-consciously quirky address and a subtitle that, quite accurately, places 'design, art and photography' before 'fashion'. Although 'craft' follows 'music' after 'fashion', the kind of fashion the magazine espouses is decidedly craft-inflected, and it rarely if ever carries any cosmetic or perfume advertising, let alone from the usual multinational companies. Features from its regular stable of writers tend to be anecdotal, even when they do (occasionally) concern celebrities. Recently, it has produced *Smith Journal*, a spin-off magazine for 'the discerning gent about town', according to its website.

The top three mass-circulation magazines, all of which started before 1950, are regarded as still catering adequately to the older women who have grown up with them and remained loyal through satisfaction or habit. Somewhat similar are the readers' own story magazines targeted at women, *Take 5* and *That's Life*, started in 1994 and 1998 respectively rapidly achieved top ten circulations. They did aim at an older grouping—indeed, neither named an upper limit—but their arrival caused little industry excitement. The lower cover price, the prominence of competitions and puzzles, the poorer quality paper and the paucity of advertising indicate that the target audience for these publications is working class—or, in media speak, down-market. The euphemistic phrase about *Take 5*'s readers on the ACP website mentions 'the heart of middle Australia'. Distinctively, these magazines ignore celebrities, having their features generated from readers' contributions, which are solicited each issue, paid for and revised by magazine staffers. These features, which are the mainstay of the publications, are supplemented by the usual service sections: cooking, fashion, beauty and advice columns.

Unlike the claims of a 'community' around more up-market magazines like the editions of *Cosmopolitan* analysed by Machin and Van Leeuwen, the readers' own story magazines operate to produce a participatory community of readers who exchange information about the events in their lives, show off their children, try to win prizes and whose vicarious involvement in others' lives is closer to that of neighbours than of looking on at the distant scandals of the famous, or an idealised world of young white-collar workers. There is something of a feminised version of the participatory world of talkback radio, but this time not organised around the public world—rather around shared domestic familial events. Although they rarely use readers' own stories, tween and teen magazines also attempt to generate a community of readers and producers through an assertion of shared activities and attitudes—particularly potent for those of an age where they want constantly to be part of an in-group.

Women move from having some choice as tweens and young teenagers to a variety of titles in their young adulthood and prime of life, returning to a more limited range from middle age on. This picture of a few callow possibilities preceding a clamouring of sleek attractive rivals followed by a restricted and rather dull range of options might seem a caricature of the life options of the conventional feminine woman. While public discourse, both feminist and medical, assures women that life does not end with menopause, and editorial content in women's magazines endorses this, the primary discourse of women's magazines—which is carried by the availability of a range of titles supported by advertisers—continues to find women much over 45 decidedly unattractive. Intermittently, there have been attempts to overcome the short-sightedness of advertisers' distaste for the older market, and thus magazine's ability to service them. *Ita, Elevator* and *Life etc.* have all tried and folded, even though the first had the experience and name of the respected editor Ita Buttrose and the last was Australian Broadcasting Corporation-badged, with television and Radio National tie-ins.

BOX 11.1: THE ARRIVAL OF NEW STYLE WOMEN'S MAGAZINES

The rise of Women's Liberation/second wave feminism in Australia from 1969 challenged the depiction of women's interests being circumscribed by domestic, family concerns. As many of the new ideas (equal pay, child care, safe abortions) gained some public purchase, they could be mentioned—just a little—in some of the existing magazines, but those ideas clustering around greater sexual freedom provided an opportunity for large media organisations to capitalise on, and retain, younger readers. In 1972, Fairfax (then the owner of

Woman's Day) bought the rights to publish an Australian edition of the American success, *Cosmopolitan*, which had been made over by a new editor, *Sex and the Single Girl* author, the pre-feminist Helen Gurley Brown. ACP needed to respond and its influential editor, Ita Buttrose, had already been pushing the owner's son Kerry Packer to address the (less radical) of the new ideas attractive to 18–24-year-old women. Buttrose succeeded, and the fully Australian *Cleo* managed to launch first. Like *Cosmopolitan*, it mixed sexual information with advice aimed to give its female readers more confidence in their role in the white-collar workforce, but its cheeky point of difference lay in the male centrefold, an assertive riposte to the pervasive use of female nudes in men's magazines and workplace calendars. *Paper Giants*, a high-rating television dramatisation of Buttrose's *Cleo* campaign, screened in 2011. The initial distinctiveness of both *Cosmopolitan* and *Cleo* in the magazine market has been eroded. They are now both owned by ACP/Bauer.

CHANGES IN MAGAZINE CONTENT

Desktop publishing has made possible a great proliferation of magazines catering to interests that might once have seemed far too marginal to support a dedicated magazine—antique tractors, for example. It has also led to the development of a significant number of independent magazines, sometimes called microzines, which may be specialised (*Sneaker Freaker*), or focus on fashion and entertainment, but with a greater concern for the quality of writing and graphic design. Megan le Masurier (2012) has analysed the phenomenon and noted the importance of their pro-am production, their design consciousness and the defiance by which their producers are digital natives committed to the production of print artefacts (2012, pp. 393–5). An international phenomenon, they may be short-lived, but Australian example *Monster Children* started in 2002 and is now, with issue 36, being published five times a year.

Food magazines represent the most recent new category to be evident in higher circulating titles. Five of the top 20 circulating magazines solely address this concern. Food has long been one of the areas considered in the service sections of mass-market magazines, and many of the home and garden titles also devote space to it, but the move to dedicated titles has come in little more than the last ten years, and it is evident across the socio-economic scale. In all instances, women dominate the readership of these magazines, though the proportions of males increase with the move upmarket. In part, this increased presence reflects the importance of lifestyle to contemporary conceptions of individuals and the societies in which they live, but it also indicates the importance of food to the concept of lifestyle. Rather than serving just to keep us alive and hopefully giving us pleasure, food now speaks of how we see ourselves and how we would like others to see us.

It is also an area where the guidance of experts is avidly sought. Nikolas Rose (1999) notes more generally how: 'Individuals act upon themselves and their families in terms of the languages, values and techniques made available to them by the professions [and proto-professions] disseminated through the apparatuses of the mass media.' (1999, p. 88) No longer is cooking solely a pursuit of women following their mothers' guidance and a limited range of cookery books. Now food preparation is a matter involving continually varying choices; it relates to fashion and change, and dishes may be derided as dated or welcomed back as sadly neglected (like the prawn cocktail). New ingredients become available and consumers need to be instructed on their use. Precisely the same situation applies to the category of home and garden magazines, although several titles preceded the prominence of lifestyle. Of the media disseminating lifestyle advice, magazines are probably second only to television.

Further instances of expertise-guided self-regulation can be seen in dedicated parenting magazines and in the proliferation of magazines looking specifically at health. As both Rosalind Coward (1989) and Rose himself (2007) note, the responsibility for personal well-being has shifted from the medical profession to the individual concerned. Magazines like the sector leader *Women's Health* and the lower circulation *Men's Health* both combine medical advice with fitness concerns to inform us about what we should be doing to take care of ourselves, especially in terms of activities and foods that promote health or contribute to disease.

There is nothing new about magazines carrying celebrity stories, but the extent to which this now constitutes a category of its own has probably only existed in Australia for fifteen years. Four of the top 20 by circulation rely on celebrity gossip, varying the proportions of admiring to exposé stories, *Who* and *OK!* being kinder than *NW* and *Famous,* although all four and the more diversified *New Idea* and *Woman's Day* contain snidely captioned paparazzi photographs.

Celebrity stories are a *sine qua non* for most high-circulation magazines, not only because celebrity is one of the principal ways in which so many public and private topics are now discussed, but also because celebrities are the prime way in which magazines attract the eye in the first place. When magazine editors other than financial and scientific ones talk of 'news', it is rare for them to be referring to anything other than celebrities. Certainly it is on this basis that *Grazia* claims to be concerned with fashion and news. Editors regularly rate celebrities by the extra number of copies sold when they are featured on the cover. Of the high-circulation magazines, only the downmarket 'readers' own stories' and the supermarket recipe magazines regularly publish issues with no celebrity content at all.

CONCLUSION

The Australian magazine industry is dominated by just three major companies, all with wider media interests. Although it does not attract a substantial proportion of the Australian advertising dollar, advertising is absolutely central to magazines' operations. The centrality of celebrity to magazine content and to media promotion, together with shared television and magazine titles, means that synergies are easy to achieve. All magazines with significant circulations now have complementary websites, which are especially important for younger readers. Women's magazines have higher circulations than men's magazines, but both genders, all ages and socio-economic groups and almost all interests are catered to—however unevenly. The persistence with which the medium provides expertise to guide readers' lifestyles and deportment is remarkable.

BOX 11.2: RESPONDING TO THE ONLINE THREAT

Discussion of the internationally observable decline in magazine circulation, and in the proportion of available advertising generally, identifies the development of online alternatives as the principal culprit. Consumers are able to get gossip, fashion, health advice, gardening tips—all the content for which they once relied on magazines—from this other source, and apparently for free. The story is a familiar one for other media, like television and newspapers.

The first magazine response has been to establish a related online presence. Deena Ingham and Alexis Weedon (2008) note how obligatory it now is for magazines to have an online presence, and the benefits this has for the reach of the title and addressing readers' time-poverty, but the print version still generates the most revenue. The ABC has developed a new measure called the Masthead Metric to allow digital editions to be counted along with print circulation. Results from the first release of this show the *AWW* with print sales of 465 477 while its digital sales are 5963, leading to a total circulation of 471 440 (MPA website). The more limited free-to-access web presence is not included here, though presumably it is more frequently visited. The industry recognises that tablets have been the technological game-changer. Critics note that both digital editions and limited free websites assume passive readers, and fail to take advantage of the interactivity that is key to online behaviour, though the increasing use of QR codes aims to address this.

Some magazines, though, have developed an expanded presence combining print with substantial online material into an integrated, interactive whole. An example here is *Mindfood* (sub-titled 'Smart Thinking'), a monthly lifestyle glossy founded in 2008 by Michael McHugh for his 'integrated media' family company. *Mindfood* addresses its readers explicitly as part of a community and combines the monthly magazine with a website updated far more frequently, which encourages visitors to sign up for daily emails and download podcasts, and promotes its app on both sites. Advertising is carried across all of its outlets. The magazine ostensibly targets both men and women, but from its content appears to tend more towards women. Internal evidence suggests 30–49 as the age range targeted.

The other response involves targeting the online world as a niche magazine market. As well as game magazines, which have also been in existence for much longer and are one of the more resilient of recent magazine categories, there are now also guides to the iPad, iPhone and other interfaces. The majority of them are imported (usually British), but there are also Australian ones, including *Australian iPhone* (in its ninth edition at the time of writing), *Australian Android Magazine* and, less precisely targeted, *Techlife Australia*.

FURTHER READING

Useful websites

Frankie: <www.frankie.com.au>
Magazine Publishers of Australia: <www.magazines.org.au>
Media Week: <www.mediaweek.com.au/magazines>
Mindfood: <www.mindfood.com>
Roy Morgan: <www.roy morgan.com>

Chapter 12

ADVERTISING AND MARKETING

JOHN SINCLAIR

Advertising, while not a medium of communication in itself, historically is the force that sustains all commercial media. More than just providing the main source of income for media owners, advertising gives the commercial media their characteristic look and sound, and orients the range of entertainment and information that the media offer us towards those audiences that advertisers want to reach. Advertising is thus a cultural industry that uses the media to connect the producers of consumer goods and services with potential markets. At its most basic, advertising is simply the most 'visible end of the marketing operation' (Caro 1981, p. 5), integrated with the manufacturing–marketing–media complex of modern societies (Sinclair 2012).

The way in which this institutional complex works is that manufacturers of consumer goods, and also service industries such as retailers and banks, buy time from the broadcast media in the form of 'spots' for commercials, page space for advertising in print media, or display or search ads on the internet. Large advertisers usually do this through an advertising agency. The selection of the medium and the schedule or position bought will depend on the size of the budget and the prospective size and type of market for the advertiser's product. For example, high-budget advertisers of mass-consumption goods and services will choose expensive prime-time television spots, while producers of 'up-market' goods and services such as investments, imported cars and international airlines will seek their prospects in the small but affluent readership of the prestige press.

Thus it is not just a question of reaching the largest number of people, but of choosing a medium that communicates with the appropriate kind of people for the advertiser. Different media reach different people in accordance with the kind of information and entertainment they carry, and for this reason some critical theorists say that media content only exists to attract an audience that the media can 'sell' to advertisers (Smythe 1977). However, if advertisers want to understand how audiences come to be sold, they need to take into account which kinds of media content appeal to which kinds of people. 'Media-buying' advertising agencies give them advice on this.

FROM SPONSORS TO SPOTS

Advertisers are still sometimes referred to as 'sponsors'. This is a term that comes from an earlier era in the development of broadcast media, when advertising agencies not only bought time and prepared advertising material for their clients, but also produced programs for them—typically plays and quiz shows. All the broadcast station had to do was put the programs to air. This system declined with the arrival of television and the advent of the 'ratings' system. Advertisers still can and do pay to have their names associated with a certain program as its 'sponsor'. However, with the notable exception of an emerging trend towards 'branded content'—such as advertiser-sponsored 'infotainment' programs on television or planted on social media (Bainbridge 2005)—advertisers and agencies do not produce the programs as they did under the old sponsorship system.

Under the current system in Australia, television stations purchase programs from production studios or produce them in house, and sell advertisers commercial spots during broadcast program breaks in accordance with the size and type of audience for that program. This audience is measured by 'the ratings', a statistical estimate of the proportion of the audience that has its sets tuned to the program, and of the demographic characteristics (age, gender, socio-economic status) of that audience.

Newspapers and magazines have their equivalent with independently audited circulation figures, so advertisers know what they are buying, while the internet measures 'click-throughs' to an advertiser's pages.

At first sight, the system of running broadcast media on the basis of ratings may seem to 'give the people what they want', and therefore to be in the public interest of a democratic society. There is no doubt that the present system is an improvement over the narrow sponsor control that once prevailed. However, critics are concerned that advertisers can still control programming in an aggregate sense—that is, program content and schedules are made to appeal to the kind of people who buy the kind of products that can be advertised in this way, so that we get 'a dramaturgy reflecting the demographics of the supermarket' (Barnouw 1979, p. 73). While all of us have to use the supermarket to some extent, there are identifiable minority audiences with low purchasing power who may be neglected in program offerings, such as the elderly, the poor and people of non-English speaking backgrounds, as well as less specific audiences with minority tastes and interests.

In the case of the press, critics have been concerned that advertisers might put pressure on editors to suppress news unfavourable to their business. Although there is evidence that this happens from time to time, some argue that it is not in the interests of an editor to accede to such pressure because of the loss of credibility that the newspaper would suffer in the long run.

ORIGINS OF ADVERTISING

How has Australia come to adopt a system of social communication in which the predominant media of information and entertainment are funded by retail chains and the manufacturers of shampoo, chocolate bars and the like? To understand this, we need to look back to the end of the nineteenth century when the production of packaged and branded household goods became widespread in all industrialised countries. Previously, manufacturers would produce generic goods in bulk, so you would have a pound of oats weighed out for you instead of picking up a packet of Uncle Toby's. Some of the best known brand names in Australia (Rosella and Fosters, for example) and the world (Heinz in the United States, Cadbury in the United Kingdom) date from this period. They were soon joined by branded 'durable' consumer goods: Gillette razors, Kodak cameras, Ford cars.

Advertising prior to this era existed just as a form of dealing in newspaper space for commission, and although there was already much retail advertising, advertised 'brands' were typically patent medicines and tonics (the origin of the world's best-known brand, Coca-Cola). From this time on, however, manufacturers in industrial capitalist societies built up national sales organisations, using advertising in conjunction with other marketing strategies in packaging and distribution. At the same time, advertising was helping itself to become established as an integral part of the new age of corporate capitalism.

All this could not have happened without the cooperation of communication media in these countries, and a corresponding process can be seen in the commercialisation of the newspaper. In Australia, this was led by Keith Murdoch (father of Rupert). He modelled the Melbourne *Herald* on the financial and editorial innovations already developed in Britain by Lord Northcliffe, particularly in the sale of 'display' advertising space rather than the columns of classified advertisements that had characterised the nineteenth century newspaper. Revenue from advertising more than covered production costs, so that the cover price could be kept low and the newspaper could become a mass rather than an elite medium, profiting from 'selling' the readership to advertisers.

Radio arrived in the 1920s, but it was not until the 1930s that it began to catch up with the press as a mass medium for advertising. This process was accelerated once newspaper companies themselves became involved in building up radio networks. Such developments prompted advertisers to pay more attention to audience measurement. Ratings and 'market research' had their beginnings as advertising sought to consolidate its position by means of the commercial application of the language and techniques of the social sciences.

The international manufacturing–marketing–media complex that we know today did not really begin to emerge until after World War II, as US corporations seized opportunities to invest overseas in industrial development and to exploit the relative affluence that accompanied it. Among these corporations were the new US television networks and the advertising agencies of Madison Avenue, as well as the consumer goods manufacturers that were growing from national into trans-national corporations at that time. Europe, Australia and the other former British dominions, as well as the newly independent developing nations, all experienced these forms of expansion to a greater or lesser extent. In Australia, it meant that foreign investment became available for industrial development, including the manufacture of consumer goods which formerly had been imported. It was precisely in this sense that General Motors could claim that the Holden that it produced here from 1948 on was 'Australia's own car'. The advent of commercial television soon followed, replete with US programs—but thanks to government regulation, carrying only Australian-made advertisements—and then, in the 1960s, the takeover of the bulk of the Australian advertising business by US agencies, which either set up their own subsidiaries or entered into various arrangements with Australian agencies (see Box 12.1 later in the chapter).

ADVERTISING AND GLOBALISATION

To understand the structure, extent and significance of the advertising industry in Australia today, it is necessary to see it not just in the context of international post-war Americanisation, but as a leading instance of more recent and intensive processes now referred to as 'globalisation'. This term covers the apparent integration of local and national economies and societies into a globally unified political, economic and cultural order. This order is not 'American', nor is it European or Japanese—even if corporations based in those countries are the prime movers in its creation and its principal beneficiaries. In fact, one of the major characteristics of globalisation is the diminished power of individual nation-states over economic decisions, relative to trans-national or 'global' corporations.

In Australia, the process is evident among advertisers, agencies and the media. In the case of the trans-national advertisers, globalisation can be seen in the increased capacity to market goods and services on a global basis—that is, corporate coordination of the production, distribution and sales of goods or services in several national markets. This has always been a defining characteristic of the 'trans-national' corporation, but it now takes more complex and dispersed forms. Even the largest of these corporations do not market just the same products everywhere. Coca-Cola and McDonald's, for example, produce different products in accordance with the cultural differences of the localities, nations and regions where they operate, a practice known as 'glocalisation' (Robertson 1995). There are also franchise operations, international brand licensing arrangements and joint ventures between trans-national corporations. In the liquor industry, to take one major category of advertisers, trans-national corporations make manufacturing, distribution and licensing arrangements between themselves so that in Australia, for example, Foster's Group markets the Miller and Grolsch beers made by its UK parent, SAB Miller, while Foster's Lager is made and distributed in North America by a Canadian brewer, Molson. Globalisation also implies that global corporations share oligopolistic dominance in the various national markets in which they operate—that is, they may use their market power to keep out or take over smaller competitors, rather than fight each other. Finally, although globalisation is characterised by a conglomeration of corporate ownership, there tends to be a dispersal of operations and management. There may no longer be a 'head office' in New York, London or Tokyo, as in the days of the multi-national corporation of the 1960s and 1970s, but rather independently managed divisions of the same conglomerate, notionally separated as if by 'Chinese walls'.

BIG SPENDERS

Each year, the trade press publishes commercial research that ranks the national advertisers according to their media advertising budgets—that is, how much they spend through their advertising agencies on media time and space. Table 12.1 lists the top 25 advertisers by estimated expenditure for 2012, as measured by global research company Nielsen Holdings, and reported in *AdNews* on 21 September 2012. It shows that just under half of the top 25 advertisers were trans-national companies or their subsidiaries. However, as usual, the trans-nationals dominated certain product categories. Most of them were in fast-moving consumer goods (FMCG)—packaged food and drink, household and/or 'personal care' goods—and fast food: Reckitt Benckiser, McDonald's, Unilever, Nestlé, Yum! Restaurants and Kraft. Some of the global motor vehicle manufacturers—Toyota, Hyundai and Volkswagen—are also on the list, although fewer of them than usual. Of the largest Australian advertisers, major retailers are prominent, as is customary and reflecting the exceptional degree of concentration of ownership in retailing in this country. Wesfarmers and Woolworths, both with their several branded chains, head the list, with Harvey Norman not far behind. As is also usual, the aggregated media advertising expenditure of the Australian federal government is found high on the list, and the governments of the Eastern states—the most populous—are also ranked. Governments are big advertisers, and so are media corporations themselves, notably represented here by News Corporation, Village and Nine Entertainment.

It is worth noting that several of the US, European and Japanese-based trans-national companies on the list are to be found with at least equal prominence in other major world advertising markets. The Anglo-Dutch FMCG giant Unilever, for instance, is one of the biggest advertisers in the world, while Toyota dominates the automotive category globally. The high expenditures of both Australian and trans-national advertisers are an indicator not just of the absolute size of their budgets, but also of the media on which the budgets are spent. Throughout the world, notwithstanding the recent and rapid growth of the internet as an advertising medium, television remains the preferred medium of trans-national mass consumer goods manufacturers. Furthermore, if we look at the relationship between the largest advertisers and the advertising agencies, we find that a relatively small number of agencies capture the majority of advertising turnover, which implies that they are dealing with the biggest spending clients, and that these clients tend towards television—the most expensive medium.

These trends have held constant in spite of the considerable impact of the GFC on advertising expenditure in Australia and the rest of the world. However huge the numbers may seem, the level of expenditure for each of the largest advertisers is down appreciably on the 2007–08 figures given in the previous edition of this book. However, the 2011–12 tallies do show a recovery from those of 2009–10, the worst years of the GFC.

Table 12.1 Top 25 advertisers

Rank 2012	Rank 2011	Advertiser group/ advertiser	2012 est. spend $m	Key brands
1	1	Wesfarmers Ltd	110–115	Coles, Bunnings, Officeworks, Kmart, Target, Liquorland, 1st Choice, Vintage Cellars
2	4	Woolworths Ltd	75–80	Woolworths, Big W, Dick Smith, Masters Home Improvement, Dan Murphy's, BWS
3	2	Commonwealth Government	70–75	Medibank Private, Australia Post, NBN Co, Australian Health Management, Meat & Livestock Australia, Departments of Health and Ageing, Human Services, Defence
4	3	Harvey Norman Holdings Limited	70–75	Harvey Norman, Domayne, Joyce Mayne
5	7	Victorian Government	40–45	Transport Accident Commission, VicRoads, Worksafe, Cancer Council, TAFE Colleges, Ambulance Victoria, Departments of Justice, and Sustainability and Environment
6	10	Reckitt Benckiser	35–40	Strepsils, Nurofen, Napisan, Finish, Airwick, Harpic, Dettol, Pine O Cleen, Easy Off Bam, Lemsip
7	15	Toyota Motor Corporation	35–40	Toyota, Lexus, Hino
8	5	NSW Government	35–40	Roads and Maritime Services, Sydney Opera House Trust, Cancer Institute, Destination NSW, Sydney Water, Departments of Health and Primary Industries
9	11	McDonald's Family Restaurants	35–40	McDonald's Family Restaurants, McCafé
10	8	Telstra Corporation Limited	35–40	Telstra, Sensis

Rank 2012	Rank 2011	Advertiser group/ advertiser	2012 est. spend $m	Key brands
11	21	News Corporation Limited	30–35	News Limited, News Digital Media, 20th Century Fox Film Distributors and Home Entertainment
12	14	Suncorp Group	30–35	AAMI, GIO, APIA, Bingle, Suncorp-Metway, Shannons
13	6	Commonwealth Bank of Australia	30–35	Commonwealth Bank, Bankwest, Colonial First State
14	17	SingTel Group	30–35	Optus, Virgin Mobile
15	27	Village Roadshow Group	25–30	Village Cinemas, Warner Village Theme Park, Roadshow Film Distributors and Home Video
16	9	Unilever Group	25–30	Dove, Lynx, Vaseline, Sunsilk, Rexona, Impulse, Omo, Lipton, Streets, Continental, Flora
17	12	Nestlé Australia	25–30	Nestlé, Uncle Tobys, Jenny Craig, Galderma, Musashi
18	29	Lion	25–30	Tooheys, Hahn, Boags, Heineken, Dairy Farmers, National Foods Milk and Dairy Foods
19	13	Queensland Government	25–30	Tourism Queensland, Queensland Health, Energex, Ergon Energy, Queensland Rail, Queensland Performing Arts, Departments of Transport and Main Roads, and Infrastructure and Planning
20	26	Hyundai	20–25	Hyundai
21	32	Yum! Restaurants Australia	20–25	KFC, Pizza Hut
22	23	Myer Limited	20–25	Myer Stores
23	30	Nine Entertainment	20–25	Nine Network, ACP Magazines, Carsales
24	24	Volkswagen AG Group	20–25	Volkswagen, Skoda
25	46	Kraft Foods Australia	20-25	Cadbury, Nabisco, Kraft, Pascall, The Natural Confectionery Co.

Source: *AdNews*, 21 September 2012.

ADVERTISING AGENCIES

The advertising agency is the key organisation in the production of advertising. Agencies are 'agents' for their 'clients', the manufacturers of goods or providers of services who are the actual advertisers. Not all advertisers engage agencies to take care of their advertising, especially for internet advertising, but nearly all the big-budget advertising for nationally distributed brand names we see in the media is handled by advertising agencies. The advertiser pays a service fee to the agency, although agencies traditionally have derived most of their income from the media, paid as a sales commission in recognition of the media time or space which the agencies purchase on behalf of their clients. This business practice was the origin of advertising agencies long before they became involved in market research or the production of television commercials, and has continued to shape the advertising agency as a form of business in Australia.

The interests of the different components of the manufacturing–marketing–media complex are not necessarily harmonious, however. As we saw above, the national advertisers are in retailing and other service industries as well as manufacturing, and a substantial proportion of them are in fact trans-national corporations. Their professional organisation is the Australian Association of National Advertisers (AANA), the members of which spend about half of all advertising expenditure in Australia. Suspicious that the media sales commission dealings between media and agencies were being done at the advertisers' expense, in 1995 the AANA aligned itself with the then Trade Practices Commission (TPC—now the Australian Competition and Consumer Commission, or ACCC) in an inquiry into the commission system, and its links to agency accreditation. Over protests from the agencies' body, the Advertising Federation of Australia (AFA) and the then Media Council of Australia (MCA), representing the media proprietors, the TPC ruled that the system be abolished. This was an effective deregulation of the industry, and advertising has never been the same since. In particular, incumbent agencies can no longer control the entry of others to the advertising business, agencies do not have to give financial guarantees to media, and the public have less opportunity to object to advertising content that it finds offensive (Bunbury 1998). On the last point, however, an Advertising Standards Board has since been established by the industry.

One peculiarity of the advertising industry that has not changed is the periodic movement of clients from one agency to another. Although there are many long-standing and stable client–agency relationships, it is the reassignment of accounts that dominates the trade press and its gossip, and that makes advertising a competitive business in which agencies must strive to attract and hold clients. There are various reasons why clients might want to reassign accounts: to find out whether another agency can produce better results or show more creativity and commitment; to get away from an agency that has taken on a competitor's business; or just because it is time for a review. Trans-national advertisers might change to the same trans-national agency that handles its advertising in other countries, a practice known as 'global alignment'. Clients watch each other's movements, and evaluate their own choices in that light, so the pressure is on agencies not only to please their own clients, but to impress all the spectators as well.

WHAT AGENCIES DO

What exactly is it that clients expect an advertising agency to do for them? The traditional 'full-service' agencies still characteristically offer clients much more than the strategic function of buying media time and space, or the creative one of preparing actual advertisements. Many clients, in fact, are more interested in 'below-the-line' agency services—for example, sports sponsorship, sales promotion in stores or direct marketing—than they are in media advertising. Direct marketing, which traditionally targets prospective consumers via 'junk mail' in the post or by phone ('telemarketing') has rapidly migrated to the mobile internet. The major advertising agencies have their direct marketing divisions and specialised digital agencies to take advantage of this trend, as well as providing strategies for viral advertising on social media, and in-game advertising on the Xbox. However, below-the-line funds can still be directed towards the mass media. For example, in addition to the notorious 'cash for comment' practice, as revealed in the 2UE scandal of 2000 (see Chapter 8), there is 'product placement', which is where an advertiser pays a fee to have their product scripted into an actual program, as with the drink brands we see being consumed by characters in a television series, or the goods used by contestants in *Big Brother* (Lawson 2002).

Even those agencies that are primarily concerned with providing advertising content may do so in conjunction with a raft of other marketing services. Advertising has thus become 'marketing communications'. It is important to appreciate the degree to which the concept and practices of marketing (as distinct from 'sales') have become the dominant professional ideology of agencies and clients alike. Marketing is 'trying to have what the consumer wants', while selling is 'trying to get the consumer to buy what you have' (Buzzell et al., quoted in Schudson 1984, pp. 29, 248). While agencies vary in the degree to which they emphasise particular elements in the integrated bundle of services that constitute marketing, such as market research or 'account planning', the full-service agency provides advertising in that whole marketing context. However, as will be seen below, in the era of the global group there has been a marked trend towards different marketing functions being 'unbundled' into specialised agencies, notably media-buying and creative functions. The global group is like a full-service corporate umbrella under which media-buying, creative and other specialist agencies are integrated.

There is always a certain tension built into the fact that marketing and advertising are business practices, but depend on the imaginative realisation of ideas and associations in words and images—the ultimate 'creative industry'. Thus the production of advertising in an agency requires some organisation to bring about the necessary fusion of commerce and art. Advertising people recognise themselves as two interdependent types: the 'suits' who manage the business as such and liaise with the clients; and the 'creatives' who generate the visual and verbal output in an indulgent environment out of the clients' sight. Some of Australia's best-known ads of past decades are said to have originated in certain Sydney pubs and restaurants (Coombs 1990). In practice, the work roles and their functional organisation are more complex, varied and mundane than this folklore suggests. Depending on the size and the 'corporate culture' of the agency, these may be organised on an ongoing team basis, servicing a specific group of clients' accounts, or the account traffic may be handled on a more bureaucratic basis through departments.

In a traditional full-service agency, management of the business side and liaison with clients are under the control of the account executives (also called account directors), but there are several other crucial non-creative positions to be filled. Ever more important are the planners and buyers in the media department who negotiate with the media for the schedules of time and space within which the advertising will appear, and check that it does so; then there is the research department, which carries out the repertoire of product and advertising testing, consumer and market research that characterises the traditional agency. The creative positions include the copywriters who devise slogans, jingles, headlines, tags and 'body copy', and visual artists who produce graphics and layouts for print media and storyboards for television commercials (TVCs), working under creative directors, art directors and so on. There may also be a production department that renders finished artwork.

However, a major part of advertising production is undertaken outside of advertising agencies by a whole range of freelance specialists such as photographers and graphic designers, and above all by production companies to whom the actual realisation of the agency's creative brief may be subcontracted: recording studios for radio ads, special effects and soundtracks, and television production houses for TVCs. These in turn will organise the recording or shooting sessions, hiring freelance musicians, voiceover people and on-camera 'talent' through casting agencies; renting costumes and props such as vintage cars; and engaging such specialists as food modellers who can make glasses look frosty and junk food tasty. They will then edit and post-produce as the agency requires (or subcontract that again to technical specialists) to yield a finished ad.

While the case of the TVC is the most extreme, it should now be clear that the production of advertising involves much more than having a good idea over a long lunch in the pub. From the point of view of the account executives, it is a question of management to achieve the coordination required of the different specialists—not only those within the agency, but also the individuals and companies who are subcontracted from outside. The realisation of the original creative idea is mediated through this organisational process, so that an advertisement is always the outcome of 'compromise, argument, bargaining and tight deadlines' (Myers 1983, p. 214).

BOX 12.1: GLOBAL LINKS

Advertising agencies, and other related marketing communications corporations, are themselves at the forefront of globalisation processes in Australia. One crucially important global trend of recent decades has been the formation of what the trade press calls 'supergroups' or 'megagroups' by several large international agencies—trans-national corporations in their own right. These groups do not operate as unified advertising agencies, but as holding companies with a management and financial coordination function at a stratospheric level around the planet. This integrates all the activities of the group's member companies in marketing communications (such as market research and public relations) with the advertising agencies and their clients on a global basis. The advertising agencies under such corporate umbrellas include both creative and media-buying agencies.

In an era of global clients, the global groups are driven by the need to manage 'client conflicts'—that is, a situation in which an agency has to pass up a prospective account because that agency already services the account of the prospective client's competitor. This becomes a problem as fewer and larger agencies serve fewer and larger clients. However, where a number of relatively autonomous agencies can be coordinated as part of the same group, and clients' marketing secrets thus separated organisationally, the group can take on the accounts of competing clients by assigning them to different agencies within the group. In practice, the large clients usually place their brands with a number of agencies, but take care that there is no competing brand within a given agency.

Table 12.2 is an alphabetical list of the leading full-service and creative agencies in Australia, not a ranking. The table also notes each agency's affiliation. It is apparent that the majority are either wholly owned divisions of global groups, or some kind of joint venture or other relationship.

Table 12.2 Top 20 advertising agencies

Agency	Affiliation
BMF	Enero (formerly Photon), a Sydney-based, publicly listed marketing communications group with offices in the United Kingdom and United States
BWM	Formerly also part of Enero, the founders bought out Enero's share in August 2012
Clemenger BBDO	A leading agency for decades, and a major part of the Clemenger Group, since 2011 majority owned by US-based global group Omnicom
DDB	This and specialist agencies wholly owned by DDB of the United States, also part of Omnicom
DraftFCB	Australian holding of DraftFCB Worldwide, part of US-based global group Interpublic
Droga5	Sydney office of New York-based agency founded by Australian David Droga
George Patterson Y&R	Well-regarded and influential agency acquired by British-based global group WPP in 2005 and merged with WPP's US-based agency, Y&R
Grey	Australian holding of Grey Group Worldwide, part of British-based global group WPP since 2005
Havas Worldwide	Formerly Euro RSCG, recent name change reflects ownership by French-based global group Havas Worldwide
JWT	Part of STW Group, an Australian-based marketing communications group, closely allied with majority owner, British-based WPP
Leo Burnett	Australian holding of Leo Burnett Worldwide, part of French-based global group Publicis
303 Lowe	Australian holding of Lowe Worldwide, part of US-based global group Interpublic
M&C Saatchi	Owned 80 per cent by M&C Saatchi Worldwide, a 'micro-network' of agencies based in the United Kingdom
McCann	Australian holding of McCann Worldgroup, part of US-based global group Interpublic

Agency	Affiliation
Ogilvy & Mather (O&M)	Part of STW Group, an Australian-based marketing communications group. O&M is a joint venture with British-based global group WPP, which owns 33 per cent of Ogilvy.
Publicis Mojo	Australian holding of French-based global group Publicis
Saatchi & Saatchi	Another Australian holding of French-based global group Publicis
Sapient Nitro	US-based digital agency Sapient took over Australian creative agency Nitro in 2009.
The Monkeys	Independent Australian creative agency
Whybin/TBWA	Owned 75 per cent by US-based global group Omnicom

Sources: 'Australia's Top Advertising Agencies', *Adbrands* 2012; 'Agency Report Card', *AdNews*, 1 June 2012.

Both George Patterson and John Clemenger were the largest agencies in Australia for many years prior to the coming of the global groups. As noted above, US agencies began to take over the Australian industry from the end of the 1950s, though J. Walter Thompson (now known as JWT, and part of WPP) had been in Australia since 1930 (Sinclair 1987, pp. 133–9). Subsequently, British- and French-based global groups, particularly WPP and Publicis, began to acquire some of the older US-based international networks in the 1980s. However, this should not lead to the conclusion that US capital has been replaced by British and French investment in the Australian advertising industry, but rather—as in most truly global industries—that the nation of origin is becoming irrelevant.

One significant and notable absence from the 2012 list is the creative agency The Campaign Palace. Dating from 1972, this was a very successful independent creative 'hot shop', which set the benchmark for Australian advertising until being acquired by WPP in 2003. In June, 2012, WPP announced that it was folding the Palace into JWT.

Turning to the media-buying agencies, the biggest by far is Mitchell & Partners, and has been for over a decade. The company was wholly owned by Harold Mitchell and family until 2010, when they sold a majority share to Aegis Media, a global media-buying group based in the United Kingdom. Then, in July, 2012, Aegis was bought out entirely by Dentsu, one of the world's oldest and largest full-service agencies and the market leader in its native Japan. This adds a very considerable Japanese dimension to the pattern of global ownership. Harold Mitchell remains on the international board, while Dentsu now controls the largest media-buying group in the Asia-Pacific. Looking down Nielsen's Top 20 Media Agency Billings list for 2011, companies linked to the global groups occupy the next twelve places—that is, it is only at fourteenth rank that Australian agencies start to appear (Nielsen Online 2012a). Clearly, the global groups dominate advertising in Australia—both creative and media-buying.

CURRENT ISSUES

Because many advertisers look for the means to communicate with a particular niche or 'target' market rather than a mass market, since the late 1980s there has been a worldwide trend towards a proportionately greater increase in expenditure to go on marketing communications avenues other than the conventional mass media (Mattelart 1991, pp. 23–4). Pay television has a growing but still very minor share of expenditure, no threat to the traditional dominance of broadcast television and the press in Australia, but the most significant technological development in which advertisers and their agencies are taking considerable interest is, of course, the relatively new 'medium' of the internet. Significantly, the internet is not a 'mass' medium like television—mainly because of its interactive nature, which means that prospective customers select themselves out by the sites that they visit, and can even buy directly over the internet itself. This is precisely why it has been so attractive to advertisers, particularly since ever more sophisticated, yet 'user-friendly', browser software has enabled the number of users to expand at a quite unprecedented rate.

However, marketing over the internet requires a quite different business model from that of traditional mass media advertising and, in spite of all the hype, that new model is still very much in the process of evolving (Sinclair 2012). In particular, small advertisers can go directly to Google or the other search engines for keyword search ads, the fastest-growing type of internet advertising. This bypasses the intermediary role that the advertising agency has always had, although large advertisers still need the wider range of functions agencies provide. Also of interest here are the various attempts to commercialise the immensely popular social networking sites, notably MySpace, Facebook and YouTube, but they too have yet to find a successful business model.

The advertising industry is facing challenges from its clients as well as from new media. One such challenge comes from the previously mentioned division of agencies into media-buying versus creative specialities. Media-buying agencies do not prepare advertising as such, but concern themselves with advertising's historical function of buying time or space on commission from the media for sale to clients, and with 'channel planning', which is giving advice to clients on where and how to place their marketing more generally. This trend to media-buying as a specialty, in conjunction with new measures of advertising effectiveness, is ensuring the total demise of the traditional agency commission system in favour of payment for service only, or by results. Furthermore, some advertisers want their agencies to 'unbundle' advertising from other marketing services so that they can contract those particular services elsewhere, while others have brought them 'in house'—that is, they perform the work themselves. As noted, the advent of the internet has made it easier for advertisers to conduct their own advertising without the benefit of an agency.

In addition to technological changes in media and measurement, and the increasingly stringent pressures exerted by advertisers, the shape of the advertising industry has been affected by regulation of various kinds, such as the self-regulatory and government codes that govern the content of advertising. An obvious historical example is the restrictions placed on the advertising of tobacco in the mass media. The harshest critics of advertising might see it as a contradiction in terms, but there is an Advertiser Code of Ethics, as well as a number of codes for specific types of products. Apart from tobacco and alcohol, these include therapeutic goods, hair and slimming products. When advertisements for some of these goods look too euphemistic or obscure, that may be attributable to the strictures of the relevant code. As noted above, the Advertising Standards Board, funded by the industry, exists to adjudicate on complaints under these codes.

As well as industry codes, there is a wide range of federal and state government legislation that directly or indirectly imposes controls upon marketing and advertising, notably the Commonwealth *Trade Practices Act* 1974. In some kinds of advertising, both legislative and self-regulatory controls apply—for example, where federal Acts are augmented by self-regulatory codes developed in conjunction with the states, the regime that brought cigarette advertising to an end. More contentious over recent decades—such as in the context of the free trade agreement (FTA) with the United States—is the regulation of Australian content in television commercials (no more than 20 per cent of all commercials transmitted can be foreign), which is administered by the Australian Communications and Media Authority (ACMA) as part of television program standards, although the networks for the most part comfortably observe this limit (Maniaty 2003).

One aspect of the advertising industry in Australia worth a final mention is its popular exposure on the ABC series, *The Gruen Transfer*. Over five seasons, well over a million viewers on average each week have enjoyed the barbed humour with which it treats advertising, and the whole world of consumption. The advertising industry is represented on the show each week by Russell Howcroft as the 'suit' in eternal conflict with Todd Sampson as the 'creative'.

CONCLUSION

Advertising continues to be a controversial and highly public phenomenon of modern societies, not least because of its constant presence in the commercial media, which it has done so much to shape. By understanding advertising as a particular kind of business geared into the ideology and practice of marketing at the heart of the manufacturing–marketing–media complex, this chapter has sought to show the workings of the changing structural environment in which advertising is produced.

FURTHER READING

A very readable history of advertising in Australia from colonial times until the recent past is Crawford (2008), *But Wait, There's More*. For an overview of advertising as a global phenomenon, see Sinclair (2012), *Advertising, the Media and Globalisation*. An excellent account of the rise of internet advertising is provided by Spurgeon (2008), *Advertising and New Media*. There is a substantial academic literature which has critically analysed the cultural and ideological effects attributable to advertising. Such research has paid particular attention to the role of advertising in presenting images of gender, notably Goffman (1979), *Gender Advertisements* and Williamson (1978), *Decoding Advertisements*. A useful introduction to the current 'cultural economy' approach to advertising is McFall (2004), *Advertising: A Cultural Economy*, while contemporary critical work on branding is well-represented by Arvidsson (2006), *Brands: Meaning and Value in Media Culture*.

Chapter 13
POPULAR MUSIC

SHANE HOMAN

What do we mean by 'popular music'? It certainly encompasses 'the forms of music and music-making that [are] most accessible to, meaningful to and enjoyed by large numbers of people' (Whiteoak 2003, p. 529). This definition includes those music forms most audible in Australian life since World War II (jazz, pop, blues, rock, country) and excludes 'high' music forms (classical, opera) that cannot be regarded as part of local popular culture. Other genres (hip hop, metal, electronic dance music, folk, 'world' music) maintain significant practitioners and audiences without being considered part of a national mainstream.

The most ostensibly 'popular' genre, Australian rock, has recently reflected on its humbler beginnings. In April 2008, Melbourne rockers Jet and US punk veteran Iggy Pop re-recorded Johnny O'Keefe's 'The Wild One' to mark the 50th anniversary of

Australia's first local chart hit in July 1958 (Donovan 2008b). In May 2008, Fremantle Arts Centre presented the *Bon Scott Project*, a celebration of the life of the former AC/DC singer. In addition, the 2002 and 2012 *Long Way to the Top* concert tours, showcasing 'heritage' acts, and the SBS *Great Australian Albums* television series underline the Australian industry's capacity to commemorate and re-examine a local history dominated by a vigorous commercial music culture at home, and few successes overseas.

More recent histories reveal a different narrative of international engagement. The global successes of Silverchair (post-grunge), The Living End (punk and ska influences), Jet (retro-rock), Keith Urban (mainstream US country), Kasey Chambers (reflective country songs from the 'Deep South' of Australia), Wolfmother (redeploying 1970s heavy metal riffs and aesthetics) and Gotye (acoustic pop) reflect the assertion that 'to look for "the Australian" element is to look for an inflection, the distinctive modification of an already internationally established musical style' (Turner 1992, p. 13). This is also evident in other locally successful acts that have ignored traditional Anglo-American influences and genres (e.g. Cat Empire, Wicked Beat Sound System, The Herd). A number of other acts purposefully play with and across genres and older divides between 'art' and 'popular' music (e.g. The Necks, Katie Noonan).

It is also important to recognise other music forms whose importance resonates beyond commercial success. The work of Archie Roach, Ruby Hunter, Leah Purcell and others has invested Indigenous music with a continuing relevance to larger political questions. Roach's compositions document his own life experiences as a product of the Stolen Generation, when he was removed from his family as a child. The inclusion of Midnight Oil and Yothu Yindi (performing 'Beds are Burning' and 'Treaty') in the 2000 Sydney Olympic Games closing ceremony has been regarded as a significant moment. The 'Sorry' apparel worn by Midnight Oil on stage during the closing ceremony was seen as a controversial statement about reconciliation between black and white Australians.

Much contemporary Aboriginal music can be viewed as a series of 'interventionist texts, making music as deliberate re-representations of [Aborigines] themselves' (Dunbar-Hall and Gibson 2004, p. 56) in the face of continuing disinterest from major recording labels, venues and broadcasting companies. Similarly dislocated from mainstream concerns, Torres Strait Islander communities have combined religious and secular traditions to produce interesting music that in some cases defies categorisation. Seaman Dan, The Mills Sisters and Christine Anu are notable examples of Islander performers who have found wider audiences and critical acclaim (Neuenfeldt 2008). Based on the true story of an Indigenous female singing group who performed for Australian troops in Vietnam in 1968, the film *The Sapphires* has provided another dimension to understandings of Indigenous performers on and off the screen. The film grossed more than $13 million in two months following its release in August 2012, with the soundtrack album (featuring Jessica Mauboy) reaching number one on the ARIA album charts (Box Office Mojo 2012).

Perhaps more than any other medium, popular music intersects with and influences the uses of other media in everyday life. Indeed, 'there is now a plethora of ways that a single song can be distributed across various media and cultural contexts: as film soundtrack, television advertisement, live concert performance, pub jukebox selection and mobile phone ringtone' (Homan and Mitchell 2008, p. 7). This chapter explores some of the implications of the increasing convergence of media platforms and audiences for the various sectors of music production and consumption. How popular music is produced, the methods by which it reaches its fans and the contexts in which it is enjoyed are undergoing the most important changes since the introduction of the phonogram in the late nineteenth century. With a long history of describing itself as proudly free market, the Australian music industry faces several challenges in satisfying its customers and maintaining profits.

LOCAL AND/OR GENERAL

In the 1990s, just five multi-national companies dominated the global recording industry. Five has now become three: Vivendi Universal (a merger of MCA and Polygram); SonyBMG (a merger of Sony and the Bertelsmann Group in 2004); and Warner Music. Despite concerns about the decline in competition (and a prior objection to Warner Music purchasing EMI), European Union regulators approved Universal acquiring EMI (and a catalogue that includes The Beatles and Coldplay) in September 2012.

The three 'majors' remain at the forefront of globalisation, increasingly seeking to employ economies of scale through vertical integration (associating with non-music media firms) and horizontal integration (purchasing other music companies and manufacturers). The Bertelsmann Group, part of Sony BMG, is a good example of horizontal integration, as the owner of print publishing (Random House books, Grune and Jahr magazines and newspapers), printing services, direct marketing groups (book and CD clubs) and online services (CDnow.com, BMG Music Service), in addition to Bertelsmann Music Group (Bishop 2005, p. 447).

The local recording industry, as Breen (1992, p. 41) asserts, 'is "Australian" only in the sense that it exists within the territorial boundaries of the country'. Australia is the sixth largest market in the world, with 3 per cent of the world's recorded music sales (Australia Council 2012). While record importers existed in the early 1900s, the recording industry did not blossom until the 1920s, when gramophone sales first overtook sales of sheet music (Laird 1999, p. 49). Smaller local labels (e.g. Regal Zonophone) coexisted with international labels such as HMV, EMI and Columbia. From the beginning, companies were concerned principally with selling imported 'serious' recordings of international stars:

> The instrumentalists and vocalists here do not compare favourably with the best English and foreign artistes, and local jealousies would militate against sales . . . Then again, one has to consider the general policy of Australia, namely, to declaim loudly the necessity of buying everything Australian but in their private life to buy imported articles and to 'swank' among their friends that these are the only ones good enough for them . . . (Gramophone Co executive James Muir, 1922–27, correspondence cited in Laird 1999, p. 128)

The Prices and Surveillance Authority (PSA) Inquiry into the Price of Sound Recordings during the 1990s revealed that this policy had not changed. The inquiry, as a process, 'exposed the entire structure and operations of the Australian music industry to public scrutiny . . . it revealed the private, invisible hand of copyright law in regulating the interests of the major record companies by maintaining their monopoly over product distribution' (Breen 1999, p. 176).

The PSA concluded that, due to the absence of domestic price competition and protection from imports afforded by the *Copyright Act*, Australian consumers paid excessive prices for CDs in comparison to those in other countries. The report recommended the end of local subsidiaries' exclusive licence agreements for CDs within Australia, weakening the multinationals' dominance of local markets. This was to be achieved by allowing non-pirate CDs—that is, those manufactured legitimately under licence of the copyright owner—to be imported without requiring the consent of the Australian copyright owner (parallel importing). The recommendation became law in July 1998. Clear battle lines emerged between the industry and the Howard Coalition government. The industry argued that copyright was not merely a contractual mechanism in the interests of the artist, but the primary means by which the recording companies established their wealth through territorial exploitation of publishing rights. The government emphasised economic benefits in its promise to consumers of significant reductions in CD prices. For musicians, it has been argued that the existence of only three truly global music companies 'gives the record labels the power to have the best of both worlds as they fashion anaemic artists contracts to obtain low-cost content, then sell that content to music buyers at inflated retail prices in the market which it controls' (Bishop 2005, p. 445).

The extent to which local industry protection ensures a satisfactory level of national cultural production is further complicated by the fact that multinational investment and distribution remain at the core of 'local' music production. Festival Records (established in 1952) and Mushroom Records (established in 1972) were the only companies of sufficient size and influence to challenge the majors in the past. These companies merged in 1998, with Festival-Mushroom becoming a part of the global News Corporation media empire, and subsequently acquired by Warner Music in 2005. A range of independent ('indie') recording companies exist, including ABC Music, Shock, Creative Vibes, Eleven, Ivy League and Obese (see the Australian Independent Record Labels Association website <www.air.org.au>). The diversity of these 'indie' interests—and organisational structures—can be noted in two examples. The Australian branch of the Hillsong Church features regularly in local Christian music charts; Hillsong Publishing's album, *Saviour King*, was listed at no. 36 in the Top 50 Australian Albums in 2007 (ARIA 2008). The local cinema/theme park/radio giant Village Roadshow has been involved in the recording industry since 1994, with notable commercial success (Savage Garden, Killing Heidi, The Butterfly Effect, Jade MacRae) through Roadshow Music. Here, non-music media interests engage in the 'core' business of artist development and licensing, while outsourcing distribution to the majors (in Roadshow's case, SonyBMG). The ongoing successes of The John Butler Trio and The Waifs have provided alternative models for acts to finance their recordings and construct lucrative touring income based upon the growth in festival events, to maintain creative control.

Other industry sectors have assumed recording company expertise, evidenced by Madonna signing a ten-year contract with touring company Live Nation for allegedly US$120 million, ending her association with Warner Music. The contract 'encompasses all of Madonna's future music and music-related businesses, including the exploitation of the Madonna brand, new studio albums, touring, merchandising, fan club/ web site, DVDs, music-related television and film projects and associated sponsorship agreements' (Waddell 2007). With the continuing decline in recording industry profits (addressed below), this new '360 degree' business model represents a shift to other revenue streams by bundling the different production and consumption sectors in the one company. Many musicians, however, are directly engaging with their fans to produce new material. Crowdfunding is not a wholly new phenomenon—Mozart and Beethoven drew upon the financial resources of their admirers—but internet calls from artists for their fans to fund new recordings is an increasingly important component of the industry. Several companies (e.g. PledgeMusic, Kickstarter, Sellaband) offer specialist services that handle advertising, contributor payments and financial planning for a range of music projects. The emergence of fans as neo-venture capitalists has proved to be a successful means of interaction between musicians and their publics. Melbourne artist Amanda Palmer raised over $1 million from 24 000 contributors for her latest album, a Kickstarter record (Kickstarter 2012); her subsequent crowdsource call for amateur musicians to play on her 2012 tour, however, attracted accusations that Palmer was exploiting her musician-fans as cheap/free labour (Geffen 2012).

PRO TOOLS, AMATEUR TOOLS

The rapidity with which MP3 technology has become commonplace has argu-ably shortened the lifespan of the compact disc as a viable music commodity. By compressing audio data and discarding those parts of the spectrum inaudible to the human ear, the MP3 file provided the central breakthrough for the distribu-tion of digital music. Launched in November 2001, the Apple iPod instigated the biggest change in personal, mobile music listening since the introduction of the Sony Walkman in 1979. By April 2007, Apple had sold over 100 million iPods (Apple Corporation 2007). With iTunes, Apple boasts an online store of over five million songs, 350 television shows and over 400 movies. Globally, iTunes had reached the 10 billion sales mark in songs by 2010. Since the launch of the Australian iTunes store in October 2005, Apple has clearly become the local market leader in an increasingly crowded market that includes BigPond, Vodafone, Optus and Jamster. Concerns that mobile listening devices will further shift music consumption from communal to private contexts (see Bull 2005) seem to be overtaken by the ways in which individual users attach emotional and symbolic value to them, in providing the 'soundtrack to their lives' (Luckman 2008a, p. 194). Music streaming services are now challenging the market dominance of iTunes. Spotify, a Swedish streaming company with ten million customers globally, opened for business in Australia in May 2012 with a library of over sixteen million songs. These services have provoked much debate about their benefits for both consumers and producers. For fans, songs aren't owned upon purchase, but simply 'leased' from the 'cloud', while musicians contemplate the marketing worth of a digital media platform that offers a royalty of only 0.33 cents for a song download.

Convergence of industries and products—music and non-music—will continue to drive innovation. From October 2007, songs playing in Starbucks stores could be downloaded on to customers' iPhones and iPods as a result of a deal between the coffee company and Apple (IFPI 2008). Starbucks has entered the market as a genuine music company, with Paul McCartney, Joni Mitchell, Dave Matthews, Lyle Lovett, Gloria Estefan and The Beastie Boys as key signings who are attracted to the substan-tial distribution networks that multinational retail stores can provide. Telephony companies increasingly are looking to drive sales of their smartphones through their own music streaming services: Google Music, established in 2011, is the best example of this.

While the CD remains the dominant format, digital sales are increasing to the point where many in the industry believe the CD to be simply a promotional tool to drive downloaded mobile phone single sales. Some 32 per cent of global music sales are now derived from digital sources (IFPI 2012). Yet the point at which digital revenues compensate (or overtake) physical (CD) revenue losses is still far away. For example, while global digital sales revenue increased by 5.3 per cent in 2010, global physical sales revenue decreased by 14.2 per cent (Smirke 2011).

BOX 13.1: THE MUSIC BUSINESS IN AUSTRALIA

According to the peak industry body the Australian Record Industry Association (ARIA), the value of recorded music product in 2011 was $382.7 million. Digital sales comprised 36.7 per cent of the market in 2011, with single track sales increasing by 39.2 per cent and digital albums revealing an increase of 45.8 per cent on 2010 sales (ARIA 2012). This has accompanied the decline in 'bricks and mortar' retail stores, with a fall from 1100 stores in the early 2000s to 600 in 2011 (Australia Council 2012). The collection societies—those responsible for distributing royalties to composers and musicians—recently increased their payments. The PPCA distributed $25.7 million derived from over 54 000 licences in relation to the use of its members' sound recordings (PPCA 2011). Royalty payments to composers and musicians for 2010–11 from public and related performances of recordings by the collection societies exceeded $160 million (APRA) and $45 million (AMCOS), an increase of 8.4 per cent. Australia remains a net importer of music product: in 2008–09, the nation received $75 million in music royalties and paid out $235 million to overseas labels/publishers (Queensland University of Technology 2010). Like most cultural industries, few artists earn substantial wages. The most recent survey of artists found that the median annual income for musicians derived from their 'creative income'—revenue earned directly from their music creativity—was $7200 (Throsby and Zednik 2010, p. 45).

'Mashups'—songs that cut, copy and paste to produce blends of lyrics, riffs and melodies—define twenty-first century recording as a messy, exciting combination of sounds, aesthetics and legalities. They have enabled some to underscore and reinforce the rock and pop canon. *Love*, the reverential 2006 Beatles mashup album, involved the band's producer, George Martin, and his son, Giles, who employed Pro Tools software to synchronise and sequence a wide mix of famous Beatles tracks. Others have exploited the absurdities produced through juxtaposition: 'I think mixing Busta Rhymes with a House tune will make people dance . . . but mixing Britney Spears with NWA [Niggas Wit Attitude] will make people dance *and* laugh.' (Eclectic Method's Jonny, cited in McLeod 2005, p. 84) In Australia in 2005, The Herd produced a critically acclaimed mashup with its hip hop treatment of Redgum's 'I Was Only 19' (an initial folk-rock hit in 1983). Their collaboration with original songwriter John Schumann transposed the song's earlier reflection upon Vietnam War veterans to contemporary debates about Australian involvement in the Iraq War.

Artists are also allowing their fans to remix songs through 'open source remixing' software. Nine Inch Nails and Radiohead have both invited their fans to contribute their own versions of album tracks:

> Despite its obvious debts to the internet era, home remixing in one sense suggests a return to the musical culture of the days before sound recording on wax cylinders, around the turn of the century. In their capacity as remixers, members of the musical public are again assuming participatory roles, interpreting compositions at home, much as late Victorians played sheet music in parlour musicales. There is also a social component to both spheres of participation, as remixers post their efforts, listen to one another's, and vote on them (Hajdu 2008).

Participation is circumscribed by the artist, however. In the case of Radiohead, the possibilities of the band's fans as 'co-authors' are constrained by a legal stipulation that all remixes remain the intellectual property of the band (Hajdu 2008). In 2003, the Australian Federal Court upheld the rights of a number of recording companies against those of the five DJs who had sold CDs containing remixed tracks. The DJs' central argument—that such remixes assisted the profile of the original artists—was not successful (Rimmer 2005, pp. 43–4). Many artists also assert their moral rights (the right of objection to derogatory treatment of their work). U2 and Island Records' court action against Negativland in 1992 stemmed from the band's belief that their song, 'I Still Haven't Found What I'm Looking For', was not only remixed without authorisation, but was a morally unacceptable use of their composition (Rimmer 2005, pp. 44–5).

COPYRIGHT: THE BATTLE FOR CONSUMERS AND REVENUE

> When music fans can say, 'I have all the music from 1950–2010, do you want a copy?'— what kind of business models will be viable in such a reality? (Johansson 2008)

It has always been hard to establish just how valuable music is in particular media contexts. In Australia, radio stations in 1970 refused to play the majors' recordings for nine months, believing the royalties paid to copyright collection bodies to be unreasonable. In the 1980s, recording companies attempted to extract fees from television stations for airing music videos, conveniently ignoring the promotional benefits of such arrangements for their artists (Stockbridge 1988). Since the phonogram era, music companies and musicians have had to contend with shifting technological platforms. As with the blank cassette debates of the 1980s, contemporary fears about piracy and trade sovereignty demonstrate once again that the transmission of music cannot be centrally controlled. Copyright is invoked in two central forms of the musical work: mechanical rights (usually asserted by recording companies as the publishers of sound recordings); and public performance rights (broadcasting rights within television, film and radio; 'on hold' telephone systems; music played in night-clubs and other businesses). The 'stimulate' and 'create' discourses of the recording companies (Laing 2003, p. 484) are based on the argument that copyright provides the proper incentives (and revenue) for the production of new works.

For metal band Metallica and the Recording Industry Association of America (RIAA), court action taken against digital file share company Napster in 2002 was not just about finances; it was also ideological: '[downloading] suggests that the copyright regime for the circulation of music goods may not be necessary at all' (Frith 2002, p. 199). ARIA followed the lead of other national recording industry bodies in a dual process of litigation and legislation. In 2003, it launched cases against three universities, citing large volumes of downloading by students using university computers. In 2004, it initiated court action against Kazaa, a file-sharing company based in Sydney, with an estimated 60 million users globally. In 2005, the Australian Federal Court ordered Kazaa to implement software changes to prevent file-sharing.

Australian federal governments have mainly been sympathetic to local recording industry requests to periodically strengthen copyright law in accordance with global changes led by the United States. The Howard Coalition government's *Copyright Amendment (Digital Agenda) Act* 2000 strengthened existing intellectual property rights, with a further promise to investigate replicating US laws protecting composers' rights in various digital environments. Its *Copyright Amendment Act* 2006 also ended some of the sillier prohibitions, legitimising 'format shifting' (moving copyright content from one media platform to another) and 'time shifting' (the recording of radio or television programs for viewing at a later time). The Act also legalised the duplication of purchased CDs for private use.

Recording industry pleas to equate cyber file sharing with retail store theft have not been successful, partly because 'copying a CD just doesn't *feel* like a property infringement' (Greenfield and Osborn 2003, p. 66). A global 2011 study argued that the high prices imposed by the majors for legitimate recordings in smaller markets (often developing nations) was a substantial factor in music piracy and little discussed in legal debates (Karaganis 2011).

The industry remains divided about the ethics of file-sharing. Many musicians argue that copyright income provides the basis for the investment in new artists—part of the reason behind companies' zealous protection of their recordings. However, many others have outlined the standard concerns expressed about recording company conduct: unethical and one-sided contracts; continual efforts to increase company ownership of copyrights; and their unwillingness to provide consumer-friendly media alternatives (Garofalo 2003).

As Crawford (2005, p. 31) points out, the copyright battle has become polarised around two competing narratives: 'thieves are downloading music and thereby exploiting struggling artists and the companies that foster their talent, or peer-to-peer services are beneficently taking profits from corrupt infotainment industries to give back to overcharged consumers'. Successive extensions of the period of copyright protection for sound recordings also remains a constant criticism because it potentially enables the majors to recoup their costs in perpetuity. This represents a shift from copyright as a 'regulatory mechanism', designed to facilitate distribution and uses in the public interest, to being a 'proprietary mechanism' of the major publishers and copyright owners (Rushton 2002, p. 56). Intellectual property projects such as the Creative Commons have called for musicians to join other creative industries authors in the use of copyright agreements that 'promote an ethos of sharing, public education, and creative interactivity' (Creative Commons 2012).

Traditional copyright mechanisms were never designed for the internet, which has combined previously distinct media—for example, radio stations and record shops, once separate businesses—in digital form. This has blurred use and distribution functions in the new millennium (Fleischer 2008). In September 2008, Radiohead offered its new album for purchase online, with fans to decide how much the album was worth (the album was also subsequently available as a boxed set including CD and vinyl versions). This strategy has provoked much debate as a potential future business model for acts of sufficient status to bypass recording companies in terms of distribution and marketing.

The music copyright debate has observed one of the key Foucauldian tenets of governance: that a failure in regulation and policing inevitably leads to greater regulation and policing (Hunt and Wickham 1994, p. 129). In this case, the failure of legislatures and the courts to enforce rights in an era of abundance leads to ever shriller calls for more legislation and enforcement based upon older eras of scarcity of distribution and content. The latest repositioning in this governmental cycle consists of attempts by ARIA to convince the federal Labor government to adopt the 'three strikes' or 'graduated response' policy (from warnings to internet disconnection) against internet service providers (ISPs) established by New Zealand in 2011. The industry has also embarked upon various educational programs: a 'Rock the Schools' tour of bands that incorporates the discussion of copyright in the digital age; a *Music for Free?* resource kit for secondary school teachers; and the establishment of an Australian Copyright Unit within the Ministerial Council on Employment, Education, Training and Youth Affairs (IFPI 2008). A 2008 Australian television debate on digital music revealed the complexities of the issue. Bringing together musicians, file sharers, recording companies and ISPs, the discussion reinforced the significant divisions between copyright owners and music fans, and how illegal downloaders base their choices upon a range of moral and economic codes (SBS 2008). The Australian music industries have joined the international Music Matters campaign (<http://anz.whymusicmatters.org/mmanz/campaign>), designed to remind fans about the value of music and reinforce legal consumption.

BOX 12.2: *ROADSHOW FILMS V IINET LTD* (2009–11)

A recent Federal Court case provides a useful window into the copyright battles for music and related audio-visual industries. In 2010, Roadshow Films and 33 other multinational film and music companies sought action against iiNet for its role as an ISP that allowed illegal downloading of film, television and music content through BitTorrent. Before the case, the Australian Federation Against Copyright Theft (AFACT) had presented iiNet with infringement evidence, demanding that a system of warning, suspension and termination be applied. The central question for the court's consideration was to determine whether iiNet's knowledge of illegal copying amounted to authorisation. After a lengthy trial, the judge found that iiNet had not condoned illegal downloading activity, and did not control the BitTorrent system or the ability to prevent downloading, and so could not be held liable. The Federal Court subsequently dismissed an appeal against the decision by the major companies; a further appeal by AFACT in the High Court in 2011 was also unsuccessful. These cases revealed a fine, but important, distinction in the positions of the courts and the audiovisual sectors. For companies such as Village Roadshow, control of *content*—who uses it, and where it flows—was emphasised in its legal arguments. For the courts, the role of the *technology* was reinforced, specifically in arguments that companies could not be held responsible for other unsanctioned forms of distribution on the internet, amidst a broader, qualified defence of net freedoms. The battle was also notable for the shift in the federal Labor government's position. In 2009, the Minister for Broadband, Communications and the Digital Economy, Senator Stephen Conroy, ridiculed iiNet's defence; in 2011, the government was seeking to talk with all ISPs about a responsible code of practice.

MUSIC BROADCASTING

Australian music radio consists of public, community and commercial sectors, each with different licensing conditions and operational objectives. Public radio—the government-funded stations operated by the ABC and SBS—operate from different legislative environments that aim to produce innovative music programs that appeal to all regions and age groups. Community radio licences are granted according to the specific needs in the market, as identified by the government, that offer alternatives to both public and commercial music radio. Its 'democratic, participatory rhetoric' (Miller and Turner 2002, p. 147) remains a key attraction to its producers interested in servicing audiences with more particular music tastes (for example, 1930s jazz, death metal, trance). For many bands, public radio (the ABC's Triple J network) and community radio (stations such as 3PBS and 3RRR) remain the only viable sources of airplay for original compositions. Triple J's 'Unearthed' strategy provides unrecorded bands with airtime and promotional opportunities denied within commercial radio environments. Like the much older 3RRR in Melbourne, Sydney station FBi has underlined the potential for community stations to support local music scenes. Since its launch in August 2003, the station has maintained a policy of playing 50 per cent Australian music, with half of this quota dedicated to Sydney artists. Radio content industry codes were amended to ensure that commercial stations aired contemporary bands and recordings within their diet of 'hits and memories'. Since October 1999, at least 25 per cent of Australian music played by mainstream rock/contemporary hits stations must be material released in the past year.

The commercial sector's syndicated formats are dominated by a few large metropolitan and regional networks that seek to match particular rock, pop and dance formats to the largest audiences and advertisers.

BOX 12.3: *PPCA V COMMERCIAL RADIO AUSTRALIA*

In 2010, one of the central collection societies, the Phonographic Performance Company of Australia (PPCA) sought in the High Court to lift the 1 per cent cap on radio broadcast royalties from sound recordings that has existed since 1969. Commercial radio broadcasters are required to pay artists and labels no more than 1 per cent of the station's gross annual revenue. The PPCA believed the cap was unfair, as it was not applied to any other royalty arrangements for broadcasting; and that the 1 per cent rate was inadequate given the substantial role of music in commercial broadcasting (see PPCA 2011). The CEO of Commercial Radio Australia, Joan Warner, aligned the cap debate with local content quotas for Australian music:

> If something happens to the 1 per cent cap because it's supposedly an unfair acquisition, what about the music quota which is forced supply of a product? . . . Is there unfair acquisition of our only product, which is air time, by a forced supply from a particular group of music companies? (cited in Sexton 2010)

The High Court ruled that the current 1 per cent rate was constitutionally valid in March 2012 (Australian Copyright Council 2012). The PPCA states that it will continue to lobby the federal government to lift the fixed broadcasting rate (PPCA 2011).

Commercial stations remain driven by 'personality radio', with the choice of presenters (such as Hamish and Andy or Kyle and Jackie O) crucial to ratings success. Comedian Judith Lucy provided useful insight into the Austereo mindset after her sacking from 2Day FM—particularly the extent to which music stations remain tied to dubious listener competitions and tightly formatted programming:

> [At 2DAY FM] the idea was that you'd get a celebrity and the example they used was Guy Sebastian, you'd get Guy to donate his sperm, and the woman who wins the competition, I don't know what the actual competition would have entailed, but she would be lucky enough to win the sperm, and get to impregnate herself. (Lucy, cited in ABC Radio National 2006)

Commercial music radio's traditional 'gatekeeper' role—based upon tight selection and repetition of key music genres and artists—is under threat from a range of internet services that duplicate some of radio's key functions and pleasures. Pandora and Last. fm, for example, offer a 'personal' internet station based upon the formulae of tastes and favoured song properties of the listener, marked by the absence of radio's 'live' properties (a talking DJ, hourly news and weather presentations, audio advertisements). Whether it can be defined as 'music radio' is debatable, yet these services' ability to fine-tune listener preferences from massive digital catalogues, providing a time-shifting 'station' that does not require a 'local' audience, accounts for their popularity (Homan 2007). Composers are also concerned that future digital radio platforms will abandon local music content quotas, allowing local stations to play fewer (or no) Australian artists.

Like commercial radio, the dominant music television programs are celebrity driven. Shows like *Australian Idol* and *The Voice* exploit a variety of media (commercial pop radio, teen and entertainment magazines, chat TV programs, internet sites, mobile phones) to ensure the broadest possible publicity for both program and groomed pop star. These new hybrids of 'reality TV' and older 1970s talent quest programs have justifiably been criticised for reinforcing dominant stereotypes of stardom, 'middle-of-the-road' music genres and unrealistic visions of the personal qualities required for successful career paths. Given the small number of acts that forge lasting careers (such as Guy Sebastian and Shannon Noll), and the emphasis upon conflict (between judges and contestants), such programs arguably remain more about classic television themes and discourses than performing an industry service in launching new artists. *The Voice*, the global franchise given an Australian makeover on Channel Nine, has been successful in part because of a format that highlights performers and is less a promotional vehicle for its celebrity music judges. The franchise airs national variants in 47 countries including Indonesia, Mexico, Ireland, Russia, Norway and China.

Music television programs are available primarily through Channel 11 (*The Loop*), the ABC (*Rage*) and on pay television (for example, Channel V). ABC's digital channel, ABC2, airs a range of concerts and music documentaries, providing a glimpse of the future possibilities of multi-channelling, although ABC1 clearly lacks sufficient funding to provide new, meaningful music programming. Music trivia quiz programs (*Rockwiz* on SBS and, until recently, *Spicks and Specks* on ABC1) have consistently produced high ratings for their respective broadcasters in recent years. An interesting development is the *Popasia* program on SBS, which airs many of Asia's most popular artists on radio, net streaming and television.

MUSIC IN THE CITY

Since the late 1980s, federal, state and local governments increasingly have recognised the role of popular music in the economic and social health of cities and regions. The Blair Labour government in Britain advocated the direction of greater governmental resources to the 'creative industries' (Smith 1998) as a means of connecting its themes of individualism and enterprise with the booming design, fashion, media, sport, theatre, advertising and software industries (Redhead 2004). While the benefits were uneven, new popular music policies aimed at urban and regional regeneration were explored. The notion of 'cultural clusters'—urban hubs of creative production and consumption—has become a fashionable concept in linking industry, government and academic thinking about popular music industries.

In Australia, state governments have turned their attention to nurturing popular music infrastructure in various ways. The Queensland government's Fortitude Valley Music Harmony Plan is a practical means of reconciling residential concerns in an area renowned for its live venues (Brisbane City Council 2008). A South Australian report similarly urged the state government to view its local music scene as an important part of the state's economy, and financial incentives subsequently were introduced by its state government to support live music and training (Live Music Working Group 2001). By late 2007, the New South Wales government had introduced key legislative changes designed to increase the provision of live music, including the streamlining of public entertainment licence processes; the creation of a special category of liquor licence for music and entertainment venues separate from hotel licences; and 'order of occupancy' guidelines for venue/resident noise disputes (Homan 2008). An early Cultural Ministers Council directive from former Midnight Oil member and federal Labor Arts Minister Peter Garrett was an investigation into a national overview of national live performance regulations and infrastructure. Live performance—once thought of simply as a supplement to and promotion of the recording product—remains critical in sustaining careers as recording profits are eroded.

The reputation of Melbourne as the live music capital of Australia was threatened in 2010 when the Victorian Director of Liquor Licensing stipulated that two 'crowd controllers' be employed at venues for every 100 patrons, in addition to the installation of CCTV cameras where recorded or amplified music was provided. This placed many small venues (pubs, music cafes and music bars) at risk of having to abandon live entertainment or face considerable security costs for even small gigs. The Tote Hotel, a Collingwood venue that had presented music since 1980, closed in January 2010, citing the security costs as an important factor. Public engagement in various forms—including a petition with 22 000 signatures tabled within parliament and a rally of 20 000 people outside parliament staged by Save Live Australian Music (SLAM)—led to a Live Music Accord signed between the music industries and the state Labor government (Homan 2010a). The SLAM rally in particular was important in countering government assertions that live music venues were the primary causes of alcohol-fuelled violence in the Melbourne CBD.

While governments and industry sectors argue about how music can best contribute as a national 'creative industry', it is employed in other spheres. The national 'Play for Life' program has successfully increased music education in primary and high schools (Play for Life 2012). Rock, pop and rap have proven to be useful creative forms within 'at-risk' youth programs, particularly for local councils. Popular music has been incorporated into youth crime prevention and social inclusion policies, and more generally included in 'identity-formation' strategies linked to urban/regional regeneration. As Mitchell (2008) points out, the simplicity of hip hop's features has allowed its use in a range of pedagogical contexts. DJ Morganics, for example, remains a key figure for his use of hip hop in teaching disadvantaged youth (including juvenile detainees, remote Indigenous young people and urban community projects) (2008, pp. 246–7). At the same time, notions of deviance and resistance—central to hip hop's founding mythologies—can be emasculated in some youth programs that strive for homogenous outcomes (Baker and Homan 2007). This reveals ongoing tensions where governments perceive some 'creative youth' programs to be actively contributing to 'troubled youth' media discourses.

The struggle for guitar bands and singer-songwriters to obtain decent incomes (or even part-time music careers) has not diminished. As recording revenues have declined, live music has become a vital income stream for most artists (see Box 12.4).

BOX 12.4: THE VALUE OF LIVE MUSIC

Live Performance Australia (2011, p. 22) estimated what it called 'non-classical' live performance (pop, rock, jazz, blues, country, etc) to be worth $659.1 million to the Australian economy in 2010. Festivals remain a substantial sector of live music circuits, worth $100.9 million to the economy in 2010 (Live Performance Australia 2011, p. 20). A 2010 arts participation survey found that 'nearly two in three (62 per cent) Australians participated in music in the past year, with over half attending live events (57 per cent) and 15 per cent creatively participating'; over one-third (41 per cent) attended a performance in the mainstream categories of pop, rock and country at least once in the year (Australia Council 2010, pp. 24–5). An Arts Victoria report underlined the worth of live music to performers as a central part of local night-time economies. The report found that the venue-based live music sector contributes around $500 million annually to the Victorian economy and creates the equivalent of 17 200 full time jobs (Arts Victoria 2011). It was estimated that there were approximately 5.4 million attendances at live venues in 2009–10, greater than attendances at AFL matches, the major winter sport in Victoria (Arts Victoria 2011, p. ii). The report also noted that venue noise issues remained a major concern, especially in high density city areas.

The 'natural' economic state—an over-supply of willing musicians and an under-supply of recording labels, live venues, radio stations and audiences—ensures that livelihoods from music activity remain difficult. These older forms of market economics have transferred to dance music cultures:

> the cost of being a DJ, in other words, buying all the equipment and everything has gone down rapidly . . . so much so that every mummy and daddy can just go out and buy their kids a set of decks, so everyone's a DJ. And if everyone's a DJ, the price of DJs goes down. (DJ, cited in Brennan-Horley 2007, p. 134)

Popular music has provided comfortable livelihoods for a few songwriters and performers, and struggling, part-time careers for the rest. Just how much music is worth, who should pay and who really profits was recently put to the test. In 2006, the Phonographic Performance Company of Australia (PPCA), a non-profit organisation that issues licences that grant businesses the right to play or broadcast protected copyright recordings, launched its campaign to increase the licence fees paid by nightclubs and dance venues for the use of sound recordings. In 2007, the Federal Court's Copyright Tribunal awarded the PPCA a substantial increase in how much dance venues should pay for recorded music, based upon parity with overseas licence fee models; the capacity for venues to accommodate increases; and the centrality of music to the venues' popularity. The venue bodies—including the Australian Hotels Association (AHA) and Clubs Australia—were unsuccessful in arguing that music was at best a secondary input into their businesses (as simply a background function to drinking and socialising) (Homan 2010b). The case was a controversial one, which highlighted the continuing battle between copyright-collection bodies protecting artists' incomes and the importance of popular music to night-time economies.

The music festival remains a popular ritual across different age groups, interests and locations. While the key festivals for youth genres may receive the bulk of media publicity (for example, the Falls Festival, Homebake, the Big Day Out), others have similar attraction and tradition, including the Wintersun Rock'n'Roll and Swing Festival (formerly at Coolangatta, now held at Coffs Harbour) and the Byron Bay East Coast Blues and Roots Festival. Music provides the 'social glue' to other cultural activities, such as wine, food and city heritage celebrations. Other festivals exploit surprising juxtapositions of commemoration, such as the Elvis Revival Festival in Parkes, New South Wales, a popular event with Baby Boomers (Gibson 2007, p. 75). Folk music communities have been particularly inventive in their use of the festival event to ensure that the genre remains 'in conversation' with other contemporary genres and performers (Smith 2007, pp. 159–62).

Music festivals have also been adopted for a range of political ends. Bush dance festivals driven by various dance music genres (especially trance and psy-trance) are now a standard feature in the rural landscape. 'Bush doofs' are often linked to specific eco-activism causes and promoted by word of mouth and 'friendship networks' (Luckman 2008b, pp. 138–40). The choice of music genres and the dance sites (remote outback or hinterland locations) is designed to provide a transcendental experience and reconnection with the land (St John 2001).

CONCLUSION: FUTURE CHALLENGES

Coffee companies signing artists; mobile phone companies entering the music sales business; fans allowed to remix and finance their favourite albums; social networking sites assuming A&R functions—what is going on? The music industries are currently subjected to remarkably fluid networks of technological change and attitudes about contemporary distribution models. And, as the spate of local litigation shows, Australian popular music is at the forefront of global legal, cultural and industrial shifts. Convergence of music content, media forms and consumer media products will continue where it makes sense for industries to exploit different markets and expertise.

Despite its recent successes in persuading governments to continually strengthen intellectual property laws in the name of stable company profits, the recording industry remains bitterly divided about the legalities of digital consumption. Its failure to construct a comprehensive, affordable digital downloading system (subsequently allowing Apple's iTunes to dominate legal sales mechanisms) says much about its inability to rise above traditional rivalries between the majors, its belief in traditional legal and production methods to maintain market share and its refusal to acknowledge the implications of changing 'digital lifestyles'.

Whether recording companies have a role in the twenty-first century will be determined by their ability to confront these issues in a fundamentally different manner. Understandings of the 'ownership' of music—both in copyright terms and with regard to what fans can ultimately do with it—will be a central battleground. The outcome will be of interest to governments and the television and film industries grappling with similar trade and intellectual property concerns.

However, we should be aware that the extent and pace of technological change have the potential to mask the central qualities of popular music as a cultural and media form. The revival of live performance as a means of experiencing our favourite artists is a reminder that some basic connections between production and consumption remain. How popular music constructs individual identities and communities of taste, which in turn shapes how we see ourselves and others, will continue to be a central question to ask in the particularly Australian context of a global chain of listening, dancing, composing and playing.

FURTHER READING

The importance of music festival circuits to Australian performers and cities is assessed in Chris Gibson and John Connell (2012), *Music Festivals and Regional Development in Australia*. Charles Fairchild (2008), *Pop Idols and Pirates: Mechanisms of Consumption and the Global Circulation of Music* provides a good examination of the rise of pop talent television franchises. Homan and Mitchell's (2007) *Sounds of Then, Sounds of Now: Popular Music in Australia* is the most recent anthology of writing on various Australian music genres and artists. Jon Stratton (2007), *Australian Rock: Essays on Popular Music* investigates key local rock performers and their social and geographical influences. Graeme Smith (2005), *Singing Australian: A History of Folk and Country Music*, provides a solid analysis of folk and country music communities. Whiteoak and Scott-Maxwell's (2003) *The Currency Companion to Music and Dance in Australia* provides a comprehensive overview of music genres, performance practices and artists. See Maxwell (2003), *Phat Beats, Dope Rhymes* and Mitchell (2001), *Global Noise* for studies on Australian hip hop. Dunbar-Hall and Gibson (2004), *Deadly Sounds, Deadly Spaces* is a useful investigation of contemporary Aboriginal music. Johnson (2000), *The Inaudible Music* is a thoughtful assessment of Australian jazz and local popular culture. For an examination of the governance of live music venues, see Homan (2003), *The Mayor's a Square: Live Music and Law and Order in Sydney*. For works examining music policy, see Breen (1999) *Rock Dogs* and Homan, Cloonan and Cattermole (2013), *Popular Music Industries and the State: Policy Notes*. The Music Council of Australia's 'Knowledge Base' (<www.mca.org.au>) is a useful source of industry statistics and current research.

Chapter 14

THE INTERNET, ONLINE AND MOBILE COMMUNICATION

GERARD GOGGIN

In the mid-2010s, as the internet enters its fourth decade, the great networked technology is everywhere. In many cases, it is now difficult to draw distinctions between what we formerly called 'media and communication', and the 'new' technology of the internet. More often than not, the great social, cultural, economic and political transformations of our time—in which media and communication matter completely—have everything to do with the internet.

Nearly 20 years ago, many thought the internet would sweep everything before it, and likened the technology to a 'tornado' or 'juggernaut' (FCC 1997). The storm bells rang a little early. By the mid-2010s, however, the internet has been at the heart of dramatic changes in television, radio, newspaper, publishing, film, games and other media. Most media companies not only have substantial internet ventures; quite a number of these internet subsidiaries or experiments are now the main game, with the digital tail well and truly wagging the media dog. For media companies, the internet is a central way by which to reach audiences. Indeed, the internet is key to how these audiences are being reshaped.

This is evident in contemporary television, for instance. We might recall that in March 2008, internet usage in Australia overtook television viewing for the first time. In 2012, television was still going strong as a prime medium for Australian audiences. The difference, in the span of just a few years, is that television practices are changing. When, where and how people watch television, what it means to them and what they make of it decisively depend on the internet and which mobile device they favour. Prime-time has been blurred, through internet downloading of programs, catch-up and time-shifting. Television is mashed up with bits of user-generated and Facebook-shared video, alongside the rise of cleverly plotted and lavishly produced home box office (HBO) DVD box-sets—complicating our ideas about the medium revolving around 'flow'.

This may come as no surprise to most of the readers of this book, especially undergraduate students proceeding to university, who have 'grown up' with the internet—or, better still, have been incubated in the contemporary cultures of the internet. The idea that there is a 'virtual world'—or, odder still, 'cyberspace'—that is weirdly separate from, and a poor imitation of, the 'offline' world makes little sense anymore (if it ever did).

In studying the internet and associated mobile media, we need to understand the histories and development of internet technologies, their associated social functions and their cultural forms. We confront a paradox at the outset: the internet is hailed as a radically global media technology—through it, we hasten towards Marshall McLuhan's vision (expressed in the early 1960s) of a 'global village' (Levinson 1999). For many, the internet is now the key player among the various media that have made 'globalisation' possible. As in many other countries, the media and communications in Australia have fundamentally been altered through the complex developments associated with the rise of the internet. Many internet users and scholars alike believe that, in the face of the internet, ideas of 'national' culture and media pale into insignificance. National gatekeepers, public service broadcasters, media corporations and barons, governments, censors and regulators struggle to stay relevant, profitable and in control, faced with the personal, broadcasting, communicating and media-making possibilities allowed by email, the web, file-sharing technologies, video-sharing, blogging, social media and other internet-based media.

Yet the eclipse of nations, their media and what historian Benedict Anderson famously called 'imagined communities' afforded by the internet needs to be set alongside the persistence of the national, and the rise of the local and regional, in a complex social and cultural shaping of the contemporary internet. Indeed, the internet can take such striking distinct guises, or incarnations, in different places and cultural settings, to justify us speaking of 'global internets'. This plurality of internets means that we both need to globalise our understanding of Australian media and communication through the advent of the internet and, at the same time, localise our amorphous understanding of global internet media, its industrial attachments and its cultures of use.

The position underpinning this chapter is that there is no single 'global internet'—invented in Cupertino, or elsewhere in California's Silicon Valley, for instance—that becomes the template, applied to bring freedom and innovation to the Australian internet, as it does the rest of the world. Rather, to understand the internet as *the* vital ingredient in contemporary media and communications, we need to understand what is specific to the Australian internet—and how it uniquely articulates into the complex international corporations, circuits and networks of international internets— which take shape in South Korea, Japan, China, Africa, the Middle East and South America as much as in North America and Europe. The Australian internet, in particular, is now very much a part of the media and cultural flows of what we loosely call the Asia-Pacific region.

In this spirit, this chapter argues that the internet needs to be studied to understand *what* it is, what its *characteristics and structures* are, and how it *fits into contemporary communications and media*. Here, detailed attention to the workings of internet and mobile cultures, consumption and production is vital—both to understand a fast-moving mediascape and to be able to place this in the broader environment of media and communications in Australia. Accordingly, the first part of this chapter provides an introduction to the basics of the internet and its historical development. The second part offers a snapshot of Australian internet users. This is followed by an overview of the commercial structures of Australia's internet industry and a discussion of characteristics of our internet consumption and use. Finally, the rise of mobile and locative media, and wireless technologies, is examined, and we will look at how the mobile internet is involved in media convergence generally.

BACK TO THE FUTURE: UNDERSTANDING INTERNET HISTORIES

The internet was officially launched in 1969, and for the first two decades of its life was largely a network used by and for researchers. By the beginning of the 1990s, the internet's role had changed radically. From a text-based network in universities and research institutions, the internet went mainstream. People experimented with the internet, pioneering new media practices and forms, and creating new ways of consuming and using media. Since 2001, the internet has dramatically changed again, with the emergence of new online technologies and cultures, often discussed under the labels of 'Web 2.0' or 'Web 3.0', including peer-to-peer (p2p) applications, blogs, podcasting, wikis, social software, social media, user-generated content, mobile and wireless internet, and many other developments, including the 'internet of things' (meaning the wireless network of connections between gadgets and everyday objects, made possible by the ubiquitous embedding of short-range transceivers).

The internet has been called a 'network of networks'. At its simplest, it is a set of protocols that allow different types of computers, operating systems and networks to be connected together (for a succinct introduction, see Clarke 2004). While being very 'scaleable'—that is, permitting great expansion in size while still functioning—the internet is quite decentralised in its fundamental workings.

The concepts underlying the internet were developed by a range of scientists in the United Kingdom, France and elsewhere (Gilles and Cailliau 2000), but were brought together and developed into the internet by a US military-funded research agency called the Advanced Research Project Agency Network (ARPANET) (Abbate 1999). In 1969, the Advanced Research Project Agency (ARPA) connected together a number of computer networks at US universities and research institutions, and the internet grew from there. More universities connected to the internet, as did more countries. Australian enthusiasts made dial-up connections over international telephone lines to the internet during the 1970s, but it was not until the advent of the Australian Computer Science network in the early 1980s that the first permanent connection was established. In May and June 1989, the University of Melbourne connected to the University of Hawaii, and so to the internet. Permanent connections to other universities followed in 1990, as the Australian Academic Research Network (AARNET) was established.

From the 1960s until the late 1980s, the US government and its agencies bore the lion's share of funding the internet's establishment and growth, and internet users were largely responsible for its technical development, coordination and governance. As the internet grew, so too did pressure on funding and governance. Governments—especially the US government—felt unable to continue funding the internet, so looked at ways for the private sector to bear the cost. For its part, the internet was for many years a commerce-free zone, with its 'acceptable use' rules prohibiting trade for profit. The ban on commerce on the internet was lifted in 1992, and commercial interests entered every area, from providing access, email addresses, website hosting and design to domain rate registration, pornography and electronic commerce.

Some commercial internet services were available in Australia from 1989, including DIALIX in Western Australia and Pegasus, operating from Byron Bay (Clarke 2004; Goggin 2003). By late 1994, use of the internet by the non-university sector was about 20 per cent of total traffic, and from the mid-1990s a competitive market in internet backbone, wholesale and retail services grew rapidly. Interestingly, with the growth of broadband internet in the early to mid-2000s, there was a perceived need for government to once again play a leading role in building the infrastructure—as the market had not delivered adequate quality networks. Hence the Rudd Labor government's National Broadband Network (NBN) initiative (discussed in Chapter 7).

One of the early functions envisaged for the internet was the sharing of scarce computer resources. By connecting mainframe computers in different sites, the use of these expensive machines could be maximised. What gradually developed, however, was a wide and diverse range of applications and technologies for the internet that enabled new kinds of communications, as well as cultural and social interactions: electronic mail and email lists; file transfer protocol; newsgroups; the World Wide Web; multi-user dungeons (MUDs) and MUDs object-oriented (MOOs), forerunners of immersive communities such as *Second Life*; internet relay chat (IRC) and other chat programs; instant messaging (IM); indexing tools (such as Archie and Veronica), forerunners of search engines like Yahoo and Google; database and server applications; streaming video and audio (such as Realplayer); p2p applications—especially music; weblogs ('blogs'); webcams; distributed computing; telephone calls and voice communications (especially through the Voice Over Internet Protocol, or VOIP); networked computer games; open news applications; photo-sharing sites; social software (Facebook, MySpace); social media (such as social bookmarking); video distribution networks (famously YouTube); user-generated content; and mobile internet software applications (apps).

MODES OF CONNECTION: AUSTRALIA'S INTERNET USERS

In mid-2012, Australia's internet subscribers passed the twelve million mark (ABS 2012a). This figure includes fixed internet connections (ADSL, fibre, cable, satellite, fixed wireless and a small percentage still with dial-up connections) as well as mobile wireless (broadband) connections (such as dongle, data card and USB modem) connections. There are another approximately 16.2 million Australians who access the internet via their mobile handsets (ACMA 2012b, p. 36). Combining all these figures, we find that Australia had a total of 28.23 million internet subscribers, up 17 per cent from the mid-2011 figure—with many subscribers having more than one internet service (hence subscriptions outnumber the total population) (ACMA 2012b, p. 36).

The vast majority of Australia's household have internet (86 per cent in 2011; Ewing and Thomas 2012, p. 1), mostly broadband (96 per cent). Most Australians use the internet currently (86.8 per cent) with just under one in ten never using it, and ex-users (people who don't use it anymore) only representing 3.6 per cent (2011 figures; Ewing and Thomas 2012, p. i). By the available measures, the internet is part of Australian everyday life, with nine out of ten people describing it in 2011 as a 'very important' or 'important' part of their life (compared with eight out of ten in 2007) (Ewing and Thomas 2012, p. v).

Similarly authoritative figures from the Australian Communications and Media Authority (ACMA) show that the internet was only more deeply embedded by mid-2012, with only 7 per cent of respondents having never used it (ACMA 2012a, p. 115). Leading online activities were communication (email, instant messaging, Skype and other VOIP services (78 per cent), research and information (77 per cent), banking and finance (67 per cent), entertainment and amusement (61 per cent), buying, selling, shopping (54 per cent), blogs and online communities (38 per cent), advertising (33 per cent) and interactive (entered competitions, registered on website) (25 per cent) (Roy Morgan June 2012 survey, quoted in ACMA 2012a, p. 118).

The longitudinal survey conducted by the ARC Centre of Excellence for Creative Industries and Innovation offers a pithy summary of this 'digital transformation':

- 'Australians are doing more online all the time.'
- 'The internet is a social technology.'
- 'The internet changes the way people access and use the media.'
- '[It] helps people share creative work, and encourages some to produce it.'
- '[It] is a major source of entertainment.'
- 'Australians love shopping online.'
- 'The internet changes politics.' (Ewing & Thomas 2012, pp. v–vi)

This picture of the intense, pervasive role of the internet in Australian everyday life needs to be leavened by at least two major qualifications and critiques. First, not everyone has access to the internet, or the financial resources, literacy or cultural capital to use it on the same terms as those in the mainstream. For instance, 91 per cent of households with income under $40 000 have broadband internet access at home, compared with 96 per cent of households with income over $120 000 (ABS 2011b).

Age is a major correlate of access and use. The most active internet users are those aged 18–44 years, characterised by highest rates of usage for most surveyed activities (ACMA 2012a, p. 118). Yet care is needed in ascertaining the exact characteristics of internet use across age demographics—it is often difficult to do in the face of stereotypes of young people as rolled-gold 'digital natives' and older people as clueless, reluctant adopters. 'Youth', for instance, is a complex category, as is 'children'—covering a wide range of different groups, especially when socio-economic and cultural circumstances are taken into consideration. For instance, 14–17-year-olds generally have lower levels of mobile phone take-up, smartphone adoption and mobile phone internet usage compared with all other groups, except older Australians—possibly because of 'young persons' reduced earning capacity and greater likelihood of relying on parental support to pay mobile phone bills' (ACMA 2012a, p. 34). Despite the stereotype, there are many older users of the internet. We can see, for example, that particular services, applications, or modes and levels of participation skew across age demographics. For instance, a higher proportion of 14–34-year-olds seek their entertainment online, whereas older internet users tend to use the internet more heavily for finances and transactions (ACMA 2012a, p. 118).

In Australia, consistent with the history of media in this country, there remain quite distinct patterns of access and use between metropolitan and non-metropolitan locations—though the gap is narrowing. This general picture is complicated when we consider the wide range of communities, infrastructures, cultures and geographies outside the capital cities, across what is typically regarded in policy as regional, rural and remote areas (e.g. see Gregg and Wilson 2011). The most striking disparities are those between Indigenous and non-Indigenous users, especially in remote locations. A 2011 study noted that 'Indigenous Australians living in remote areas are the least likely to have access to the internet from home' (ARC CoE 2011, p 16). Just 20 per cent of Indigenous households in remote and very remote Australia had an internet connection in 2006, compared with 60 per cent of their non-Indigenous counterparts living in the same area. In Central Australia, takeup was as low as 2.2 per cent for Indigenous households (compared with 57 per cent of comparable non-Indigenous counterparts) (2006 ABS figures, quoted in ARC CoE 2011, p. 16). The overall low level of internet users has consequences for all, as Thomas and Rennie (2012) note:

> [When] we look at people elsewhere in Australia who don't use the internet, a substantial number turn out to be 'proxy users'. Many are older, and while they don't use the internet themselves, they can ask family or friends to do things online for them—buy air tickets, for example, or complete an online form for a government agency. In remote Australia, where there are significantly fewer active users across generations, there are correspondingly fewer proxy users.

Disability is another area where internet access and use by Australians are often quite different in nature, and where real barriers to access and digital participation are evident. The available statistics show that in 2009 just over half (53 per cent) of persons with a disability used the internet (up from 39 per cent in 2003) (ABS 2011b), yet 71 per cent had access to a computer at home (up from 55 per cent in 2003), and 62 per cent had internet access at home (41 per cent in 2003) (ABS 2011b).

Such figures should prompt us to acknowledge the kinds of social exclusion in which the internet is involved—but this is only the first step to establishing the new social relations in which the internet has such a significant place. Moreover, we still do not understand much about the modes of connection such pervasive internet use entails, and what their implications are.

Much public debate and social anxiety turns on this—for instance, Australian versions of the internet-as-silly-and-superficial argument, or worries that the internet or, worse still mobile technology, will alter the structure of our brains (Carr 2010). Of course, the implications of any technology are very important to understand, especially when it comes to harnessing their potential while addressing pitfalls. What can help ground such discussions is an understanding of what connecting to the internet in its contemporary Australian forms actually involves—and here research and public debate lag well behind the cutting edge of conversation and experiment among groups in the networked 'public spheres' and the everyday meaning-making interactions with the internet by ordinary users.

COMMERCIAL STRUCTURES

The internet industry is difficult to define and measure because of the diverse range of services and products it encompasses, and the new kinds of media organisation it involves. This is signalled by the fact that the internet industry is represented by a number of industry associations: the Internet Industry Association (<www.iia. net.au>), the Australian Interactive Media Association (<www.aimia.com.au>), the Australian Computer Society (<www.acs.org.au>) and the Australian Information Industry Association (<www.aiia.com.au>). Not surprisingly, reliable information on the size and revenue of the internet industry is difficult to obtain.

Once the internet became a zone of commerce and an internet industry developed in earnest in the 1990s, a fever gripped previously nonplussed investors, managers and technologists (Lovink 2003). From 1997 to 2000, Australia experienced its own 'dot.com bubble', and its own 'crash' (Goggin 2004a). Extraordinary claims were made that the internet was not only the 'next best thing' as a new industry, but that it was part of a 'new economy' that suspended the rules of business and economics. Since 2000, a more cautious approach has been taken in the internet industry, with the recognition that user behaviour needs to be carefully studied and new business models developed in order for sustainable and profitable enterprises to be established. This has occurred, with many new kinds of businesses created—including non-traditional business types (for instance, drawing on open source, Creative Commons or social entrepreneurship models). Since 2008, the burgeoning internet and mobile media industries, including new players, have been grappling with the profound economic difficulties posed by the GFC. The economics of internet innovation—and the search for the business models they entail—remain at the heart of trying to figure out whether a particular internet form (Facebook, for instance) is just a flash-in-the-pan (remember MySpace?) or a genuinely lasting part of how we communicate.

Internet infrastructure

The pioneering organisation AARNET still plays an important role in the Australian internet, operating the National Research and Education Network (NREN)—the internet for universities and the Commonwealth Scientific and Industrial Organisation (CSIRO), currently connecting across 10 gigabit per second links. Now it is just one of a wide variety of internet infrastructures and delivery modes—something that stands to be dramatically transformed by the rollout of the NBN—if it continues after the 2013 federal election (see Chapter 7).

In 2012–13, however, internet access technologies in Australia still mostly comprised dial-up; digital subscriber line (ADSL), using the existing copper-based access network; hybrid fibre coaxial (HFC) cable; mobile internet; fibre; and satellite (ACMA 2012a, p. 43). At June 2011, there were 97 broadband internet service providers (ISPs), representing a consolidation of the industry since the heyday of dial-up internet (ACMA 2012a, p. 25). There were only four providers whose offerings were underpinned by their own broadband cable network: Telstra and Optus (via their cable TV—fibre coaxial cable—network, laid in the mid-1990s); Canberra's pioneering provider TransACT (acquired by iiNet in late 2011); and Neighbourhood Cable (a subsidiary of TransACT serving Mildura, Bendigo and Geelong). Telstra and Optus have struck agreements to transfer their customers to the NBN, basing their services on the new national infrastructure.

Supported by the Australian Broadband Guarantee, satellite broadband has been the only real option for most people living in low-population areas—with an estimated 106 000 satellite internet subscribers at June 2011. At this time, the NBN launched its interim satellite offering, the centrepiece now of government policy for rural citizens outside the reach of the fixed-line NBN.

ISPs are regulated by a range of different bodies, such as ACMA in matters of appropriate content, as well as some areas of consumer protection and technical standards, and the Australian Competition and Consumer Commission (ACCC)—especially regarding anti-competition conduct, and deceptive and misleading conduct. Like telecommunications carriage service providers, ISPs offering services to residential consumers are obliged to join the Telecommunications Industry Ombudsman scheme. ISPs are also subject to self-regulatory codes of practice developed through the Internet Industry Association (for instance, in the area of appropriate content). Because of their key role in consumer internet, the ISPs have been in the thick of recent policy debates on internet censorship, media classification and freedom of expression—seen as a gatekeeper, particularly by government.

Under internet infrastructure, it is now important to note the main providers of mobile internet infrastructure—the mobile carriers and service providers. In 2013, there were three mobile carrier networks across second- , third- and fourth-generation mobiles—operated by Telstra, Optus and Vodafone Hutchison Australia (VHA).

In addition to household, mobile and wireless connections, users access internet services in a wide range of public, semi-public and private settings, such as internet cafes, kiosks, community access centres (especially in rural and remote areas), libraries, workplaces and educational institutions (ABS 2012a).

Domain name services

As the internet grew exponentially in the early 1990s, and the web blossomed, web addresses grew in their personal, cultural and commercial significance. Web addresses were linked to an underlying alphanumerical system of identifying internet addresses, domains and hosts—the domain name registration system. This moved into the hands of private, competitive providers and became an immensely profitable—if volatile—industry as it matured (Goggin 2004a).

In 1999, auDa (.au Domain Administration Ltd, <www.auda.org.au>) was established as a non-profit company, and is part of the international framework, recognised in 2001 by the Internet Corporation for Assigned Names and Numbers (ICANN). auDa operates the .au domain space under a self-regulatory model. Another company, AusRegistry, is the actual registry operator, and the wholesale provider for all commercial and non-commercial .au domain names. The retail providers—or auDA registers—are companies that provide services to anyone who wishes to register a domain name.

Email

Email remains an important form of communication in its own right. There are broadly two types of email services: email accounts provided by an ISP, or by a workplace or educational institution (often via a dedicated ISP); and 'free' email accounts, still dominated by Gmail (Google Mail), Yahoo! Mail or Windows Live Hotmail (formerly MSN Hotmail, and before that simply Hotmail). The free accounts are supported by advertising, and the value of having subscribers use other services offered by providers. Following the lead of Google, Yahoo! and Windows now offer substantial email and file storage, and server-based applications and services such as 'cloud-computing' (meaning users use the internet to access computing services, resources and files, not needing to hold data locally). Despite the scourge of spam, scams and viruses, email remains important for many communication contexts and practices, not least the email list and its 'list cultures' (Lovink 2002).

The web industry

The World Wide Web revolutionised the internet because it provided a way to easily link together and find resources. It put media tools in the hands (or rather screens, keyboards and mice) of the masses. Some 20 years since its widespread takeup, there is now a substantial industry associated with the web. There are companies that specialise in hosting websites, which provide a range of functionality. Most large Australian ISPs are happy to do this, but it is often cheaper to have a site hosted overseas.

Websites became important to communications and media more generally from the mid-1990s onwards. The first websites were established by people in universities such as ANU Professor David Green's 1992 Life (<life.csu.edu.au>), which claimed to be the first website in Australia, and the Botanic Gardens Site (<www.anbg.gov.au>), but were then followed by a slew of other sites, including by commercial organisations, especially communication and media organisations (such as *Rolling Stone* magazine's Next website).

While slow to appreciate the pre-web internet, the dominant media interests of print, radio and television eventually established dedicated digital media sections and secured a web presence. Their existing brand names provided reassuring familiarity for internet 'newbies', or for those finding the navigation of the internet difficult. The rise of portals, for instance, suited the established players quite well.

Hence most established media companies have a dedicated digital division or subsidiary as part of their cross-platform strategy—for example, Fairfax Digital (for the Fairfax press stable), ninemsn (joint venture between Channel 9 and Microsoft, established in 1997) and News Digital Media (for Rupert Murdoch's News Limited titles). These outlets now play a very influential role in media consumption. For instance, during June 2012, approximately 12.27 million Australians accessed online news sites, with ninemsn Nine News the most accessed site (ACMA 2012b, p. 32). Nonetheless, these companies have been challenged by a multitude of digitally conceived alternatives, such as the long-running *Crikey*, *New Matilda* and the university-supported sites *Inside Story* and *The Conversation*, as well as smaller blogs, Twitter feeds and websites. While the traditional titans of Australian media—especially the broadcasters, press and magazines and advertisers—have strong stakes in the Australian internet, the tech companies—old and new—have taken the commanding heights (cf. Castells 2009), as Table 14.1 reveals.

Table 14.1 Top ten online brands, July 2012

Brands	Unique audience (millions)
Google	13.61
Facebook	11.36
ninemsn/MSN	10.64
YouTube	9.92
Microsoft	8.82
Yahoo!7	8.37
Wikipedia	7.28
eBay	7.12 n
Apple	6.56
Blogger	4.83

Source: Nielsen Online, *Australian Online Landscape Review*, July 2012 (<www.nielsen.com/au/en/news-insights/press-room/2012/australian-online-landscape-review-july-2012.html>); [permission to be sought for reproduction]

While the basic architecture of the web has remained the same, its core protocols have become more complex and sophisticated, and important new web, networking and media technologies have emerged.

Search engines

With the advent of the web, search engines became a lucrative business in their own right. Google is the dominant player in Australia, as elsewhere, possessing some technology development capacity locally as well as growing policy influence. Internationally, Yahoo!, the once proud pioneer of search, is in demise—but still retains an important place in Australia through its joint venture Yahoo!7.

The largest home-grown competitor in search remains Telstra's Sensis online and mobile search based on its older telephone directories business. For a long time, directories dominated media advertising spend, but with the phenomenal growth of online advertising and search, Sensis has been forced to drastically cut staff—despite reorienting its operations to online.

Social media

The area of enormous growth in the internet since 2005 has been in what was termed Web 2.0 and now social media. Under the banner of social media are typically included user-generated content, mash-ups, easy-to-use tools for creating and distributing multimedia content, social networking, content feeds, image and video sharing, commenting, tagging and recommending. Web 2.0 has been displaced by the term 'social media', often used just as loosely to indicate social networking systems (like Facebook and LinkedIn), image or video-sharing (Instagram, Flickr, YouTube), micro-blogging (Twitter) or even mobile or locative media (Foursquare, Facebook Places, apps) (see Chapter 11). Research on the structure of social media industries is nascent (Albarran 2013), but while some of the big, enabling players—such as Facebook—have a presence in Australia, they are mostly based overseas (especially in the United States). Typically, the Australian social media companies are focused on providing applications and tools for social media—a lucrative new area of internet media (see Chapter 25 on apps).

Cloud computing

The provision of applications, tools, computing and file storage from remote services, rather than them being installed on devices themselves, is a fast-growing reality of the contemporary Australian internet. Much cloud computing is provided by global concerns, with applications like Dropbox widely used by households and workplaces (despite security concerns). The structure of the nascent industry, its characteristics and implications—especially in the Australian context—are still unclear. However, many Australians already use cloud-based services, as an April 2011 survey showed, for: sending and receiving email (95 per cent); webmail (68 per cent); social networking sites (60 per cent); storing personal photos online (43 per cent); applications such as Google docs or Adobe Photoshop Express (41 per cent); storing personal video online (11 per cent); backing up their hard drive to an online site (7 per cent); and paying to store computer files online (6 per cent) (ACMA 2012a, p. 162).

BOX 14.1: INDUSTRY PROFILE OF ONLINE AND INTERACTIVE SERVICES

Internet access services

- Backhaul transmission network providers
- Internet service providers (97)
- Broadband internet providers (three carriers)
- Satellite (33 providers)
- Wireless internet providers
- Mobile carriers (three carriers)

Key internet services

- Email providers
- Domain name services (38 auDA accredited registrars)
- Website hosting and design services
- Search engines
- VOIP (176 providers)
- Cloud computing

Key forms of interactive technology and services

- Social media platforms (Facebook, Twitter, LinkedIn)
- Chat
- Messaging
- p2p applications
- Blogs
- Photo-sharing sites (such as Instagram and Flickr)
- Video-sharing sites (such as YouTube)
- Wikis (collaborative websites and databases)
- Immersive communities (such as *Second Life*)
- Maps and navigation (Google Maps)
- Geospatial web (images, maps and annotation, such as tagging)
- Wireless sensor networks ('the internet of things')

Source for figures: ACMA (2012a, pp. 24–5).

INTERNET CONSUMPTION AND CULTURES OF USE

Over the almost four decades of its existence, the many technologies, applications and services associated with the internet have created new forms of media consumption and cultures of use. Of key interest to students of communications and media—and wider, ongoing public fascination—is understanding these new internet cultures, and placing them in the historical and comparative context with other communications and media practices. While some of these new forms of interactivity have been extensively discussed and studied (such as email, web and online communities of various sorts), there has still not been a great deal of work on the Australian context, especially when it comes to the most recent internet technologies.

Chat, virtual and immersive worlds

The desire of internet users to find spaces in which to interact with each other has been evident for a long time. A number of Australians were avid users of early 'chat' programs, such as MOOs and MUDs, which drew on role-playing game models and cultures such as *Dungeons and Dragons*. There were also pre-internet models in 'bulletin boards' and early online communities, and in the early Australian ISP Pegasus's 'cafes' (Goggin 2003b).

An early technology that pioneered chat and meeting people was internet relay chat (IRC). The IRC client allowed people to meet others and talk over many dedicated channels. IRC was displaced by web-based chat. Chat became popular for all sorts of social interaction, but most famously as a mode of forming amorous and erotic relationships. Meeting people over the web is now a well-established way of finding partners across all sexual cultures, especially for members of sexual minorities who have long been on the margins of public space. Chat remains important, and now is embedded across a wide range of platforms and applications—often used interchangeably with file-sharing and video chat (as in Skype or Google Hangout). Another form of 'synchronous' online communication has been instant messaging, pioneered in the ICQ program. Instant messaging found popularity among tech-savvy users, and then with the much more commercially positioned MSN Messenger (now Windows Live Messenger), was widely adopted by young Australian users.

The antecedent forms of online communities, chat and messengers have found their way into virtual worlds and immersive communities. One of the most popular in Australia remains Linden Lab's *Second Life*, with a dedicated group of users across a range of settings, especially in universities, businesses, art circles and elsewhere. Debates continue about immersive, virtual worlds—such as what kind of social life *Second Life* constitutes, or the representation of disability (Ellis and Kent 2013; Hickey-Moody and Wood 2008)—but to a great extent they are now taken for granted as an important part of how Australians use the internet.

Peer-to-peer (p2p) applications, photo-sharing and video-sharing websites

Peer-to-peer networks use direct connections between computer clients (peers) rather than relying on server–client relationships. The popularity of programs such as

BitTorrent, which allows TV shows and movies to be downloaded from the internet (<www.bittorrent.com>) ushered in user choice and interactivity promised by digital television (Meikle and Young 2009). Video-sharing platforms such as YouTube have combined with downloading to continue to be a prime force in the redefinition of contemporary television.

Such user cultures continue to challenge the strategies of free-to-air and pay television broadcasters, seeking to guide and profit from consumer behaviour through the carefully controlled introduction of personal video recorders, recordable set-top boxes, portable digital devices and mobile media, TV and video apps, and ultimately the NBN (which, if fully implemented, will see broadband internet enshrined as the major alternative to digital television broadcasting). Photo-sharing sites such as Flickr (acquired by Yahoo! in 2005) have sought to survive by integrating with the most popular photo software such as Apple's iPhoto. Otherwise, users now typically share mobile and digital photos via social media platforms, and the apps integrated into them, such as the popular Instagram.

Blogs and wikis

Weblogs (blogs) developed as an online journal, offering new ways to distribute ideas, images and sounds, and to comment on and link to others' work. The word was coined in 1997, and usage spread rapidly in 1999 with the arrival of blogging tools such as Blogger, WordPress and Tumblr. Blogs became popular after the September 11, 2001 New York tragedy, and rapidly assumed an important role in alternative news-gathering and dissemination on the left and right—especially during the Second Gulf War from 2003.

In Australia, blogging has been an important source of innovation in internet media culture. Bloggers have developed a role in politics—signalled early on, for instance, with journalist Margo Kingston's pioneering web diary for the *Sydney Morning Herald* starting in 2000 (now available at <http://webdiary.com.au/cms>) or during the 2004 federal election. Established media organisations now routinely include blogs as part of their cross-platform offerings, notably as part of the contributions of newspaper or broadcast journalists.

Debate has raged for some time about whether blogs add illumination or just noise to the public sphere (Lovink 2007), although now social media more broadly tend to be seen as the culprit in making for a loutish public sphere. In many ways, the furore about the blogosphere is beside the point as, like websites, blogs have initiated new practices, opened new spaces for a multitude of communities and interests and made a discernible contribution to media diversity (Bruns and Jacobs 2006; Bruns 2008; Russell and Echchaibi 2009). With the advent of social media, blogs are less prominent as a 'stand-alone' internet platform for opinion, views, news, links and commentary. Rather, they form part of an integrated set of communication—in which pundits and publishers will move between website, Twitter, photo-sharing, Facebook and their blog, depending on audience or desired form of communication.

Wikis are collaborative websites, made famous through the indispensable Wikipedia. Wikis allow users to freely create and edit web content. They have been widely used on the Australian internet, for a range of education, cultural, professional and personal projects. The high-water mark of wikis has probably passed, but there remain a number of interesting uses by institutions using wikis to allow greater access and involvement from their end-users and audiences (for instance, by the National Library of Australia).

Social networking systems

In Australia, Facebook and LinkedIn dominate internet-based social networks, with YouTube, Twitter, Tumblr and others also being significant.

Facebook is most popular, with nearly eight million Australians accessing it at its monthly peak in the first half of 2011 (ACMA 2012a, p. 164). The professionally oriented social networking software LinkedIn has consolidated its place in Australia, with many sectors reporting it is a prime tool for recruitment. It claimed nearly three million users in June 2011 (ACMA 2012a, p. 164). Twitter makes up in influence among networked public spheres what it lacks in raw numbers—approximately one million in June 2011 (ACMA 2012a, p. 164). Doubtless Australians are using many other social networking applications—including those popular in China, Korea, Japan, and other countries in the Asia-Pacific region. However, there are no easily available figures to give a clear sense of the Australian internet's location in the babble of international internets and social media.

Most types of social networking software revolve around a user inviting a friend or colleague to join their group. Social software provides a semi-open, regulated way of building new friendships and other relationships by mobilising trust. In its mass medium phase, social software has also offered a new media form—making it possible to circulate information, send invitation to events, post photos and create identities in ways that other internet technologies (whether email, messaging or websites) would previously have been required to do. With the user fatigue that has set on in the face of a bewildering range of social networking systems, the most popular platforms build in interconnectivity—allowing log-in via another trusted account (typically Facebook or Twitter).

Social networking systems have now been fully integrated into social media at large and, further still, into electronic and mobile commerce, entrenching the user and industrial trends evident from the 2007 onwards. Advertising, retail information, 'liking' of goods, services and commercial providers, and other kinds of commercial and consumer activity are widespread, if disliked by many users.

Social networking systems are also well entrenched as an important feature of the communicative, promotional and political cultures of many organisations, something that can be charted in successive federal elections—from the use of Facebook and MySpace in the 2007 Kevin Rudd ('Kevin '07') campaign through to its sophisticated, near-seamless incorporation by Labor, the Coalition and The Greens in the 2013 election.

WIRELESS TECHNOLOGIES AND MOBILE MEDIA

As we have seen, the contemporary reality of the Australian internet for many users is a mobile one, with users increasingly attracted to the idea of accessing the internet anywhere using a range of wireless and mobile devices.

Wireless internet was introduced commercially in Australia in 2003–04, with initially slow takeup rates. In the tradition of early internet notions of public access and the gift economy, 'hacker' culture and community or cooperative networking, Wi-Fi was celebrated as offering a way for citizens to escape the thrall of large ISPs and providers (Sandvig 2004). Not only could anyone potentially set up a Wi-Fi network and offer it to passers-by, they could also join anyone else's network—a vision of the 'wireless commons' (Benkler 2006). In various Australian locales, community-based Wi-Fi was an important experiment in digital cultures (Jungnickel 2013). Wi-Fi is now widely available in hotels, cafes, airports, tourist destinations and on university campuses. Wi-Fi has also been enormously popular in the home—where many Australian households now access the internet via a wireless router (Goggin and Gregg 2007).

Another important area of wireless access to the internet and online services comes not so much from the internet and computing world, but from mobile telecommunications. Users were not enthusiastic about the first versions of internet for mobiles (the infamous Wireless Access Protocol or WAP, released in 1997). What users did quickly adopt, however, was short text messaging (SMS). SMS was avidly taken up—especially by young people and also by deaf users, but then across society—and has proved a very successful and flexible form of mobile media. Because of its relative ubiquity and security, SMS has become part of mobile commerce, advertising, and banking. A service that builds upon SMS is multimedia messaging services (MMS), which allows mobile users to send pictures and short videos. MMS services became an important and lucrative path for interactivity in television (voting, video downloads) and, with SMS, underpinned a lucrative premium mobile services industry (consumers paying more than standard rates for SMS/MMS). Premium mobile services remain lucrative, with ACMA, as the regulator, finally tackling poor industry practices towards consumers. However, premium mobile services have been eclipsed by the rise of apps—with many mobile service and software developers now focusing on apps and app stores (like Apple iTunes), rather than carrier-controlled mobile channels.

From 2010 onwards, there was steady growth in the use of the mobile phone for purposes other than calls and text messages—mostly centred on mobile internet. Thus the top uses of mobile phones, on 2012 figures, were: voice calls (23 per cent); texting (22 per cent); sending and receiving emails (14 per cent); visiting and browsing websites and searching (12 per cent); obtaining information (12 per cent); banking (4 per cent); reading or editing documents online (3 per cent); and buying things online (1 per cent) (AIMIA 2012, p. 29). The use of social media on mobiles commenced in earnest from 2009 (Goggin and Crawford 2010), and now involves a wide range of applications, not least Facebook, Twitter and Instagram.

Mobile television trials were introduced to Australia in 2004–05, and it was then offered commercially in 2006. Direct broadcast of television to mobiles was a much-anticipated vision of digital television in Australia, but has not eventuated in a widespread form (Goggin 2012a). The annual industry Mobile Lifestyles study found that only 21 per cent of its 2012 users surveyed had used mobile TV (up from 16 per cent in 2009) (AIMIA 2012, p. 47). However, for those who are 'high-level' users of mobile entertainment (that is, people who used particular services daily), mobile TV was the second most popular service (after games) (AIMIA 2012, p. ix). Much television is being designed, delivered and consumed for mobile, tablets and laptop computers, but very much via the new forms of apps, video-sharing sites (YouTube), and peer-to-peer file sharing—across a mix of wireless and mobile networks. Thus the distribution of online video via mobiles, like the internet (Curtis, Given and McCutcheon 2012), has become a vital part of the new television ecologies.

This is also now the case with mobile film. With the mobile phone referred to as the 'fourth screen' (after the silver screen, television and the computer), industry, producer and filmmaker attention since the early 2000s has been directed to the prospect of reconfiguring cinema for the mobile platform (Goggin 2012b). Shorter films and videos have proven to be more compatible with mobile phone culture, as well as small, comparatively low-quality screens. Thus mobile videos have become part of the turn to short film, especially in film festivals, but also as a handy component of programming for mobile phone companies and users more accustomed to 'snack content'.

Finally, locative media is now a significant and growing area of the Australian internet, in which mobile media forms are key. There are various positioning technologies available through the mobile network and handsets that can also be used in conjunction with Global Positioning System (GPS). Location-based services have been slow to appear on mobiles, but with mapping software, satellite navigation devices in the domestic vehicle and pedestrian markets and, finally social media and apps, location media has become a diverse, rich and lucrative area of the Australian internet. Two of the most popular locative media applications—Foursquare and Facebook Places—have not made the same splash here as they have in the United States, for instance; however, location-based capabilities are now being incorporated into—and indeed underpinning—a very wide range of services and applications, especially courtesy of smartphones. Users are now routinely asked whether their location information can be used by applications, and many consent.

CONCLUSION

The internet is a relatively new phenomenon in Australia, with its widespread use beyond a research network spanning little more than 20 years. Already the technology has significantly transformed communications and media in this country. The internet did not immediately spell an end to the newspaper, book, radio or television; it failed to make fortunes out of air (or bytes); it didn't become an untameable, lawless, wild frontier; nor was it completely colonised by commercial interests.

Instead, the internet has produced new cultures of consumption and use that do redraw the boundaries and relationships among user, producer and distributor, creating new cultural intermediaries and spaces. It has created alternative media spaces for many communities and users who have not been well catered for or represented in traditional media. It has also radically internationalised the habits, preferences and options of Australian consumers, allowing content from other places and peoples to be readily viewed, read and apprehended.

In doing so, the internet forms a central part of the portfolios of the large transnational communications and media companies that still dominate the Australian scene, and these have developed important new forms of mass and niche consumption that consumers have avidly taken up. As a consequence, the internet has further opened up our national media to international forces and structures, posing challenges to national policy and regulation.

FURTHER READING

It wouldn't be the internet if you couldn't get a wealth of resources about the technology online. Basic information on internet and mobiles in Australia can be found in relevant Australian Bureau of Statistics publications (<www.abs.gov.au>), and also the reports from the Australian component of the World Internet Survey (undertaken by Swinburne Institute of Social Research). ACMA (<www.acma.gov.au>) offers an excellent series of research reports on aspects of internet, mobiles, digital media and economy—a good starting point being its annual *Communications Report*. Digital industry association AIMIA has useful resources, including its annual *Australian Mobile Phone Lifestyle Report* (<www.aimia.com.au>).

Roger Clarke's site (<www.anu.edu.au/-people/Roger.Clarke>) has a wide range of resources on internet technologies, policy and privacy issues. An important email list and archive for discussions of internet policy and practice remains the Link mailing list (<mail-man.anu.edu.au/pipermail/link>). Useful websites about the internet and mobiles include those of the Internet Society of Australia (<www.isoc-au.org.au>), the Australian Computer Society (<www.acs.org.au>), the Internet Industry Association (<www.iia.net.au>), the Australian Mobile Telecommunications Association (<www. amta.org.au>) and the Australian Interactive Media Industry Association (<www. aimia.com.au>).

On the development of the Australian internet, see Gerard Goggin (ed.) (2004b), *Virtual Nation*; Glenda Korporaal (2009), *AARNET: 20 Years of the Internet in Australia: 1989–2009*; and Maureen Burns (2008), *ABC Online: Becoming the ABC*.

For an introduction to the internet and mobiles by Australian scholars, see: Gerard Goggin (2006), *Cell Phone Culture*; Axel Bruns (2008), *Blogs, Wikipedia, Second Life, and Beyond*; Jean Burgess and Josh Green (2013), *YouTube* (rev. ed.); Gerard Goggin and Mark McLelland (eds) (2009), *Internationalizing Internet Studies*; Lelia Green (2009), *The Internet*; Larissa Hjorth (2009), *Mobile Media in the Asia-Pacific*; Adrian Mackenzie, (2010), *Wirelessness*; Larissa Hjorth, Jean Burgess and Ingrid Richardson (eds) (2012), *Studying Mobile Media*; Katie Ellis and Mike Kent (2013), *Disability and New Media*; Peter Chen (2013), *Australian Politics in a Digital Age*; Melissa Gregg (2012), *Work's Intimacy*; K. Weller et al. (eds) (2013), *Twitter and Society*; Rowan Wilken and Gerard Goggin (eds) (2014), *Locative Media*; and Matthew Allen and Tama Leaver (2014), *Web Presence*. An earlier but still helpful account is H. Brown et al. (2001), *Politics of a Digital Present*.

Chapter 15

GAMES: MOBILE, LOCATIVE AND SOCIAL

LARISSA HJORTH

A Singaporean teenage girl waiting for friends in a café takes a picture with her iPhone and uploads to her location-based service (LBS) mobile web application, Foursquare, to show her late friends she has arrived. In Tokyo, a young male plays *Angry Birds* on his iPhone while commuting to and from work. In Seoul, a group of friends play *World of Warcraft* (WoW) in a *PC bang* (internet room) while surfing on their phones and checking social media. In Melbourne, a mother gives her toddler her iPhone to play one of the numerous toddler game apps available while they wait in line at the supermarket. Over in Shanghai, a mother keeps in regular online contact with her university student daughter by playing *Happy Farm*.

This paints a picture of how games have become an integral part of everyday life in many locations globally. With the rise of smartphones and the mainstreaming of LBS mobile games, the types of games, their platforms and media—along with the modes of co-presence and engagement—are changing rapidly. Across a variety of platforms, media, contexts and modes of presence, games are being played by a growing number of people: young and old, male and female, individuals and families. Cutting across cultures, generations and media contexts, games are no longer contained by distinctions such as 'casual' and 'serious'. In what Jesper Juul (2009) defines as a 'casual revolution', games as everyday media reflect the complex practices and relationships that inhabit contemporary life. By 2013, PriceWaterhouseCoopers estimates that the games industry will grow to A$70 billion globally. As a vehicle for popular culture, games provide great insight into cultural and media practice globally. Rubrics like 'video games' are no longer adequate placeholders—especially as games, through the rise of smartphones, converge locative, social and mobile media realms. While not everyone owns a computer, the ubiquity of mobile phones has caused the number and extent of games to burgeon. And in this ubiquity, three key features have emerged: *mobile, locative* and *social*.

In Australia, the demise of local key game companies like Blue Tongue has given way to the rise in small, independent companies specialising in mobile games. Companies such as Robot Circus, Firemonkeys and Tin Man Games are all indicative of this new type of independent game developer that focuses upon the burgeoning of mobile games. With 75 per cent of all mobile downloads being games, and mobile games generating $12 billion dollars in 2011 alone, the mobile gaming industry is predicted to reach $54 billon by 2015. While not every independent company will be like Rovio and make the next *Angry Birds* (having a billion downloads as of mid-2012), mobile gaming has afforded many designers and programmers—like players—with more choices about game genres, gameplay and aesthetics.

Games can be understood as cultural artefacts, industries, social communities, material cultures and media practices. In their various convergent formats—computer, mobile, online, console—games have become one of the central forms of entertainment in the twenty-first century. From 'massively multiplayer online games' (MMOGs) and consoles such as the Sony PlayStation 3, Nintendo Wii and Microsoft's Xbox, to the rise of mobile gaming on devices such as the iPhone, game content, genres and platforms have expanded to reflect the burgeoning diversity and heterogeneity of player demographics. In the debates around the politics of platforms in an age of convergent media (Gillespie 2010; Montford and Bogost 2009), games have been exemplary.

The expansion of gaming as one of the dominant entertainment industries of the twenty-first century has been accompanied by increasing levels of cultural, technological and economic convergences that have, in turn, reworked twentieth-century models of consumption and production within 'packaged media' paradigms (Jenkins 2006a). As opposed to the older model of media packaged for consumption, twenty-first-century networked media promotes audiences to be active co-producers of meaning and content. In the case of the games industry, the rise in the importance of interactivity and participation has resulted in an erosion of the old binaries such as casual (that is, puzzle and mobile phone) games versus serious (role-playing) games, as well as a collapsing of the distinction between the labour of players and that of game developers. The rise of new modes of player participation—what Julian Kücklich (2005) calls 'playbour'—can be found within the various forms of gaming user-created content (UCC) genres such as machinima ('machine cinema', or movies made from game engines) and modding (computer modification). This UCC playbour phenomenon highlights that the birth and rise of gaming owe their success to hacking and a hybridisation of player-producer roles.

Given that games converge and blur platforms, media, contexts and modes of engagement, it is not surprising that this is reflected in the debates and different schools of thought within games studies. For example, with the rise of smartphone games, there is a need to distinguish between portable and mobile media platforms such as the difference between playing games on an iPhone and on a PlayStation Portable (PSP). As Ingrid Richardson (2012) notes in her study of haptic (touch) screen mobile gaming such as iPhone games, the medium creates a particular relationship with the body that is based on interruptibility (that is, maneouvring between calls and gameplay) and distinct modalities of place, presence and being-in-the-world. While this chapter cannot cover all of the debates in games studies, it will provide a window on to the invention of games and one of the most salient earlier debates—ludology versus narratology. This will then be followed by a discussion of game studies through approaches that have underlined many of the methods in media and communications: the social and cultural analysis of technology. The chapter then turns to a case study of one of the key emergent areas in gaming: location-based service (LBS) games. As a realm that was once only occupied by experimental pedagogical and artistic exploration, location-based games have grown into part of mainstream mobile media applications.

THE HISTORIES OF GAMING

Gaming has many histories, depending on what discipline and approach one takes. This interdisciplinary background—drawing from film and TV studies, literary and art theory as well as approached from the perspectives of media, communication and cultural studies—makes game studies both fascinating and perplexing. Games, like other popular media such as TV, have often attracted moral criticism in the media. In particular, as a form of 'youth media', games have been accused of contributing to a range of social problems; these accusations often mobilise simplistic adult definitions of children, which see them as passive consumers and as highly vulnerable to media influence. To some extent, games share the problem that contributes to moral panics about television due to their location—that is, personal computers, like TV, occupy domestic spaces.

For Leslie Haddon (1999), the history of games can be best understood in relation to the messy and increasingly unbounded space of domesticity. While semi-public versions of gaming could be viewed in arcade games—with more recent guises in the form of PC rooms—much of the rise of gaming has been orchestrated around the ubiquity of domestic technologies (both inside and outside the home) within contemporary lifestyles. The 'home' for playing games can also be outside the physical domain of the domestic sphere—as evidenced in the rise of PC rooms in which guilds play online and offline together, and the emergence of the casual mobile game market. Interestingly, both of these aspects (online and mobile) have captured the attention of predominantly female players for their casual and social dimensions. Yet, despite these synergies with other domestic technologies, games differ dramatically from other media such as TV, as this chapter highlights.

Hactivism: The birth of gaming

Given that play is one of the most creative and innovative (Sutton-Smith 1997) yet misunderstood notions, it is no accident that the birth of games began with hackers (Haddon 1999), and that the advent of games within the global popular imaginary has been marked by subversive and independent subcultures. The invention of 'video games' can be linked to the founding of computer science as a discipline in the 1950s and 1960s at MIT—secured by the investment of US military funding in areas such as Artificial Intelligence (AI). The establishment of the MIT's computer science lab granted then-student Steve Russell the technological opportunities for his group, the Tech Model Railway Club (TMRC), to create the first game, *Spacewar*, in 1962. This first incarnation of *Spacewar* was designed for the PDP-1 computer at MIT and was not capable of simultaneous two-player interaction. It was in 1971 that Nolan Bushnell took *Spacewar* and transformed it into one of the first arcade games under the title *Computer Space*. Bushnell went on to make the popular *Pong*, and to establish the legendary Atari game company that dominated the 1970s entertainment industries; he was also responsible for spearheading the shift of games into the arcades.

The significance of the US military backing was also pertinent in the conception of the video game as domestic technology. The defence company Sanders Electronics was responsible for developing the first game technology for the TV in 1972, with the Magnavox Odyssey machine. The Odyssey was the first home console, and featured twelve puzzle and maze games. One key game was Ralph Baer's *Tennis for Two,* which was later adapted by Atari and released in 1975 as a reworking of Bushnell's *Pong.* By 1976, consoles contained microprocessors, allowing them to be programmable—in short, hardware and software could be separated. This meant that games, like other popular media such as vinyl records, could be 'bought, collected and compared' (Haddon 1999).

The late 1970s and early 1980s saw the games industry going from strength to strength. In 1979, Atari released its global success story, *Space Invaders.* The early 1980s saw the introduction of many home consoles from Atari, Nintendo, Sega, Microsoft and Sony. This phenomenon was concurrent with the development of personal home computers such as the Commodore 64, Apple II and Sinclair Spectrum, which also allowed users to experiment, hack and make their own games.

The history of gaming can broadly be categorised under seven generations. The first generation (c. 1971) saw the dawn of the arcade game and console gaming (the Magnavox Odyssey system, 1972). The rise of both university mainframe computers and the home computer helped ensure the development of games. In 1976, the introduction of the ROM cartridge format—spearheaded by the release of the Fairchild Video Entertainment System (VES) and Atari's Video Computer System (VCS, later called the Atari 2600) in 1977—marked the birth of the second generation of gaming. By the early 1980s, often known as the 'Golden Age of Arcade Games', the once-burgeoning games industry began to experience a slowdown. This period also fostered the rise of two of the most enduring directions in gaming—online and mobile gaming. Early online gaming could be seen in the form of dial-up Bulletin Board Systems (BBS—a precursor to Web 2.0 social networking systems), which allowed for some of the first examples of MUDs (multi-user dungeons) and basic, textual fantasy role-playing games that would eventually evolve into Massively Multiplayer Online Role-Playing Games (MMORPGs). Concurrently, we see the rise of mobile handheld gaming in the form of Nintendo's Game & Watch (initiated in 1980)—the spirit of this phenomenon can be seen in the recent success of the Nintendo DS portable and the Wii.

This second generation was marked by one of the defining periods in the games industry—the North American video game crash of 1983. This was marked by the unsuccessful adaptation of blockbuster films into games, most notably the video game version of Steven Spielberg's film *E.T.* (1982). Not only was *E.T. the Game* dubbed the all-time worst video game in history, but it also marked the beginning of the end for Atari; it was one of the company's biggest commercial failures. Tens of thousands of *E.T.* game cartridges were buried in a New Mexico landfill—a symbolic grave not only for Atari but for the games industry as well. After the software and hardware peak of 1982, the boom was over—suddenly production dwindled and declined.

After the crash of 1983, the gaming industry was partly resuscitated, marking the third generation (1985–89), with Nintendo's release of the eight-bit console Famicom (or Nintendo Entertainment System NES). During the 1990s, arcades declined dramatically in the face of the rise of handheld gaming and MMOGs. During this fourth generation (1989–96), CD-ROM drives and 3D graphics such as flat-shaded polygons were introduced. The fifth generation (1994–99) saw Nintendo's departure from CD-ROMs in favour of the cheaper-to-produce cartridges (Nintendo 64), with disastrous consequences. Since CD-ROMs could hold more data than the cartridges, at a time when games were increasing their graphics and thus requiring more memory, companies such as SquareSoft (producers of the legionary *Final Fantasy* series) quickly shifted from Nintendo to PlayStation platforms. By the end of the fifth generation, PlayStation led the market globally while Nintendo only experienced success in Japan.

By the end of this phase in the development of games, two key features became apparent: the growing significance of the portable (mobile) game systems (Sony Play-Station Portable [PSP], Nintendo DS) and the rise of the online, networked UCC in the form of game 'modding' (whereby players could remodel games environments and gameplay). The integral role of the player—and their labour or 'playbour'—in the production and consumption of gaming cultures can be found in the modding of games such as *Counter-Strike*, *Half-Life*, *Unreal Tournament* and *The Sims*. Game companies began including customising tools as a part of this playbour phenomenon. The sixth generation saw the exit of Sega, with Sony gaining an increasing hold over the market and the entrance of Microsoft. During this time, online gaming continued to grow while 'casual gaming' shifted from consoles to the PC.

Paralleling the growth in portable (handheld) game systems was the growth in games for mobile phones. As mobile phones shifted from extensions of the landlines to third-generation (3G) convergence *par excellence*—incorporating Web 2.0 features of social and locative media—games were pivotal to the transformation. In Japan, the main telecommunications provider, iMode, featured numerous games aimed at diverse demographics not normally associated with gaming. In South Korea, companies such as GOMID (now defunct) made haptic games exclusively for the mobile phone. Within the Western world, Nokia's N-Gage phone, while not hugely successful, marked the shift towards mobile phones as entertainment technologies. This was given momentum by the launch of Apple's iPhone in 2007—by 2008, more than half of the iPhone's applications sold were games. Now games generate a billion dollars in revenue. Over this time—known as the seventh generation (2004–present)—the market for mobile game consoles became a war between Sony PSP and Nintendo DS. Nintendo managed to gain control by its introduction of the haptic console, Nintendo's Wii.

Since 2000, the increasing dominance of games within the popular culture imaginary has become evident. This period was also marked by the rise of game studies as a serious interdisciplinary field. Within the field of game studies, there are various contested approaches and perspectives from empirical, player-based studies (Taylor 2006) to more theoretical, abstract or formalist studies (Bogost 2009). However, in order to comprehend game studies, we need to gain a context for games with general approaches to social media technologies.

APPROACHES TO SOCIAL TECHNOLOGIES

Given that the area of game studies draws from a variety of disciplines and media, an important part of defining the field came from trying to differentiate what constituted 'games' as opposed to other media. How are games similar to other media? How are they different from them? How do they converge and how do they remediate other media? Two of the distinctive features that separated games from other media (such as TV and film) were the function of *interactivity* and *simulation*. These two elements played a key role in defining early game studies through the ludology versus narratology debate (Egenfeldt-Nielsen, Smith and Tosca 2008; Wolf and Perron 2008).

On one side of this debate, narratologists have argued that narratives underpin all types of media—from literature and film to games. We use narratives, they point out, to make sense of the world. On the other side, drawing on the Latin word for 'game' (*ludus*), ludology aimed to establish a discipline that studied game and play activities (Frasca 2003). Ludologists such as Espen Aarseth (2005) argued that, while narratives do operate within games, they are almost *incidental* to the specific interactive and simulative dimensions of gameplay. This can be seen in the fact that game genres have predominantly been defined around player interaction—that is, first-person shooter (FPS) role-playing games—rather than in relation to the underlying narrative of the game.

For key theorist Gonzalo Frasca (2003), one way to understand the difference between ludology and narratology is through the distinction between *ludus* (game) and *paidea* (play). Traditionally—certainly for children—*games* are conceived as having rules while *play* does not. However, Frasca highlights how even child's play still has rules and conventions (for example, if one is playing being a bird, then one does not run around sounding like a car). Thus, if both *play* and *games* have rules, the difference lies in their result—games define a winner or loser, while play does not. Although puzzle and traditional video games genres such as first-person shooters had a pre-designated goal, more recently—with the rise of 'sandbox' (coined from the notion of the sandbox playing in which socialising and play are more important than goals and action) online social games such as *The Sims*—gameplay has moved increasingly towards notions of play rather than game modality.

The ludology versus narratology debate enjoyed great traction in the early stages of games studies (Juul 2006). However, such a divisive debate around formal properties of games neglected to address the ways in which games have been key vehicles for convergence and remediation. Games are unique, but they are also relational to the media and technological affordances. Remediation—that is, Bolter and Grusin's (1999) notion that new and old media have a cyclic and dynamic relationship, has taken on particular characteristics in gaming. Gaming borrows as it revises from other media genres and modes of engagement. Like older media such as TV, games reflect social and cultural mores and literacies.

Since the ludology debate, games have grown to encompass and revise numerous traditions and methods. Within the interdisciplinary realm of social and cultural technologies, some main approaches have dominated: science and technology studies (STS)/social construction of technology (SCOT), cultural studies and domestication theory. These approaches have sought to investigate the role of media, technology and consumption in social and cultural life.

While it is said that STS started in the 1960s, STS as we know it today—that is, what Steve Woolgar (1991) terms the 'turn to technology'—is attributed to the ground-breaking books *Social Shaping of Technology* (MacKenzie and Wajcman 1985) and *The Social Construction of Technological Systems* (Bijker, Hughes and Pinch 1987). Within STS, there have been three main approaches: substantive, social constructivism and affordances. The substantive approach had a publicly popular face in the form of its sub-set—technological determinism or 'media effects'. This model was criticised for its simplistic understandings of technologies and users, especially negating the multi-dimensional agency of the user and context in which the technologies/media were deployed. Canadian media theorist Marshall McLuhan was often described as exemplifying this approach, and the method gained further currency with the rise of cyberculture studies (Jones 1997; Bell 1998; Featherstone and Burrows 1995; Green 2001).

In order to address the problems with the first approach, an inverse model was outlined: social constructivism, or SCOT. This approach was developed in response to some of the early analysis of television by one of the founding figures in British cultural studies, Raymond Williams (Williams 1974; During 1999). However, this model neglected to address the multi-directional nature of social technologies by which technologies can often shape users as much as users shape technologies—a phenomenon particularly apparent in the ubiquity of lifestyle technologies from mobile phones and gaming consoles to MP3 players, which function on numerous levels—both *symbolic* and *material*. With this in mind, theorists such as Bruno Latour (1987) developed an approach that sat in between the substantive and social constructivist models: actor network theory (ANT), or the 'affordances' approach, whereby technologies and people are seen as 'actors'. The affordances approach, developed by Donald Norman in *The Design of Everyday Things* (1988), draws upon the principles of human-centred design and attempts to consider not only the actors'/users' physical capabilities but also their motivations, plans, values and history. Rather than focusing on subjective or essentialist positions, the affordances approach seeks a more 'ecological' and relational understanding of the ways in which media and technologies become—or can be designed to become—part and parcel of users' everyday lives.

One example of an approach that incorporates all three models to explore the dynamic and social dimension of the uptake of technologies is the domestication approach developed in the work of Roger Silverstone (Silverstone and Haddon 1996; Haddon 2004; Silverstone and Hirsch 1992; Miller 1987). The British tradition of domestication approaches grew out of media studies and interest in consumption studies, as well as anthropological work that explored how objects become part of identity and social life. The approach identifies new technologies as having become embedded in everyday life and household social relations; this results in new technologies and media not only being a site for making and remaking meaning. Groundbreaking case studies such as Paul du Gay et al.'s (1997), *Doing Cultural Studies: The Story of the Walkman* are indicative of how useful this approach could be when it was employed as a means of understanding the functions of lifestyle technologies within everyday life.

There have been a variety of applications of the domestic technologies approach within game studies—in particular, Jon Dovey and Helen Kennedy's (2007) *Game Culture: Computer Games as New Media* and T.L. Taylor's (2006) ethnographies of online gaming communities. Despite gaming trends heading outside the home—via either physical (handheld) or virtual (online) mobility—an understanding of them as domestic technologies remains central to work on how we play and engage in communities. Ironically, despite the potential physical and electronic movement afforded by mobile devices, most mobile games are played in bed. In other words, while the domestic increasingly becomes unbounded and mobile (Berker et al. 2006; Bakardjieva 2006; Lim 2006), technologies like games and mobile media become progressively embedded within practices of belonging. With the rise of location-based websites and games like Foursquare and *Jiepang*—in which users 'check in' to locations, both physically and electronically—and augmented reality mobile apps, the ways in which games, mobility and place overlap are changing. As a reflection of broader socio-cultural shifts in which work and leisure are blurring (Wajcman et al. 2009), mobile games and their 'wireless leash' capacities harness new forms of engagement that move unevenly across modes of co-presence (being both here and there, online and offline), net presence (online presence) and tele-presence (technologically mediated presence such as augmented reality).

LOCATING GAME STUDIES: A CASE STUDY OF LOCATION-BASED SERVICE GAMES

All over the globe, location-based services such as the Global Positioning System (GPS), geotagging and Google Maps have become a pervasive part of everyday life through platforms and devices such as smartphones, Android devices, tablets and portable gaming devices. Moving beyond printed maps, mobile digital devices now frame and mediate our ability to traverse, experience, share and conceptualise place. Mobile, networked technologies not only transform how we understand place in everyday life; they also remind us that place is more than just physical geographic location. More importantly, places are constructed by an ongoing accumulation of stories, memories, and social practices (Massey 1999; Harvey 2001; Soja 1989). This is particularly the case within the realm of urban mobile gaming, which seeks to challenge everyday conventions and routines that shape the cityscape.

Although location-based services (LBS) have been available in mobile devices since the early 1990s, it has only been fairly recently that they have become a feature of smartphones, and so have started to become available to people who would not otherwise have gone out to purchase a separate device such as a GPS unit. While locative media, like the internet, has its history in the military, GPS was quickly adapted for commercial use. The transition of LBS can be thought of in terms of generations. The first generation of LBS were available through custom devices that provided a single-use device—often seen in countries such as the United States and Australia only in higher-end motor vehicles. The use of first-generation LBS saw some innovative experiments with play, but was constrained largely to experimental uses by early adopters. Second-generation LBS have emerged as GPS and GPS-like services that are embedded in consumer devices as just one of many features on those devices. With the more general accessibility of LBS, the experimental uses of the technology have been commodified, and are moving beyond gaming and into other applications. The most immediate impact of these second-generation LBS for users of smartphones is through services like Google Maps, where an interactive map can pinpoint a user's location and calculate the fastest route to almost any destination. Although the navigational capabilities this affords are important, the feature only represents a fraction of the implications of LBS, particularly when they converge with networked media. It should also be noted that while this convergence of mobile, locative and social media is quite new in some countries (particularly in the Anglophone world), in other countries—such as Japan—the mobile phone (*keitai*) has been associated with social and locative media for over a decade (Hjorth 2003; Ito 2005). Now, with the increasingly widespread use of smartphones and the convergence of mobile, social and locative technologies in these devices, the implications of this phenomenon are being seen in many places.

The first generation of locative-based mobile games was developed from an experimental and creative context by the likes of UK new media group Blast Theory (de Souza e Silva and Hjorth 2009). They sought to transform urban spaces into playful places. Much of the first-generation experimentation and exploration of mobile media artwork from the late 1990s onwards has taken the form of hybrid reality and location-based mobile games (de Souza e Silva 2004, 2006; Davis 2005) as they challenge the role of co-presence and everyday life, forging questions around the boundaries between the virtual and actual, online and offline, haptic (touch) and cerebral (mind), delay and immediacy (Hjorth 2007, 2009). Examples include the Pac-Manhattan (United States), Proboscis's *Urban Tapestries* (United Kingdom), Blast Theory (United Kingdom), aware (Finland), Mogi game (Japan) and INP (Interactive and Practice) *Urban Vibe* (South Korea). Unlike the first generation, which took an experimental and creative angle, the mainstreaming of locative media mobile sites such as Foursquare sees different effects and affects.

Although second-generation LBS websites and games like *Foursquare* and *Jiepang* are still in their infancy, they represent an area of growing diversity and complexity within mobile media and communication. In LBS mobile games, we see an overlaying place with the social and personal, whereby the electronic is superimposed on to the geographic in new ways. For Adriana de Souza e Silva and Daniel Sutko (2009), LBS mobile gaming is indicative of what the authors call net locality—that is, the process whereby location-aware technologies create a perpetual, evolving dynamic between information as place and place as information. While urban spaces have always been mediated by technologies, according to Eric Gordon and de Souza e Silva (2011, p. 91), net localities 'produce unique types of networked interactions and, by extension, new contexts for social cohesion' and so 'co-presence is not mutually opposed to networked interaction—and as emerging practices of technology develop, drawing the line in the sand becomes increasingly difficult'.

Although the area of locative media has attracted much critical and rigorous attention of late as a convergence between urban, gaming and mobile media studies (Gordon and de Souza e Silva 2011; de Souza e Silva and Frith 2012; Farman 2011), some gaps remain. Specifically, given the field's infancy, there is a need for longitudinal studies that emphasise that media practice is embedded within everyday life. As mobile media—as a portal for locative and social media—increasingly becomes all-pervasive, the distinctions between game and non-game, online and offline spaces converge. While LBS mobile games remind us of the early debates around online and offline identity practices evoked by cyberculture discourses (Bell and Kennedy 2000), they also are dramatically different. As Ingrid Richardson and Rowan Wilken (2012) note, LBS mobile games require a particular embodied experience with the screen that opens up an array of differing modes of presence and impact upon practices of place as 'stories so far' (Massey 2005). LBS mobile games, as Frans Mäyrä (2003) notes in his examination of the experimental first generation, remind us that place and the social have always been pivotal to gameplay. While the social importance of place may have been lost on early video games, mobile games are rapidly rectifying this problem by providing a complex weave of co-present, highly social, haptic and networked play spaces.

CONCLUSION

In an age of cross-platform convergent and divergent media (Jenkins 2006), games are providing a variety of both alternative and mainstream forms of storytelling. Relationships between players and the industry are no longer as clearly demarcated as they once were, as modes of playbour become increasingly pervasive. No longer mere 'video games' confined to fixed play spaces, games have embraced three key features: mobile, locative and casual. With games moving to centre stage as a dominant part of creative industries, the demographics of players have expanded dramatically to include young and old, male and female.

As locative media become more part of mainstream culture through the rise of smartphones, the implication of location awareness is increasingly apparent. This has led to websites such as pleaserobme.com (<http://pleaserobme.com>) to make people aware of what location awareness is doing to change how we practise privacy. LBS mobile games also highlight how notions like online participation and privacy are culturally specific. For example, the uptake of LBS mobile game *Jiepang* in Shanghai, China reflects a Chinese notion of privacy that is informed by *guanxi* (social relations)— vastly different from Western examples of Foursquare, in which surveillance and even überveillance (Michael and Michael 2011) have entered the debate. As Alison Gazzard (2011) notes, LBS applications like Foursquare interpellate the player as stalker.

While games are becoming more inclusive in their genres, platforms and content, the gender inequalities with games continue, especially in terms of women in the industry. Although this problem has been acknowledged, and there are attempts to address it through education and recruitment practices in the industry, the fact that female game developers constitute only 5 per cent of the Australian industry—compared with 12 per cent worldwide (International Game Developers Association 2008)—suggests that *much* more work needs to be done.

As noted earlier, thinking about game studies in terms of the domestic technologies approach not only makes us consider the social, cultural and economic dimensions of games, but also the ongoing role *context* plays in informing the *content*, meanings and practices around gameplay. As the 'staycation' (stay-at-home vacation) and user-friendly consoles such as the Wii become key factors in the rise of family gaming, it is important to consider how the domestic sphere has functioned to construct particular modes of gendered behaviour, as well as how technologies such as TV and games are modelling types of gendered and generational interaction. While there has been a body of literature in game studies exploring gendered gaming consumption and production (Jenkins and Cassell 1997)—particularly around gendered representation and role models (Kennedy 2002)—the gendered domain of the context of gameplay (that is, at home or in an internet cafe) is still in need of analysis. This is especially the case given that many mobile games are still played in the bedroom.

Furthermore, as gendered genres and platforms such as 'casual' mobile phone games become more widespread as a consequence of the rise of networked multimedia devices such as the iPhone, more studies of gendered modes of gaming and the role of multiple screen engagement are needed. Indeed, to explore 'casual' mobile gaming is, as mentioned previously, a gendered issue with most of the players being women (Casual Games Association 2008). Mobile convergent, cross-platform devices such as the iPhone have become key repositories for new types of game storytelling with a female focus (Hjorth and Richardson 2009). Maybe, with the rise of independent game companies in the burgeoning market of smartphone games, more women will get involved as programmers and managers, not just designers and administrators.

However, one must be cautious of granting the mobile games industry too much agency in a liberation for game-makers, especially as there is still a gap between the potential of mobile games to make profit for the independent designer, with global corporations like Apple taking their (un)fair share of financial profits. Some Australian companies such as Firemonkey and Halfbrick have focused specifically on developing an innovative industry model for mobile games (Banks 2012). But games also need to acknowledge the politics of labour, especially as companies such as Apple have been complacent in exploitative work conditions for workers (Qiu 2012). While game cultures are global, their practices (both consumption and production) are very much informed by the local. As this chapter has outlined, games have unevenly developed into a mainstream activity across three key areas: *locative*, *social* and *mobile media*.

FURTHER READING

The following books provide a good theoretical and conceptual overview of game studies: Dovey and Kennedy (2007), *Game Culture: Computer Games as New Media*; Egenfeldt-Nielsen, Smith and Tosca (2008), *Understanding Video Games: The Essential Introduction*; Wolf and Perron (2003), *The Video Game Theory Reader 2*; Hjorth (2010), *Games & Gaming*. For students interested in game studies specifically within the Asia-Pacific region, see Hjorth and Chan (2009), *Games of Locality: Gaming Cultures in the Asia-Pacific Region*. For a case study of the iPhone, see Hjorth, Burgess and Richardson (2012), *Studying Mobile Media*. For location-based services (LBS) mobile gaming, see de Souza e Silva and Sutko (eds) (2009), *Digital Cityscapes*, de Souza E Silva and Hjorth (2009), 'Urban spaces as playful spaces: A historical approach to mobile urban games' and Farman (2011), *Mobile Interface Theory*.

PART III

Issues

Chapter 16

SOCIAL MEDIA

JEAN BURGESS AND JOHN BANKS

In the space of the past decade, the technologies, business models, everyday uses and public understandings of social media have co-evolved rapidly. In the early to mid-2000s, websites like MySpace, Facebook and Twitter were garnering interest in both the press and academia as places for amateur creativity, political subversion or trivial time-wasting on the behalf of subcultures of geeks or 'digital natives', but such websites were not seen as legitimate, mainstream media organisations, nor were they generally understood as respectable places for professionals (other than new media professionals) to conduct business. By late 2011, online marketing company Comscore was reporting that social networking was 'the most popular online activity worldwide accounting for nearly 1 in every 5 minutes spent online', reaching 82 per cent of the world's internet population, or 1.2 billion users (Comscore 2011).

Today, social media is firmly established as an industry sector in its own right, and is deeply entangled with and embedded in the practices and everyday lives of media professionals, celebrities and ordinary users. We might now think of it as an embedded communications infrastructure extending across culture, society and the economy—ranging from local government Facebook pages alerting us to kerbside collection, to Tumblr blogs providing humorous cultural commentary by curating animated .gifs, to Telstra Twitter accounts responding to user requests for tech help, and to Yelp reviews helping us find somewhere to grab dinner in a strange town. As well as at least appearing to be near-ubiquitous, social media are increasingly seen as highly significant by scholars researching issues as diverse as journalistic practice (Hermida 2012), the coordination of government and community responses to natural disasters (Bruns and Burgess 2012) and the activities of global social and political protest movements (Howard and Hussain 2013). Furthermore, social media platforms are increasingly regarded as a highly valuable source of 'big data', not only for marketers but also for scientists from the natural and social sciences—the millions of tweets we generate every day, for example, are being mined right now, for everything from analysing global mood swings (Golder and Macy 2011) to predicting stock market trends (Bollen, Mao and Zeng 2011).

THE PLATFORM PARADIGM

The term 'social media' first came to mainstream prominence in the mid-2000s alongside other neologisms like 'Web 2.0', 'blogging', 'user generated content' and 'social networking sites', but it has only been since around 2010 that it has come to dominate all others. We argue that the emergence of 'social media' as an organ-ising concept—a paradigm—for the business, practice and study of these formerly disparate phenomena has occurred for three interconnected reasons. First, a few key commercial service providers, or 'platforms' like Facebook, YouTube and Twitter, have risen to international prominence, largely defining what it means to participate online for large proportions of the population. Second, the past few years have seen a dramatic expansion and legitimation of participation in the activities afforded by those platforms—across populations, and across sectors of the society and economy. Third, a key characteristic of these key, dominant platforms is the way they produce convergences among interpersonal communication, creative content and mainstream media consumption—hence the resonance of the term 'social media'.

Throughout her critical history of social media, *Culture of Connectivity*, José Van Dijck (2013) highlights this convergence of user-created content and social connec-tion. In defining social media as a term, she adopts Kaplan and Haenlein's definition of it as 'a group of Internet-based applications that build on the ideological and technological foundations of Web 2.0, and that allow the creation and exchange of user-generated content' (Kaplan and Haenlein 2010, p. 61), adding that social media platforms constitute a 'new online layer through which people organize their lives' (2013, p. 4), producing a widely experienced 'platformed sociality' (2013, p. 23) that has emerged in less than a decade. As mundane and embedded as this new platform paradigm may seem, social media are still sometimes seen as new and disruptive. For example, issues and controversies surrounding privacy and cyberbullying remain persistent areas of social concern, and receive prominent and regular attention in the media (see Chapters 17 and 20).

THE BUSINESS OF SOCIAL MEDIA

Social media platforms are now big media businesses in their own right. Facebook, Twitter and YouTube in particular are now some of the most powerful players in global digital economy, with complex relationships to more traditional media sectors like broadcast television, telecommunications and advertising. The reach and breadth of social media's uses have also given rise to new kinds of media management and communication professions, as well as ancillary businesses like social media marketing and analytics.

The platform paradigm is a shift from the Web 2.0 paradigm, which saw a wide range of content and connection genres and competing services in each genre category, to the rise of more monolithic companies capturing large slices of the global market—YouTube for web video, Facebook for social networking, Pinterest and Tumblr for networked scrapbooking, Twitter for short messaging and microblogging, Instagram for photo-sharing and so on. According to the *Nielsen Social Media Report 2012* (Nielsen 2012, p. 8), in 2012 Facebook was still the dominant social media platform in the United States, with some 152 226 000 unique PC-based visitors; Twitter recorded a 13 per cent year-on-year increase to 37 033 000 unique PC visitors, while the emerging 'niche' platform Pinterest recorded a staggering 1047 per cent year-on-year growth to 27 223 000 unique PC visitors—and these numbers don't even account for mobile users inside the United States, let alone the rest of the world. But the most striking development in 2012 was the staggering growth in mobile apps used to access these social media platforms. The report notes that time spent on mobile apps and mobile web account for 63 per cent of the year-over-year growth in time spent using social media; and 30 per cent of people's mobile time is spent on social media apps (Nielsen 2012, p. 4).

Here in Australia, social media usage statistics such as those regularly published on the SocialMediaNews Website, (<www.socialmedianews.com.au>) tell a similar story of growth. Social media are also becoming important to government, businesses, charities and other organisations, as they recognise that these online networks and platforms provide them with an opportunity to connect with hundreds of thousands of users, citizens and consumers. Sensis's (2012) *Yellow Social Media Report* suggests that the effective use of social media by businesses requires daily updates, diverse content and engagement strategies, including competitions, giveaways and discounts (Sensis and AIMIA 2012, pp. 42–50). But most companies are still quite tentatively exploring how to use social media. The need for Australian businesses to develop more mature strategies is demonstrated by the #qantasluxuy PR disaster, in which Qantas launched a frivolous giveaway campaign too soon following a serious period of industrial disruption. As Bruns (2012) notes, 'choosing Twitter as the platform for their promo activities . . . Qantas didn't have access to [familiar] forms of censorship; once unleashed, there was nothing they could do to stop the barrage of criticism'. (For further discussion of the challenges of social media for brand communication, see Nitins and Burgess 2013; for a description of the #qantasluxury incident, see Glance 2011.)

REGULATION AND GOVERNANCE ISSUES

Intellectual property law, terms of service (TOS) agreements and end-user licence agreements (EULAs) provide much of the regulatory frameworks that govern user-created content and social-network platforms. However, these terms and conditions are not always compatible with the diverse and rapidly evolving ways in which people participate in co-creative media and online social networks. Rather, these legal instruments and institutions emerged to deal with rights and responsibilities of primarily corporate participants in the industrial systems of media production and distribution. In new media environments, increasingly difficult questions are arising around the rights and responsibilities of users in relation to those of platform-providers and copyright-holders. When participating on a social networking site like Facebook, for example, who owns and controls the personal information and photographs that you post to the site? Should you be able to take your content and connections with you if you decide to leave Twitter? Should uploading a favourite song to YouTube without the permission of the copyright-holder be treated as 'piracy'?

Instagram was acquired by Facebook in early 2012 for $1 billion. In December 2012, Instagram announced a change to its terms of service and privacy policy that was to come into effect in January 2013. The changes were designed to allow Instagram to share data with Facebook, but their wording alarmed the user community, giving the impression that Instagram was going to hand over user data (including user-created photos) to other businesses for profit. In the announcement, Instagram commented:

Our updated privacy policy helps Instagram function more easily as part of Facebook by being able to share info between the groups. This means we can do things like fight spam more effectively, detect system and reliability problems more quickly, and build better features for everyone by understanding how Instagram is used. (Instagram 2012)

Many users were not convinced by the Instagram spin that this change was in their best interests. Very quickly after the announcement, many of them took to Twitter and other social media platforms—including posting protest photos to Instagram itself—to express their anger and concern regarding this change to the Instagram privacy policy, using hashtags such as #instascam, #leavinginstagram and #byeinstagram. They quickly noticed and spread the word through social media that the new terms also permitted Instagram to reserve the right to sell access to users' photos to companies that wanted to use them in advertisements without the users' knowledge or consent, and without providing them with a share of the revenues that might be generated from that use. Users then started announcing on Facebook, Twitter and Instagram that they were deleting the Instagram app from their devices, with many adding they were considering migrating to Flickr, at the same time attracting significant global media attention and negative publicity for Instagram. In the end, the company was forced to reword the new policy in order to make not only the new rules but also the company's corporate intentions more transparent to users (Systrom 2012).

Such controversies, which emerge regularly on Facebook—and also Twitter—are processes of social learning in which we are starting to see norms emerge about the appropriate and acceptable uses that platform owners can make of users' content and data. Controversies like this raise all kinds of dilemmas about the ownership and control of user-created content, as well as privacy issues, and reveal the often limited extent to which participants in online social networks understand the full legal implications of the terms of their participation. As in this example, though, controversies can also create visibility and discussion, leading to new knowledge and in some cases even forcing a partial renegotiation of these terms of participation, and the regulations that encode them.

Chapter 17
SOCIAL SELVES
ROWAN WILKEN AND ANTHONY McCOSKER

It is widely acknowledged that, through processes of globalisation, the end of the twentieth century saw the rise of a 'reflexive modernity', with both an increased emphasis on individualism and broad societal-level challenges to 'the very idea of controllability, certainty or security' (Beck 1999, p. 2). These are developments that impact directly on how self-identity is formed (Giddens 1991), reformed and performed (Hall 1992). Faced with such upheavals, it is suggested that the individual increasingly 'must produce, stage and cobble together their biographies themselves' (Beck 1994, p. 13); they must self-reflexively and continuously 'invent' themselves. These processes take place in relation to social networks that are becoming increasingly diverse, and are facilitated by media and communication technologies. We use media, communication devices such as mobile phones and social networking sites, as well as other forms of consumption, to 'choose, construct, interpret, negotiate, display who [we] are to be seen as' (Slater 1997, p. 84). This chapter examines the ways in which we use social media and communication devices as tools of social self-formation, and probes some of the tensions they raise regarding our control over our public availability, visibility and 'locatability'.

Self-presentation takes place increasingly through online profiles containing personal details, with varying degrees of public access. Being 'always-on', as danah boyd (2012) puts it, establishes 'an ecosystem in which people can stay peripherally connected to one another through a variety of microdata', exchanged across a range of networks and with varying degrees of 'publicness' (2012, p. 73). Social network sites, for example, enable constant communication and connection, while encouraging increasingly public levels of self-disclosure or exposure. In these contexts, networks are developed and maintained through self-expression, communication and sharing. Identity narratives and social connections are created in the *bricolage* or assemblage of media objects, likes (and dislikes), interests and activities. This could be the simple act of sharing videos through sites such as YouTube, or on Facebook or Twitter, which 'can support social networks by facilitating socialization among dispersed friends', but also by helping to 'project identities that affiliate with particular social groups' on the basis of the types of content produced and shared (Lange 2007, p. 361). Negotiating the self and social networks among the massive flow of data becomes a process of managing attention and relevance, both of which come to define and sequester participation even within generally open, unrestricted public platforms like YouTube or Twitter.

One of the culturally resonant issues associated with these forms of participation and interaction is often described as the dramatic dissolution of the boundaries between spaces or contexts that are considered private or public. This is reflected in the 'pursuit of visibility' (Blatterer 2010, p. 79) associated with practices of self-disclosure through social network sites such as Facebook and in our willingness to circulate photos and videos reflecting ourselves and aspects of our intimate everyday lives. However, it is not that we inhabit two distinct spheres—one public and the other private—that have been broken down by emerging forms of social media and social networking tools. Rather, we are always managing the aspects of ourselves that we make accessible to others, and communication tools simply afford new possibilities to increase the extent of our visibility, in the process creating new opportunities and new anxieties. The two examples discussed here are taken from quite different contexts, and illustrate both the opportunities and anxieties confronting our practices of self-formation through social media and mobile communication devices.

A first example, touching on many of the ways we use media and social networking tools to manage a personal, cultural and networked sense of self, can be found in the viral circulation of a YouTube video. In September 2011, numerous Māori *hakas* were performed as flash mob events in public spaces during the six-week Rugby Union World Cup held in New Zealand. The first was performed on Sunday, 4 September at Sylvia Park Shopping Centre in Auckland, and was recorded by several low-resolution cameras and uploaded to YouTube that on the same day. One version, titled 'Flashhaka@SilviaPark,4.Sept.11' (<www.youtube.com/watch?v=puXad30DSfg>), uploaded by eyiboom43, gained the most attention as it was reposted across a wide variety of sites including *BBC News*, *The Guardian* and CNN. In the almost two-minute video, the camera is positioned at the edge of an open atrium area that is part of the Sylvia Park Shopping Centre, and initially shows people crossing the space or milling within it before the initiating call of the Maui Potiki *haka* is heard off camera, and a small group starts the responding calls and movements with others gradually entering the space to join in.

One year on from the event, there were close to 1.4 million views, more than 2800 comments, around 7000 likes and 250 dislikes, which is a remarkable level of visibility for a video taken at a shopping centre in suburban New Zealand. As with flash mobs generally, the *haka* was performed in a public space, bringing together passers-by and those who view the video online as both audience members and participants. The overall spectacle is reliant for its effect on its broader public accessibility as a YouTube video, and required both the attention generated through commercial media networks. But it also relied on the highly localised networks, and the collaborative production and distribution efforts of those involved in the performance, its videoing and its upload. A great deal of the attention is also built through YouTube's own social network and the thousands of comments and lengthy discussions generated by those with a YouTube channel or profile. This is a locally produced video, filmed in a typical yet specific suburban shopping centre but with global visibility, functioning as an object to engage with and through in the act of projecting identity and affiliating with social groups (Lange 2007).

Within YouTube's user networks, interesting interactions took place, also illustrating some of the ways we manage our sense of self socially through media and social network platforms. When people engaged with the video and with others through YouTube's comment field, it was typically lively and continued on for many months. The vast majority of comments expressed cultural and national pride as a public performance of affiliation. As is typical of YouTube interaction, some involved antagonism and even vitriol. More interesting, though, was the fact that many comments expressed affiliation of differing levels—in some cases referring directly to someone recognised in the video. For example, cultural affiliation was established through lengthy discussion of Māori and Polynesian traditions, often as a response to those who were hostile in their comments. At all levels and stages, these were acts of projecting and expressing identities and affiliation that revolved around the video object, the people and performance it recorded, and the comments and interactions that followed.

The second example of how we manage those aspects of ourselves we make accessible to others relates to our everyday uses of mobile media technologies. Mobile phones are widely understood as crucial devices in the construction of our sense of self-identity (Castells et al. 2007, p. 112), and in how we negotiate social network relations (Rainie and Wellman 2012)—our 'social selves'. With the rise of location-based mobile social networking platforms, such as the check-in service Foursquare, another crucial element is added to this mix: that of place or location (see also Chapter 16). Where we are—our 'presentation of location'—now extends the 'presentation of self', as Erving Goffman (1959) puts it, which has been greatly enriched by social networking sites. The phrase 'presentation of location', which was coined by Adriana de Souza e Silva and Jordan Frith (2012), captures the two-way process through which locations have become important to people's self-formation and, at the same time, are actively formed as sites, places and locations with which we interact and increasingly embed digital information (2012, pp. 167, 169).

Through our everyday use of location-enabled mobile devices, the embedded geographic information that is linked to our actions is routinely stored and disclosed to others in the form of check-ins, geo-tagged photos, location-specific tweets and so on. These forms of location disclosure through mobile use are especially significant in the context of wider public interest in and anxiety around privacy—concerns that appear heightened when the location of a Twitter, Facebook or Foursquare user becomes publicly accessible (de Souza e Silva and Frith 2010, p. 118). Playing on these fears, in 2010 the Dutch website Please Rob Me (<http://pleaserobme.com>) created controversy by posting real-time updates from social media users as they checked into locations other than their homes (Hough 2010). The aim of the site was to raise awareness about the risks of over-sharing by pointing out to Foursquare users who 'push' their check-in activities to linked Twitter accounts that they are making their location *publicly* available, rather than available to just their friends on the closed networks of Foursquare.

Personal disclosure, though, is only one of a number of concerns surrounding the aggregation of location-based social data. For instance, de Souza e Silva and Frith (2012) draw on the work of Solove (2008) to argue that transparency, and exclusion and aggregation, are key issues for geo-tagged social data. With respect to transparency, their argument is that the privacy policies of popular location-based services rarely disclose whether 'they share location information with third parties, how they share the information, or if location information is stored' (de Souza e Silva and Frith 2012, p. 128). With respect to the second, interrelated concerns of exclusion and aggregation, they suggest that the issue here is that while more and more data is collected by companies that themselves benefit from creating sophisticated profiles of social media users, 'people have little recourse to access what information has been collected or whether that information is correct', and so we have very little control over what is done with that information (2012, pp. 128–9).

As with our uses of social networking sites and producing and sharing of media through platforms like YouTube, the issues raised by location disclosure and aggregation need to be considered in terms of two complicating factors: the importance of the specific medium, and our willingness to use technologies and sites that capture location data in order to take advantage of the (social) benefits they afford. With respect to the former, location information must be understood as shifting from platform to platform: 'Sharing location with a small group of friends in Foursquare is different from allowing anyone that uses Whrrl to see one's location, which is also different from sharing one's location via Twitter openly on the Web.' (de Souza e Silva and Frith 2012, p. 131) In light of this, social media users need to have adequate provision to control the context in which they share their location information—something of which both Twitter and Foursquare are evidently aware, given the detailed information they provide to users on how to manage location settings, and the explanations they give of the risks associated with location disclosure. But because users usually pay little attention to this information, and given that so many people are willing to use these technologies anyway, it can be argued that use of location-aware technologies and social networking sites becomes just one aspect of the way we negotiate the self-constituting act of 'finding' (someone or something) and 'being found' (Elmer 2010), and how we manage our visibility (Blatterer 2010) in highly mediated and networked social environments.

In this chapter, we have explored briefly two distinct examples—one involving YouTube user networks, the other concerning location-based mobile social networking—that illustrate the opportunities and anxieties confronting our practices of self-formation through our uses of social and mobile media. By exploring some of the tensions generated by social and locative media regarding our control over our public availability, visibility and 'locatability', we are able to illustrate how social media platforms and communication devices function in very distinct ways as crucial tools of social self-formation.

Chapter 18

'WHITE BREAD' MEDIA

TANJA DREHER

Firass Dirani can attest to both the successes and the challenges of multiculturalism in Australian media. The Logie award-winning actor of Lebanese descent has starred in critically acclaimed television dramas including *Underbelly: The Golden Mile* (Nine, 2010) and *The Straits* (ABC, 2012). However, in 2012 he accused commercial TV producers of a 'white Australia' policy, claiming that the all-Anglo families of soaps such as *Packed to the Rafters* and *Neighbours* don't reflect 'who we are in 2012' (Byrnes 2012). While the complex characters of *The Straits* were a landmark in media representation of Indigenous Australians, Dirani's colleague Jay Laga'aia, who is of Samoan descent, echoed his concerns. Having been recently cut from the long-running soap *Home and Away*, Laga'aia tweeted: 'As someone who lost his job on *H&A* because they couldn't write two ethnics that weren't together, I'd like a chance to ply my trade freely.' (Wilkins 2012)

Given their central social, cultural and political role, it is no great surprise that the media are often criticised. A notable cause for concern in recent years has been the role of the media in inflaming community tensions and contributing to racism in Australia. In the aftermath of the Cronulla riot in 2005, for example, many media commentators, community leaders and politicians argued that talkback radio in particular had whipped up anger against Lebanese and Muslim communities in south-western Sydney and encouraged a nationalist fervour directed at 'claiming back the beach' for Anglo-Australians (Marr 2005). Following complaints from listeners, the Australian Communications Media Authority (ACMA) investigated comments broadcast by high-profile 'shock jock' Alan Jones, and found that certain broadcasts 'encouraged violence and brutality and were likely to vilify people of Lebanese and Middle Eastern background on the basis of their ethnicity' (ABC Online 2007).

The depth and consistency of the criticism lodged against the media with regard to multicultural Australia are important for our understandings and experiences of diversity and difference. Public debates about 'white bread media' remind us just how much the media matter. And they matter because they do not merely reflect, but are also players in, key public debates, providing representations and frameworks that shape understandings and action. In this chapter, I discuss some recent debates in relation to the media's treatment of Muslim Australians, as well as the response of the communities concerned.

PARADOXES OF MEDIA AND MULTICULTURALISM

While public debate focuses on racism in the media, scholarly research on media and multiculturalism paints a more complex picture. Indeed, recent research finds that the media are central to both relatively unproblematic experiences of 'everyday multi-culturalism' *and* to everyday experiences of racism in Australia. This apparent paradox is typical of Australian multiculturalism more generally. Even while most Australians consume diverse cultural products, and mix and mingle across cultures in their daily lives, certain stereotypes and pockets of resistance to cultural diversity persist (Ang et al. 2002). Media studies research has focused on both the positive and the negative potential of the media's representational function in multicultural Australia.

Audience studies reveal the importance of media in the everyday negotiations of cultural difference and hybrid identities experienced by migrant communities. Marie Gillespie (1995) introduced the concept of 'TV talk' in her study of young Punjabi Londoners, highlighting the ways in which media representations function as a shared cultural resource in mundane conversations through which audiences explore various axes of difference and identity, including gender, generation, ethnicity, religion and nation (see also Barker 1999). *Floating Lives* (Cunningham and Sinclair 2000) surveys media consumption among a number of Asian Australian diasporic communities, and identifies three major uses for the wide range of transnational media: for heritage maintenance, for cultural negotiation and for assertive hybridity. Media here are understood as central to developing a sense of belonging and a cosmopolitan world-view.

Working in a different paradigm, an earlier research tradition focuses on identifying racism in the media, largely through the analysis of media content. Many reports reveal evidence of stereotyping, invisibility, sensationalism and racist representations in soaps, advertising and news and current affairs (Coupe, Jakubowicz and Randall 1992), with a particular focus on the coverage of Indigenous Australians (Goodall 1990), Asian Australians during the 1990s (Jacubowicz et al. 1994) and of Arab and Muslim Australians in more recent years (Poynting et al. 2004). A number of large-scale national consultations have also found that news media reporting can contribute to an environment in which racist violence occurs (Royal Commission 1991; HREOC 1991, 2004). News media and talkback radio have been found to be routine contributors to the waves of 'moral panic' directed at migrant or ethnic communities assumed to be inherently criminal, threatening or 'un-Australian'.

While this research has primarily focused on mainstream media, it is important to remember that the media in Australia are in fact highly diverse. The media in Australia include mainstream commercial media characterised by highly concentrated ownership; the relatively under-funded public broadcasters ABC and SBS; the rapidly growing Indigenous media sector; transnational media available via satellite, cable and internet; the lively field of community media and public-access radio; as well as a plethora of commercially operated newspapers, radio and television targeting specific language communities and many more outlets.

SBS: AUSTRALIA'S MULTICULTURAL NATIONAL BROADCASTER

Perhaps the most unique and significant of Australia's major media institutions is the Special Broadcasting Service (SBS). This was founded in 1975 with experimental ethnic radio stations in Melbourne and Sydney, expanding to broadcast television in 1980 and now available in urban and regional centres across the country. Required by its charter to 'provide multilingual and multicultural radio and television services that inform, educate and entertain all Australians, and in doing so reflect Australia's multicultural society', the SBS has no equivalent anywhere else in the world. It is arguably the most significant and the most visible institutional manifestation of Australia's official policy of multiculturalism (Jakubowicz 1987).

The most recent comprehensive study of the SBS (Ang, Hawkins and Dabboussy 2008) found that the organisation is innovative precisely because it takes the idea of difference and diversity as central and normal, developing innovative strategies to pluralise what we hear and see on TV and radio. New forms of TV and radio pioneered at SBS range from radio broadcasting in dozens of languages other than English—which enables newly arrived migrants to negotiate settlement and belonging—through to high-quality television dramas exploring contemporary issues, and world music radio programming produced by hip second- and third-generation cultural activists addressing youth taste cultures in global Englishes. Ang, Hawkins and Dabboussy (2008) contend that, far from simply a 'niche' or 'ethnic' broadcaster, in fact SBS reflects three versions of multiculturalism operating in some tension. The early days of SBS Radio were characterised by 'ethno-multiculturalism' addressed to the special needs and interests of migrants and ethnic communities, while the advent of SBS TV foregrounded 'cosmopolitan multiculturalism', which encourages all Australians—regardless of cultural background—to embrace global cultural diversity. The late 1990s, however, saw a shift towards 'popular multiculturalism', in which 'the emphasis is no longer on actively promoting multicultural diversity, but on treating it as an increasingly ordinary, taken-for-granted feature of everyday life' (Ang, Hawkins & Dabboussy 2008, p. 20). The history of SBS is also touched on in Chapter 10.

MEDIA AND THE 'ARAB OTHER'

While an exploration of the role of SBS highlights the innovative and productive possibilities for multicultural media, much research on the media representation of Muslim and Arab Australians since 2001 demonstrates the prevalence and persistence of racism. The news reporting of 'ethnic gang rapes' in western Sydney, asylum seekers arriving primarily from Afghanistan and Iraq, the 'Pacific Solution' and the events of September 11, 2001, followed by the 'war on terror', have been the subject of much public debate and considerable scholarly analysis. These events were linked in media discourse through the involvement of people categorised as 'Middle Eastern', 'Muslim' or 'Arab' (Poynting et al. 2004; Anti-Discrimination Board 2003), and the naming and framing of these events in news reporting contributed to 'the emergence of the "Arab Other" as the pre-eminent "folk devil" of our time' (Poynting et al. 2004, p. 3), with the production of refugees, Arab and Muslim Australians as 'the new "others"' (Jacka and Green 2003).

In much news reporting of the gang rapes in Bankstown, asylum seekers, 'border protection' and the 'war on terror', complex events have been explained in terms of their relationship to essentialised Arab or Muslim 'cultures'. Poynting and colleagues

(2004) describe this as a 'racialised frame' in public discourse, which not only contributed to the discursive linking of these events, but also privileged a moral frame of explanation rather than a focus on social causes. Peter Manning (2004) also notes the conflation of 'ethnic crime', 'border protection' and terrorism in news and current affairs reporting of this period. Both local communities and asylum seekers described as 'Middle Eastern' have been criminalised in news reporting (Anti-Discrimination Board 2003), and journalists as well as researchers have argued that asylum seekers have been dehumanised in media coverage—a tendency exacerbated by federal government restrictions on access to information about individual asylum seekers, which might have given their predicament a human dimension, and to immigration detention centres (Green 2003; Manning 2004; Klocker and Dunn 2003; Saxton 2003; Slattery 2003).

COMMUNITY MEDIA INTERVENTIONS

Strategies for speaking up and talking back to news media have become an integral part of anti-racism and community relations work in Australia, and researchers and government bodies increasingly recommend funding for community media responses to and interventions in their media representation (Anti-Discrimination Board 2003; HREOC 2004; Dunn 2003). News intervention strategies target the mainstream media and aim to shift the ways in which communities and issues are reported, framed and defined (Dreher 2003, 2010).

In response to racialised representations, Arab and Muslim communities have developed a wide variety of strategies, from media monitoring and complaints to creative cultural production and comedy, and from media advocacy and skills training to satire. The comedy sketch and panel TV show *Salam Café* encapsulates the shift in representations of Australian Muslims in mainstream media. Originally aired on community television in Melbourne, in 2008 the program was picked up for national broadcast by SBS TV. The show featured young, media-savvy Muslim Australians as regular panellists, discussing issues in the news and their daily experiences. The program received positive reviews:

> Clearly intended to influence perceptions of young Muslims in the current global climate, this series wants to show that being a Muslim can be as much about going to the footy as to the mosque and that Muslims have no trouble laughing at themselves and the way they are misrepresented . . . it's refreshing to see Muslim comics and community leaders taking ownership of the prejudice they feel to make it funny and entertaining. (Duthie 2008)

The program represented a significant opportunity for young Muslim Australians to set the media agenda, chatting about everyday concerns such as popular culture and mobile phones, as well as addressing controversial issues that more commonly feature in mainstream media representations of Islam. Using self-reflexive comedy, panellists both normalised their everyday experiences in multicultural Australia and satirised contemporary public debate and its obsessive scrutiny of Islam.

CONCLUSION

In contemplating media and multiculturalism in Australia, there is much to celebrate, and also significant challenges. The SBS is a unique public broadcaster that has pioneered innovative multicultural media, not least by popularising cultural diversity for all Australians and developing programming that addresses the hybrid lives of young Australians who negotiate differences every day. While a racialised media frame served to demonise Arab and Muslim communities in the early years of the new millennium, tireless efforts by people working with those communities have created productive media interventions. While the scrutiny of Muslim Australians in particular continues, there is evidence of shifting representations and attempts by media professionals to produce more diverse and balanced representations as well.

If programs like *The Straits* or *Salam Café* suggest increasing diversity in Australian media, there are also reminders of the need for continued vigilance with regard to the persistence of 'white bread media'. For example, in 2008 the Australian soap *Neighbours* was slammed by UK viewers for being 'too white' (Byrnes 2012), and in 2007 youth workers and African community representatives were compelled to challenge sensationalised news reporting of youth crime in Melbourne's Noble Park, which led to calls for a reduction in immigration from Sudan. While such moral panics may shift in focus and intensity, nevertheless the media continue to play a central role in understandings of Australian multiculturalism and immigration. The media in multicultural Australia continue to grapple with the apparent paradox of everyday diversity and the prevalence of everyday racism.

Chapter 19
CELEBRITY CULTURE

GRAEME TURNER

It is not uncommon to hear that we now live in a 'culture of celebrity'. Usually, that is regretted: while selected celebrities may get good press, 'celebrity culture' does not. Celebrity culture is seen as encouraging shallow and narcissistic performances of the self, while flooding the public sphere with meretricious (and possibly fictional) versions of the news. Nonetheless, and notwithstanding the regular criticism of the promotion of celebrities—or those arguments which suggest that the public good might be better served through a more traditional news agenda—celebrity has become an increasingly pervasive presence in Australian public culture. Even the quality end of the print media—newspapers such as *The Age* or *The Australian*, which do not include much in the way of celebrity material in their pages—nevertheless find plenty of room for it on their websites. The rise of video aggregators like YouTube and social networking sites like Facebook has opened up new platforms for the consumption and distribution of celebrity material, extending the reach of individual media outlets and developing a transnational market for celebrity content that has been taken from its original platform and repurposed for online consumption.

The industries that produce celebrity—publicity, promotions, public relations and so on (for an account of the Australian industry, see Turner, Bonner and Marshall 2000)—are now fundamental structural components of the media in Australia. Celebrity's commercial importance as an attractor of audience interest has had a major effect on the nature of the content our media carry. The focus of Australian mass-market women's magazines has dramatically changed since the 1980s; celebrity has become a standard component of television news and current affairs and, most significantly, free-to-air TV programming in Australia has constructed a virtual production line for creating and circulating celebrity through its takeup of transnational reality and talent quest formats such as *Idol*, *Big Brother*, *So You Think You Can Dance*, *Dancing with the Stars*, *The Voice*, *MasterChef* and so on.

More broadly, celebrity culture is seen as now exercising a significant influence on the construction of identity within Western societies (Rojek 2011). The identities performed in programs such as *Big Brother* are one important element in this—that is, they are seen as promoting a particular version of selfhood as if it were a desirable model to emulate (Wood and Skeggs 2011). There is also the avid interest in particular celebrities, which produces what has been called 'parasocial' interaction: the development of 'relationships' with people you never actually meet face to face. Celebrity is a key site for this, although the desire for parasocial interaction has been connected to changes in the structures of our communities. Today, it is argued, we find ourselves in communities where many of the traditional structures have faded: the extended family, neighbourhood networks and so on no longer play the central role in everyone's lives they once occupied. In their place, it is suggested, we are constructing relations with people we know only through the media: celebrities, talk show hosts, sports stars and the like. In a related development, the objective of achieving celebrity has also become more integrated into the expectations of a person's everyday life. As celebrity becomes more pervasive, it can seem like a realistic goal or aspiration for ordinary people—even for those with no particular achievements or talents. There have been a number of research projects dealing with teenagers, in particular, which report that celebrity is regarded as a genuine career option among the teenage subjects investigated, even when the area of activity in which that celebrity might be achieved is regarded as a secondary consideration (Lumby 2011).

WHAT IS CELEBRITY?

In its most common usage today, 'celebrity' is attached to a particular kind of cultural figure: they will usually have emerged from the sports or entertainment industries; they will be visible through the media; and their private lives will attract greater public interest than their professional lives. Among the markers of contemporary celebrity, as distinct from previous versions of fame, is the fact that the contemporary celebrity's prominence does not necessarily depend on the position or the achievements that brought them to our attention in the first instance. Rather, their fame is likely to have outstripped the claims to prominence developed within that initial location. Indeed, it is a mark of the modern celebrity that they may claim no special achievements other than their exorbitant visibility; as Boorstin (1971) put it many years ago, they are 'famous for being famous'. It is for this reason that many media commentators have criticised the level of public interest generated by celebrities today as disproportionate: celebrity, for such commentators, constitutes the epitome of the inauthenticity of today's popular culture. For many others, however, it is the very excessiveness and arbitrariness of celebrity that constitutes its appeal to a media-savvy and 'postmodern' (Gamson 1994) culture.

That said, it is worth pointing out that celebrity should not simply be regarded as a property of particular individuals. In *Understanding Celebrity* (Turner 2004), I argue that celebrity is at least four things. First, the celebrity is a commodity that is manufactured, managed and traded through the media. Second, celebrity is a mode of media representation—that is, celebrity is a property of how particular individuals are treated by the media, and central to this is an interest in their private rather than their professional lives. Third, celebrity is the effect of such media representations—that is, the changes to the cultural meanings of the individual who is their subject as well as how they are circulated. Fourth, celebrity also seems now to be integrated into a form of social relations: available through media representations and operated through patterns of social consumption, celebrity is now a part of the community's common currency for conversation, gossip and the like. It is within this last location that it has become most implicated in the construction of social identities.

RECENT SHIFTS IN THE PRODUCTION OF CELEBRITY

As I suggested earlier, the celebrity who is known for being well known rather than for any particularly outstanding personal achievement has now become, more or less, the standard. Indeed, the less their fame is connected to their achievements, the more they depend upon its active commodification and promotion, and the more we can expect to see the results of that produce a steady stream of paparazzi pictures in *Who* magazine, leaked stories about personal dramas, personal appearances on television chat shows, newsworthy personal website revelations, 'candid' videos online and so on. The management of celebrity has become an industry on its own, and it is now separable from its origins as a support structure for the publicising of other media projects.

Recently, we have seen a steady shift that has taken us from the exploitation of individuals who have achieved some prominence already, and therefore are in some sense already an elite group, to the development of 'ordinary' people as popular personalities through their participation in particular media platforms or products (Turner 2010). As noted earlier, the key development here has been the explosion of reality TV, confessional and docu-formats: docu-soaps, docu-dramas, reality game shows, reality dating shows, confessional talk shows, reality talent contests and so on. The number of hybrid TV genres that have contributed to this shift is extraordinary. The extraordinary cultural prominence of *Big Brother*, however—its status as a high-profile popular culture event in so many countries around the world—has had the effect of normalising the media's suddenly enhanced demand for ordinary people desiring 'celebrification'. (In Malaysia, the fifth series of that country's version of *Fame Academy*, *Akademi Fantasia*, attracted seven million applicants!) Not only do these programs enlist ordinary people to live parts of their lives—albeit not a very ordinary part—on television, but the radical 'liveness' of these programs engenders a sense that they have become part of our own everyday lives. I am referring here not only to the fact that the programs are transmitted live in stripped slots across the week, but also to the many forms of real-time interactivity they provide (the voting, the interaction with the website, the opportunity for attending the live evictions and so on). It is as if television has found a way to shrink the difference between the reality it constructs and its audiences' own realities, so that TV becomes increasingly 'ordinary' even as it turns its 'ordinary' subjects into celebrities.

Of course, among the consequences of this accelerated process of celebrification—for example, those who take part no longer 'pay their dues' by performing for years, they just audition for *Australian Idol*—is the increased speed of the life-cycle for the products of this process. The industrial rhythm of use and disposal has radically accelerated in response to the demand created by new media formats. The appeal of successive series of *Big Brother* or *Survivor* depends in part upon their superseding their predecessors; the contestants from each series must give way to the next crop. These are replaceable celebrities: with little to distinguish them in the first place; with little in the way of career options to develop after the series has ended; and with only a six-month contract (in the case of the Australian version of *Big Brother*, although longer in the case of some of the US series—see Collins 2008) tying them to the network's promotional schedule after the program is completed. As a result, very few of the contestants from *Big Brother* or *Idol* have managed to use their experience to leverage a continuing career in the Australian media or the music industry.

To some extent, one could argue that the cultural placement and meaning of celebrity have themselves mutated. As the opportunity for celebrity has spread beyond elites of one kind or another and into the experience of the population in general, it has shifted from being an elite and magical condition to the point where it has become almost a reasonable expectation to have of one's own life. At the same time, the production of celebrity has become increasingly systematised. Today, the media have learnt how to mass-produce celebrity as and when it is required. Rather than merely exploiting the popular appeal of those who have already been established through other means, television in particular has engaged in a process of vertical integration: instead of marketing the celebrity developed elsewhere, the media now discover, produce, market and sell on their celebrities from scratch. There have been many who have questioned the ethical basis on which this has been done. Both Andrejevic (2004) and Collins (2008), for instance, have published research that points to the exploitative nature of the contracts offered by reality TV to their contestants, the powerlessness of the individual contestant to broker the kind of deal that might lead to a continuing career, and the misleading nature of the promises made and advice given to the contestants before they sign up.

CONCLUSION

There are genuine ethical issues about the expansion of the opportunities for celebrity in our celebrity culture, as well as about the kinds of identities recommended by way of the current formations of celebrity articulated via the dominant distribution platforms. Chris Rojek's *Fame Attack* (2011) has recently raised the issue of whether we need to more closely consider the social and psychological consequences of the current versions of fame—both on the celebrities themselves and upon the public understanding of what it is to be a successful person. While the last decade of work on celebrity has helped us to better understand the fundamental role played by celebrity, and the industries that trade in it, in the contemporary mediascape there is still much more to be done to help us to better understand the broader cultural and social functions of a celebrity culture.

Chapter 20
THE ETHICS OF PRIVACY

KATE BOWLES

> Facebook is a global communications platform embraced by over 10 million Australians because we give them the power and controls to share what they want, when they want, with whom they want. When it comes to privacy, we are focused on transparency, control, and accountability. (Garlick 2012)

Reminders about the delicate nature of privacy are pervasive across the networks of our everyday online lives. Free email services rapidly adjust their advertising to you according to the topics you're writing about in private communications. YouTube makes recommendations that expose the themes of your recent searches. You are automatically tagged by Facebook in photos uploaded by your friends. And most websites you visit now ask you to consent to a privacy policy in relation to the cookies that leave a trail of crumbs wherever you go on the internet. All of this is part of our understanding of privacy as something ordinary, troubling and vague. But mainstream discussions of media privacy still seem focused on ideals of privacy that are both more concrete and much more scandalous than our everyday experiences: grainy photographs of pregnant celebrities, tabloid phone hacking, the controversial release of secure military and diplomatic communications, and the revelations of high-status affairs documented in the emails, sex tapes, intimate photographs and texts that individuals expected to stay private forever.

Despite contemporary attention on privacy as some kind of inalienable right of citizenship, privacy is a relatively limited privilege, and its boundaries are shrinking. Historically, it has been offered only to citizens of particular status, who have the means to safeguard the ways in which they are represented by others, and the capacity to demand the protection of the state for the security of their identity in the public realm. Slaves in the American South, for example, enjoyed very limited rights to privacy; while the privacy of children is typically subordinated to the oversight of their parents or guardians. Prisoners or people suspected of criminal or terrorist activity can lose many of their rights to privacy in the interests of public safety, and holders of public office can find their private lives treated as legitimate matters of national or even international interest. But more recently, we have become used to the ways in which the privacy of employees, students, internet users and indeed anyone who walks down a street watched by CCTV can be overruled by security and even business risks.

The right of celebrities to curb media surveillance of their private lives, as well as to control the personal brand that they have cultivated for themselves, is of longstanding interest to media and news corporations (Rahimi 1995). We now also pay attention to the privacy of ordinary media users, as new networks, technologies and data-processing capabilities enable us to capture the details of other people's homes, relationships and misfortunes, and to transmit this information to the kinds of global audiences previously only reached by media corporations (Blatterer, Johnson and Markus 2010). These changes are placing significant pressure on traditional privacy principles, as major media companies try to work out how to manage privacy as a potential constraint on their emerging business activities. To understand the complex terrain of media privacy, and to think about our place in it, we can begin with a very simple and familiar illustration: the paradoxically isolating experience of falling down in public.

Some time in 2011, an anonymous woman walking down an urban back street in Belo Horizonte, Brazil tripped and fell full length on the pavement. Across the road, a small group noticed and laughed. Earlier in the same year, a woman walking through a mall in Wyomissing, Pennsylvania fell headlong into a fountain while texting, watched by a mall cleaner. These two minor incidents occurred in public space, and in snapshot simply represent the social predicament of our presence as private individuals in the company of strangers. What happens to the normal rules of social privacy when someone falls over? In most contexts, someone tripping over in public triggers a banal interpersonal dilemma: whether to look sympathetically or to look away discreetly. It is the onlookers themselves who convert a physical tumble into a social one; by looking, or looking away, they make visible the normally hidden boundary around privacy that strangers learn to offer one another in crowded places.

Neither of these two incidents was exceptional in itself, unlike the kinds of privacy malfunctions that we typically discuss—the moments where celebrities are caught by paparazzi smoking, or shopping in unflattering trackpants. What makes these two incidents important to the study of media and communications practices, however, is their status as viral media events, and the questions they raise about media technology and the surveillance of public space (Quay and Damico 2012). They expose the technologies and channels that have changed our expectation of privacy in everyday life: CCTV, Google Street View, YouTube and vernacular news content—pratfalls, pranks and disaster footage contributed by users who were on the scene with their mobile phones. Both events involved a familiar surveillance technology that harvested unfortunate footage in the course of its normal operation.

The woman who fell down in Belo Horizonte did so just as a Google Street View car drove past. Her stumble found its way into the many websites like streetviewfun. com that revel in Google's accidental discovery of embarrassing moments in everyday life—people caught coming out of sex shops, urinating in the street, lying in the gutter or falling off their bicycles. Before-and-after montages of her walking, tripping and getting up again appeared on blogs and video sharing sites, and in January 2012 her image on Google Street View was abruptly blurred—or 'censored', as one blog described it. As it happens, Google's image blurring technology is available to any complainant who seeks either to have their own identifying data (faces, vehicle licence plates or properties) removed from public view. As Google puts it:

> The Street View team takes a number of steps to help protect the privacy and anonymity of individuals when images are collected for Street View, including blurring faces and license plates. You can easily contact the Street View team if you see an image that should be protected or if you see a concerning image. (Google Street View 2013)

Anonymisation through blurring, pixellation or voice manipulation are all familiar media practices; they ask us to accept that actual privacy is redundant, providing a reasonable level of de-identification is achieved. In the case of the anonymous woman who fell down in Belo Horizonte, Google's normal practice was evidently insufficient to manage her growing celebrity, and a more comprehensive blurring was eventually applied to her whole body, as though notoriety required her to be erased completely from public view. Her actual privacy remains moot, however, as it is still very easy to find unblurred images of her fall that were captured and circulated at the time. Google cannot reasonably be expected to remove them from across the internet, and indeed Google itself provides the search capability that finds them quickly in response to the simple search: 'woman falling down in Brazil street'.

When the individual concerned is identifiable, however, the stakes in relation to privacy are raised. The woman who fell into the fountain in a Pennsylvania mall was a mall employee. The footage was captured on official CCTV, and noticed by security staff, who then used their private mobile phones to film the footage as they replayed it on equipment owned by their employer, before uploading the footage to YouTube. When this footage was rebroadcast on television around the world, the woman identified herself and in media interviews indicated that she was prepared to take legal action against the management of the mall, first for the distress caused by the fact that no one came to her aid, but more importantly for failing to prevent their CCTV footage from being remixed as global YouTube LOL (Praetorius 2011). As she reported her reaction to the event: 'I didn't get an apology. What I got was, "At least nobody knows it was you",' Marrero said. 'But I knew it was me.' (Chang 2011)

This commonsense test—that someone whose image is broadcast feels that an element of their identity has been revealed without their consent, whether or not they are actually identifiable by others—invites us to reflect on the beliefs we hold about privacy. How much control do we have over the way in which we are represented by others? What test of public interest applies to the private behaviour of prominent individuals? Is privacy culturally specific, or are there universal principles to which all citizens should be able to appeal, in the tradition of international human rights? Within this broad and very complicated cultural realm, the area typically singled out for legislative attention is the protection of personal and identifying data. The Australian *Privacy Act*, for example, expects that agencies that collect data will use it only for intended purposes, that they will dispose of it correctly, and that the people to whom it refers will in general retain the right to access it. This is an important protection for the wealth of sensitive data that both public and private agencies collect about individuals, including health and credit data. But there are other aspects of media privacy managed by different standards: the privacy of people using telephones is covered under the *Telecommunications Act*, and news and current affairs producers are required by the *Broadcasting Services Act* to develop and implement codes of practice for balancing the right to privacy against the public interest. In the case of the behaviour of individuals who violate one another's privacy, however, regulation is much more limited, and can often be applied only where the information that is exposed is also offensive, demeaning or libellous, rather than merely private.

Emerging technologies and practices—spyware, identity theft and hacking, for example—are challenging the viability of all these traditional privacy protection regimes. Many advocates of open information are alarmed at any suggestion that legislative reach over privacy should be extended. At the same time, the commercial value of personally identifying data is increasing, and this does suggest the need to protect the interests of individuals in relation to the harvesting of data that can be deployed in commercial partnerships or to attract advertising. To give a sense of the importance of these safeguards, we can return to the car that accidentally captured (or perhaps caused) the moment where an anonymous woman fell down in Belo Horizonte. Like many other large media corporations, Google Inc. has recently experienced a very public stumble of its own. In 2010, the company admitted that its Street View cars had been harvesting and storing private data from domestic wireless networks, using code that had been written for that purpose. Around the world, Google was forced to explain itself and to promise to have this compromising data destroyed. In Australia, for example, the Australian Privacy Commissioner found that Google had clearly breached the *Privacy Act* by collecting this data, and required the company to issue a public apology and have the destruction of the data verified by an independent third party (OAIC 2010).

This, then, is one way of understanding Google Street View's tactical promotion of its investment in privacy, just as Facebook is keen to promote its commitment to 'transparency, control and accountability'. Both companies have suffered significant reputational harm in relation to their exploitation of users' private data. In order to protect Google Inc.'s primary operations in relation to its search algorithm, to which its advertising revenue is closely coupled, Google Street View is used to promote the company's commitment to privacy as a commonsense composite of dignity, anonymity and security in the public domain. The blurred faces and licence plates on Street View communicate more than a simple corporate ideal about the fact that people who fall over in the street should be allowed to do it privately. They are also a form of corporate advertising, displaying on every screen Google's paradoxical status as a privacy champion, continually attempting to blur the company's own investment in the aggregation and manipulation of personal data on a global scale.

Chapter 21
SPORTS MEDIA
DAVID ROWE

THE MEDIATISATION OF SPORT

Sport has, over the last two centuries, become pivotal to the development of news and entertainment media across the world. It draws consistent and sometimes enormous audiences, providing very large amounts of both staple and exceptional media content. At the same time, without media publicity and finance through broadcast media rights, professional sport would be a much smaller, less conspicuous cultural activity. This 'marriage made in heaven' is described by Wenner (1998) as a singular phenomenon—'mediasport'—while others see media and sport as forming a single 'complex' (Jhally 2006; Maguire 1999) involving production, consumption and cultural exchange. This 'media sports cultural complex' is now a pervasive global phenomenon (Rowe 2004, 2011). However, as applies to all relationships—both institutional and personal—questions of power cannot be sidestepped, and there is a persistent anxiety that the media now dominate sport and use it for their own ends in ways that diminish sport's independence and integrity.

Enthusiasm for watching sport on television is often regarded as a 'health hazard', with couch-bound sports viewers seen as 'outsourcing' their physical activities to sportspeople performing for them on screen. According to the national Census, Australians expend 42 million person hours per day watching television, and only 6.2 million daily person hours engaging in sport and outdoor activity (ABS 2011a, 2012c). While not all television watching involves sport, it is a significant component of it, with almost three million Australians watching the Opening Ceremony of the London 2012 Olympics. Sport annually features heavily among the most-watched programs on Australian free-to-air television, and completely dominates them on pay TV. Long-standing concerns about the *quantity* of sport media use is accompanied by an equivalent anxiety about its *quality*. What happens to sport when it is in the hands of the media?

THE IDEOLOGICAL USES AND CONSEQUENCES OF MEDIA SPORT

The media do much more than represent sport, they also attach a range of socio-cultural meanings to it. Wenner (2007) calls this the 'communicative dirt' that is sprinkled around via the media, picking up different connotations and being put to different symbolic uses. For example, media sport overwhelmingly focuses on men, with international studies consistently showing that sports journalism mostly involves men writing about other men, with women's sport generally well below 10 per cent of all-media coverage (Horky and Nieland 2011; Bruce, Hovden and Markula 2010). When sportswomen do garner some media coverage, their status as athletes is frequently denigrated as inferior to that of men and unduly focuses on their sexuality (Australian Sports Commission 2010; Coakley et al. 2009, Chs 8 and 12; Marjoribanks and Farquharson 2012, Ch. 5). While masquerading as a politics-free domain (Whannel 2008), media sport privileges men and marginalises women, thus playing a significant role in the perpetuation of sexual and gender inequality.

Similar critiques of the sports media as vehicles for oppressive ideologies have been advanced in many other areas, such as racial and ethnic discrimination (Adair 2012; Carrington 2010), homophobia (Caudwell 2006; Miller 2001) and national chauvinism and xenophobia (Bairner 2001; Tomlinson and Young 2006). In each case it is argued, with various permutations, that the coverage of sport typically involves damaging stereotypes that are 'naturalised' within a media sport world dominated by affluent, white heterosexual men, which then influentially resonates across whole societies in ways that reinforce that domination. Of course, the relationships between sport, media, culture, politics and society are much more complex and contested than such brief summations allow. 'Mediasport' can, in various ways, be seen as an important space where ideas, values and practices clash, and thereby advance public debates on a range of social issues in a popularly accessible way. This is demonstrably the case during periodic media sport scandals that range from the treatment of women by sportsmen and clubs to the ethical conduct of sport celebrities such as Tiger Woods and Lance Armstrong (Rowe 2011, Ch. 6). Here, the 'sport dirt' described above by Wenner can move into places that expose the politics of sport and society in novel ways, and so helps to disabuse sport fans of any illusion that sport somehow sits above the world of politics in isolated 'purity'. Certainly a sound grasp of the political economy of media sport is an effective antidote to such naivety.

MEDIA VERSUS SPORT

It is commonplace to assert that sport is now a business like any other, and that the media, in particular, have made it so by turning everyday pastimes into a commodity. This is the main argument of the critical political-economic approach to the sports media. It is undeniable that the media—especially television—have played a pivotal role in commercialising sport which, until barely a century ago, involved people playing physical games for little if any money, in front of comparatively small, mostly local and co-present crowds. With continuing commercialisation and technological innovations such as colour, satellite and high definition, televised sport events became increasingly vivid global spectacles. The viewing statistics for mega media sport spectacles are remarkable, such as the almost 900 million people estimated to have watched at least some of the London 2012 Olympics Opening Ceremony, or the almost 910 million television viewers of the 2010 FIFA World Cup Final.

Enabling people all over the world, who would otherwise find it impossible to 'share the moment', to watch live sport events could be seen as a positive example of media power. Television also provides enormous resources to support sport by paying for the rights to broadcast them. NBC, for example, has spent approximately US$10 billion on acquiring the US rights to all Summer and Winter Olympics between 2000 and 2020, while the Australian Seven and Nine Networks (in association with, variously, Foxtel, Fox Sports and Telstra) have both paid over A$1 billion in both cash and so-called 'contra' (free advertising and promotion) to display, respectively, the Australian Football League (AFL) (2012–16) and the National Rugby League (NRL) (2013–17) live on a range of media platforms. But the media becoming the most powerful economic force in sport inevitably brings demands to 'pay the piper'. Media power over sport has therefore been exerted by reshaping its forms, rules and rhythms to suit the demands of television. Such media-induced 'innovations' include tie breaks in tennis to prevent disruption to television schedules, timeouts in basketball for the insertion of advertisements and TV-friendly forms like one-day and Twenty20 cricket.

Television can also influence when sport events occur, with boxing bouts after midnight and Olympic marathons in the heat of the day scheduled to accommodate pay per view and network audiences in the most important media sport market—the United States. 'Staggered' event timing within and across days in competitions such as the AFL, NRL and the England Premier League (EPL) maximise television audiences, while during multi-sport events like the Olympics, 'live' action is packaged 'as live' or 'plausibly live' to give the impression to viewers that what has already happened is happening now. More profoundly, television has reshaped the whole experience of sport spectatorship through multiple camera angles, rapid-fire editing, replays, slow motion, close-ups and commentary that are now integral to its visual imagination (Rowe 2004). For this reason, instead of such domestic television devices being used to compensate viewers for not 'being there' at the sport stadium, giant screens are routinely imported into stadia in order to compensate paying spectators for not staying at home and watching the event on television. At the same time, pay television has introduced the 'electronic turnstile' at home, in the process raising questions about citizens' rights to sport on television.

MEDIA, CULTURAL CITIZENSHIP AND SPORT BEYOND TELEVISION

When subscription television was introduced to Australia in 1995, one of its major selling points was that it could include much more dedicated sport programming than free-to-air television. Not only were the commercial TV networks—especially Network Nine under the politically influential Kerry Packer—keen to prevent the loss of profitable sports rights to pay TV, but viewers were concerned that the exclusive capture of those rights by pay TV would force them (as had occurred, for example, in the United Kingdom and since in New Zealand) to subscribe to watch major sport events. As a result, an 'anti-siphoning' regime was introduced that listed 'events of national importance and cultural significance'—all of which were sporting events, including the football codes, cricket and tennis. Pay TV broadcasters could not therefore televise listed events before free-to-air television broadcasters had purchased the rights. The listed events in Australia (the most extensive list in the world) have been subject to many reviews and revisions, with constant pressure from pay TV to reduce or abandon the list, as well as complaints that media convergence has rendered the code an anachronism (Department of Broadband, Communications and the Digital Economy 2010, 2011). That no major Australian political party has supported the abandonment of the list is an indication of the popular sentiment that major televised sport events are part of the 'national estate', so viewing them is a right of 'cultural citizenship'. This debate over access to free TV sport (Scherer and Rowe 2013) is being played out in various ways across a world where broadcast TV sport is undergoing challenge as the dominant delivery mode in the burgeoning era of 'networked media sport' (Hutchins and Rowe 2012). With proliferating sport screens (digital channels, computer, tablet, mobile and game console) and widespread use of social media by sport fans, both to bypass and interact with institutional 'legacy' media, the media–sport nexus is undergoing substantial change.

CONCLUSION: THE 'SPORTIFICATION' OF THE MEDIA

This chapter commenced by discussing the historical anxiety that the media have 'taken over' sport and reduced its quality for players and spectators alike. Conversely, sport has insinuated itself into an increasing range of media organisations, practices and texts. This 'sportification' of the media involves not only their heavy reliance on sport's capacity to assemble large audiences—especially in a digital, multi-channel, multi-platform environment. It is also demonstrated by the proliferation of 'sport-like' characteristics of media genres, such as competitive 'reality' and 'talent' television shows with uncertain outcomes (score-keeping and live/mediated audiences), news and current affairs constructed around a contest framework that closely resembles sports encounters (a striking example being scoring who 'won' the 2012 Obama–Romney US presidential election debates) and the ubiquitous use of sport iconography and meta-phors in advertising, with liberal invocations of 'races', 'hurdles' and 'finishing lines' (Jackson and Andrews 2005). The media sports cultural complex, then, continues to repay close, systematic attention for all who are interested in the socio-cultural ramifications of popular media and communication.

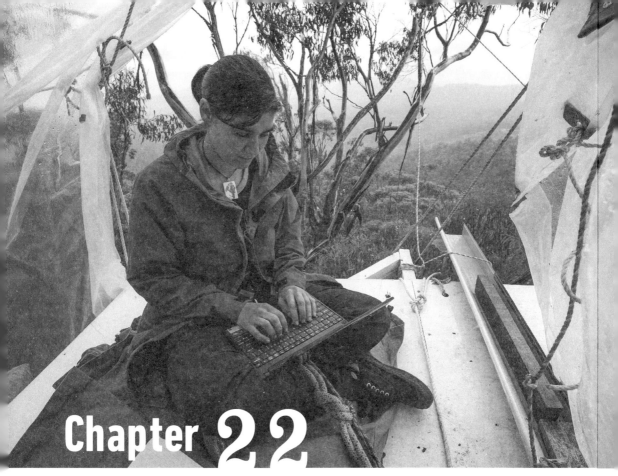

Chapter 22
MEDIA AND THE ENVIRONMENT

LIBBY LESTER

It is a long way to Miranda Gibson's tree. The drive from Australia's most southerly city, Hobart, to the edge of the World Heritage wilderness area is slow. Then there is the hour-long walk along wet and muddy bush tracks. The going is easier once the tracks open on to industrial forestry coupes, but climbing the slopes of the small mountain on which the tree sits is tough, particularly for those carrying fresh water supplies to send up the tree to Gibson. The tree itself is 80 metres high; it is a 60-metre thigh-breaking climb to Gibson's platform.

Gibson's tree is indeed remote. That is its point. The symbolism of a lone young woman perched on a small platform observing the surrounding threatened eucalypt forests through a Tasmanian summer and winter is powerful. It resonates across vast and complicated networks of political decision-making, commercial investments and interests, and local and cosmopolitan concern to protect environments and limit environmental harm. Gibson and her colleagues in the environment movement chose the tree for its isolation, which helps create symbols, images, messages and meanings that might impact on debate and decisions about the forest's future. However, there is another, more pragmatic, reason this tree was chosen. A new telecommunications tower had recently been constructed on the side of a nearby mountain, expanding 3G coverage in the region and allowing Gibson's tree-sit to serve as the hub of a sophisticated environmental communications strategy. Among other activities, she produces a daily blog, directs cyber actions against Japanese and other international buyers and retailers of Tasmanian timbers, circulates press releases to media outlets around the globe, and conducts Skype interviews with journalists and classroom talks to students in faraway locations (The Observer Tree 2012). Gibson's tree therefore is a media and communications powerhouse for the environment, not only producing powerful symbols of resistance and value, but sending them to the world.

Public environmental debate and decisions have long relied on the power of certain images and meanings to cut through the complexity of the science or the politics that underlie environmental problems. The polar bear on the small ice floe; the bloodied decks of Japanese whalers in the Southern Ocean; the belching emissions from cooling towers—these resonate to engage audiences with environmental concerns, even to the point that individuals and publics might respond and act. By their very nature, media carry such symbols with more ease than they can represent the uncertainties with which scientists speak of environmental risk or the complex policies enacted by governments to mitigate against environmental harm. When they do need to tackle the science or politics, media—and news in particular—often fall back on the safety of the he said, she said 'duelling sources' formula for balance. The cost, according to some, is a dumbed-down, emotion-laden understanding of environmental problems, which leaves individuals and publics ill-equipped to judge their severity and adopt viable, sound solutions. Instead, intractable conflicts can arise, fuelled by increasingly well-funded public relations campaigns by the industries and governments accessing and developing the environment and natural resources, and sophisticated uses of the media and communications by environmentalists such as Gibson.

REPORTING THE ENVIRONMENT

Media are the most important means we have for learning about environmental problems that exist beyond our own backyards. They adopt multiple roles in this process: carrying the words and images that produce meanings and understandings of the environment and associated problems (Anderson 1997); providing an arena in which protagonists voice concerns, fight over the right to use or protect natural resources and places, or contest the scientific and other representations of environmental harm (Hansen 2010); and, often as a player, investigating the causes of environmental damage, pushing for industries or governments to act to prevent or repair this damage, or dampening the messages of environmental activists who they perceive to be working against community or state interests (Lester 2010).

News is central to public awareness and communication of environmental risk (Beck 2009)—and as such its role has been closely scrutinised in recent years. Focusing in particular on the way the news has reported climate change internationally and in Australia, numerous studies have found media practices wanting: in presenting the science as unsettled or exaggerating the level of uncertainty (Pollack 2005); in giving equal air time or column space to non-expert 'sceptics' as climate scientists (Boykoff 2011, pp. 124–8); in adopting ideological positions of governments, industries or campaigners (Carvalho 2007); and in failing to maintain interest in the topic beyond extreme weather events or major international political debate (see Boykoff and Mansfield 2012 for tracking of news coverage since 2004).

Journalists who regularly cover the environment for Australian news outlets identify several related obstacles in their work (see Lester forthcoming). Climate change reporting alone can require in-depth knowledge of renewable energies, carbon production and storage, ice melt, international and taxation laws, and consumer power demands. The breadth, depth and complexity of environmental issues mean that with limited time and resources on top of deadline demands, journalists will often fall back on known sources for their stories. While on one hand this limits the range of voices that can participate in debate, on the other the journalistic practice of balance is met by providing an opposing viewpoint, which also helps avoid flak, or constant negative feedback about stories (Herman and Chomsky 1988, pp. 3–30). In the case of the heated ideological debate that surrounded climate change, this led many journalists and editors to turn to climate change 'sceptics' or 'deniers' (Painter 2011). News media also often exaggerate or dismiss uncertainty in the science, finding it difficult to portray a range of possibilities within accepted media frames as anything other than absolute risk or unsettled science (Cox 2010, pp. 309–314). Finally, environmental coverage has always been prone to the 'ups and downs' of public opinion (see Downs 1972 for an early attempt to understand the relationship). When climate change was finally perceived as a serious issue by media in the mid-2000s, editors provided more space and developed a seemingly insatiable demand for content. After the fizzle of the Copenhagen COP15 international meeting in late 2009, opportunities to produce and place climate change stories were quickly limited.

Nevertheless, it is also clear that, despite these professional and practical obstacles, news media can and do generate pressure for action. A study of television news and current affairs in six countries found that in 2004, just prior to climate change becoming a major international issue, there were numerous examples of journalism presenting the issue as a serious threat requiring urgent action (Lester and Cottle 2009). It did this in a variety of ways. First, it drew on iconic images of environmental risk, such as palm trees bent to the ground by extreme weather, people laden with personal belongings wading through mud and water, or houses perched precariously on eroded cliffs. Second, it signified the credibility and effectiveness of scientific and political sources via live crosses to scientists working in busy laboratories, or images of politicians with sleeves rolled up inspecting renewable energies, or in the field with journalists bearing witness to the impacts of climate change. Third, it produced and circulated emotional images of and interviews with the victims of climate change—with an Inuit family forced to move from its home, a bogged lorry taking food to the victims of Haiti floods, of the official of a small Pacific island surveying the inundated remnants of the local church and cemetery.

BYPASSING THE MAINSTREAM

The contemporary Australian environment movement emerged in the late 1960s and early 1970s, opposing plans to flood Lake Pedder in Tasmania's southwest, uranium shipments from Victorian docks, sand mining on Queensland's Fraser Island and development in Sydney's historic inner suburbs (Lohrey 2002). The fledgling movement quickly learned that a successful communications strategy involved more than the often vain hope of attracting news media attention by putting on spectacular protest events. Journalists were quickly bored by these protests, worse still seeing them as a challenge to journalistic control over the news agenda (Lester 2007). So, while news media coverage remained 'the main game', the movement drew on a variety of tactics to get its message to the public and to influence decision-makers, including town hall meetings, direct lobbying, newsletters, and newspaper and television advertising when access to financial and human resources allowed.

The advent of the internet was understandably greeted as a game-changer for the environment and other social movements pushing for change from outside the centre of power. Here was the means to bypass mainstream news media, which for too long had functioned as a 'nasty gatekeeper' over movement activities (Wolfsfeld 1997, pp. 1–5), or to avoid expensive forms of media advertising, and to communicate directly and tactically with vast numbers of potential supporters and the voting public. Most significantly, here was the opportunity to speak to influential consumers and decision-makers in distant places and markets: tourists who might change travel plans on the basis of damage to the natural environment; home owners who might choose eco-friendly flooring over that sourced from old-growth forests; members of international organisations willing to intervene to protect natural environments.

In many ways, the internet is satisfying the expectations of the movement. An email directs recipients to a YouTube clip, which encourages donations to buy television advertising. A single click generates an email in Japanese to managers of major companies, several steps along a complicated supply chain from the tropical forests of Sarawak to Japanese homes. A tweet calls supporters to a protest about to begin on the lawns of Parliament House. Activist-filmed footage of a clash with whalers on the Southern Ocean is posted on the campaign website, and media releases alert journalists of its presence and availability for their use. What has emerged is a complex network of flows and bridges between different forms of media, with mainstream news remaining an important and influential part of the mix (Cottle and Lester 2011).

Yet, while the internet is expanding the visibility of social and environmental problems and opportunities for different voices to be heard in debating issues and negotiating solutions, this cannot be treated as an uncontested given. Like all public spaces, it is not equally accessible, nor is its value universally recognised. As with news, it is vulnerable to being swamped by the loudest, best-resourced voices; to strategies and tactics of campaigners, lawyers and public relations consultants; to the banalities and popularities of celebrity and tabloid politics (Brockington 2009).

CONCLUSION

There are those whose interests are better served by issues or by their actions remaining invisible, and by public debate about environmental futures being contained and controlled (Lester and Hutchins 2012). Yet new media opportunities to communicate with distant audiences, supporters and consumers are still emerging, and they are changing the way local and global environmental risks and conflicts are understood, negotiated and perhaps resolved. Journalism, for all its embedded professional and organisational constraints, retains an important, influential and often committed role. This is illustrated by a study from Reporters Without Borders (2009, p. 1), which found that the environment is now at the heart of 15 per cent of all cases the press freedom group monitors. Yet, beyond its role in transferring information and suppressing or pushing for action, the media and communications' own contribution to environmental degradation and harm also needs to be considered. The massive growth in mobile communications and associated equipment and technologies has created new and increasing demands for resources, and produced new pressures on local resources, places and communities. These inevitably are leading to new conflicts (Maxwell and Miller 2012). Media and communications have always played a multi-faceted, sometimes contradictory role in the production and circulation of knowledge about the environment, and this role continues to evolve; the forests near Gibson's tree, after all, might now serve as a media hub and a mediated symbol for environmental protection, but they were once pulped to supply newsprint for many of Australia's newspapers.

Chapter 23
PUBLIC SERVICE BROADCASTING

MAUREEN BURNS

Predictions about the future of public service media institutions in Australia and elsewhere usually and necessarily include discussions of digital media, participatory culture and globalisation. Such discussions ask how will organisations that were designed to be national, one-to-many analogue broadcasters adapt to a globalised, participatory, digital environment. Do we still need Australian public service media in such an environment, and if so, then how are we to think about their futures? Should the ABC and the SBS provide participatory sites for deliberative democracy, and can they do so more effectively than exclusively online providers (Flew et al. 2008; Iosifidis 2011)? Should the future be one where public service media institutions provide news and current affairs content (among other branded items) to commercial providers (Burns 2012)? Should public service media provide searchable digital archives, as has been suggested by Andrejevic (2013)? Should the ABC in particular maintain and reinvigorate its focus on local content as has been suggested by Manning (2004)? Is the role of public service media to manage difference, and to allow for the creation of publics, as Hawkins proposes (2013)?

The answer to these questions is 'yes'—and more. The very diversity of these issues illustrates the perils of making predictions about public service broadcasting. These questions are historically specific—some could not have even been imagined at the inception of public service broadcasting, and others need our very recent media environment to make any sense at all.

Public service media do more than provide news and current affairs, despite the news and current affairs focus of much academic and policy discussion. They do more than screen high-quality wildlife documentaries, and they do more than adapt and adopt new technologies. They do more than allow for discussion, and they do more than 'reflect' national culture. I argue that the strength of public service media institutions (as, arguably, of other public institutions) lies in the productive tension they afford between stability and flexibility. This position relies on several well-rehearsed arguments, such as that public service media institutions—given adequate budgets—can take risks that commercial operators cannot, and that they can, on occasion, subsidise less financially successful experiments with those that are more successful. They can act as research and innovation divisions for the industry more broadly. Their value—even if understood only as devices to provide what cannot be provided in the commercial arena—is significant. Public service media have demonstrated a remarkable level of technological flexibility as new platforms, media and business models emerged (Burns 2000; Martin 2002), in some cases building on lessons learned through innovation failure (Burns 2012). They are also important institutions for reminding the nation of its forgetfulness of its own past. First, though, some historical details.

Since the 1920s, when Lord Reith argued that the newly founded BBC should inform, entertain and educate, public service broadcasters have either been criticised as elitist and paternalistic, or defended as institutions that offer equal access to all citizens. The future of public service media institutions has been questioned frequently and almost continuously since their inception, though for varying historical reasons. Over the past few years, commercial operators such as Rupert and James Murdoch have challenged the continuing need for public service broadcasters in the digital era. Given that increased media diversity in a digital era should address market failure, they argue, public service media organisations are at an unfair advantage because they receive government funds that are not available to commercial players. Such arguments became louder as media outlets and technologies proliferated, and as media moguls learnt to reconstruct and manipulate the digital media economy.

There is certainly not much merit in defending either of Australia's public service broadcasters by claiming that they have a 'pure' public economy—that is, no commercial entanglements. As well as being statutory authorities that function at 'arm's length' from government, but receive government funds, both the ABC and SBS have complex commercial arrangements that are easily identified, even on their web pages. Nor can they be understood merely as broadcasters. Indeed, if you refer back to Part II of this book, with reference to the ABC and SBS (see Chapter 10), you will note that both organisations are involved in many of the industries listed. The ABC and the SBS publish magazines, have online, mobile and web applications including games, and offer broadcast radio and television services. Both the ABC and SBS offer multiple media platforms—although the ABC, with a much larger budget, is ahead of SBS in its adoption of new technologies, having been one of the first media institutions in the world to have an online presence (Burns 2000).

Innovation in digital media at the ABC and SBS is ongoing, with staff continuously redefining what public service media are, and are for. Very soon after the ABC implemented its online service, it offered the first online forum, *Frontier Online*—which was presented along with the three-part documentary television series *Frontier* in early 1997. Henry Reynolds' (1996) history book on which the *Frontier* television series and website were based documented the wars between white invaders and Aboriginal people. Before its publication, the accepted history had it that Aboriginal people gave up their land without a fight. The book, and then the television series, documented the fierce territorial wars of that period, rewriting what had been a history of 'settlement' into one of 'invasion'. After each episode, there was a live online forum with Henry Reynolds and Professor Marcia Langton. On this site, public memory was negotiated in between the exemplary one-to-many interaction of the public service broadcasting idea and the many-to-many networked interaction of the internet idea. Both *Frontier* the television series and *Frontier* the web forum were designed to help the public understand its future by an understanding of its past and present. They existed very much in the public arena, and the web forum enabled different perspectives. In turn, the major thrust of commentary was not the past but serious contemporary matters of Indigenous–non-Indigenous relations. The forum made for confronting reading about Australia's race relations. On the *Frontier* forum, the interactivity and accessibility of the technology enabled an easier and faster intersection between the vernacular and the official. In exchanges about beliefs and ideas of the past, serious matters in the present were discussed—in this case, race relations.

Satirical television series and online site *The Games* is another example of the ABC using what were new technologies to examine the future through the present and the past. Early in 2000, when Prime Minister John Howard was refusing to apologise on behalf of non-Indigenous Australia for injustices done to Indigenous Australians, and when the hype about the upcoming Olympics in Sydney was inescapable, the ABC screened a mock documentary TV series called *The Games*. *The Games* satirised the bureaucracy of the Sydney Olympics, and interrupted the accepted relations between ABC television and ABC Online. Until this point, online services were secondary to television and radio. In this instance, however, the scripts for each television episode were 'leaked' to *The Games* website before the television show was screened, so ardent user/viewers could get a 'scoop' on ardent viewers. In one episode, an actor (also named John Howard), after eulogising the advantages of Australia including the fact that Australia has the longest coastline in the world, apologised to Indigenous Australians. The responses to this speech on *The Games* website were amazingly supportive and impassioned. One even compared the speech to Martin Luther King's 'I have a dream' speech. Here is another response:

> John Howard's apology to the Aboriginal people, that was posted on your site, exhibits a depth of insight, foresight, and feeling that is wholly unexpected when one bears in mind the vapid appellation of your commentator. But while your Mr Howard appears to exhibit the promise of embracing 'the whole vision thing' with much more gusto than his lesser namesake, he does however share the latter's habit of getting the details wrong: Canada boasts the world's longest coastline. (Lostsole 1999)

Authority was not always entirely vested in the public service broadcaster, but could be gently mocked. *The Games* website encouraged the viewer/user to 'bat on', encouraging an irreverent attitude to the ABC and to the jingoism that accompanied the upcoming Sydney Olympics. The television program and site, like the *Frontier* site, also revisited the past to discuss serious issues of race in the present. *The Games* (TV series and online site) unravelled the more prevalent Olympic yarn of a unified nation.

The historical cases of multi-platform projects *Frontier* and *The Games* demonstrate some of the complexities of imagining futures for public service media. Since then, there has been a general shift in thinking at the ABC from one where the ABC imagines itself as speaking to the people, to one where it imagines itself as being in dialogue with its publics, to one where it sometimes imagines itself as being outside the conversations that evolve between self-creating publics. According to an ABC producer for the 'Pool' interactive art site, for example:

> [T]here's a lot of work going into how we design a site that allows people to find and communicate with each other easily. But it's just one piece of the puzzle. We'll still use Flickr and Vimeo, we're on Twitter and Facebook, we're experimenting with Instagram

and Freesound. What we're interested in isn't just about connecting people with the ABC online, but ultimately about how the ABC can help people create meaningful connections amongst themselves. (Dwyer 2012)

There are still, however, instances where one-to-many platforms take precedence. In 2012, the ABC screened the six-part television series *Redfern Now*. The series featured Indigenous Australian theatre, film and television stars, including Deborah Mailman, Leah Purcell, Dean Daley-Jones and Miranda Tapsell. It was produced by Blackfella Films and funded by Screen Australia, Screen NSW and the ABC. The ABC offered very little by way of user created content options, or *virtual* interactive elements (an *actual* street party was held in Redfern for the premiere), though timeshifting via iView was possible. The production and screening of this series is perhaps an example of what Hawkins (2013) describes as the ABC 'pluralising the mainstream'. Hawkins argues that the advent of digital media and multi-platforming allowed the ABC to resist its homogenising tendencies, and this was perhaps the case with the examples of *Frontier* and *The Games* cited above. The appearance of high-end television drama *Redfern Now* so late in the ABC's history suggests that the regime of choice allowed by the digital multi-platform era affords scope for such series that did not exist before. What might this old-fashioned high-end television drama series tell us about the future of public service media in Australia?

Perhaps, as I have argued above, it demonstrates the ways in which a stable public service institution affords flexibility across platforms and content areas. Such flexibility, diversification of services and technological innovation are afforded by the stability of an organisation that can absorb some level of experimentation—a capacity that is less likely in either the commercial or community sector. If there is to be a future for public service media institutions—and this is perpetually in doubt—it will be one that maintains this balance between stability and flexibility, and allows for examinations of the future to be based on re-examinations of the national construction of the past.

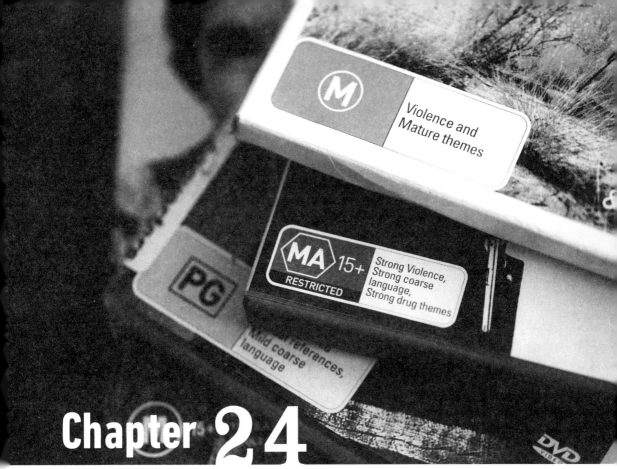

Chapter 24
CLASSIFICATION AND REGULATION

TERRY FLEW

THE POLICY CHALLENGE OF MEDIA CONVERGENCE

Australia's media landscape is changing rapidly. Today, Australians have access to a greater range of communications and media services than ever before. Developments in technology and increasing broadband speeds have led to the emergence of innovative services not previously imagined . . . Users are increasingly at the centre of content service delivery. They are creating their own content and uploading it to social media platforms . . . Despite these dramatic changes, Australia's policy and regulatory framework for content services is still focused on the traditional structures of the 1990s—broadcasting and telecommunications. The distinction between these categories has become increasingly blurred and these regulatory frameworks have outlived their original purpose. These frameworks now run the risk of inhibiting the evolution of communications and media services. (Convergence Review 2012, p. vii)

A major challenge for governments all over the world is how to adapt their media policies for the challenges of convergence. In the twentieth century, media policy was typically platform based. There were policies for broadcasting, telecommunications, film, newspapers and magazines. In the twenty-first century, content moves seamlessly across media platforms, virtually all media content is accessible via the internet, all media companies now see themselves as being multi-platform content and service providers, and companies such as Microsoft, Google and Apple increasingly are operating in the media space.

Perhaps most significantly, there has been a fundamental shift in media producer–consumer relations in the age of convergent media. In the twentieth century, mass communications media consisted of a finite number of media 'gatekeepers' who distributed professionally produced content to audiences, and were often vertically integrated—that is, they produced content, controlled production facilities, managed distribution and so on. In the twenty-first century, content-hosting platforms have become open and porous, enabling user-created content to reach larger audiences on the internet. This has allowed media consumers themselves to become the producers and distributors of media content, as media audiences transform from being passive consumers to media content co-creators and participants in global media culture (Jenkins 2006; Hartley 2012).

A series of policy reviews were undertaken in Australia during 2011–12 to address the challenges of convergence for media policy in the face of such changes. The reviews undertaken included the following:

- *The Convergence Review*, an independent inquiry undertaken through the Department of Broadband, Communications and the Digital Economy, was asked to 'review the operation of media and communications legislation in Australia and to assess its effectiveness in achieving appropriate policy objectives for the convergent era' (Convergence Review 2012, p. 110). There is further discussion of review in Chapter 5.
- *The Review of the National Classification Scheme* was undertaken by the Australian Law Reform Commission; its final report was titled *Classification—Content Regulation and Convergent Media* (Australian Law Reform Commission 2012).
- *The Independent Media Inquiry* was established in 2011 to review the adequacy of media codes of practice and related matters, and was chaired by Ray Finkelstein QC (Independent Inquiry into the Media and Media Regulation 2012).

These reviews occurred alongside a range of other media law and policy-related reviews, including the development of a new National Cultural Policy, undertaken through the Office for the Arts in the Department of Prime Minister and Cabinet, and a review of Australia's copyright laws, conducted by the Australian Law Reform Commission (ALRC).

MEDIA CLASSIFICATION IN AUSTRALIA

Media classification is primarily involved with providing information to consumers about the nature of media content, typically in relation to violence, nudity and sexually explicit content, language, and depictions of 'adult themes' such as suicide, drug use and so on. While different countries apply classification in different ways, it characteristically involves information about the age-appropriateness of particular films, television programs, computer games and other media content. At the higher levels of classification, there will also be obligations to restrict access, such as material that is only to be available to adults. Some media content may be prohibited entirely. This is referred to as censorship, and in Australia such material is deemed to be refused classification (RC). Examples of material likely to be RC would include that which depicts certain fetishes and 'abhorrent' behaviour, material that depicts sexual violence, sexual activity involving children and minors, content instructing how to commit crimes and, most recently, material deemed to be advocating a terrorist act.

The history of censorship and classification has involved a gradual shift from a strong censorship regime to one that primarily revolves around classification, with the outright banning of material only occurring in exceptional cases (Sullivan 1997; Flew 1998). Prior to the 1970s, the Chief Censor had virtually unlimited powers to ban material he deemed likely to 'deprave or corrupt'. Subsequent to the 1968 *Crowe v Graham* case, where the High Court required that a 'community standards' test be applied to censorship decisions, the Minister for Customs and Excise, Don Chipp, and the subsequent Whitlam Labor government, shifted the Australian approach from a closed and highly interventionist censorship model to a more open, liberal and accountable regime based around classification.

The 1970s saw the introduction of an 'R' rating for films, and the establishment of three core principles of the National Classification Code designed to inform censorship and classification decisions:

- the principle that 'adults should be able to read, hear and see what they want'
- the principle that 'minors should be protected from material that is likely to harm or disturb them'

- the principle that 'everyone should be protected from unsolicited material that they find offensive'.

Associated with these principles that underpin the 'community standards' test has been the expectation that those involved in making classification decisions should be broadly representative of the community, and that their decisions should be both public and open to appeal. Since the 1990s, the National Classification Code has also required that classifiers need to take account of community concerns about 'depictions that condone or incite violence, particularly sexual violence' and 'the portrayal of persons in a demeaning manner' (Australian Government 2012).

The National Classification Scheme was established with the passing of the *Classification Act* (Cth) 2005, and covers films, some publications and computer games. It developed out of the recommendations of the ALRC in its 1991 Review of Censorship and Classification (Australian Law Reform Commission 1991) and involved the establishment of a cooperative national scheme and an independent Classification Board, as well as a Classification Review Board.

While the National Classification Scheme addressed anomalies in the preexisting framework, some problems remained. There continued to be different laws between the Commonwealth and the states, particularly in relation to sexually explicit 'X'-rated material, which is legal in the Australian Capital Territory and parts of the Northern Territory but illegal in most states. The failure to approve an 'R' rating for computer games would lead to over a decade of campaigning before such a rating was finally passed through the federal parliament in 2012 (Humphreys 2009). Broadcast television had developed an industry-based co-regulatory model with the *Broadcasting Services Act* 1992, which was extended to online content in the late 1990s (Coroneos 2008; Crawford and Lumby 2011). Importantly, laws passed in the mid-1990s were pre-internet laws, and could not have understood the extent to which media convergence would undercut platform-based media regulations.

FUTURE-PROOFING MEDIA CLASSIFICATION REGULATIONS

When asked to review the National Classification Scheme by the Attorney-General in 2011, the ALRC needed to be alert to the megatrends that were rapidly reshaping the Australian media and communications landscape, and would continue to do so in the future. In addition to technological and industry convergence, and the growing fluidity of the relationship of media content to distribution platforms, it also needed to consider whether community attitudes towards government regulation of media content had shifted. This could be a result of people having both a wider array of media choices, and greater user control over the content accessed through their own media devices, through catch-up TV services such as the ABC's iView, IPTV services such as BigPond TV and Fetch TV, and personal video recorders such as TiVo and Foxtel's IQ2, and televisions connected to the internet.

The federal government's commitment to developing a National Broadband Network was also relevant, as it would enable more Australian homes and businesses to download video content more rapidly from all over the globe. To take one example, it was estimated that in January 2012, 60 hours of video were being uploaded on to YouTube every minute, and four billion videos were being viewed every day from that site alone, with at least 200 million videos a month being viewed from YouTube by an estimated six million Australian users (ALRC 2012, pp. 66–7).

In such an environment of rapid technological change and growing access to a seemingly infinite array of media content, including social media and user-created content, one can ask whether national government policies such as those that governed media classification in the twentieth century would continue to have any relevance. In their 2011 report *The Adaptive Moment*, Kate Crawford and Catharine Lumby captured this dilemma when they observed that:

> Nation state governments clearly have a remit to enforce the laws of their country and to protect public policy priorities when it comes to cultural and social parameters. Their ability to enforce this remit is restricted, however, due to the sheer volume of media content, as well as the decentralisation and vast number of media producers. (Crawford and Lumby 2011, p. 40)

There has been a notable absence of political consensus in Australia about future directions for media regulation. This was seen most clearly in relation to the Finkelstein Review which called for a statutory regulator for the print media in order to ensure journalists and newspapers better met their contract with society. This led to accusations that the Finkelstein Review was proposing an Orwellian government watchdog aimed at silencing critics and denying the public access to a free press (Jolly 2012).

But whether media regulation is framed around notions of social responsibility of the media, or more libertarian arguments to let access to all forms of content flourish and multiple points of view contend, there will continue to be key issues emerging for any revised suite of media legislation to be developed in Australia in the 2010s. The first concerns the question of who should be subject to future media regulations. If it is accepted that large media organisations should be subject to different regulatory requirements than user-created content that is primarily about online self-expression and peer communication, then the question exists of where the line should be drawn. The Convergence Review and the National Classification Scheme Review proposed that the focus should be on content intended primarily for Australians that has significant audience reach and that is produced primarily by media professionals. Organisations that meet these criteria would be subject to local content production and community standards requirements—including news standards—but it is uncertain who would be included in such requirements, particularly given the commercial benefits of not being subject to these obligations.

The second issue concerns who is a media company. Until very recently, this was largely confined to the major print and broadcast media interests, recognising also the existence of smaller players in these sectors. But it is now apparent that, in a variety of different ways, companies as diverse as Apple, Google, Microsoft, Facebook and Telstra are all engaged in the distribution of media content to consumers. This raises a variety of issues, including parity of treatment between different media content providers (broadcast networks as against IPTV services, or YouTube), addressing different service delivery platforms (for example, console-based computer games compared with apps), the parity of treatment between nationally based media companies and global media content providers, and the likelihood that the platforms themselves will be constantly shifting in influence in a highly dynamic and convergent technological environment (Flew 2012).

Finally, there is the issue of what should be set in media law, and what should be subject to regulator discretion. The most common criticism of Australia's media classification system is that it is out of date, both in terms of changes in community standards and expectations, and in its applicability across media platforms. A media content regulation framework that was adaptive and flexible enough to be quickly modified for future developments would require considerably more regulator discretion about the development and application of laws and policies, and a closer working relationship with the media content industries themselves. This may prove to be too radical a step for governments that wish to preserve the sovereignty of parliament, establish legal certainty and be able to set the laws with which media companies have to comply. But the inability to adapt current classification laws to changing technological and industry developments suggests that this will not prove to be sustainable or particularly credible with Australian media consumers.

Chapter 25
THE APPS INDUSTRY

BEN GOLDSMITH

The first recorded use of 'app' as shorthand for 'application'—meaning a computer software program—was in 1985, when Apple released the MacApp programming tool. However, the term did not enter common parlance until after the launch of the Apple App Store and the iPhone 2 in July 2008. It is now generally understood to refer principally to software programs designed to run on mobile platforms and devices, although apps have now been developed for a range of devices from televisions to cars. Apps development has boomed in recent years with the rise of the mobile web, smartphones and tablets, coupled with business realisation that apps enable innovation in market development and work practices, as well as being conduits to investment and new revenue streams.

THE AUSTRALIAN APPS INDUSTRY

Australian apps developers typify global industry segmentation, varying in function, focus, employment situation and background. They range from freelancers contracted to build apps on demand and venture capital-backed or bootstrapped start-ups, to specialist app studios and full-service digital agencies for whom apps are one among many services that may include web development, marketing, advertising, business strategy, branding and games development.

In keeping with the findings of the Creative Industries National Mapping Project conducted by the ARC Centre of Excellence for Creative Industries and Innovation, a substantial proportion of apps developers are 'embedded' or employed in sectors not normally thought of as being part of the creative industries, such as government, education, manufacturing and finance (Cunningham 2013, pp. 125–45). In the latter sector, several of the major banks routinely contract out apps development to apps studios and digital agencies. The Westpac Group—comprising Westpac, St George, BankSA and the Bank of Melbourne—is a partial exception, with a mixture of in-sourcing, engagement of external design and development consultants, and limited out-sourcing. St George released an internally developed iPad app to coincide with the launch of Apple's tablet device in May 2010; these designers and developers became the core of an in-house team responsible for creating and building a series of internal and customer apps for use across the group. The team, numbering approximately 50, spent a year developing the Tabula iPad app, which allows Westpac's board members to securely access and annotate documents. At the same time, the group built the Broker iPad app for mortgage brokers, as well as the award-winning customer-focused Westpac iPad app, released in July 2012. In a quarterly earnings announcement in March 2013, Westpac reported that since its launch, the iPad app had been downloaded 227 000 times, with users recording 4.7 million sessions, and almost A$2 billion in payments processed. Westpac chose not to develop a parallel Android app immediately—in part because of the proliferation of devices running various versions of the Android operating system with a variety of screen resolutions, in marked contrast to Apple's more limited and controlled ecosystem. A version of the Westpac iPad app was developed for the global launch of Windows 8 in October 2012, with Westpac the only bank with an app available when the new operating system was introduced (Muir 2012).

Like other 'born digital' creative industries, apps development is not anchored to particular locations in the same way as manufacturing or mining traditionally have been. While the largest clusters of apps companies are to be found in Sydney and Melbourne, successful and innovative Australian apps developers can be found all around the country. Brisbane game and app developer Halfbrick's *Fruit Ninja* was named in March 2012 as the second most downloaded paid app worldwide since the Apple App Store opened in 2008 (Viticci 2012). Other examples include Magic Kingdom, an Adelaide-based games, apps and web development company, which built a video modelling app for the Telstra Foundation and Autism SA's iModeling social development group project for children with Autism Spectrum Disorder, and Filter Squad, a Perth apps studio responsible for the Discovr series of apps, which collectively have been downloaded over three million times.

Filter Squad's experience illustrates the global and export-oriented character of the apps industry. The studio's apps are designed to assist users to discover movies, music, people and other apps via interactive tree maps. Filter Squad works exclusively within Apple's ecosystem, meaning that its apps are only sold through the Apple App Store. Upon Apple's approval, developers can choose the countries in which their apps will be available; Filter Squad has routinely made its apps available in all territories. As a result, they have been sold in over 110 countries and downloaded in over 130 since the first, Discovr Music, was published in January 2011. Discovr Music has reached number one in the music category in over 50 countries, and has been translated into 20 languages. The Australian market accounts for only around 3 per cent of total downloads for all of Filter Squad's apps, and returns only around 12 per cent of the company's total profits. Japan is the most profitable market (followed by the United States, Australia, Germany and the United Kingdom), despite the fact that the company is unable to collect affiliate revenue (from in-app purchases) because it is not domiciled in Japan and cannot open a Japanese bank account (McKinney 2012).

Apps have slightly different payment and revenue models to digitally distributed 'traditional' content. Between 80 and 90 per cent of apps downloaded from the various app stores are free, a figure that is predicted to grow even further (Lunden 2012; Holgersson 2012). Both free and pay-per-download apps can generate revenue from in-app advertising, product placement, 'in-app purchases'—meaning the sale of features, game levels, virtual goods or content after download—or recurring subscription, a model adopted by many magazine publishers. 'Freemium' apps are free to download but offer paid upgrades. 'Paymium' apps are pay-per-download with paid upgrade options. 'Premium' apps provide all content or game play for a one-off fee. Other revenue models include commissions from businesses or organisations wanting custom-built apps; royalties from apps pre-loaded on a device; exclusive distribution deals, where apps are distributed through one particular app store or vendor; purchase intermediation, when a fee or share is taken from third-party transactions enabled by the app; and investment in return for equity by angel investors or venture capitalists—a typical model for start-ups (Vision Mobile 2012, p. 43).

As the above examples show, Australian apps not only serve a local audience, but can potentially reach a worldwide market. The industry is globally networked through international ownership structures and partnership arrangements, and through companies expanding into overseas markets. Sky Technologies exemplifies all of these connections. This Melbourne-based company developed a mobile enterprise application platform (MEAP) that enables a business's workforce, customers and vendors to access back-end systems via 'micro-apps' deployed on any mobile device. Through a number of strategic alliances and partnerships with companies around the world, Sky Technologies services clients in 35 countries through offices in Australia, the United States and the United Kingdom. In August 2012, Sky Technologies was bought by American MEAP provider Kony Solutions for an undisclosed sum. Other noteworthy international takeovers of Australian apps companies include Apple's purchase of iOS and Android app discovery service Chomp in February 2012. The service's Android search capacity was immediately discontinued, before it was closed down entirely upon the release of the iOS 6 operating system in September 2012.

Many Australian apps companies have expanded into overseas markets and opened offices around the world, with some relocating abroad after local success. BigTinCan for example, which began life in Sydney as the developer of an app that enabled discount calls on smartphones, went on to set up offices in Singapore, Paris and Kiev before moving its company headquarters to Boston in October 2012 and focusing on its innovative enterprise-oriented information and content-delivery platform. One of the first Australian companies working in this space to realise the potential of the Chinese market, Sydney-based digital agency and software/apps developer Gruden, opened an office in a technology park in Qingdao in 2008, initially to provide services to Western companies based in China and to source local talent because of a perceived digital skills shortage in Australia. After establishing a reputation as a centre for training and development in China, Gruden partnered with another Australian software developer, SmartTrans, to build an Android-based apps store for one of the leading telecommunications companies, China Mobile, in the process increasing its local workforce from an initial cohort of six to over 30. Gruden's desire to be a major player in the Asia-Pacific was made evident again in mid-2012, when the company announced the purchase of a Malaysian company specialising in 3D and augmented reality apps and games. As well as servicing the local apps market, the mobile and tablet specialist team in Kuala Lumpur expands Gruden's global reach (Trevillion 2012).

APPS BEYOND MOBILE

Over 80 per cent of almost 5000 mobile developers around the world surveyed in mid-2012 predicted that they would be likely to be building mobile applications for televisions within three years (Appcelerator/IDC 2012, p. 3). Almost three-quarters of these developers anticipated building mobile apps for connected cars, over 70 per cent expected to be developing apps for games consoles and more than two in three forecast apps development for Google's Project Glass, the augmented reality headset unveiled in early 2012.

Television is by far the most advanced of these new markets, with increasing numbers of broadband-enabled 'smart', 'hybrid' or 'connected' television sets, and set-top boxes such as TiVo, Roku and Boxee, as well as other companion devices such as games consoles entering the market. Some pay television services, such as Foxtel in Australia, have developed apps for games consoles like the Xbox 360, and at present broadcaster catch-up services, YouTube, and video-on-demand services dominate the TV apps market. Communications and social networking services such as Skype, Facebook and Twitter are also popular, although the library of TV apps is considerably smaller than that for mobiles. Many developers are reluctant to build apps for television because different brands and set-top boxes use various, often proprietary, operating systems and platforms. Some manufacturers, such as LG, have even installed different systems in different models, with some using the Netcast platform, and a browser engine based on Webkit, others running on a modified Android interface and others still based on open standards such as HTML5, CE-HTML and HbbTV (hybrid broadcast broadband TV).

Device fragmentation is perhaps the most pressing issue for developers and publishers seeking wide reach, not only in television but also—and to a much larger degree—in mobile. As Deloitte Australia noted in its annual *Technology, Media and Telecommunications Predictions* in 2012:

> To reach more than 90 per cent of all app users, a developer may need to create versions for five different operating systems (plus HTML5), five major languages, three different processor speeds, and four different screen sizes. In other words, 360 variants of a single app may need to be created in order to fully cover the global market. (Deloitte 2012, p. 42)

Fragmentation is a particular issue for Android developers. There are multiple versions of the Android operating system, not only the versions produced by Google (Gingerbread, Ice Cream Sandwich, Jelly Bean, etc.), but also those customised by carriers and device-makers. There are multiple versions of the SDK, with each one specific to a version of Android, meaning that developers may have to produce several iterations of their app in order to reach the largest possible number of users. The challenge for developers is further complicated by the variety of brands running Android, many of which contain different hardware and software features. In May 2012 the operators of OpenSignal, an app that collates data on signal strength readings and

Wi-Fi access points around the world, reported that over the previous six months their app had been downloaded to almost 4000 distinct Android devices, representing almost 600 distinct brands, with multiple different screen resolutions or aspect ratios (Open Signal 2012).

CONCLUSION

The apps industry has grown phenomenally quickly on the back of the popularity of smartphones and tablet computers. Fragmentation of devices and operating systems has been an issue for developers for some time, while ensuring an app can be discovered amid the hundreds of thousands of apps on offer in the various app stores remains a challenge. Australian companies like Chomp and Filter Squad are addressing these, and other challenges, in what is an extraordinarily dynamic and fast-changing industry. At present, games represent the largest and most profitable sector of the apps market, but there has been substantial growth in areas such as health and finance, as well as in apps for business and enterprise. Apple's 2008 slogan 'There's an app for that' appears more and more prescient by the day.

Chapter 26
MEDIA ETHICS
CATHARINE LUMBY

In December 2012, two commercial radio presenters at 2DayFM performed a busi-ness-as-usual stunt on their program. Presenters Mel Greig and Michael Christian called a UK hospital where the Duchess of Cambridge, Katherine Middleton, was being treated for an extreme form of morning sickness in the first trimester of her pregnancy. The female presenter pretended to be the Queen and the male presenter aped Prince Charles in the background. To their shock, they were put through to the Duchess's private nurse, who disclosed personal information about her illness. The call was pre-recorded but the station decided to put it to air.

Three days later, the nurse who put the call through committed suicide. The chain of events triggered an intense reaction in the United Kingdom. Media profes-sionals and other public commentators ferociously condemned the stunt as unethical.

Licensee Southern Cross Austereo, which owns 2DayFM, acknowledged that the stunt had been legally vetted and cleared for broadcast. The case illustrates the complex reality of media ethics in practice. Much Australian commercial FM radio competes for listeners by using allegedly humorous stunts that sometimes push the boundaries of ethical behaviour. 2DayFM DJ Kyle Sandilands is notorious for interviewing a 14-year-old girl about her sex life while she was attached to a lie detector. Goaded by Sandilands, the angry girl revealed that she had been raped at the age of 12.

The potentially damaging consequences of such stunts are clear. But where does the responsibility for policing ethics in this commercially driven environment lie? Does it rest with the presenters—many of whom have had no formal training in journalistic ethics and see themselves as entertainers? With the producers who decide to put this material to air? With the station owners and the board who are ultimately responsible for broader culture of their radio stations? Or with the regulator that oversees commercial radio station compliance with commercial radio codes of prac-tice—the Australian Communication and Media Authority (ACMA)?

Media ethics are one thing in theory and quite another in practice. Ethics take us into a complex set of decision-making steps, where journalists and entertainers are under increasing pressure to draw audiences to traditional print, radio and television media. Advertising revenue, which supports most media production in Australia, is increasingly moving online. Audiences have a vast array of choices about what media they consume, and much of the content is produced or redistributed by other media users.

An important feature of this new media landscape, when considering media ethics, is the fact that many media users are also media producers who are not signed up to codes of conduct and who may have no training in ethical reflection on what they produce, how they source it and where they distribute it.

Many textbooks on media ethics focus on traditional journalistic ethics and the core issues journalists have to confront in their daily practice (Goc and Tynan 2008; Hirst and Patching 2005). Such issues are also addressed in the Australian Media Entertainment and Arts Alliance (MEAA) Code of Ethics. They include:

- the importance of editorial independence
- the need to respect privacy, including private grief
- the need to disclose any payments or conflicts of interest
- the need to strive for objectivity or balance in reporting
- the need to avoid racial or other forms of discrimination in reporting.

As Brian McNair argues, journalistic codes of ethics 'have complex socio-historical roots which reflect the values and idea of the societies in which they emerged'.

Journalism is a profession, like medicine or law, and a code of ethics acts as a contract with the public that guarantees journalists' trustworthiness (McNair 1998, p. 64).

Today, however, professional journalists who may feel bound by a code of ethical practice play an increasingly minor role in the professional media sphere. Entertainment values have thoroughly infiltrated news values (Turner 2005; Lumby 1999) and news production is largely driven by ratings and readership, not by serving the public interest but by serving up material that interests the public.

The second decade of the twenty-first century has seen growing concern across the Western world about a perceived decline in journalistic standards and ethics. In the United Kingdom, revelations that journalists employed by Rupert Murdoch's company, News International, had hacked into the phones of celebrities and ordinary people caught up in tragic circumstances led to the government establishing the Leveson Inquiry. Chaired by Lord Justice Leveson, the inquiry examined the culture, ethics and practices of the British press. His report not only sharply criticised journalists, but also police who had failed to investigate reporters and editors, and politicians who pandered to proprietors and editors to ensure favourable coverage (Leveson 2012). As David McKnight (McKnight 2012, p. 5) writes, 'The phone hacking scandal shed light not only on the unethical and criminal behaviour of Murdoch's tabloid editors, but also on the web of political influence exerted on governments in Britain for many years.' The report recommended the establishment of a new statutory independent body to investigate complaints.

The revelations that UK journalists and editors had engaged in unethical and even criminal practices provoked calls for a similar investigation into the Australian media. The federal government responded by setting up an independent inquiry into media and media regulation chaired by Ray Finkelstein QC. The report of that inquiry also recommended the establishment of an independent body—the News Media Council—to set journalistic standards in consultation with the industry and to handle complaints made by the public when those standards are breached (Finkelstein 2012). Unlike the body recommended in the Leveson Report, the News Media Council recommended by the Finkelstein Report would have dealt with breaches in all forms of media, including online media.

Not surprisingly, the recommendation was attacked by many media organisations, particularly by Rupert Murdoch's News Limited newspaper *The Australian*. In Australia, to date, newspapers have been largely self-regulating and the public's only avenue for lodging complaints about unethical or inaccurate reporting has been the Australian Press Council (APC), a body that considers complaints about unethical practice and makes rulings about corrections and apologies. However, newspaper groups are under no obligation to join the APC or to heed its direction.

Also in 2012, a second Australian government review—the Convergence Review (see Chapters 5 and 24)—also recommended establishing a new industry-led body to promote news standards, adjudicate on complaints and provide timely remedies to parties who had been wronged by the media. The report notes that 'news and commentary play a vital role in any democracy', and that 'news and commentary should meet appropriate journalistic standards in fairness, accuracy and transparency regardless of the delivery platform' (Convergence Review 2012, p. x).

Both reports arguably raise more questions than they answer when we map their recommendations back on to the complexities of the contemporary online, mobile and social media landscape.

In understanding how we might regulate media content—including news and current affairs content—we need to see ethical principles as part of a continuum that includes legal forms of regulation. In ideal terms, our laws are based in legislation and common law that reflect community standards. They are meant to protect those standards and to make it clear what constitutes acceptable and unacceptable behaviour. Sanctions range from prison terms to fines or an order to pay damages to recompense an injured party, as well as orders to restrain an individual or corporation from engaging in a particular behaviour.

We have laws that regulate media content. Defamation laws give a right of action to individuals whose reputation has been unfairly smeared by media practitioners. Contempt of court laws prevent media outlets from publishing material that might prejudice a fair criminal trial. There are also laws that regulate how media material is classified, who can access it and what kinds of material are prohibited. There are, however, many forms of media content and practice that are not covered by legal regulation, and that the media have traditionally self-regulated, with varying degrees of care.

In the era when most media content was produced and distributed by a narrow range of organisations across print, radio and television, it was in the interests of proprietors, journalists and editors or producers to avoid accusations of unethical conduct. In a world where much media content is produced and distributed by amateurs and where such content is often sourced and redistributed by professional media outlets, the incentives for traditional forms of self-regulation have been substantially weakened.

The social and online media environment means that content is often produced and distributed without regard for, or even knowledge of, existing laws and codes of ethics. An example of this was the online and social media response to the rape and murder of a Melbourne woman, Jill Meagher, in 2012. When the police apprehended a suspect and charged him with the crime, social media outlets—including Twitter and Facebook—exploded in outrage. Numerous participants in these forums posted images of the accused and information about his alleged prior convictions. As is often the case in the online sphere, the commentary was highly personal and abusive. Jill Meagher's husband, Tom Meagher, appeared outside the court where the accused was brought before a magistrate and appealed to the public to avoid making comments on social and online forums that may prejudice legal proceedings. He also asked that the media respect the privacy of his wife's family ('Accused killer of Jill Meagher appears in court' 2012).

The case is a good example of how much commentary and information in the convergent media era is produced and circulated in ways that escape traditional forms of legal and ethical regulation. While it is still possible to charge an individual with contempt of court for material they publish, it is outside the capacity of our courts to charge everyone who distributes prejudicial material in the social media world. Similarly, many participants in this new media sphere do not feel bound by, or even understand, journalistic codes of ethics.

Framing and regulating media ethics is replete with new challenges in the online and social media era. It is an era in which content no longer circulates vertically in distinct media silos (print, radio and television) that are individually regulated, but flows horizontally across platforms. Content also flows back and forth between professional media contexts and sites of amateur distribution and production. The sheer volume of media content that circulates in this manner now outstrips the capacity of any government or industry group to regulate all material.

It is a media ecology that arguably asks us to rethink the regulation and governance of media content, in both a legal and ethical sense. The largest challenge lies in encouraging ordinary media users—who are also producers and distributors of media content—to reflect and act on ethical principles of media practice. We need to find ways of encouraging participants in this new ecology to see themselves as part of a community—as digital citizens, perhaps—in the same way that many journalists have traditionally felt themselves bound to a code of ethics by virtue of their membership of a professional group. Educating Australians about ethical media production and engagement will be important. Equally, however, government and industry have an important role to play in enhancing the agency of media users to govern content and work together as communities in different areas of social and online media to evolve ethical frameworks and identify and sanction unethical practices (Crawford and Lumby 2010).

Chapter 27
CRISIS COMMUNICATION

AXEL BRUNS

While a substantial part of the discourse around social media continues to focus on concerns over cyberbullying and other undesirable practices, the important role that such media play in information dissemination—especially in the context of natural disasters and other acute events—is also being realised. A series of natural and human-made crisis events since 2011, including several major natural disasters in Australia, have highlighted this role.

As both a country and a continent, Australia has always been exposed to natural disasters: it experiences climate extremes from scorching heat through widespread flooding rains to cyclonic storms on an annual basis. This propensity for natural disasters places significant stresses on Australian emergency services, as well as on Australian media in their role as emergency media. Indeed, it may be argued that the significant size and population spread of the Australian mainland mean that media play an especially important role in the emergency response process, compared with more geographically compact nations that may be served more efficiently by centralised emergency services: for many remote and rural communities, emergency alerts disseminated electronically through broadcast and online media may reach them well before emergency personnel and equipment are able to make their way to potential disaster zones. Similarly, given the wide dispersal of official personnel, local communities also play an especially important role as information sources on the environmental conditions on the ground. Effective two-way communication between locals and emergency responders is of particular importance in the context of anthropogenic climate change which is set to intensify these weather patterns even further. In Australia, long-term drought is likely to increase the chance of devastating bushfires in southern states, while greater cyclonic activity in the tropics may increase the frequency and severity of floods in the north. Additionally, the prospect of rising sea levels due to the shrinking of polar ice caps poses a threat to the substantial majority of Australians who live in coastal areas.

Australian and international crisis events in 2011 and 2012 point to the emergence of a new ecology of emergency media, which now incorporates conventional mass media (and, in particular, broadcast media such as radio and television) alongside many-to-many channels from SMS to social media. Indeed, what is becoming clear is that it is not any one of these media forms and platforms, but the interweaving of these different channels, that ensures effective crisis communication. The 2011 crisis calendar began with substantial flooding across most of the Australian state of Queensland during January, followed by a devastating earthquake in Christchurch, New Zealand. In each case, research has pointed to the importance of recent social media platforms such as *Facebook* and *Twitter* in the dissemination of information and the coordination of community responses (e.g. see Bruns et al 2012; Bruns and Burgess 2012).

In the immediate aftermath of a sudden disaster—such as an earthquake—social media can serve as an important first-hand information source, enabling locals to provide immediate situational information reports that are also of significant use to first responders in planning their activities (Palen et al. 2010; Vieweg et al. 2010). Over the longer term—as in a more gradually unfolding flooding event—locals can also serve as a network of human 'sensors', who regularly updates on the situation on the ground at a level of detail that is often beyond what may be achieved by the limited staff and resources of emergency and media organisations (Shklovski, Palen and Sutton 2008; Hughes and Palen 2009). Indeed, in the aftermath of the third major disaster of early 2011, the earthquake, tsunami and nuclear meltdown that affected the northeastern

Japanese coastline, activists set up a network of locals who used cheap Geiger counters to monitor the progress of nuclear contamination across the provinces surrounding the stricken Fukushima reactors (Hakatte.jp 2012).

Such crowdsourcing of information is of increasing interest to emergency services and media organisations. During the Queensland flood crisis of early 2011, for example, the Australian Broadcasting Corporation (ABC) trialled an emergency mapping system based on the *Ushahidi Maps* platform (previously used in collating information in the aftermath of Kenyan election violence and the Haiti earthquake—see Goolsby 2010) to collect and present official as well as user-generated information on the current situation in affected areas (ABC 2011), while emergency services are similarly exploring best practices for the greater incorporation of crowdsourced information into their processes. Key challenges in this context are the verification of user-provided information (distinguishing solid first-hand information from widely circulating rumours), and the tracking of situational changes (acute crisis messages are generally circulated more widely than end-of-emergency notifications—cf. Mendoza, Poblete and Castillo 2010; Starbird and Palen 2010). More sophisticated tools for the tracking, triangulation and evaluation of information circulating through social media may be able to assist in this process. These may take into account, for example, the social media track records of participating users, or distinguish widely re-shared messages from individual, independent alerts about the same local situation. However, it is likely that significant manual supervision and evaluation will continue to be necessary.

Additionally, social media also play an important role in the further dissemination of emergency alerts and other messages, and in the community self-organisation of local responses. Research has shown that the social media response to crisis situations is far from random; rather, key information sources receive disproportionate attention by social media communities, and thereby gain substantially greater levels of visibility for themselves and their messages. Such sources may include conventional emergency services (the account of the Queensland Police Service Media Unit, @QPSMedia, became the central information source on Twitter during the 2011 Queensland floods, for example—see Bruns et al. 2012) or media organisations (the account of newspaper site *New Zealand Herald*, @nzherald, played a similar role in the 2011 Christchurch earthquake—see Bruns and Burgess 2012), but other traditional or new emergency actors may also emerge to prominence. Such actors include NGOs and other civic organisations, but also other internet actors (staff working for Google's philanthropic arm *Google.org* were prominent in the Christchurch earthquake as they shared their *Peoplefinder* site) and locals who are engaged in sharing first-hand information or organising emergency-response activities.

In the days following the Queensland floods, for example, Brisbane residents who had not been directly affected by flooding took to social media to organise the Baked Relief campaign, which organised volunteers to prepare and deliver home-cooked meals to flood clean-up volunteers. Organised through a Facebook page and the #bakedrelief Twitter hashtag, the effort was a notable success, generating further media coverage and resulting in spin-off activities during further natural disasters in Australia and elsewhere (Baked Relief 2011). Other groups and individuals contributed to 'working the crisis' by setting up unofficial websites to mirror and collate official information, thereby relieving stress from often overloaded government webservers; frequently, they also converted official information materials into formats that were more easily accessible and searchable for users with smartphones and other mobile devices. Such self-organised activities play an important role in enhancing community resilience, and can assist official emergency relief efforts by transferring responsibility for a range of ancillary activities from official organisations to the wider community.

The strategies of emergency services organisations must also recognise the significant interweaving of social and other online media with conventional broadcast and print media. The current, complex nature of the wider media ecology means that it is no longer appropriate to treat each media form and platform as a separate entity, but the rapid and frequent transition of messages and information from one medium to another must be anticipated (and encouraged, to ensure maximum dissemination—especially for crucial emergency advisories). During the 2011 Queensland floods, for example, updates were posted via the @QPSMedia Twitter account, and the corresponding Facebook page, directly from the situation briefings involving Premier Anna Bligh and the heads of the emergency services; in addition to being shared by social media users themselves, these messages were then also picked up and disseminated through the live tickers included in the major networks' television broadcasts; encountered through these broadcasts, they were then also shared further by other social media users, who posted about what they saw on screen. Finally, local social media users often also shared their information with neighbours and friends through their offline social networks. Such complex transmission paths for emergency information point to the fact that social media complement rather than replace more conventional media channels, at least in emergency situations.

In this context, it is important to note that the nature of the emergency situation will also impact on the media mix available for crisis communication activities. Floods, for example, for the most part tend to leave intact the local mobile and landline communications infrastructure; mobile phone towers usually have independent battery power supplies even if network power fails, for example. To some extent, this is also true during earthquakes: while mobile communication networks may be affected as various individual access points fail, a network-wide failure is less common. Bushfires, on the other hand, are known for their far more devastating effects on overground communications infrastructure: phone and electricity cables, as well as mobile phone towers, are usually unable to withstand direct exposure to intense fire and heat.

Crisis communication strategies must take such differences into account: social media—especially as accessed through mobile devices—may never play a significant role in bushfire contexts, for example, while the proliferation of internet-capable smartphones in Australia positions them as an especially important component of the crisis communication process in the aftermath of floods, storms and earthquakes. Consequently, recent emergency preparedness campaigns in Queensland and other Australian states have begun to recommend the purchase of phone-charging equipment that may be used in cars, to ensure access to emergency information even if landline power and communications connections fail; similarly, the restoration of mobile communications infrastructure is now a priority task in the aftermath of major natural disasters.

Overall, however, it has become clear that social media are now an integral part of the crisis communication infrastructure: for disseminating official advice to the public, for gathering information from affected locals and for enhancing the resilience of communities by providing them with an additional means of self-organisation. Emergency services and emergency media organisations throughout the world are now exploring the ways to integrate social media into their communications strategies; ongoing changes in the social media landscape mean that this is a process that will continue for some time to come.

References

Aarseth, E. 2005, 'Narrativism and the art of simulation', in P. Harrigan and N. Wardrip-Fruin (eds), *First Person*, MIT Press, Cambridge, MA, pp. 45–55.

Abbate, J. 1999, *Inventing the Internet*, MIT Press, Cambridge, MA.

ABC News 2012, 'Artist anger as Spotify launches in Australia', 23 May, <www.abc.net.au/news/2012-05-22/artist-anger-as-spotify-launches-in-australia/4026998> (accessed 20 February 2013).

ABC Online 2007, 'ACMA links Alan Jones to Cronulla Violence', *ABC News Online*, <www.abc.net.au/news/newsitems/200704/s1893477.htm> (accessed 20 March 2013).

ABC Radio National 2006, 'Judith Lucy', *The Media Report*, 29 June, <www.abc.net.au/rn/mediareport/stories/2006/1674731.htm> (accessed 20 March 2013).

Abdela, L. 2001, 'So many male stupidities', *The Guardian*, 9 January.

Abercrombie, N., Hill, S. and Turner, B. 1980, *The Dominant Ideology Thesis*, Allen & Unwin, Sydney.

'Accused killer of Jill Meagher appears in court 2012, *ABC News*, 28 February, <www.abc.net.au/news/2012-09-28/accused-killer-of-jill-meagher-appears-in-court/4285668> (accessed 20 March 2013).

Adair, D. (ed.) 2012, *Sport: Race, Ethnicity and Identity: Building Global Understanding*, Routledge, London.

Adams, P. 2011, 'Beware: bigotry is back' *The Weekend Australian*, 1–2 November, p. R36.

Anti-Discrimination Board (NSW) 2003, *Race for the Headlines: Racism and Media Discourse*, Anti-Discrimination Board of NSW, Sydney.

Adbrands 2012, 'The top advertising agencies in Australia', <www.adbrands.net/au/top_advertising_agencies_australia.html> (accessed 24 October 2012).

AdNews 2012, 'Agency report card' 2012, 1 June, pp. 21–35.

Adorno, T. 1976, *The Positivist Dispute in German Sociology*, Heinemann, London.

Albarran, A.B. (ed.) 2013, *Social Media Industries*, Routledge, London.

Allen, M. and Leaver, T. 2014, *Web Presence: Staying Noticed in a Networked World*, Chandos, Cambridge.

Allen, R.C. 1992, *Channels of Discourse Reassembled*, Routledge, London.

Alterman, E. 2008, 'Out of print: The death and life of the American newspaper', *The New Yorker*, 31 March.

Althaus, C., Bridgman, P. and Davis, G. 2012, *The Australian Policy Handbook*, 5th ed., Allen & Unwin, Sydney.

American Psychological Association (APA) 2007, *Sexualization of Girls*, American Psychological Association, Washington, DC, <www.apa.org/pi/women/programs/girls/report.aspx> (accessed 28 June 2013).

Anderson, A. 1997, *Media, Culture and the Environment*, Routledge, London.

Andrejevic, M. 2004, *Reality TV: The Work of Being Watched*, Rowman and Littlefield, Lanham, MD.

—— 2013 'Public service media utilities: Rethinking search engines and social networking as public goods', *Media International Australia*, no. 146, pp. 123–32.

Ang, I. 1991, *Desperately Seeking the Audience*, Routledge, London.

Ang, I., Brand, J., Noble, G. and Wilding, D. 2002, *Living Diversity: Australia's Multicultural Future*, SBS, Sydney.

Ang, I., Hawkins, G. and Dabboussy, L. 2008, *The SBS Story*, UNSW Press, Sydney.

Anonymous 2008, *Boned*, Penguin/Michael Joseph, Melbourne.

Appcelerator/IDC 2012, *Voice of the Next-Generation Mobile Developer: Q3 2012 Mobile Developer Report*, <www.Appcelerator.com> (accessed 20 February 2013).

Apple Corporation 2007, '100 Million iPods Sold', 9 April, <www.apple.com/pr/library/2007/04/09ipod.html> (accessed 20 February 2013).

Appleton, G. 1988, 'How Australia sees itself: The role of commercial television', in *The Price of Being Australian*, conference report, 31 August–1 September 1987, Australian Broadcasting Tribunal, Sydney, pp. 190–246.

APRA/AMCOS 2011, 'Year in review: An overview of the 2011 financial year results', <www.apra-amcos.com.au/downloads/file/ABOUT/ApraYIR2011D8.pdf> (accessed 20 February 2013).

ARIA 2012, 'Australian sales at wholesale value (physical product) for the year ended 31 December', <www.aria.com.au/pages/documents/physical-salesxvalue.pdf> (accessed 20 February 2013).

Armstrong, M. 1982, *Broadcasting Law and Policy in Australia*, Butterworths, Sydney.

—— 1986, 'Deregulation of radio', *Media Information Australia*, no. 41, pp. 45–9.

Arts Victoria 2011, *The Economic, Social and Cultural Contribution of Venue-based Live Music in Victoria*, 20 June, Deloitte Access Economics, Melbourne.

Arvidsson, A. 2006, *Brands: Meaning and Value in Media Culture*, Routledge, London.

Askew, K. 2011, *Dot.Bomb Australia*, Allen & Unwin, Sydney.

Australia Council 2010, *More Bums on Seats: Australian Participation in the Arts*, Australia Council, Sydney.

—— 2012, 'Artfacts: music', <http://artfacts.australiacouncil.gov.au/global> (accessed 20 February 2013).

Australia Copyright Council 2012, 'High Court upholds 1% cap on broadcast royalties for sound recordings', 28 March, <www.copyright.org.au/news-and-policy/details/id/2056> (accessed 20 February 2013).

Australian Association of National Advertisers (AANA) 2008, *AANA Food & Beverages Advertising & Marketing Communications Code 2008*, <www.aana.com.au/pages/codes.html> (accessed 20 June 2013).

Australian Broadcasting Authority (ABA) 2003, *Understanding Community Attitudes to Radio Content*, ABA, Sydney.

—— 2004, *Annual Report 2003/04*, <www.abc.net.au/corp/ar04> (accessed 20 February 2013).

Australian Broadcasting Corporation 2011, "ABC Qld Flood Crisis Map." https://queensland-floods.crowdmap.com/, (accessed October 15th, 2012).

Australian Bureau of Statistics (ABS) 2008, *Australian National Accounts: National Income, Expenditure and Product, September Quarter,* cat. no. 5206.0, ABS, Canberra.

— 2011a, *Arts and Culture in Australia: A Statistical Overview.* http://www.abs.gov.au/Ausstats/ABS@.nsf/0/32049C1F6913E595CA257968000CB4B2?opendocument cat. no. 4172.0

— 2011b, *Household Use of Information Technology, Australia, 2010–11,* cat. no. 8146.0, ABS, Canberra.

— 2012a, *Internet Activity, Australia, June 2012,* cat no. 8153.0, ABS, Canberra.

— 2012b, *Australian National Accounts: National Income, Expenditure and Product, September Quarter,* cat. no. 5206.0, ABS, Canberra.

— 2012c, *Participation in Sport and Physical Recreation,* Australia, 2011–12, cat. no. 4177.0, ABS, Canberra.

Australian Communications Authority (ACA) 2001, *Telecommunications Performance Report 2000/01,* ACA, Melbourne.

Australian Communications and Media Authority (ACMA) 2007, *Media and Communications in Australian Families,* ACMA, Sydney.

— 2012a, *2011–12 Annual Report,* ACMA, Sydney.

— 2012b, *Communications Report 2011/12,* ACMA, Melbourne.

— 2012c, *Communications Report: Report 2—Australia's Progress in the Digital Economy: Participation, Trust, and Confidence,* ACMA, Sydney.

Australian Competition and Consumer Commission (ACCC) 2009, *Snapshot of Telstra's Customer Access Network as at 31 December 2008,* ACCC, Melbourne.

— 2013, *Telecommunications Competitive Safeguards for 2011–12,* ACCC, Canberra.

Australian Government 2012, *National Classification Code,* <www.classification.gov.au/ClassificationinAustralia/Legislation/Pages/TheCode.aspx> (accessed 20 February 2013).

Australian Independent Record Labels Association 2013, Website <www.air.org.au> (accessed 20 February 2013).

Australian Labor Party (ALP) 2007, *New Directions for Communications: A Broadband Future for Australia—Building a National Broadband Network,* ALP, Canberra.

Australian Law Reform Commission 1991, *Censorship Procedure,* Report No. 55, Sydney, ALRC, Sydney.

— 2012, *Classification—Content Regulation and Convergent Media,* Final Report, No. 108, ALRC, Sydney.

Australian Interactive Multimedia Industry Association (AIMIA) 2012, *Australian Mobile Phone Lifestyle Index,* 8th ed., AIMIA, Sydney, <www.aimia.com.au/ampli> (accessed 20 February 2013).

Australian Journalists' Association (AJA) 1991, *Submission to the House of Representatives Select Committee on Print Media,* AJA, Sydney.

Australian Recording Industry Association (ARIA) 2012, *Australian Sales at Wholesale Value (Physical Product) for the Years ended 31 December,* <www.aria.com.au/pages/documents/physical-salesxvalue.pdf> (accessed 20 February 2013).

— 2012, 'ARIA releases wholesale figures for 2011', <www.aria.com.au/documents/2011wholesalefigures.pdf> (accessed 20 February 2013).

Australian Research Council Centre of Excellence (ARC CoE) 2011, *Home Internet for*

Indigenous Communities, Institute for Social Research, Swinburne University of Technology, Melbourne.

Australian Sports Commission 2010, *Towards a Level Playing Field: Sport and Gender in Australian Media*, <www.ausport.gov.au/__data/assets/pdf_file/0007/356209/Towards_a_Level_Playing_Field_LR.pdf> (accessed 20 February 2013).

Bainbridge, J. 2005, 'Branded Content Takes Hold', *B&T*, 2 August, <www.bandt.com/au/news> (accessed 20 February 2013).

Bairner, A. 2001, *Sport, Nationalism, and Globalization: European and North American Perspectives*, State University of New York Press, Albany, NY.

Bakardjieva, M. 2006, 'Domestication running wild: From the moral economy of the household to the mores of a culture', in T. Berker, M. Hartmann, Y. Punie and K. Ward (eds), *Domestication of Media and Technology*, McGraw-Hill, Maidenhead, pp. 62–78.

Baked Relief 2011, Website, <http://bakedrelief.org>, (accessed 15 October 2012).

Baker, S. and Homan, S. 2007, 'Rap, recidivism and the creative self: A popular music programme for young offenders in detention', *Journal of Youth Studies*, vol. 10, no. 4, pp. 459–76.

Ball, J. and Lewis, P. 2011, 'Twitter and the riots: How the news spread', *The Guardian*, 7 December, <www.guardian.co.uk/uk/2011/dec/07/twitter-riots-how-news-spread> (accessed 15 October 2012).

Balnaves, M. and O'Regan, T. 2002, 'The ratings in transition: The politics and technologies of counting', in M. Balnaves, T. O'Regan and J. Sternberg (eds), *Mobilising the Audience*, University of Queensland Press, Brisbane, pp. 29–64.

Banks, J.A. 2012, 'The iPhone as innovation platform: Reimagining the videogames developer', in L. Hjorth, J. Burgess and I. Richardson (eds), *Studying Mobile Media: Cultural Technologies, Mobile Communication, and the iPhone*, Routledge, New York, pp. 155–72.

Barker, C. 1999, *Television, Globalization and Cultural Identities*, Open University Press, Philadelphia, PA.

Barker, M. and Petley, J. (eds) 2001, *Ill Effects*, Routledge, London.

Barnouw, E. 1979, *The Sponsor: Notes on a Modern Potentate*, Oxford University Press, New York.

Barr, T. 2000, *newmedia.com.au*, Allen & Unwin, Sydney.

Barry, P. 2003, *Rich Kids: How the Murdochs and Packers Lost $950 Million in One.Tel*, Bantam Books, Sydney.

Barthes, R. 1968, *The Elements of Semiology*, Hill and Wang, New York.

Bartholomeusz, S. 2013, 'Vodafone bides for a rebirth', *Business Spectator*, 8 February.

Beaton, J. and Wajcman, J. 2004, *The Impact of the Mobile Telephone in Australia*, Academy of the Social Sciences in Australia, Canberra.

Beattie, S. and Beal, E. 2007, *Connect + Converge: Australian Media and Communications Law*, Oxford University Press, Melbourne.

Beazley, K. (Minister for Transport and Communications) 1991, 'Second Reading Speech on the Telecommunications Bill 1991', *Hansard*, House of Representatives, 7 May, p. 3094.

Beck, U. 1994, 'The reinvention of politics: Towards a theory of reflexive modernization', in U. Beck, A. Giddens and S. Lash (eds), *Reflexive Modernization: Politics, Tradition and Aesthetics in the Modern Social Order*, Polity Press, Cambridge, pp. 1–55.

—— 1999, *World Risk Society*, Polity Press, Malden, MA.

—— 2009, *World at Risk*, Polity Press, Cambridge.

'Beginner's Guide to Sexism, A' 2000, *Tertangala*, University of Wollongong SRC, no. 6, 2000, p. 28.

Bell, D. and Kennedy, B. (eds) 2000, *The Cybercultures Reader*, Routledge, London.

Bell, P. 1998, 'Television', in P. Bell and R. Bell (eds), *Americanization and Australia*, UNSW Press, Sydney, pp 193–209.

Benkler, Y. 2006, *The Wealth of Networks: How Social Production Transforms Markets and Freedom*, Yale University Press, New Haven, CT.

Bennett, T. 1992, 'Useful culture', *Cultural Studies*, vol. 6, no. 3, pp. 395–408.

Bennett, W.L. 2005, News: *The Politics of Illusion*, 6th ed., Pearson/Longman, New York.

Berelson, B. 1949, 'What missing the newspaper means', in P. Lazarsfeld and F. Stanton (eds), *Communication Research 1948–1949*, Harper and Brothers, New York, pp. 36–47.

Berg, C. 2012, *In Defence of Freedom of Speech: From Ancient Greece to Andrew Bolt*, Institute of Public Affairs, Melbourne.

Bertrand, I., McFarlane, B. and Mayer, G. 1999, *The Oxford Companion to Australian Film*, Oxford University Press, Melbourne.

Bignell, J. 2008, *An Introduction to Television Studies*, Routledge, London.

Bijker, W., Hughes, T. and Pinch, T. (eds.) 1987, *The Social Construction of Technological Systems: New Directions in the Sociology and History of Technology*, MIT Press, Cambridge, MA.

Bishop, J. 2005, 'Building International Empires of Sound: Concentrations of Power and Property in the "Global" Music Market', *Popular Music and Society*, vol. 28, no. 4, pp. 443–71.

Blatterer, H. 2010, 'Social Networking, Privacy, and the Pursuit of Visibility', in H. Blatterer, P. Johnson and M. R. Markus (eds), *Modern Privacy: Shifting Boundaries, New Forms*, Palgrave Macmillan, Basingstoke, pp. 73–87.

Blatterer, H., Johnson, P. and Markus, M. (eds) 2010, *Modern Privacy: Shifting Boundaries, New Forms*, Palgrave Macmillan, Basingstoke.

Blumler, J.G. and Katz, E. (eds), 1974, *The Uses of Mass Communication: Current Perspectives on Gratification Research*, Sage, Thousand Oaks, CA.

Bodey, M. 2008, 'ABC boss behind Aunty's sparkle', *The Australian*, 15 December.

Bogost, I. 2009, 'You played that? Game studies meets game criticism', <www.bogost.com/writing/you_played_that_game_studies_m.shtml> (accessed 18 March 2013).

Bollen, J., Mao, H. and Zeng, X. 2011, 'Twitter mood predicts the stock market', *Journal of Computational Science*, vol. 2, no. 1, pp. 1–8.

Bolter, J. and Grusin, R. 1999, *Remediation: Understanding New Media*, MIT Press, Cambridge, MA.

Bonner, F. 2003, *Ordinary Television*, Sage, London.

Bonney, B. and Wilson, H. 1983, *Australia's Commercial Media*, Macmillan, Melbourne.

Boorstin, D.J. 1971, *The Image: A Guide to Pseudo-events in America*, Atheneum, New York.

Bowman, D. 1988, *The Captive Press*, Penguin, Melbourne.

Bowman, M. and Grattan, M. 1989, *Reformers*, Collins Dove, Melbourne.

Box Office Mojo 2012, '*The Sapphires*', <http://boxofficemojo.com/movies/intl/?id=_fTHESAP PHIRES01&country=AU&wk=2012W37&id=_fTHESAPPHIRES01&p=.htm> (accessed 16 December 2012).

Boyd, D. 2012, 'Participating in the always-on lifestyle', in M. Mandiberg (ed.), *The Social Media Reader*, New York University Press, New York, pp. 71–6.

Boykoff, M. 2011, *Who Speaks for the Climate? Making Sense of Media Reporting of Climate Change*, Cambridge University Press, Cambridge.

Boykoff, M.T and Boykoff, J.M. 2004, 'Balance as bias: Global warming and the US prestige press', *Global Environmental Change*, no. 14, pp. 125–36.

Boykoff, M. and Mansfield, M., 'Media coverage of climate change/global warming', <http://sciencepolicy.colorado.edu/media_coverage>.

Braman, S. (ed) 2003, *Communication Researchers and Policy-making*, MIT Press, Cambridge, MA.

—— 2006, *Change of State: Information, Policy, and Power*, MIT Press, Cambridge, MA.

Braudy, L. 1986, *The Frenzy of Renown: Fame and its History*, Oxford University Press, New York.

Breen, M. 1992, 'The Inquiry into the Prices of Sound Recording', *Media Information Australia*, no. 64, pp. 31–41.

——1992, 'The music industry and pop culture: The Case for an Australian Study', *Perfect Beat*, vol. 1, no. 1, pp. 63–74.

——1999, *Rock Dogs: Politics and the Australian Music Industry*, Pluto Press, Sydney.

Brennan-Horley, C. 2007, 'Work and play: Vagaries surrounding contemporary cultural production in Sydney's dance music culture', *Media International Australia*, no. 123, pp 123–37.

Brisbane City Council 2008, 'Valley Music Harmony Plan', <www.brisbane.qld.gov.au/BCC:BASE::pc=PC_74> (accessed 20 December 2012).

Brockington, D. 2009, *Celebrity and the Environment: Fame, Wealth and Power in Conservation*, ZED Books, London.

Bronner, S. and Kellner, D. (eds) 1989, *Critical Theory and Society: A Reader*, Routledge, New York.

Brown, A. 1990, *Deregulation of Australian Metropolitan Radio*, Institute for Cultural Policy Studies, Griffith University, Brisbane.

Brown, H., Lovink, G., Merrick, H., Rossiter, N., The, D. and Wilson, N. (eds) 2001, *Politics of a Digital Present: An Inventory of Australian Net Culture, Criticism and Theory*, Fibreculture, Melbourne.

Bruce, T., Hovden, J. and Markula, P. (eds) 2010, *Sportswomen at the Olympics: A Global Content Analysis of Newspaper Coverage*, Sense, Rotterdam.

Bruns, A. 2008, *Blogs, Wikipedia, Second Life, and Beyond: From Production to Produsage*, Peter Lang, New York.

—— 2012, 'How not to use Twitter: Lessons from Qantas and Westpac', *The Conversation*, 15 February, <http://theconversation.com/how-not-to-use-twitter-lessons-from-qantas-and-westpac-5342> (accessed 18 September 2012).

Bruns, A. and Burgess, J. 2012, 'Local and global responses to disaster: #eqnz and the Christchurch earthquake', *Proceedings of the Australian & New Zealand Disaster and Emergency Management Conference, Brisbane, 16–18 April*, AST Management Pty Ltd, Brisbane, pp. 86–103.

Bruns, A., Burgess, J., Crawford, K. and Shaw, F. 2012, *#qldfloods and @QPSMedia: Crisis Communication on Twitter in the 2011 South East Queensland Floods*. Brisbane: ARC Centre of Excellence for Creative Industries and Innovation, <http://cci.edu.au/floodsreport.pdf> (accessed 15 October 2012).

Bruns, A. and Jacobs, J. (eds) 2006, *Uses of Blogs*, Peter Lang, New York.

Budde, P. 2009, *Global–Mobile–Equipment–Mobile Handsets*, Buddecom, Bucketty, NSW.

Budde, P. and McNamara, S. 2012, *Australia Telecoms Industry Statistics and Forecasts*, 25th ed., Buddecom, Bucketty, NSW.

Bull, M. 2005, 'No dead air! The iPod and the culture of mobile listening', *Leisure Studies*, vol. 24, no. 4, pp 343–55.

Bunbury, R. 1998, 'Ad industry policing lacks weapons', *The Australian*, 26 March.

Burgess, J. and Green, J. 2009, *YouTube: Online Video and Participatory Culture*, Polity Press, Cambridge.

—— 2013, *YouTube: Online Video and Participatory Culture*, rev. ed., Wiley, New York.

Burnley, I. and Murphy P. 2004, *Sea Change: Movement from Metropolitan to Arcadian Australia*, UNSW Press, Sydney.

Burns, M. 2000, 'ABC Online: A Prehistory', *Media International Australia*, no. 97, pp. 92–104.

—— 2008, *ABC Online: Becoming the ABC. The First Five Years of the Australian Broadcasting Corporation Online*, VDM Verlag, Rotterdam.

—— 2012, 'Protecting the brand: A history of ABC Online news–as–commodity', in M. Burns and N. Brügger (eds), *Public Service Broadcasters on the Web: A Comprehensive History*, Peter Lang, New York.

Burns, M. and Brügger, N. 2012, *Public Service Broadcasters on the Web: A Comprehensive History*, Peter Lang, New York.

Butler, D. and Rodrick, S. 2007, *Australian Media Law*, 3rd ed., Law Book Co., Sydney.

Byrnes, H. 2012, 'Actor Firass Dirani urges TV bosses to show our true colours', *Daily Telegraph*, 15 February, <www.news.com.au/entertainment/television/actor-firass-dirani-urges-tv-bosses-to-show-our-true-colours/story-e6frfmyi-1226271245464> (accessed 28 January 2013).

Canberra Times 2011, 'Giving pollies the right look', *Canberra Times*, 13 November.

Caro, A. 1981, 'Advertising—an Introduction', in K. Fowles and N. Mills (eds), *Understanding Advertising: An Australian Guide*, TAFE Educational Books, Sydney, pp. 5–17.

Carr, N. 2010, *The Shallows: What the Internet is Doing to our Brains*, W.W. Norton, New York.

Carrington, B. 2010, *Race, Sport and Politics: The Sporting Black Diaspora*, Sage, London.

Carvalho, A. 2007, 'Ideological cultures and media discourses on scientific knowledge: Rereading news on climate change', *Public Understanding of Science*, vol. 16, pp. 223–43.

Castells, M. 2009, *Communication Power*, Oxford University Press, New York.

Castells, M., Fernández-Ardèvol, M., Qiu, J.L. and Sey, A. 2007, *Mobile Communication and Society: A Global Perspective*, MIT Press, Cambridge, MA.

Casual Games Association 2012, Website, <www.casualgamesassociation.org> (accessed 20 November 2012).

Caudwell, J. (ed.) 2006, *Sport, Sexualities and Queer/Theory*, Routledge, London.

Chadwick, P. 1989, *Media Mates: Carving up Australia's Media*, Macmillan, Melbourne.

Chandler, D. 2006, *Media Representation*, <www.scribd.com/doc/109805233/Representation-David-Chandler> (accessed 31 August 2012).

Chang, J. 2011, 'Fountain-falling texter in court for alleged debt', *ABC News Online*, <http://abcnews.go.com>, 20 January (accessed 28 October 2012).

Chen, P. 2013, *Australian Politics in a Digital Age*, ANU e-Press, Canberra.

CIMB Securities 2012, 'Company Note—iiNet', 12 December.

—— 2013 'Flash Note: SingTel', 14 February.

Clark, P. 1988, 'More FM stations on the way', *Sydney Morning Herald*, 10 August, p. 2.

Clarke, R. 2004, 'An internet primer: Technology and governance', in G. Goggin (ed) *Virtual Nation: The Internet in Australia*, UNSW Press, Sydney, pp. 13–27.

Coakley, J., Hallinan, C., Jackson, S. and Mewett, P. 2009, *Sports in Society: Issues and Controversies in Australia and New Zealand*. McGraw-Hill, Sydney.

Cole, J. 2011, 'Is America at a digital turning point?' *USC Annenberg News*, 14 December.

Collingwood, P. 1997, *Commercial Media Since the Cross-Media Revolution*, Communications Law Centre, Sydney.

Collins, F. and Davis, T. 2005, *Australian Cinema After Mabo*, Cambridge University Press, Cambridge.

Collins, S. 2008, 'Making the most out of 15 minutes: Reality TV's dispensable celebrity', *Television and New Media*, vol. 9, no. 2, pp. 87–110.

Commonwealth Parliament, Senate Standing Committee on Environment, Communication and the Arts 2008, *Report of Inquiry into Sexualisation of Children in the Contemporary Media*, <www.aph.gov.au/senate/committee/eca_ctte/sexualisation_of_children/report/ index. htm> (accessed 20 September 2012).

Community Radio National Listener Survey: Summary Report of Findings 2008, McNair Ingenuity Research, Sydney, 28 July.

Comscore 2011, *It's a Social World: Top 10 Need-to-Knows About Social Networking*, <www.comscore. com/Insights/Presentations_and_Whitepapers/2011/it_is_a_social_world_top_10_ need-to-knows_about_social_networking> (accessed 20 November 2013).

Conley, D. 2002, *The Daily Miracle: An Introduction to Journalism* (2nd ed.), Oxford University Press, Oxford.

Convergence Review 2012, *Convergence Review Final Report*, Department of Broadband, Communications and the Digital Economy, Canberra.

Conroy, S. 2012, 'Renewal decision provides certainty for mobile consumers', Media Release, 10 February.

—— 2009, 'New National Broadband Network', Joint Media Release with Prime Minister, Treasurer and Minister for Finance, 7 April.

Coombs, A. 1990, *Adland: A True Story of Corporate Drama*, Heinemann, Melbourne.

Coroneos, P. 2008, 'Internet content policy and regulation in Australia', in B. Fitzgerald, F. Gao, D. O'Brien and S.X. Shi (eds), *Copyright Law, Digital Content and the Internet in the Asia-Pacific*, Sydney University Press, Sydney, pp. 49–65.

Coster, A., McMahon, K. and Epstein, J. 2011, 'PM develops a passion for fashion', *Herald Sun*, 17 June.

Cottle, S. and Lester, L. (eds) 2011, *Transnational Protests and the Media*, Peter Lang, New York.

Couldry, N. 2003, *Media Rituals: A Critical Approach*, Routledge, London.

—— 2004, 'Theorising media as practice', *Social Semiotics*, vol. 14, no. 2, pp. 115–32.

Counihan, M. 1982, 'The formation of a broadcasting audience: Australian radio in the twenties', *Meanjin*, vol. 41, no. 2, pp 196–209.

—— 1992, 'Giving a chance to a youthful muse: Radio, records and the first Australian music quota', *Media Information Australia*, no. 64, pp. 6–16.

—— 1996, 'Summer in the suburbs: HITZ FM and the reinvention of teen radio', in H. Ericksen (ed.), *The Media's Australia*, The Australian Centre, University of Melbourne, Melbourne, pp. 17–30.

Coupe, B., Jakubowicz, A. and Randall, L. 1992, *Nextdoor Neighbours: A Report for the Office of Multicultural Affairs on Ethnic Group Discussions of the Australian Media*, AGPS, Canberra

Coward, R. 1989, *The Whole Truth: The Myth of Alternative Health*, Faber and Faber, London.

Cowley, M. 2012, 'Seebohm curses social media fixation after falling for own hype', *Sydney Morning Herald*, 31 July, <www.smh.com.au/olympics/swimming-london-2012/seebohm-curses-social-media-fixation-after-falling-for-own-hype-20120731-23boi.htm> (accessed 22 January 2013).

Cox, R. 2010, *Environmental Communication and the Public Sphere*, Sage, Thousand Oaks, CA.

Craig, G. 2000, 'Perpetual crisis: The politics of saving the ABC', *Media International Australia*, no. 98, pp. 105–16.

Crawford, K. 2005, 'Adaptation: Tracking the ecologies of music and peer-to-peer networks', *Media International Australia*, no. 114, pp. 30–9.

Crawford, K. and Lumby, C. 2011, *The Adaptive Moment: A Fresh Approach to Convergent Media in Australia*, Journalism and Media Research Centre, University of New South Wales, Sydney.

Crawford, R. 2008, *But Wait, There's More: A History of Australian Advertising 1900–2000*, Melbourne University Press, Melbourne.

Creative Commons 2012, Website, <http://creativecommons.org> (accessed 20 February 2013).

Crook, J. 2012, 'Instagram will share user data with Facebook according to its new privacy policy', *TechCrunch*, <http://techcrunch.com/2012/12/17/instagram-will-share-users-data-with-facebook-according-to-its-new-privacy-policy> (accessed 20 January 2013).

Cunningham, S. 1992, *Framing Culture: Criticism and Policy in Australia*, Allen & Unwin, Sydney.

—— 2000, 'History, contexts, politics, policy', in G. Turner and S. Cunningham (eds), *The Australian TV Book*, Allen & Unwin, Sydney, pp. 13–32.

—— 2013, *Hidden Innovation: Policy, Industry and the Creative Sector*, University of Queensland Press, Brisbane.

Cunningham, S. and Bridgstock, R. 2012, 'Say goodbye to the fries: Graduate careers in media, cultural and communication studies', *Media International Australia*, no. 145, pp. 6–17.

Cunningham, S. and Sinclair, J. (eds) 2000, *Floating Lives: The Media and Asian Diasporas*, University of Queensland Press, Brisbane.

Cunningham, S. and Turner, G. (eds) 1993, *The Media in Australia*, Allen & Unwin, Sydney.

Curran, J. 1990, 'The new revisionism in mass communication research: A reappraisal', *European Journal of Communication*, no. 5, pp 130–64.

Curthoys, A. 1986, 'The getting of television: Dilemmas in ownership, control and culture 1941–56', in A. Curthoys and J. Merritt (eds), *Better Dead Than Red: Australia's First Cold War 1941–1956*, vol. 2, Allen & Unwin, Sydney.

Curtis, R., Given, J. and McCutcheon, M. 2012, 'Online video in Australia', *International Journal of Digital Television* vol. 3, no. 2, pp. 141–62.

Dahlgren, P. and Sparks, C. 1991, *Communication and Citizenship: Journalism and the Public Sphere in the New Media Age*, Routledge, New York.

Daily Telegraph 2010, 'Being quick to cotton on to smart new look', *Daily Telegraph*, 7 July.

Dale, D. 2004, 'Fairytale is over as nice girls finish last at the movies', *Sydney Morning Herald*, News and Features, 10 May, p. 3.

D'Alpuget, B. 1982, *Robert J. Hawke: A Biography*, Schwartz, Melbourne.

Darian-Smith, K. and Turnbull, S. (eds) 2012, *Remembering Television: Histories, Technologies, Memories*, Cambridge Scholars Publishing, Newcastle Upon Tyne.

Davis, A. 2005, 'Mobilising phone art', *RealTime*, <www.realtimearts.net/article/issue66/7782> (accessed 20 August 2005).

Davis, L. and Mackay, S. 1996, *Structures and Strategies: An Introduction to Academic Writing*, Macmillan, Melbourne.

Day, M. 2002, 'FM talk sounds sweet to new US generation', *The Australian*, Media, 12 December, p. 5.

Deloitte 2012, *Technology, Media and Telecommunications Predictions 2012*, 24 April, Deloitte, Sydney.

Dempster, Q. 2000, *Death Struggle: How Political Malice and Boardroom Powerplays are Killing the ABC*, Allen & Unwin, Sydney.

Department of Broadband, Communications and the Digital Economy (DBCDE) 2010, *Sport on Television: A Review of the Anti-Siphoning Scheme in the Contemporary Digital Environment*, <www.dbcde.gov.au/__data/assets/pdf_file/0017/131462/Review_Report_-_Sport_on_Television-the_anti-siphoning_scheme_in_the_contemporary_digital_environment_-_25-11-2010.pdf> (accessed 20 November 2012).

—— 2011, *Convergence Review Discussion Paper: Media Diversity, Competition and Market Structure*, <www.dbcde.gov.au/__data/assets/pdf_file/0004/139270/Paper-2_Media-diversity_competition_access.pdf> (accessed 20 November 2012).

Department of Communications, Information Technology and the Arts (DCITA) 2004, *Introduction of Digital Radio Issues Paper*, December, DCITA, Canberra.

Dermody, S., Docker, J. and Modjeska, D. (eds) 1982, *Nellie Melba, Ginger Meggs and Friends: Essays in Australian Cultural History*, Kibble Books, Malmsbury.

Dermody, S. and Jacka, E. 1987, *The Screening of Australia, Volume 1: Anatomy of a Film Industry*, Currency Press, Sydney.

—— 1988a, *The Imaginary Industry: Australian Film in the Late '80s*, Australian Film, Television and Radio School, Sydney.

—— 1988b, *The Screening of Australia, Volume 2: Anatomy of a National Cinema*, Currency Press, Sydney.

de Souza e Silva, A. 2004, 'Art by telephone: From static to mobile interfaces', *Leonardo Electronic Almanac*, vol. 12, no. 10, <http://mitpress2.mit.edu/e-journals/LEA/TEXT/Vol_12/lea_v12_n10.txt> (accessed 4 January 2006).

—— 2006, 'From cyber to hybrid: Mobile technologies as interfaces of hybrid spaces', *Space and Culture*, vol. 9, no. 3, pp. 261–78.

de Souza e Silva, A. and Frith, J. 2010, *Mobile Interfaces in Public Spaces: Locational Privacy, Control, and Urban Sociality*, Routledge, New York.

—— 2012, 'Locational privacy in public spaces: Media discourses on location-aware mobile technologies', *Communication, Culture and Critique*, vol. 3, no. 4, pp. 503–25.

de Souza e Silva, A. and Hjorth, L. 2009, 'Playful urban spaces: A historical approach to mobile games', *Simulation and Gaming*, vol. 40, no. 5, pp. 602–25.

de Souza e Silva, A. and Sutko, D. (eds) 2009, *Digital Cityscapes*, Peter Lang, Berlin.

Donovan, P. 2008a, 'Ashamed Wheatley aims to re-earn his stripes', *The Age*, 28 August.

—— 2008b, 'Iggy pops in to help Jet go wild about Johnny', *The Age*, 10 April.

Dovey, J. and Kennedy, H.W. 2007, *Game Culture: Computer Games as New Media*, Open University Press, Maidenhead.

Downie, L. Jr and Schudson, M. 2009, *The Reconstruction of American Journalism*, Columbia University Graduate School of Journalism, New York, 20 October.

Downs, A. 1972, 'Up and down with ecology: The "issue–attention" cycle', *The Public Interest*, no. 28(Summer), pp. 38–50.

'Do YOU need satellite radio programming?' 1988, *Broadcast*, vol. 3, no. 4, pp. 13–15.

Dreher, T. 2003, 'Speaking up and talking back: Media interventions in Sydney's "othered" communities', *Media International Australia*, no. 119, pp. 121–37.

—— 2010, 'Muslim community media interventions—"a command performance"', J. Ewart and H. Rane (eds), *Muslims and the Media in Australia*, Melbourne University Press, Melbourne.

Du Gay, P., Hall, S., Janes, L., Mackay, H. and Negus, K. (eds) 1997, *Doing Cultural Studies: The Story of the Walkman*, Sage, London.

Dunbar-Hall, P. and Gibson, C. 2004, *Deadly Sounds, Deadly Spaces: Contemporary Aboriginal Music in Australia*, UNSW Press, Sydney.

Dunleavy, P. and O'Leary, B. 1987, *Theories of the State: The Politics of Liberal Democracy*, Macmillan, London.

Dunn, K. 2003, 'Using cultural geography to engage contested constructions of ethnicity and citizenship in Sydney', *Social and Cultural Geography*, vol. 4, no. 2, pp. 153–65.

During, S. 1999, *The Cultural Studies Reader*, 2nd ed., Routledge, London.

Duthie, K. 2008, '*Salam Cafe*', *The Age*, 6 May, <www.theage.com.au/news/tv-reviews/salam-cafe/2008/05/06/1209839627629.html> (accessed 20 November 2012).

Dwyer, T. 2008, 'Ownership changes', in T. Dwyer, *The State of the News: Print Media in Australia*, Australian Press Council, Sydney.

—— 2012, 'Is community the right word for what happens online?', <http://about.abc.net.au/2012/09/is-community-the-right-word-for-what-happens-online> (accessed 23 December 2012).

Dyer, R. 1997, *White*, Routledge, London.

Economist, The 2008, 'Feeling the pinch', 6 December, p. 76.

Edgar, P. 1977, *Children and Screen Violence*, University of Queensland Press, Brisbane.

Egenfeldt-Nielsen, S., Smith, J. and Tosca, S. 2008, *Understanding Video Games: The Essential Introduction*, Routledge, London.

Eichler, A. 2012, 'Instagram terms of service change sparks revolt: The Instascam backlash as told by the users', *Huffington Post*, <www.huffingtonpost.com/2012/12/20/instagram-terms-of-service-change_n_2333284.html?utm_hp_ref=technology> (accessed 20 January 2013).

Ellis, K. and Kent, M. 2013, *Disability and New Media*, Routledge, New York.

Elmer, G. 2010, 'Locative networking: Finding and being found', *Aether: The Journal of Media Geography*, vol. 5A, pp. 18–26.

Emerson, C. 2006, *Vital Signs, Vibrant Society: Securing Australia's Economic and Social Wellbeing*, UNSW Press, Sydney.

Ergas, H. 2008, *Wrong Number: Resolving Australia's Telecommunications Impasse*, Allen & Unwin, Sydney.

Ernesto 2012, 'Game of Thrones Most Pirated TV-Show of 2012', *Torrentfreak*, 23 December, <http://torrentfreak.com/game-of-thrones-most-pirated-tv-show-of-2012-121223> (accessed 20 January 2013).

Errington, W. and Miragliotta, N. 2012, *Media & Politics: An Introduction*, 2nd ed., Oxford University Press, Melbourne.

Este, J. 2008, 'Is going private the answer to media woes?' *Crikey*, 9 September.

Evans, P. 2012, *Asia—Mobile Operators*, 10th ed., Buddecom, Bucketty, NSW.

Ewing, S. and Thomas, J, 'CCi digital futures 2012: The internet in Australia', 1 September,

<http://ssrn.com/abstract=2144214> (accessed 20 November 2012).

Fairchild, C. 2008, *Pop Idols and Pirates: Mechanisms of Consumption and the Global Circulation of Music*, Ashgate, Aldershot.

Fallows, J. 2010, 'How to save the news', *The Atlantic*, June.

Farman, J. 2011, *Mobile Interface Theory*, Routledge, London.

Featherstone, M. and Burrows, R. (eds) 1995, *Cyberspace, Cyberbodies, Cyberpunk: Cultures of Technological Embodiment*, Routledge, London.

Federal Communications Commission, Office of Plans and Policy (FCC) 1997, *Digital Tornado: The Internet and Telecommunications Policy*, OPP Working Paper Series, no. 29, FCC, Washington, <www.fcc.gov/Bureaus/OPP/working_papers/oppwp29.pdf>.

Finkelstein, R. (assisted by M. Ricketson) 2012, *Report of the Independent Inquiry into the Media and Media Regulation*, Report to the Minister for Broadband, Communications and the Digital Economy, Commonwealth Government, Canberra.

Fiske, J. 1989, *Understanding Popular Culture*, Unwin Hyman, London.

Fiske, J., Hodge, B. and Turner, G. 1987, *Myths of Oz*, Allen & Unwin, Sydney.

Fleischer, R. 2008, 'The future of copyright', *Cato Unbound*, 9 June, <www.cato-unbound.org/2008/06/09/rasmus-fleischer/the-future-of-copyright> (accessed 20 November 2012).

Fletcher, P. 2009, *Wired Brown Land? The Battle for Broadband*, UNSW Press, Sydney.

Flew, T. 1995, 'Images of nation: Economic and cultural aspects of Australian content regulations for commercial television', in J. Craik, J.J. Bailey and A. Moran (eds), *Public Voices, Private Interests: Australia's Media Policy*, Allen & Unwin, Sydney, pp. 73–85.

—— 1998, 'From censorship to policy: Rethinking media censorship and classification', *Media International Australia*, no. 88, pp. 89–98.

—— 2005, 'The social contract and beyond in broadcast media policy', *Television and New Media*, vol. 6, no. 2, pp. 247–70.

—— 2007, *Understanding Global Media*, Palgrave Macmillan, Houndmills.

—— 2009, 'The cultural economy moment?', *Cultural Science*, vol. 2, no. 1, <http://cultural-science.org/journal/index.php/culturalscience/article/viewArticle/23/79> (Accessed 20 November 2012).

—— 2012, *The Convergent Media Policy Moment*, Institute for Culture and Society Occasional Paper 3(3), <www.uws.edu.au/__data/assets/pdf_file/0004/396373/ICS_Occasional_Paper_Series_3_3_Flew_Final.pdf> (accessed 20 February 2013).

Flew, T., Cunningham, S., Bruns, A. and Wilson, J. 2008, 'Social innovation, user-created content and the future of the ABC and SBS as public service media', submission to ABC and SBS Review, Department of Broadband, Communications and the Digital Economy, 12 December.

Forde, H., Meadows, M. and Foxwell, K. 2002, *Culture, Commitment, Community: The Australian Community Radio Sector*, Griffith University, Brisbane.

Franklin, B. 2008, *Pulling Newspapers Apart: Analysing Print Journalism*, Routledge, London.

Fransman, M. 2002, *Telecoms in the Internet Age: From Boom to Bust to . . . ?*, Oxford University Press, Oxford.

Frasca, G. 2003, 'Simulation versus narrative: Introduction to ludology', in B. Perron and M. Wolf (eds), *The Video Game Theory Reader*, Routledge, London.

Freedman, D. 2008, *The Politics of Media Policy*, Polity Press, London.

Frith, S. 2002, 'Illegality and the music industry', in M. Talbot (ed.), *The Business of Music*, Liverpool University Press, Liverpool, pp. 195–216.

Frow, J. and Morris, M. (eds) 1993, *Australian Cultural Studies: A Reader*, Allen & Unwin, Sydney.

Gamson, J. 1994, *Claims to Fame: Celebrity in Contemporary America*, University of California Press, Berkeley, CA.

Garfinkel, H. 1967, *Studies in Ethnomethodology*, Prentice-Hall, Englewood Cliffs, NJ.

Garlick, M. 2012, 'Facebook's data use policy response', letter to Australian Privacy Commissioner, 30 July.

Garnham, N. 1979, 'Contribution to a political economy of mass communication', *Media, Culture and Society*, vol. 1, no. 2, pp. 123–46.

Garofalo, R. 2003, 'I want my MP3: Who owns internet music?' in M. Cloonan and R. Garofalo (eds), *Policing Pop*, Temple University Press, Philadelphia, PA.

Gazzard, A. 2011, 'Location, location, location: Collecting space and place in mobile media', *Convergence: The International Journal of Research into New Media Technologies*, vol. 17, no. 4, pp. 405–17.

Geffen, S. 2012, 'Amanda Palmer "can't afford" to pay her backing band', *Prefix*, <www.prefixmag.com/news/amanda-palmer-cant-afford-to-pay-her-backup-band/69017> (accessed 20 February 2013).

Gibson, C. 2007, 'Music festivals: Transformations in non-metropolitan places and in creative work', *Media International Australia*, no. 123, pp. 65–81.

Gibson, C. and Connell, J. 2012, *Music Festivals and Regional Development in Australia*, Ashgate, Aldershot.

Giddens, A. (ed.) 1974, *Positivism and Sociology*, Heinemann, London.

—— 1991, *Modernity and Self-Identity: Self and Society in the Late Modern Age*, Polity Press, Cambridge.

—— 2001, *The Global Third Way Debate*, Polity Press, Malden.

—— 2002, *Where Now for New Labour?* Blackwell, Malden, MA.

Gilles, J. and Cailliau, R. 2000, *How the Web was Born: The Story of the World Wide Web*, Oxford University Press, Oxford.

Gillespie, M. 1995, *Television, Ethnicity and Cultural Change*, Routledge, London.

Gillespie, T. 2010, 'The politics of platforms', *New Media & Society*, vol. 12, no. 3, pp. 347–64.

Given, J. 2003, *Turning Off the Television: Broadcasting's Uncertain Future*, UNSW Press, Sydney.

—— 2010, 'We're all tech heads now', *Inside Story*, 23 August, <http://inside.org.au/we-are-all-tech-heads-now> (accessed 1 March 2013).

Glance, D. 2011, '#QantasLuxury: A Qantas social media disaster in pyjamas', *The Conversation*, 23 November, <http://theconversation.edu.au/qantasluxury-a-qantas-social-media-disaster-in-pyjamas-4421> (accessed 20 December 2012).

Goc, N. and Tynan, L. 2008, 'Ethics in communication', in J. Bainbridge, N. Goc and J. Tynan (eds), *Media and Journalism: New Approaches to Theory and Practice*, Oxford University Press, Melbourne.

Goffman, E. 1959, *The Presentation of Self in Everyday Life*, Doubleday, New York.

—— 1979, *Gender Advertisements*, Macmillan, London.

Goggin, G. 2003, 'Digital rainbows: Inventing the internet in northern New South Wales', in H. Wilson (ed.), *Belonging in the Rainbow Region*, Southern Cross University Press, Lismore, pp. 227–46.

—— 2004a, 'Antipodean internet: Placing Australian networks', in G. Goggin (ed.), *Virtual*

Nation: The Internet in Australia, UNSW Press, Sydney, pp. 1–12.

—— 2004b, 'Net acceleration: The advent of everyday internet', in G. Goggin (ed.), *Virtual Nation: The Internet in Australia*, UNSW Press, Sydney, pp. 55–70.

—— (ed.) 2004c, *Virtual Nation: The Internet in Australia*, UNSW Press, Sydney.

—— 2006, 'Cool phone: Nokia, networks, and identity', in G. Goggin (ed.), *Cell Phone Culture: Mobile Technology in Everyday Life*, Routledge, Abingdon, pp. 41–62

—— 2006, *Cell Phone Culture: Mobile Technology in Everyday Life*, Routledge, New York.

—— 2012a, 'The eccentric career of mobile television', *International Journal of Digital Television*, vol. 3, no. 2, pp. 119–40.

—— 2012b, 'The evolution of Australian mobile screens: New technology, new formats, new business models', *Studies in Australasian Cinema*, vol. 6, no. 3, pp. 263–77.

Goggin, G. and Crawford, K. 2010, 'Moveable types: The emergence of mobile social media in Australia', *Media Asia Journal*, no. 37, pp. 224–31.

Goggin, G. and Gregg, M. (eds) 2007, 'Wireless cultures and technologies', special issue of *Media International Australia*, no. 126.

Goggin, G. and McLelland, M. (eds) 2009, *Internationalizing Internet Studies: Beyond Anglophone Paradigms*, Routledge, New York.

Golder, S. and Macy, M. 2011, 'Diurnal and seasonal mood vary with work, sleep, and daylength across diverse cultures', *Science*, vol. 333, no. 6051, pp. 1878–81.

Goldsworthy, A. 2013, *Unfinished Business: Sex Freedom and Misogyny: Quarterly Essay* 50, Melbourne.

Goodall, H. 1990, *Racism, Cultural Pluralism and the Media: A Report to the Office of Multicultural Affairs*, Department of Prime Minister and Cabinet, Office of Multicultural Affairs, Canberra.

Good Universities Guide 2009, Hobsons Australia, Melbourne.

—— 2013, Hobsons Australia, Melbourne.

Google Inc v ACCC, 2013, HCA 1, 6 February.

Google Street View 2013, 'Privacy', <www.google.com/help/maps/streetview/privacy.html> (accessed 13 January 2013).

Goolsby, R. 2010, 'Social media as crisis platform: The future of community maps/crisis maps', *ACM Transactions on Intelligent Systems and Technology*, vol. 1, no. 1, <http://doi.acm.org/10.1145/1858948.1858955> (accessed 4 January 2012).

Goot, M. 1979, *Newspaper Circulation in Australia, 1932–1977*, Centre for the Study of Educational Communication and Media, La Trobe University, Melbourne.

Gordon, E. and de Souza e Silva, A. 2011, *Net Locality*, Wiley-Blackwell, London.

Gould, E. 2012, 'Talk radio and the open-line: A history of commercial talkback radio in Australia', PhD thesis, Macquarie University.

Grant, A. and Howarth, D. (ed) 2011, *Australian Telecommunications Regulation*, 4th ed., CCH Australia, Sydney.

Gray, J. and Lotz, A.D. 2012, *Television Studies*, Polity Press, Cambridge.

Green, J. 2001, 'More Than TV: Channel Ten and diversity in free-to-air broadcasting', *Media International Australia*, no. 100, pp. 49–63.

—— 2008, 'Why do they call it TV when it's not on the box? "New" television services and old television functions', *Media International Australia*, no. 126, pp. 95–105.

Green, L. 2001, *Technoculture: From Alphabet to Cybersex*, Allen & Unwin, Sydney.

—— 2003, 'The new "others": Media and society post-September 11', *Media International Australia*, no. 109, pp. 7–13.

—— 2009, *The Internet: An Introduction to New Media*, Berg, London.

Greenacre, J. 2012, 'Say goodbye to the branch—the future for banking is upwardly mobile', *The Conversation*, 19 October, <http://theconversation.edu.au/say-goodbye-to-the-branch-the-future-for-banking-is-upwardly-mobile-10191> (accessed 20 November 2012).

Greenfield, S. and Osborn, G. 2003, 'Remote control: Legal censorship of the creative process', in M. Cloonan and R. Garofalo (eds), *Policing Pop*, Temple University Press, Philadelphia, PA.

Greenslade, R. 2003, *Press Gang: How Newspapers Make Profits from Propaganda*, Pan Books, London.

Gregg, M. 2012, *Work's Intimacy*, Polity Press, Cambridge.

Gregg, M. and Wilson, J. 2011, *Willunga Connects: A Baseline Study of pre-NBN Willunga*, Department of Further Education, Employment, Science and Technology, Government of South Australia, Adelaide.

Griffen-Foley, B. 2003, *Party Games: Australian Politicians and the Media from War to Dismissal*, Text, Melbourne.

—— 2004, 'From the Murrumbidgee to Mamma Lena: Foreign-language broadcasting on Australian commercial radio', unpublished Australian & New Zealand Communication Association conference paper, University of Sydney.

—— 2009, *Changing Stations: The Story of Australian Commercial Radio*, UNSW Press, Sydney.

Habermas, J. 1989, *The Structural Transformation of the Public Sphere*, trans. T. Burger and F. Lawrence, MIT Press, Cambridge, MA.

Haddon, L. 1999, 'The development of interactive games', in H. Mackay and T. O'Sullivan (eds), *The Media Reader: Continuity and Transformation*, Sage, London, pp. 305–27.

——2004, *Information and Communication Technologies in Everyday Life: A Concise Introduction and Research Guide*, Berg, New York.

Hadju, D. 2008, 'Fans transfixed by the remix', *The Australian*, 20 June, <www.theaustralian.news.com.au/story/0,25197,23890642-16947,00.html> (accessed 20 November 2012).

Hakatte.jp 2012, Website, <http://hakatte.jp> (accessed 15 October 2012).

Hall, S. 1973, *Encoding and Decoding in the Television Discourse*, Centre for Contemporary Cultural Studies, University of Birmingham, Birmingham.

—— 1992, 'The question of cultural identity', in S. Hall and T. McGrew (eds), *Modernity and Its Futures*, Polity Press, Cambridge, pp. 274–316.

—— 1997a, 'The work of representation', in S. Hall, *Representation: Cultural Representations and Signifying Practices*, Sage, London, pp. 13–64.

—— 1997b, *Representation: Cultural Representations and Signifying Practices*, Sage, London.

Hall, S., Hobson, D., Lowe, A. and Willis, P. (eds) 1980, *Culture, Media, Language: Working Papers in Cultural Studies, 1972–79*, Hutchinson, London.

Halliday, J. 2011, 'Government backs down on plan to shut Twitter and Facebook in crises', *The Guardian*, 25 August 2011, <www.guardian.co.uk/media/2011/aug/25/government-plan-shut-twitter-facebook> (accessed 15 October 2012).

Halsbury's Laws of Australia 2004, vol. 18, 275 Media and Communications, Broadcasting Services, 15 June.

Hansen, A. 2010, *Environment, Media and Communication*, Routledge, London.

Harcourt, E. 1987, *Taming the Tyrant: The First Hundred Years of Australia's International Communication Services*, Allen & Unwin, Sydney.

Harding, S. 2010, *Centre for Policy Development Issue Brief: Media Ownership and Regulation in Australia*, <http://cpd.org.au/wp-content/uploads/2011/11/Centre_for_Policy_Development_Issue_Brief.pdf> (accessed 20 November 2012).

Harrington, S., Highfield, T. and Bruns, A. 2012, 'More than a backchannel: Twitter and television', in J.M. Noguera (ed.), *Audience Interactivity and Participation*, COST Action ISO906 Transforming Audiences, Transforming Societies, Brussels.

Hartley, J. 1992, *Tele-ology: Studies in Television*, Routledge, London.

—— 1993a, 'Invisible fictions', in J. Frow and M. Morris (eds), *Australian Cultural Studies: A Reader*, Allen & Unwin, Sydney.

—— 1993b, *The Politics of Pictures*, Routledge, London.

—— 1996, *Popular Reality: Journalism, Modernity, Popular Culture*, Edward Arnold, London.

—— 1999, *Uses of Television*, Routledge, London.

—— 2012, *Digital Futures for Cultural and Media Studies*, Wiley-Blackwell, Malden, MA.

Harvey, D. 2001, *Spaces of Capital: Towards a Critical Geography*, Routledge, New York.

Hawke, J. 1995, 'Privatising the Public Interest: The Public and the *Broadcasting Services Act 1992*', in J. Craik, J.J. Bailey and A. Moran (eds), *Public Voices, Private Interests: Australia's Media Policy*, Allen & Unwin, Sydney, pp. 33–50.

Hawkins, G. 1996, 'SBS: Minority television', *Culture and Policy*, vol. 7, no. 1, pp. 45–64.

—— 2010, 'Public service media in Australia: Governing diversity', in P. Iosifidis (ed.), *Reinventing Public Service Communication: European Broadcasters and Beyond*, Palgrave Macmillan, Basingstoke.

—— 2013, 'Enacting public value on the ABC's *Q&A:* From normative to performative approaches', *Media International Australia*, no. 146, pp. 82–92.

Herd, N. 2012, *Networking: Commercial Television in Australia—A History*, Currency House, Sydney.

Herman, E. and Chomsky, N. 1988, *Manufacturing Consent: The Political Economy of the Mass Media*, Pantheon, New York.

Hermida, A. 2012, 'Social journalism: Exploring how social media is shaping journalism', in E. Siapera and A. Veglis (eds), *The Handbook of Global Online Journalism*, Wiley-Blackwell, Malden, MA, pp. 309–28.

Herzog, H. 1941, 'On borrowed experience: An analysis of listening to daytime sketches', *Studies in Philosophy and Social Science*, vol. 9, pp. 65–93.

Hesmondhalgh, D. 2007, *The Cultural Industries*, 2nd ed., Sage, London.

Hibberd, J. 2013, '*Game of Thrones* early DVD sales breaking HBO records', *Inside TV*, 22 February, <http://insidetv.ew.com/2013/02/22/game-of-thrones-dvd-sales-breaking-hbo-records> (accessed 30 March 2013).

Hickey-Moody, A. and Wood, D. 2008, 'Virtually sustainable: Deleuze and desiring differentiation in *Second Life*', *Continuum*, vol. 22, no. 6, pp. 805–16.

Hill, A. 2005, *Reality TV: Audiences and Popular Factual Entertainment*, Routledge, London.

Hirst, M. and Patching, R. 2005, *Journalism Ethics: Arguments and Cases*, Oxford University Press, Melbourne.

Hjorth, L. 2007, 'The game of being mobile: One media history of gaming and mobile technologies in Asia-Pacific', *Convergence: The International Journal of Research into New Media Technologies*, Gaming special issue, vol. 13, no. 4, pp. 369–81.

—— 2009, *Mobile Media in the Asia Pacific: Gender and the Art of Being Mobile*, Routledge, London.

—— 2010, *Games & Gaming*, Berg, London.

Hjorth, L., Burgess, J. and Richardson, I. (eds) 2012, *Studying Mobile Media: Cultural Technologies, Mobile Communication, and the iPhone*, Routledge, New York.

Hjorth, L. and Chan, D. (eds) 2009, *Games of Locality: Gaming Cultures and Place in the Asia-Pacific*, Routledge, London.

Hjorth, L. and Richardson, I. 2009, 'The waiting game: Complicating notions of (tele)presence and gendered distraction in casual mobile gaming', *Australian Journal of Communication*, special issue: 'Placing Mobile Communication' (eds) G. Goggin, C. Lloyd and S. Rickard, vol 36, no 1, pp. 23–35.

—— (2010) 'Playing the waiting game: Complicated notions of (tele)presence and gendered distraction in casual mobile gaming', in H. Greif, L. Hjorth, A. Lasén and C. Lobet-Maris (eds), *Cultures of Participation: Media Practices, Politics and Literacy*, Peter Lang, Berlin, pp. 111–25.

Holgersson, T. 2012, 'Do free apps really account for 89% of all downloads?' *Mobile Trends*, 17 September, <http://ebctyho.blogspot.com.au/2012/09/do-free-apps-really-account-for-89-of.html> (accessed 24 April 2013).

Homan, S. 2003, *The Mayor's a Square: Live Music and Law and Order in Sydney*, Local Consumption, Sydney.

—— 2007, 'Classic hits in a digital era: Music radio and the Australian music industry', *Media International Australia*, no. 123, pp. 95–108.

—— 2008, 'Introduction: Locating Australian popular music', in S. Homan and T. Mitchell (eds) *Sounds of Then, Sounds of Now: Popular Music in Australia*, ACYS, Hobart, pp. 1–18.

—— 2010a, 'Dancing without music: Copyright and Australian nightclubs', *Popular Music and Society*, vol. 33, no. 3, pp. 377–93.

—— 2010b, 'Governmental as anything: Live music and law and order in Melbourne', *Perfect Beat*, vol. 11, no. 2, pp. 103–18.

Homan, S., Cloonan, M. and Cattermole, J. 2013, *Popular Music Industries and the State: Policy Notes*, Routledge, London.

Homan, S. and Mitchell, T. (eds) 2007, *Sounds of Then, Sounds of Now: Popular Music in Australia*, ACYS, Hobart.

Horky, T. and Nieland, J.-U. 2011, *First Results of the International Sports Press Survey*, <www.playthegame.org/fileadmin/image/PTG2011/Presentation/PTG_Nieland-Horky_ISPS_2011_3.10.2011_final.pdf> (accessed 20 November 2012).

Hough, A. 2010, 'Please Rob Me website causes fury for "telling burglars when Twitter users are not home"', *Telegraph*, 19 February, <www.telegraph.co.uk/technology/twitter/7266120/Please-Rob-Me-website-tells-burglars-when-Twitter-users-are-not-home.html> (accessed 20 November 2012).

Howard, P. and Hussain, M. 2013, *Democracy's Fourth Wave? Digital Media and the Arab Spring*, Oxford University Press, New York.

Hughes, A.L. and Palen, L. 2009, 'Twitter Adoption and Use in Mass Convergence and Emergency Events', *International Journal of Emergency Management*, vol. 6, nos 3–4, pp. 248–60.

Huber, A. 2007, 'Top 40 in Australia: Popular music and the mainstream', in S. Homan and T. Mitchell (eds), *Sounds of Then, Sounds of Now: Popular Music in Australia*, ACYS, Hobart, pp. 271–88.

—— 2004, *Isma—Listen: National Consultations on Eliminating Prejudice Against Arab and Muslim Australians*, Human Rights and Equal Opportunity Commission, Sydney.

Human Rights and Equal Opportunity Commission (HREOC) 1991, *Racist Violence: Report of the National Inquiry into Racist Violence in Australia*, AGPS, Canberra.

—— 2004, *A Last Resort? Report of the National Inquiry into Children in Immigration Detention*, AGPS, Canberra.

Humphreys, S. 2009, 'Computer games: Co-creation and regulation', *Media International Australia*, no. 130, pp. 50-2.

Hunt, A. and Wickham, G. 1994, *Foucault and Law: Towards a Sociology of Law as Governance*, Pluto Press, Sydney.

Hutchins, B. and Rowe, D. 2012, *Sport Beyond Television: The Internet, Digital Media and the Rise of Networked Media Sport*, Routledge, New York.

International Federation of the Phonographic Industry (IFPI) 2008, *IFPI Digital Music Report 2008*, <www.ifpi.org/content/section_statistics/index.html> (accessed 20 October 2012).

International Federation of the Phonographic Industry (IFPI) 2012, *Digital Music Report 2012*, <www.ifpi.org> (accessed 20 February 2013).

Independent Inquiry into the Media and Media Regulation 2012, *Report of the Independent Inquiry into the Media and Media Regulation*, Department of Broadband, Communications and the Digital Economy, Canberra.

Ingham, D. and Weedon, A. 2008, 'Time well spent: The magazine publishing industry's online niche', *Convergence*, vol. 14, no. 2, pp. 205-20.

Inglis, F. 2010, *A Short History of Celebrity*, Princeton University Press, Princeton, NJ.

Inglis, K. 1983, *This is the ABC: The Australian Broadcasting Commission 1932–1983*, Melbourne University Press, Melbourne.

—— 2006, *Whose ABC? The Australian Broadcasting Corporation 1983–2006*, Black Inc., Melbourne.

Instagram 2012, 'Privacy and terms of service changes on Instagram', *Instagram Blog*, <http://blog.instagram.com/post/38143346554/privacy-and-terms-of-service-changes-on-instagram> (accessed 20 January 2013).

International Federation of the Phonographic Industry 2004, 'Report summary', <www.ifpi.org/ site-content/statistics/worldsales.html> (accessed 20 November 2012).

—— 2008, *IFPI Digital Music Report 2008*, <www.ifpi.org/content/section_statistics/index.html> (accessed 20 November 2012).

—— 2012, *Digital Music Report 2012*, <www.ifpi.org> (accessed 16 January 2013).

International Game Developers Association (IGDA) 2012, Website, <www.igda.org> (accessed 20 November 2012).

Iosifidis, P. 2011, 'The public sphere, social networks and public service media', *Information, Communication, & Society*, vol. 14, no. 5, pp. 619-37.

Ito, M. 2003, 'Mobiles and the appropriation of place', *Receiver*, no. 8, <http://academic.evergreen.edu/curricular/evs/readings/itoShort.pdf> (accessed 20 November 2012).

Jacka, E. 1990, *The ABC of Drama 1975–1990*, AFTRS, Sydney.

—— 1994, 'Researching audiences: A dialogue between cultural studies and social sciences', *Media Information Australia*, no. 73, pp. 93-8.

—— 2006, 'The future of public broadcasting', in S. Cunningham and G. Turner (eds), *The Media and Communications in Australia*, 4th ed., pp. 344–56, Allen & Unwin, Sydney.

Jacka, E. and Green, L. (eds) 2003, 'The new "others": Media and society post-September 11', special edition of *Media International Australia*, no. 109.

Jackson, R., Stanton, M. and Underwood, R. 1995, 'The portrayal of Aboriginal people in West Australian newspapers: Less than a lily-white record', paper presented to Australian and New Zealand Communication Association National Conference, Perth, July.

Jackson, S. 2008, 'Gossip magazines hit hardest in slide', *The Australian*, 17 November, p. 32.

—— 2012, 'ACP owner Yvonne Bauer shuns publicity despite high-profile media role', *The Australian*, 5 September.

Jackson, S. and Andrews, D. (eds) 2005, *Sport, Culture and Advertising: Identities, Commodities and the Politics of Representation*, Routledge, London.

Jakubowicz, A.H. 1987, '*Days of Our Lives*: Multiculturalism, mainstreaming and "special" broadcasting', *Media Information Australia*, no. 45, pp. 18–32.

Jakubowicz, A., Goodall, H., Martin, J., Mitchell, T., Randall, L. and Seneviratne, K. 1994, *Racism, Ethnicity and the Media*, Allen & Unwin, Sydney.

Jakubowicz, A. and Newell, K. 1995, 'Which world? Whose/who's home? Special broadcasting in the Australian communication alphabet', in J. Craik, J.J. Bailey and A. Moran (eds), *Public Voices, Private Interests: Australia's Media Policy*, Allen & Unwin, Sydney, pp. 130–45.

Javes, S. 2003, 'The light's on but nobody's home', *Sydney Morning Herald*, The Guide, 13 October, pp. 4–5.

—— 2008, 'Up late for the latest', *Sydney Morning Herald*, The Guide, 29 September, p. 5.

Jay, M. 1974, *The Dialectical Imagination: A History of the Frankfurt School and the Institute of Social Research*, 1923–1950, Heinemann, London.

Jenkins, H. 1992, *Textual Poachers: Television Fans and Participatory Culture*, Routledge, London.

—— 2006a, *Fans, Bloggers, and Gamers, Essays on Participatory Culture*, New York University Press, New York.

—— 2006b, *Convergence Culture: Where Old and New Media Collide*, New York University Press, New York.

Jenkins, H. and Cassell, J. 1997, *From Barbie to Mortal Kombat*, MIT Press, Cambridge, Mass.

Jenkins. H. with K. Clinton, R. Purushotma, A.J. Robison and M. Weigel 2006, *Confronting the Challenges of Participatory Culture: Media Education for the 21st Century*, Macarthur Foundation, <www.digitallearning.macfound.org/atf/cf/%7B7E45C7E0-A3E0-4B89-AC9C-E807E1B0AE4E%7D/JENKINS_WHITE_PAPER.PDF> (accessed 20 February 2013).

Jericho, G. 2013, 'Grab some popcorn, we're doing fine', *The Drum Opinion*, 30 January, <www.abc.net.au/unleashed/4489102.html> (accessed 20 February 2013).

Jhally, S. 2006, *The Spectacle of Accumulation: Essays in Culture, Media, and Politics*, Peter Lang, New York.

Johansson, D. 2008, 'The future of private copying', *Digital Renaissance*, 27 March, <www.digitalrenaissance.se/2008/03/27/the-future-of-private-copying>.

Johnson, B. 2000, *The Inaudible Music: Jazz, Gender & Australian Modernity*, Currency Press, Sydney.

Jolly, R. 2012, *Media Reviews: All Sound and Fury?*, Parliamentary Library Background Note, Parliament of Australia, Department of Parliamentary Services, <www.aph.gov.au/About_Parliament/Parliamentary_Departments/Parliamentary_Library/pubs/BN/2012-2013/MediaReviews>.

Jones, S. (ed) 1997, *Virtual Culture: Identity and Communication in Cybersociety*, Sage, Thousand Oaks, CA.

—— (ed.) 2007, *Cybersociety*, Sage, Thousand Oaks, CA.

Jonker, E. 1992, 'Contemporary music and commercial radio', *Media Information Australia*, no. 64, pp. 24–30.

Jowett, G. and O'Donnell, V. 1992, *Propaganda and Persuasion*, 2nd ed., Sage, Newbury Park, CA.

Jungnickel, K. 2013, *WiFi Makers: An Ethnography of a Wireless Digital Culture*, Palgrave, Basingstoke.

Juul, J. 2006, *Half-Real: Video Games Between Real Rules And Fictional Worlds*, MIT Press, Cambridge, MA.

—— 2009, *A Casual Revolution: Reinventing Video Games and Their Players*, MIT Press, Cambridge, MA.

Kaplan, A. and Haenlein, M. 2010, 'Users of the world, unite! The challenges and opportunities of social media', *Business Horizons*, vol. 53, no. 1, pp. 59–68.

Karaganis, J. (ed.) 2011, *Media Piracy in Emerging Economies*, Social Sciences Research Council, Washington, DC.

Kennedy, H. 2002, 'Lara Croft: Feminist icon or cyberbimbo? On the limits of textual analysis', *Game Studies*, vol. 2, no. 2, <www.gamestudies.org/0202/kennedy> (accessed 20 November 2012).

Kenyon, A. 2007, *TV Futures: Digital Television Policy in Australia*, Melbourne University Press, Melbourne.

Kickstarter 2012, 'Amanda Palmer: The new record, art book, and tour', <www.kickstarter.com/projects/amandapalmer/amanda-palmer-the-new-record-art-book-and-tour?ref=most-funded> (accessed 20 February 2013).

Klocker, N. and Dunn, K. 2003, 'Who's driving the asylum debate? Newspaper and government representations of asylum seekers', *Media International Australia*, no. 109, pp. 71–92.

Kohler, A. 2008, 'Newspapers are the new vinyl', *Crikey*, 8 October.

Kompare, D. 2006, 'Publishing flow: DVD box sets and the reconception of television', *Television and New Media*, vol. 7, no. 4, pp. 335–60.

Korporaal, G. 2009, *AARNET: 20 Years of the Internet in Australia*, AARNET, Sydney, <http://mirror.aarnet.edu.au/pub/aarnet/AARNet_20YearBook_Full.pdf> (accessed 20 January 2013).

Kücklich, J. 2005, 'Precarious *Playbour*: Modders and the digital games industry', *Fibreculture Journal*, no. 5, <http://journal.fibreculture.org/issue5/kucklich.html> (accessed 23 July 2008).

Laing, D. 2003, 'Copyright', in *Continuum Encyclopedia of Popular Music of the World*, vol. 1, pp. 480–5.

Laird, R. 1999, *Sound Beginnings: The Early Record Industry in Australia*, Currency Press, Sydney.

Lange, P. 2007, 'Publicly private and privately public: Social networking on YouTube', *Journal of Computer-Mediated Communication*, vol. 13, no. 1, Article 18, <http://jcmc.indiana.edu/vol13/issue1/lange.html (accessed 20 November 2012).

Latour, B. 1987, *Science in Action: How to Follow Scientists and Engineers Through Society*, Harvard University Press, Cambridge, MA.

Lawe Davies, C. 1998, 'SBS and its amazing world', *Media International Australia*, no. 89, pp. 89–108.

Lawson, A. 2002, '*Big Brother*, Big Business', *The Age Green Guide*, 28 June, pp. 8–9.

Le Masurier, M. 2012, 'Independent magazines and the rejuvenation of print', *International Journal of Cultural Studies*, vol. 15, no. 4, pp. 383–98.

Lester, L. 2007, *Giving Ground: Media and Environmental Conflict in Tasmania*, Quintus, Hobart.

—— 2010, *Media and Environment: Conflict, Politics and the News*, Polity Press, Cambridge.

—— 2013, 'On flak, balance and activism: The ups and downs of environmental journalism', in S. Tanner and N. Richardson (eds), *Investigative Journalism in the Digital Age*, Oxford University Press, Melbourne, pp. 221–232.

Lester, L. and Cottle, S. 2009, 'Visualizing climate change: Television news and ecological citizenship', *International Journal of Communication*, no. 3, pp. 17–26.

Lester, L. and Hutchins, B. 2012, 'The power of the unseen: Environmental conflict, the media and invisibility', *Media, Culture & Society*, vol. 34, no. 7, pp. 832–46.

Leveson, Lord Justice Brian 2012, *An Inquiry into the Culture, Practices and Ethics of the Press: Report*, <www.levesoninquiry.org.uk> (accessed 20 February 2013).

Levin, J. 2009, 'An industry perspective: Calibrating the velocity of change', in J. Holt and A. Perren (eds), *Media Industries: History, Theory and Method*, Wiley-Blackwell, Malden, MA, pp. 256–63.

Levinson, P. 1999, *Digital McLuhan: A Guide to the Information Millennium*, Routledge, New York.

Liberal–National Coalition 2013, 'The Coalition's plan for fast broadband and an affordable NBN', Liberal Party, Canberra.

Lim, S.S. 2006, 'From cultural to information revolution: ICT domestication by middle-class Chinese families', in T. Berker, M. Hartmann, Y. Punie and K. Ward (eds), *Domestication of Media and Technology*, McGraw-Hill, Maidenhead, pp. 185–201.

Live Music Working Group 2001, *Live Music in South Australia*, report prepared for the South Australian Minister for Transport and Urban Planning, Adelaide.

Live Performance Australia 2011, *Ticket Attendance and Revenue Survey 2010*, <www.liveperformance.com.au/site/_content/document/00000184-source.pdf> (accessed 20 November 2012).

Livingstone, S. 2004, 'The challenge of changing audiences: Or, what is the audience researcher to do in the age of the internet?', *European Journal of Communication*, vol. 19, no. 1, pp. 75–86.

Local, The 2008, 'Newspapers see sales and ad revenue climb', 2 June.

Lohrey, A. 2002, *Groundswell: The Rise of The Greens: Quarterly Essay*, no. 8, pp. 1-86.

Lovink, G. 2002, *Dark Fibre: Tracking Critical Internet Culture*, MIT Press, Cambridge, MA.

—— 2003, *My First Recession: Critical Internet Culture in Transition*, V2_NAI, Rotterdam.

—— 2007, *Zero Comments: Blogging and Critical Internet Culture*, Routledge, London.

Lowery, S.A. and de Fleur, M.L. 1983, *Milestones in Mass Communication Research*, Longman, New York.

Lucas, P. 1964, *The Constant Voice: Radio Australia*, Australian Broadcasting Commission, Sydney.

Luckman, S. 2008a, 'Music and the internet: File sharing, the iPod revolution and the industry of the future', in S. Homan and T. Mitchell (eds), *Sounds of Then, Sounds of Now: Popular Music in Australia*, ACYS, Hobart, pp. 181–98.

—— 2008b, 'Doof, dance and rave culture', in S. Homan and T. Mitchell (eds), *Sounds of Then, Sounds of Now: Popular Music in Australia*, ACYS, Hobart, pp. 131–50.

Luft, O. 2008, 'Rupert Murdoch: The internet won't destroy newspapers', *The Guardian*, 17 November.

Lumby, C. 1997, *Bad Girls: The Media, Sex and Feminism in the 90s*, Allen & Unwin, Sydney.

— 1999, *Gotcha: Life in a Tabloid World*, Allen & Unwin, Sydney.

— 2003, 'Real appeal: The ethics of reality TV', in C. Lumby and E. Probyn (eds), *Remote Control: New Media, New Ethics*, Cambridge University Press, Melbourne, pp. 18–38.

— 2008, 'Art, not porn. Or vice versa?' *Sunday Age*, 25 May.

— 2011, 'Doing it for themselves? Teenage girls, sexuality and fame', in S. Redmond and S. Holmes (eds), *A Reader in Stardom and Celebrity*, Sage, London, pp. 341–52.

Lunden, I. 2012, 'Free apps account for 89% of all downloads', *TechCrunch*, 11 September, <http://techcrunch.com/2012/09/11/free-apps> (accessed 24 April 2013)

Lunt, P. and Livingstone, S. 2012, *Media Regulation: Governance and the Interests of Citizens and Consumers*, Sage, London.

Machin, D. and van Leeuwen, T. 2003, 'Global schemas and local discourses in *Cosmopolitan*', *Journal of Sociolinguistics*, vol. 7, no. 4, pp. 493–512.

— 2007, *Global Media Discourse: A Critical Introduction*, Routledge, London.

Mackenzie, A. 2010, *Wirelessness: Radical Empiricism in Network Cultures*, MIT Press, Cambridge, MA.

MacKenzie, D. and Wajcman, J. (eds) 1999, *The Social Shaping of Technology: How the Refrigerator Got Its Hum*, 2nd ed., Open University Press, Milton Keynes.

MacLean, S. 2005, 'Stay tuned as the word spreads', *The Australian*, Media, 3 February, p. 17.

Macleay, J. 2000, 'Internet thrills the radio stars', *The Australian*, Media, 22 June, pp. 6–7.

Magazine, The 2000, 'Austar TV Guide', EMAP Contract and Austar Communications, November, p. 115.

Maguire, J. 1999, *Global Sport: Identities, Societies, Civilizations*, Polity Press, Cambridge.

Maguire, T. 2007, 'In the need of a little help from friends', *Daily Telegraph*, 3 June, p. 15.

Maniaty, T. 2003, 'That's not entertainment', *The Weekend Australian*, 16–17 August, p. 25.

Manning, P. 2004, *Dog Whistle Politics and Journalism: Reporting Arabic and Muslim People in Sydney Newspapers*, The Australian Centre for Independent Journalism, University of Technology, Sydney.

Maras, S. 2004, 'Thinking about the history of ANZCA: An Australian perspective', *Australian Journal of Communication*, vol. 31, no. 2, pp. 13–51.

Marcato, P. 2004, 'In exquisite stereo: A history of commercial FM radio in Australia', Bachelor of Media Studies Honours thesis, La Trobe University.

Marjoribanks, T. and Farquharson, K. 2012, *Sport and Society in the Global Age*, Palgrave Macmillan, Houndmills.

Marr, D. 2005, 'One-way radio plays by its own rules', *Sydney Morning Herald*, 13 December, <www.smh.com.au/news/national/oneway-radio-plays-by-its-own-rules/2005/12/12/1134236005956.html>.

Marshall, P.D. 1997, *Celebrity and Power: Fame in Contemporary Culture*, University of Minnesota Press, Minneapolis, MN.

— (ed.) 2006, *The Celebrity Culture Reader*, Routledge, London.

Martin, F. 2002, 'Beyond public service broadcasting? ABC Online and the user/citizen', *Southern Review: Communication, Politics and Culture*, vol. 35, no. 1, pp. 42–62.

Martin, I. 2013, Personal communications, 6 and 28 February.

Massey, D. 1993, 'Questions of locality', *Geography*, no. 78, pp. 142–9.

Masters, C. 2006, *Jonestown: The Power and the Myth of Alan Jones*, Allen & Unwin, Sydney.

Mattelart, A. 1991, *Advertising International*, Routledge, London.

Mattelart, A. and Siegelaub, S. (eds) 1983, *Communication and Class Struggle. Volume 1: Capitalism, Imperialism*, International General, New York.

Maxwell, I. 2003, *Phat Beats, Dope Rhymes: Hip Hop Down Under Comin' Upper*, Wesleyan University Press, Middletown, CT.

Maxwell, R. and Miller, T. 2012, *Greening the Media*, Oxford University Press, Oxford.

Mayer, H. 1964, *The Press in Australia*, Lansdowne Press, Melbourne.

Mäyrä, F. 2003, 'The city shaman dances with virtual wolves—researching pervasive mobile gaming', *receiver*, no. 12, <www.receiver.vodafone.com> (accessed 20 May 2005).

McChesney, R.W. 2008, The *Political Economy of Media: Enduring Issues, Emerging Dilemmas*, Monthly Review Press, New York.

McCutcheon, M. 2006, 'Is Pay TV meeting its promise?' PhD thesis, Murdoch University.

McFall, L. 2004, *Advertising: A Cultural Economy*, Sage, London.

McKee, A. 2001, *Australian Television: A Genealogy of Great Moments*, Oxford University Press, Melbourne.

—— 2003, *Textual Analysis: A Beginner's Guide*, Sage, Thousand Oaks, CA.

—— 2004, 'Is *Doctor Who* political?' *European Journal of Cultural Studies*, vol. 7, no. 2, pp. 223–59.

—— 2005, *The Public Sphere: An Introduction*, Cambridge University Press, Cambridge.

McKee, A., Albury, K. and Lumby, C. 2008, *The Porn Report*, Melbourne University Press, Melbourne.

McKinney, D. 2012, founder, Filter Squad. Interview with author, 19 October.

McKnight, D. 2012, *Rupert Murdoch: An Investigation of Political Power*, Allen & Unwin, Sydney.

McLeod, K. 2005, 'Confessions of an intellectual (property): Danger Mouse, Mickey Mouse, Sonny Bono and my long and winding path as a copyright activist-academic', *Popular Music and Society*, vol. 28, no. 1, pp. 79–93.

McNair, B. 1998, *The Sociology of Journalism*, Arnold, London.

McQuail, D. 2010, *McQuail's Mass Communication Theory*, 6th ed., Sage, London.

McQueen, H. 1977, *Australia's Media Monopolies*, Widescope, Melbourne.

Meade, A. 2008, 'Religion presenter Stephen Crittenden blasts ABC Radio National for cutting show', *The Australian*, 15 October.

Meadows, M. 1992, *A Watering Can in the Desert: Issues in Indigenous Broadcasting Policy in Australia*, Institute for Cultural Policy Studies, Griffith University, Brisbane.

Meikle, G. 2002, *Future Active: Media Activism and the Internet*, Routledge and Pluto Press, New York and Sydney.

Meikle, G. and Young, S. (eds) 2008, 'Beyond Broadcasting', special issue of *Media International Australia*, no. 126.

Mendoza, M., Poblete, B. and Castillo, C. 2010, 'Twitter under crisis: Can we trust what we RT?', paper presented to 1st Workshop on Social Media Analytics (SOMA '10), ACM, Washington, DC.

Mercer, C. 1994, 'Cultural policy: Research and the governmental imperative', *Media Information Australia*, no. 73.

Meyer, P. 2004, *The Vanishing Newspaper: Saving Journalism in the Information Age*, University of Missouri Press, London.

Michael, M.G. and Michael, K. 2010, 'Towards a State of Überveillence', *IEEE Technology and Society Magazine*, vol. 29, no. 2, pp. 9–16.

Michaels, E. 1986, *The Aboriginal Invention of Television in Central Australia, 1982–1985*, Australian Institute of Aboriginal Studies, Canberra.

Miller, D. 1987, *Material Culture and Mass Consumption*, Blackwell, London.

Miller, T. 1995, 'Striving for Difference: Commercial Radio Policy', in J. Craik, J.J. Bailey and A. Moran (eds), *Public Voices, Private Interests: Australia's Media Policy*, Allen & Unwin, Sydney, pp 86–100.

——2001, *Sportsex*, Temple University Press, Philadelphia, PA.

——2010, *Television Studies: The Basics*, Routledge, London.

Miller, T. and Turner, G. 2002, 'Radio', in S. Cunningham and G. Turner (eds), *The Media and Communications in Australia*, Allen & Unwin, Sydney.

Miller, T., Lawrence, G., McKay, J. and Rowe, D. 2001, *Globalisation and Sport: Playing the Field*, Sage, London.

Mills, C. Wright 1959, *The Sociological Imagination*, Oxford University Press, New York.

Mitchell, T. 2001, *Global Noise: Rap and Hip Hop Outside the USA*, Wesleyan University Press, Middletown, CT.

——2008a, 'Australian hip hop's multicultural literacies: A subculture emerges into the light', in S. Homan and T. Mitchell (eds), *Sounds of Then, Sounds of Now: Popular Music in Australia*, ACYS, Hobart, pp. 231–52.

——2008b, 'Culture and Economy', in T. Bennet and J. Frow (eds), *The Sage Handbook of Cultural Analysis*, Sage, London, pp. 447–66.

Molloy, B. 1990, *Before the Interval: Australian Mythology and Feature Films, 1930–1960*, University of Queensland Press, Brisbane.

Molloy, M. and Lennie, J. 1990, *Communication Studies in Australia: A Statistical Study of Teachers, Students and Courses in Australian Tertiary Institutions*, Communication Centre, Queensland University of Technology, Brisbane.

Montford, N. and Bogost, I. 2009, *Racing the Beam: The Atari Video Computer System*, MIT Press, Cambridge, MA.

Moores, S. 1993, *Interpreting Audiences: The Ethnography of Media Consumption*, Sage, London.

Moran, A. 1985, *Images and Industry: Television Drama Production in Australia*, Currency Press, Sydney.

Morley, D. 1980, *The 'Nationwide' Audience, Structure and Decoding*, British Film Institute, London.

—— 1992, *Television, Audiences, and Cultural Studies*, Routledge, New York.

——1999, 'Finding out about the world from television news: Some difficulties', in J. Gripsrud (ed.), *Television and Common Knowledge*, Routledge, London.

Mosco, V. 1996, *The Political Economy of Communication*, Sage, London.

Moyal, A. 1984, *Clear Across Australia: A History of Telecommunications*, Thomas Nelson, Melbourne.

Muir, I. 2012, Customer Experience Manager, Westpac, interview with Ben Goldsmith, 6 November.

Mulhern, F. 1979, *The Moment of 'Scrutiny'*, New Left Books, London.

Mulvey, L. 1975, 'Visual Pleasure and Narrative Cinema', *Screen*, vol. 16, no. 3, pp. 35–47.

—— 1989, *Visual and Other Pleasures*, Indiana University Press, Bloomington, IN.

Munster, A. 2009, 'The Henson photographs and the "network condition"', *Continuum—Journal of Media and Cultural Studies*, no. 23, pp. 3–12.

Murdock, G. and Golding, P. 1974, 'For a political economy of mass communication', in R. Miliband and J. Saville (eds), *Socialist Register*, Merlin Press, London.

Murphy, K. 2012, 'After a sudden, shocking event, it's time to connect again', *The Age*, 10 December, <www.smh.com.au/opinion/politics/after-a-sudden-shocking-event-its-time-to-connect-again-20121209-2b3en.html>.

Murray, S. (ed.) 1995, *Australian Film 1978–1994*, 2nd ed., Oxford University Press, Melbourne.

Mutter, A. 2011, 'Newspaper ad sales head to new low: $24B', *Reflections of a Newsosaur*, 5 December.

Myers, K. 1983, 'Understanding advertisers', in H. Davis and P. Walton (eds), *Language, Image, Media*, Basil Blackwell, Oxford, pp. 205–23.

Neuenfeldt, K. 2008, '"Ailan style": An overview of the contemporary music of Torres Strait islanders', in S. Homan and T. Mitchell (eds), *Sounds of Then, Sounds of Now: Popular Music in Australia*, ACYS, Hobart, pp. 167–80.

New Zealand Ministry of Business Innovation and Employment and Australian Department of Broadband, Communications and the Digital Economy 2013, *Trans-Tasman Roaming: Final Report*, New Zealand Government and Australian Government, Wellington and Canberra.

Nicoll, F. 2001, *From Diggers to Drag Queens: Configurations of Australian National Identity*, Pluto Press, Sydney.

Nielsen 2012, *State of the Media: The Social Media Report 2012*, <www.nielsen.com/us/en/reports/2012/state-of-the-media-the-social-media-report-2012.html> (accessed 20 March 2013).

Nielsen Online 2012a, 'Top twenty agency billings', *Mumbrella*, 9 March, <http://mumbrella.com.au/only-five-from-top-20-agencies-grow-as-media-market-shrinks-78341> (accessed 20 March 2013).

Nielsen Online 2012b, *Australian Online Landscape Review*, July, <www.nielsen.com/au/en/news-insights/press-room/2012/australian-online-landscape-review-july-2012.html> (accessed 20 March 2013).

Nielsen, R.K. 2012, *Ten Years That Shook the Media World: Big Questions and Big Trends in International Media Developments*, Reuters Institute for the Study of Journalism, University of Oxford.

Nightingale, V. 1993, 'What's "ethnographic" about ethnographic audience research?', in J. Frow and M. Morris (eds), *Australian Cultural Studies: A Reader*, Allen & Unwin, Sydney, pp. 164–178.

Nitins, T. and Burgess, J. 2013, 'Twitter, brands, and user engagement', in K. Weller, A. Bruns, J. Burgess, C. Puschmann and M. Mahrt (eds), *Twitter and Society*, Peter Lang, New York.

Noble, G. 1975, *Children in Front of the Small Screen*, Constable and Sage, London and Beverly Hills, CA.

Norman, D. 1988, *The Design of Everyday Things*, Basic Books, London.

The Observer Tree 2012, Website, <http://observertree.org> (accessed 14 October 2012).

Office of the Australian Information Commissioner (OAIC) 2010, 'Australian Privacy Commissioner obtains privacy undertakings from Google', <www.privacy.gov.au/materials/a-z?fullsummary=7103> (accessed 12 February 2013).

OECD Broadband Portal 2010, *News in the Internet Age*, OECD, Paris.

—— 2011, *OECD Communications Outlook 2011*, OECD, Paris.

O'Connor, J. 2009, 'Creative industries: A new direction?', *International Journal of Cultural Policy*, vol. 15, no. 4, pp. 387–402.

O'Donnell, P., McKnight, D. and Este, J. 2012, *Journalism at the Speed of Bytes. Australian Newspapers in the 21st Century*, the Walkley Foundation, Sydney.

Open Signal 2012, 'Android fragmentation visualised', <http://opensignal.com/reports/fragmentation.php> (accessed 24 April 2013).

O'Regan, T. 1990, 'TV as cultural technology: The work of Eric Michaels', *Continuum: A Journal of Media and Culture*, vol. 3, no. 2, pp. 53–98.

—— 1994, 'The Janus face of Australian television: Local and imported programming', in A. Moran (ed.), *Film Policy: An Australian Reader*, Institute for Cultural Policy Studies, Griffith University, Brisbane, pp. 87–104.

—— 1996, *Australian National Cinema*, Routledge, London.

Owen, B. and Wildman, S. 1992, *Video Economics*, Harvard University Press, Cambridge, MA.

Painter, J. 2011, *Poles Apart: The International Reporting of Climate Scepticism*, Reuters Institute for the Study of Journalism, Oxford.

Palen, L., Starbird, K., Vieweg, S. and Hughes, A. 2010, 'Twitter-based information distribution during the 2009 Red River Valley flood threat', *Bulletin of the American Society for Information Science and Technology*, vol. 36, no. 5, pp. 13–17.

Papandrea, F. 1997, *Cultural Regulations of Australian Television Programs*, Bureau of Transport and Communications Economics, Occasional Paper 114, AGPS, Canberra.

Pavlik, J.V. 1996, *New Media Technology: Cultural and Commercial Perspectives*, Allyn and Bacon, Boston.

Pearce, M. 2000, 'Perspectives of Australian broadcasting policy', *Continuum*, vol. 14, no. 3, pp. 367–82.

Petersen, N. 1993, *News Not Views: The ABC, the Press, and Politics, 1932–1947*, Hale & Iremonger, Sydney.

—— 1999, 'Whose news? Organisational conflict in the ABC, 1947–1999', *Australian Journalism Monographs*, nos 3–4, May–November.

Pew Research Center The Databank 2012, '23%—number of Americans who read print newspapers continues decline', 15 October.

Phonographic Performance Company of Australia (PPCA) 2011, *Phonographic Performance Company of Australia Annual Report 2011*, <www.ppca.com.au/IgnitionSuite/uploads/docs/PPCA%20AR%202011.pdf> (accessed 20 October 2012).

Pike, A. and Cooper, R. 1998, *Australian Film 1900–1977*, Oxford University Press, Melbourne.

Play for Life 2012, 'Music. Play for Life', <www.musicplayforlife.org> (accessed 20 February 2013).

Pollack, H.N. 2005, *Uncertain Science . . . Uncertain World*, 2nd ed., Cambridge University Press, Cambridge.

Popper, K. 1959, *The Logic of Scientific Discovery*, Basic Books, New York.

Potter, W. 1999, *On Media Violence*, Sage, Thousand Oaks, CA.

Potts, J. 1989, *Radio in Australia*, UNSW Press, Sydney.

Poynting, S., Noble, G., Tabar, P. and Collins, J. 2004, *Bin Laden in the Suburbs: Criminalising the Arab Other*, Sydney Institute of Criminology, Sydney.

Praetorius, D. 2011, 'Cathy Cruz Marrero, "Fountain Girl", falls in mall fountain while texting, considering lawsuit', *Huffington Post*, 25 May.

Putnam, R.D. 2000, *Bowling Alone: The Collapse and Revival of American Community*, Simon & Schuster, New York.

Putnis, P. 2000, *An Investigation of the Growth and Current Status of Communications and Media Studies Courses in Australian Universities*, DEST Evaluations and Investigations Programme, Canberra.

Qiu, J.L. 2012, 'Network Labor: Beyond the shadow of Foxconn', in L. Hjorth, J. Burgess and I. Richardson (eds), *Studying Mobile Media: Cultural Technologies, Mobile Communication, and the iPhone*, Routledge, New York, pp. 173–89.

Quay, S.E. and Damico, A.M. 2012, 'Ten years of watching *Falling Man*', *Media Ethics*, vol. 24, no. 1, <www.mediaethicsmagazine.com> (accessed 20 January 2013).

Queensland University of Technology 2010, *A Data Picture of Australia's Arts and Entertainment Sector 2010*, Creative Industries Faculty, Queensland University of Technology, Brisbane.

Quigley, A. 2006, 'Julia's image is better right than left', *Daily Telegraph*, 6 December.

'Radio National plans program cuts to save money' 2012, *ABC News*, 25 September, <www.abc.net.au/news/2012-09-25/radio-national-plans-program-cuts-to-save-money/4279846> (accessed 29 November 2012).

Rahimi, T.J. 1995, 'The power to control identity: Limiting a celebrity's right to publicity', *Santa Clara Law Review*, vol. 35, no. 2, p. 72.

Rainie, L. and Wellman, B. 2012, *Networked: The New Social Operating System*, MIT Press, Cambridge, MA.

Redhead, S. 2004, 'Creative modernity: The new cultural state', *Media International Australia*, no. 112, pp. 9–27.

Reporters Without Borders 2009, *The Dangers for Journalists Who Expose Environmental Issues*, Reporters Without Borders, Paris.

Reynolds, H. 1996, *Frontier: Aborigines, Settlers and Land*, Allen & Unwin, Sydney.

Rimmer, M. 2005, 'The Grey Album: Copyright law and digital sampling', *Media International Australia*, no. 114, pp. 40–53.

Richardson, I. 2011, 'The hybrid ontology of mobile gaming', *Convergence: The International Journal of Research into New Media Technologies*, vol. 17, no. 4, pp. 419–30.

—— 2012, 'Touching the screen: A phenomenology of mobile gaming and the iPhone', in L. Hjorth, J. Burgess and I. Richardson (eds), *Studying Mobile Media: Cultural Technologies, Mobile Communication, and the iPhone*. Routledge, New York, pp 133–53.

Richardson, I. and Wilken, R. 2012, 'Parerga of the third screen: Mobile media, place, and presence', in R. Wilken and G. Goggin (eds), *Mobile Technologies & Place*, Routledge, New York.

Robertson, R. 1995, 'Glocalization: Time–space and homogeneity–heterogeneity', in M. Featherstone, S. Lash and R. Robertson (eds), *Global Modernities*, Sage, London, pp. 25–44.

Rojek, C. 2001, *Celebrity*, Reaktion Books, London.

—— 2012, *Fame Attack: The Inflation of Celebrity and Its Consequences*, Bloomsbury, London.

Roscoe, J. 2001, 'Real entertainment: New factual hybrid television', *Media International Australia*, no. 100, pp. 9–20.

Rose, N. 1999, *Powers of Freedom: Reframing Political Thought*, Cambridge University Press, Cambridge.

—— 2007, *The Politics of Life Itself: Biomedicine: Power and Subjectivity in the Twenty-first Century*, Princeton University Press, Princeton, NJ.

Rosen, J. 2006, 'The people formerly known as the audience', *Pressthink*, 27 June, <http://archive.pressthink.org/2006/06/27/ppl_frmr.html> (accessed 20 November 2012).

Ross, K. and Nightingale, V. 2003, *Media and Audiences: New Perspectives*, Open University Press, Maidenhead.

Ross, S. 2008, *Beyond the Box: Television and the Internet*, Blackwell, Malden, MA.

Rosten, L. 1939, 'A "Middletown" study of Hollywood', *The Public Opinion Quarterly*, vol. 3, no. 2, pp. 314–15.

Rowe, D. 2004, *Sport, Culture and the Media: The Unruly Trinity*, 2nd ed., Open University Press, Maidenhead.

—— 2011, *Global Media Sport: Flows, Forms and Futures*, Bloomsbury Academic, London.

Royal Commission into Aboriginal Deaths in Custody 1991, *National Report* by Elliott Johnston, AGPS, Canberra.

Roy Morgan Research 2006, 'Australian media viewed with scepticism—TV remains our first stop when chasing the news', 18 December.

Ruddock, A. 2001, *Understanding Audiences*, Sage, London.

—— 2007, *Investigating Audiences*, Sage, London.

Rush, E. and La Nauze, A. 2006, *Corporate Paedophilia: Sexualisation of Children in the Media*, Australia Institute, Canberra.

Rushton, M. 2002, 'Copyright and freedom of expression: An economic analysis', in R. Towse (ed.), *Copyright in the Cultural Industries*, Edward Elgar, Cheltenham, pp. 48–62.

Russell, A. and Echchaibi, N. (eds) 2009, *International Blogging: Identity, Politics and Networked Publics*, Peter Lang, New York.

Salomon, M. 2009, 'Alpha male is online political beta', *The Age*, 12 February.

Sanders, K. 2003, *Ethics and Journalism*, Sage, London.

Sandvig, C. 2004, 'An initial assessment of cooperative action in Wi-Fi networking', *Telecommunications Policy*, no. 28, pp. 579–602.

Saxton, A. 2003, '"I certainly don't want people like that here": The discursive construction of "asylum seekers"', *Media International Australia*, no. 109, pp. 109–20.

SBS 2008, 'Mitunes', *Insight*, SBS TV, 3 June, <http://news.sbs.com.au/insight/episode/index/id/19#overview>.

Scherer, J. and Rowe, D. (eds) 2013, *Sport, Public Broadcasting, and Cultural Citizenship: Signal Lost?* Routledge, New York.

Schiller, H. 1969, *Mass Communication and American Empire*, Kelly, New York.

Schudson, M. 1978, *Discovering the News: A Social History of American Newspapers*, Basic Books, New York.

—— 1984, *Advertising: The Uneasy Persuasion*, Basic Books, New York.

Schultz, J. 1998, *Reviving the Fourth Estate: Democracy, Accountability and the Media*, Cambridge University Press, Melbourne.

Screen Australia 2009, 'The top 20 programs shown on television 1998–2009', <www.screenaustralia.gov.au/research/statistics/archwftvtopprog.aspx>.

—— 2012, 'Subscriber numbers, total and by operator, 1995–2011', <www.screenaustralia.gov.au/research/statistics/archwptvsubsxops.aspx> (accessed 20 November 2012).

Seiter, E. 1990, 'Making distinctions in TV audience research: Case study of a troubling interview', *Cultural Studies*, vol. 4, no. 1, pp. 61–84.

Senate Standing Committee 2007, *Sexualisation of Children in the Contemporary Media*, 26 June, <www.aph.gov.au/SENATE/committee/eca_ctte/sexualisation_of_children/index.htm> (accessed 20 November 2012).

Sensis and the Australian Interactive Multimedia Industry Association 2012, *Yellow Social Media Report*, 2nd ed., <http://about.sensis.com.au/IgnitionSuite/uploads/docs/FinalYellow_SocialMediaReport_digital_screen.pdf> (accessed 20 February 2013).

Sexton, E. 2010, 'Sound and fury over *Copyright Act* cap', *The Examiner* (Hobart), 13 October, <www.examiner.com.au/news/national/national/general/sound-and-fury-over-copy-right-act-cap/1967126.aspx?storypage=1> (accessed 20 February 2013).

Seymour-Ure, C. 1991, *The British Press and Broadcasting Since 1945*, Basil Blackwell, Oxford.

Shanahan, J. and Morgan, M. 1999, *Television and Its Viewers: Cultivation Theory and Research*, Cambridge University Press, Cambridge.

Shand, A. 2002, 'Chisholm pivotal in Point Piper Accord', *Australian Financial Review*, 6 March, p. 41.

Shawcross, W. 1992, *Rupert Murdoch: Ringmaster of the Information Circus*, Pan Books, London.

Sheridan, S. with Baird, B., Borrett, K. and Ryan, L. 2002, *Who Was that Woman? The Australian Women's Weekly in the Postwar Years*, UNSW Press, Sydney.

Shirley, G. and Adams, B. 1987, *Australian Cinema: The First Eighty Years*, Currency Press, Sydney.

Shklovski, I., Palen, L. and Sutton, J. 2008, 'Finding community through information and communication technology in disaster response', *Proceedings of the ACM 2008 Conference on Computer Supported Cooperative Work—CSCW '08*, ACM, San Diego, p. 127.

Silverstone, R. and Haddon, L. 1996, 'Design and domestication of information and communication technologies: Technical change and everyday life', in R. Silverstone and R. Mansell (eds), *Communication by Design: The Politics of Information and Communication Technologies*, Oxford University Press, Oxford, pp. 44–74.

Silverstone, R. and Hirsch, E. (eds) 1992, *Consuming technologies: Media and information in domestic spaces*, Routledge, London.

Simons, M. 2008, 'Kirk sorts the crap from the self-serving garbage', *Crikey*, 5 June.

—— 2012, *Journalism at the Crossroads*, Scribe, Melbourne.

Sinclair, J. 1987, *Images Incorporated: Advertising as Industry and Ideology*, Croom Helm and Methuen, London and Sydney.

——2012, *Advertising, the Media and Globalisation*, Routledge, London.

Sinclair, J. and Davidson, J. 1984, *Australian cultural studies = Birmingham + Meanjin, OK?*, Humanities Department, Footscray Institute of Technology.

Sinclair, L. 2011, 'Australian advertising market growth smashes forecasts', *The Australian*, 28 February.

Slater, D. 1997, *Consumer Culture and Modernity*, Polity Press, Cambridge.

Slater, P. 1977, *Origin and Significance of the Frankfurt School: A Marxist Perspective*, Routledge and Kegan Paul, London.

Slattery, K. 2003, 'Drowning not waving: The "children overboard" event and Australia's fear of the "other"', *Media International Australia*, no. 109, pp. 93–108.

Smirke, R. 2011, 'IFPI 2011 report: Global recorded music sales fall 8.4%', *Billboard*, <www.billboard.biz/bbbiz/industry/global/ifpi-2011-report-global-recorded-music-sales-1005100902.story> (accessed 20 November 2012).

Smith, A. 1980, *Goodbye Gutenberg: The Newspaper Revolution of the 1980s*, Oxford University Press, Oxford.

Smith, C. 1998, *Creative Britain*, Faber and Faber, London.

Smith, G. 2005, *Singing Australian*, Pluto Press, Melbourne.

—— 2007, 'Folk music: Movements, scenes and styles', in S. Homan and T. Mitchell (eds), *Sounds of Then, Sounds of Now: Popular Music in Australia*, ACYS, Hobart, pp. 151–66.

Smith, S.E. 2012, 'Model with Down Syndrome heads up Dolores Cortes US kids swimwear catalogue', *xoJane*, <www.xojane.com/issues/model-down-syndrome-heads-dolores-cortes-us-kids-swimwear-catalogue> (accessed 24 July 2012).

Smythe, D. 1977, 'Communications: Blindspot of Western Marxism', *Canadian Journal of Political and Social Theory*, vol. 1, no. 3, pp. 1–27.

Soja, E. 1989, *Postmodern Geographies: The Reassertion of Space in Critical Social Theory*, Verso, New York.

Solove, D. 2008, *Understanding Privacy*, Harvard University Press, New York.

Sparks, G. 2002, *Media Effects Research: A Basic Overview*, Wadsworth/Thomson Learning, Belmont, CA.

Spearritt, P. and Walker, D. 1979, *Australian Popular Culture*, George Allen & Unwin, Sydney.

Special Broadcasting Service (SBS) 2012, *Annual Report 2011–2012*, SBS, Sydney.

Spurgeon, C. 2008, *Advertising and New Media*, Routledge, London.

Standard Telephone Service Review Group 1997, *Review of the Standard Telephone Service*, Department of Communications, Information Technology and the Arts, Canberra.

Starbird, K. and Palen, L. 2010, 'Pass It On? Retweeting in Mass Emergency', *Proceedings of the 7th International ISCRAM Conference*, ISCRAM, Seattle.

Stelter, B. 2010, Water-cooler effect: Internet can be TV's friend, *New York Times*, <www.nytimes.com/2010/02/24/business/media/24cooler.html> (accessed 20 November 2012).

St John, G. 2001, *FreeNRG: Notes from the Edge of the Dance Floor*, Common Ground Press, Melbourne.

Stockbridge, S. 1988, 'The pay-for-play debate: Australian television versus the record companies, and the myth of "public benefit"', in T. Bennett, L. Grossberg, W. Straw and G. Turner (eds), *Rock Music: Politics and Policy*, Institute for Cultural Policy Studies, Griffith University, Brisbane, pp. 13–20.

Stone, G. 2007, *Who Killed Channel 9?* Pan Macmillan, Sydney.

Stratton, J. 2007, *Australian Rock: Essays on Popular Music*, API Network Books, Perth.

Sullivan, B. 1997, *The Politics of Sex: Prostitution and Pornography in Australia Since 1945*, Cambridge University Press, Cambridge.

Sutton-Smith, B. 1997, *The Ambiguity of Play*, Routledge, London.

Swingewood, A. 1977, *The Myth of Mass Culture*, Macmillan, London.

Systrom, K. 2012, 'Updated terms of service based on your feedback', *Instagram Blog*, <http://blog.instagram.com/post/38421250999/updated-terms-of-service-based-on-your-feedback>.

Tanner, L. 1999, *Open Australia*, Pluto Press, Sydney.

—— 2012, *Sideshow*, 2nd ed., Scribe, Melbourne.

Taylor, T.L. 2006, *Play Between Worlds*, MIT Press, Cambridge, MA.

Thomas, D. and McCarthy, B. 2013, 'Mobile operators challenge Google and Apple', *Financial Times*, 24 February.

Thomas, J. and Rennie, E. 2012, 'Nobody uses the internet because the government says they should', *Inside Story*, 1 October, <http://inside.org.au/nobody-uses-the-Internet-because-the-government-says-they-should> (accessed 2 February 2013).

Thornley, P. 1995, 'Debunking the "Whitlam" myth: The annals of public broadcasting revisited', *Media International Australia*, no. 77, pp. 155–64.

—— 1999, 'Broadcasting policy in Australia: Political influences and the federal government's role in the establishment and development of public/community broadcasting in Australia—a history 1939 to 1992, PhD thesis, University of Newcastle.

Throsby, D. and Zednik, A. 2010, *Do You Really Expect to Get Paid? An Economic Study of Professional Artists in Australia*, Australia Council for the Arts, Sydney.

Tiffen, R. 1989, *News and Power*, Allen & Unwin, Sydney.

—— 1994a, *Mayer on the Media: Issues and Arguments*, Allen & Unwin, Sydney.

—— 1994b, 'Media policy', in J. Brett, J. Gillespie and M. Goot (eds), *Developments in Australian Politics*, Macmillan, Melbourne.

Tiffen, R. and Gittins, R. 2009, *How Australia Compares*, 2nd ed., Cambridge University Press, Melbourne.

Tomlinson, A. and Young, C. (eds) 2006, *National Identity and Global Sports Events: Culture, Politics, and Spectacle in the Olympics and the Football World Cup*, State University of New York Press, New York.

Toohey, P. 2010, 'Fashion funds push for Julia', *The Mercury*, 6 July.

'Top 150 companies up to close of trade, Friday March 1' 2013, *The Weekend Australian—Business*, 2–3 March, p. 33.

Totaro, P. 2010, 'Gillard's first appearance on international stage as PM', *Sydney Morning Herald*, 4 October, <www.smh.com.au/world/gillards-first-appearance-on-international-stage-as-pm-20101004-1644u.html> (accessed 20 October 2012).

Toynbee, P. 2005, 'Why vote Labour? The answer is in the *Daily Mail*', *The Guardian*, 16 March.

Trevillion, T. 2012, CEO, interview with the author, 17 October.

Tunstall, J. 1971, *Journalists at Work*, Constable, London.

—— 1996, *Newspaper Power: The New National Press in Britain*, Clarendon Press, Oxford.

Turnbull, M. (Shadow Minister for Communications and Broadband) 2012, Address to CommsDay Melbourne Congress, 9 October.

Turner, G. 1986, *National Fictions*, Allen & Unwin, Sydney.

—— 1992, 'Australian popular music and its contexts', in P. Hayward (ed.), *From Pop to Punk to Postmodernism: Popular Music and Australian Culture from the 1960s to the 1990s*, Allen & Unwin, Sydney.

—— 1993a, 'Introduction: Moving the margins—theory, practice and Australian cultural studies', in G. Turner, *Nation, Culture, Text: Australian Cultural and Media Studies*, Routledge, London, pp. 1–13.

—— 1993b, 'Who killed the radio star? The death of teen radio in Australia', in T. Bennett, S. Frith, L. Grossberg, J. Shepherd and G. Turner (eds), *Rock and Popular Music: Politics, Policies and Institutions*, Routledge, London, pp. 142–55.

—— 1996, 'Maintaining the news', *Culture and Policy*, vol. 7, no. 3, pp. 127–64.

—— 2003, *British Cultural Studies: An Introduction*, 3rd ed., Routledge, London.

—— 2004, *Understanding Celebrity*, Sage, London.

—— 2005, *Ending the Affair: The Decline of Television Current Affairs in Australia*, UNSW Press, Sydney.

—— 2010, *Ordinary People and the Media: The Demotic Turn*, Sage, London.

—— 2012, *What's Become of Cultural Studies?*, Sage Publications, London.

Turner, G., Bonner, F. and Marshall, P.D. 2000, *Fame Games: The Production of Celebrity in Australia*, Cambridge University Press, Melbourne.

Turner, G. and Cunningham, S. (eds) 2000, *The Australian TV Book*, Allen & Unwin, Sydney.

Turner, G. and Tay, J. (eds) 2009, *Television Studies After TV: Understanding Post-broadcast Television*, Routledge, London.

Van Dijck, J. 2013, *The Culture of Connectivity: A Critical History of Social Media*, Oxford University Press, Oxford.

Varian, H. 2010, 'Newspaper economics: Online and offline', presentation to Federal Trade Commission Workshop, 'How Will Journalism Survive the Internet Age?', Federal Trade Commission Conference Centre, Washington DC.

Verghis, S. 2000, 'No, colour, please. We're the eternally white Aussies', *Sydney Morning Herald*, 26 October, p. 12.

Vision Mobile 2012, *Developer Economics 2012: The New Mobile App Economy*, Vision Mobile, Sydney, 24 April.

Vieweg, S., Hughes, A., Starbird, K. and Palen, L. 2010, 'Microblogging during two natural hazard events', *Proceedings of the 28th International Conference on Human Factors in Computing Systems—CHI '10*, ACM, Atlanta, p. 1079.

Viticci, F. 2012, 'Apple reveals new "all-time top apps"', 3 March, *Macstories*. <www.macstories. net/news/apple-reveals-new-all-time-top-apps-following-25-billion-downloads> (accessed 24 April 2013).

Vodafone Group 2012, 'Background presentation 2012', <www.vodafone.com/content/dam/ vodafone/investors/factsheet/group_presentation.pdf> (accessed 30 January 2013).

Waddell, R. 2007, 'Update: Madonna, Live Nation sign global pact', *Billboard*, 16 October, <http://billboard.biz/bbbiz/content_display/industry/e3i172f2c4d34dd5766e64291d77 52db92d?imw=Y> (accessed 20 October 2013).

Wajcman, J., Bittman, M. and Brown, J. 2009, 'Intimate connections: The impact of the mobile phone on work/life boundaries', in G. Goggin and L. Hjorth (eds), *Mobile Technologies: From Telecommunications to Media*, Routledge, New York, pp. 9–22.

Waldman, S. 2011, 'The information needs of communities', in S. Waldman, *The Changing Media Landscape in a Broadband Age*, Federal Communications Commission, Washington DC.

Walsh, K.A. 2013, *The Stalking of Julia Gillard*, Allen & Unwin, Sydney.

Ward, I. 2002, 'Talkback radio, political communication, and Australian politics', *Australian Journal of Communication*, vol. 29, no. 1, pp. 21–38.

Wasko, J., Murdock, G. and Sousa, H. (eds) 2011, *Handbook of Political Economy of Communications*, Blackwell, Oxford.

Weller, K., Bruns, A., Burgess, J., Mahrt, M. and Puschmann, C. (eds) 2013, *Twitter and Society*, Peter Lang, New York.

Wenner, L.A. (ed.) 1998, *MediaSport*, Routledge, London.

—— 2007, 'Towards a dirty theory of narrative ethics: Prolegomenon on media, sport, and commodity value, *International Journal of Media and Cultural Politics*, vol. 3, no. 2, pp. 111–29.

Western, J. and Hughes, C. 1971, *The Mass Media in Australia*, University of Queensland Press, Brisbane.

Westfield, M. 2000, *The Gatekeepers: The Global Media Battle to Control Australia's Pay TV*, Pluto Press, Sydney.

Whannel, G. 2008, *Culture, Politics and Sport: Blowing the Whistle, Revisited*. Routledge, London.

Wheelright, E.L. and Buckley, K. (eds) 1987, *Communications and the Media in Australia*, Allen & Unwin, Sydney.

Whiteoak, J. 2003, 'Popular music', in J. Whiteoak and A. Scott-Maxwell (eds), *The Currency Companion to Music and Dance in Australia*, Currency Press, Sydney, p. 529.

Whiteoak, J. and Scott-Maxwell, A. (eds) 2003, *The Currency Companion to Music and Dance in Australia*, Currency Press, Sydney.

Wilken, R. and Goggin, G. (eds) 2014, *Locative Media*, Routledge, New York.

Wilkins 2012, 'Star hits out at *Home and Away* racism', *Sydney Morning Herald*, 12 February, <www.smh.com.au/entertainment/tv-and-radio/star-hits-out-at-home-and-away-racism-20120216-1ta23.html> (accessed 20 November 2012).

Williams, R. 1974, *Television: Technology and Cultural Form*, Fontana/Collins, London.

—— 1977, *Marxism and Literature*, Oxford University Press, Oxford.

Williamson, J. 1978, *Decoding Advertisements: Ideology and Meaning in Advertising*, Boyars, London.

Wilson, H. 2006, '30 years of *MIA*: A commemorative editorial', *Media International Australia*, no. 119, pp. 3–20.

Windschuttle, K. 1988, *The Media*, 2nd ed., Penguin, Ringwood.

Wolf, M.J.P. and Perron, B. (eds) 2003, *The Video Game Theory Reader*, Routledge, New York.

—— 2008, *The Video Game Theory Reader 2*, Routledge, New York.

Wolfsfeld, G. 1997, *Media and Political Conflict: News from the Middle East.* Cambridge University Press, Cambridge.

Wood, H. and Skeggs, B. (eds) 2011, *Reality Television and Class*, Palgrave Macmillan, London.

Woolgar, S. 1991, 'The turn to technology in social studies of science', *Science, Technology & Human Values*, vol. 16, no. 1, pp. 20–50.

Index

Abbott, Tony 39
ABC
 abolition of fees 177
 audience loyalty 6
 Australian content 177
 bias, perception of 182
 broadcasting regulation 79
 budget cuts 182
 charter 144
 comedies 183
 commencement 174–5
 demographic appeal
  182–3
 emergency mapping system
  353
 innovation 329–30
 iView 189–90, 337
 legislation 79
 loyalty to 6
 Mansfield Review 182
 multi-channelling
  capacities 240
 news and current affairs
  176, 182, 183–4
 1970s and 1980s 177
 1990s and 2000s 182–4
 'perpetual crisis' 182
 political bias 182
 'Pool' interactive art site
  330–1
 radio 144–6, 238
 satirical comedy 183
 services, expansion and
  re-branding 183–4
 structural changes 183–4
 studies 193
ABC Online 184

Aboriginal people see
 Indigenous people
ACP Magazines 194, 202
ADSL (asymmetrical digital
 subscriber line) 129, 251,
 255
Advanced Research Project
 Agency Network
 (ARPANET) 250
advertising
 agencies 210, 217–22
 agency services 218–20
 audience research see
  audience
 branded content 211
 budgets 214–16
 channel planning 223
 code of ethics 224
 commerce and art, fusion
  219
 commercial media
  sustained by 209
 competition 217–18
 deregulation 217
 direct marketing 218
 freelance specialists 219–20
 global links 220–2
 globalisation 213
 income derived from 65
 infotainment 210
 internet 223, 224
 legislation 224
 magazines 197–8
 media-buying agencies 210,
  223
 medium, choosing 210
 misleading 129–30

 national advertisers 214
 nature of 209
 newspapers 96, 99, 104–5,
  107–8
 niche marketing 223
 non-national advertising 214
 online 198, 259
 operation of 209–10
 origins 211–12
 product placement 218
 radio 143–4
 ratings-based 210–11
 regulation 224
 social networking sites 223
 sponsors 210–11
 spots 210–11
 telecommunications
  industry 129–30
 telemarketing 218
 television 176, 223
 television commercials
  (TVCs) 219–20
 top advertisers 214, 215–16
 top agencies 221–2
 transnational advertisers
  214, 218
 viral 218
Advertising Federation of
 Australia (AFA) 84, 217
Advertising Standards Board
 217, 224
Advertising Standards Bureau
 (ASB) 83
Afghan refugees 300
The Age 99, 103, 303
American empiricism 16–17,
 22–3

American Telegraph and
  Telephone (AT&T) 113
Android 122, 168, 278, 340,
  342, 343–4
Angry Birds 269, 270
Apple 232, 334, 341
Apple iPhone 122, 208, 232,
  269, 270, 271, 274–5, 281,
  339
Apple iPhoto 262
Apple iPods 4, 232
Apple iTunes 7, 122, 164, 169,
  232, 244, 265
apps 2, 122, 259, 265, 287–8
  Australian industry 340–2
  banks 340
  cars, for 343
  development 339
  device fragmentation 343
  distribution 341
  markets 341–2
  mobile devices 342, 344
  national developers 340–1
  non-creative company
    involvement 340
  outsourcing 340
  revenue 341
  televisions, for 342–3
Arab Australians 299, 300–1
ARC Centre of Excellence for
  Creative Industries and
  Innovation 28, 252, 340
Arnold, Matthew 18
the arts, regulation of 80
Asian Australians 299
Associated Press 103
Atari 272, 273, 274
ATN 7 174, 175
audience
  academic interest in 68
  active 69, 70
  advertising and 65
  concept of 59–60
  consumers 61
  'cultural dopes' 17
  'effects tradition' 68–9
  encoding/decoding 71
  ethnographic approach 71
  fans and fandom 69

global 60–1
globalisation 67
government interests in
  65–7
industry interests in 64–5
interpretations by 35–6, 37,
  38–9
'invisible fictions' 24
nature of 59–63
old versus new 59–62
passive 68–9, 69–70
'produser' 61
public interests in 65–7
quantitative and qualitative
  measures 65
ratings 64, 65, 176
research 65, 68–72
social and civil
  participation 62
tele-participation 63–4
theory and method in
  research 68–72
Audit Bureau of Circulation
  98, 193
AUSSAT 113, 118
Austereo 239, 345–6
Australia and New Zealand
  Communication
  Association (ANZCA) 26
Australia Council 80, 152
Australia Institute 66
Australia-US Free Trade
  Agreement 3, 155, 158
The Australian 38, 105, 144,
  303, 347
Australian Academic Research
  Network (AARNET) 250,
  255
Australian Associated Press
  (AAP) 104
Australian Association of
  National Advertisers
  (AANA) 84, 217
Australian Broadband
  Guarantee 255
Australian Broadcasting
  Commission *see* ABC
Australian Broadcasting
  Corporation *see* ABC

Australian Broadcasting
  Tribunal (ABT) 177
Australian Business Arts
  Foundation 80
Australian Children's
  Television Foundation
  (ACTF) 75, 84
Australian Communications
  and Media Authority
  (ACMA) 68, 81–2, 114, 143,
  169, 252, 255, 298, 346
Australian Communications
  Consumer Action Network
  (ACCAN) 129
Australian Competition and
  Consumer Commission
  (ACCC) 80, 81, 82, 88–9,
  114, 217, 256
Australian Computer Science
  network 250
Australian Computer Society
  254
Australian Constitution 77,
  112
Australian Council of Trade
  Unions (ACTU) 105
Australian cultural identity 46
Australian culture
  sexist, whether 31–4
Australian Film Commission
  152, 153
Australian Film Development
  Corporation (AFDC) 152
Australian Film Institute (AFI)
  160
Australian Financial Review 87,
  105, 199
Australian Fine Music
  Network 147
Australian Hotels Association
  242–3
Australian Idol 180, 239, 306–7
Australian Information
  Industry Association 254
Australian Interactive
  Multimedia Industry
  Association (AIMIA) 254
*Australian Journal of
  Communication* 26

Australian Journal of Cultural Studies 23
Australian Journalists' Association 101
Australian Law Reform Commission (ALRC) 335, 336
Australian media and communications 10–12
Australian media studies 26–7
Australian Mobile Telecommunications Association (AMTA) 84
Australian Press Council 78, 82–3, 347
Australian Record Industry Association (ARIA) 229, 233, 235, 236
Australian Research Council 24
Australian Subscription Television and Radio Association (ASTRA) 84, 148
Australian theoretical traditions 23–8
Australian Women's Weekly 193, 195, 196, 198, 200–1
Autism SA 341
Autohome 116

Ballmer, Steve 96
Bandura, Albert 69
Barr, Trevor 76
Barthes, Roland 71
Bauer Media Group 194
BBC iPlayer 189
Berners-Lee, Tim 3
Big Brother 63–4, 66, 68, 179–80, 304, 306–7
BigPond 232, 337
BigPond Movies 115
BigTinCan 342
Birmingham School 19
BitTorrent 8, 237, 262
Bligh, Anna 354
The Block 180
Blogosphere 3, 7
blogs 262–3

Blue Tongue 270
Bobo doll studies 69
Bond, Alan 178
Boxee 343
British cultural studies 18–19
British press 96, 102–3, 347
broadband
    DSL technology 123, 124, 126
    National Broadband Network (NBN) 77, 81, 87, 117, 124, 126–8, 130, 131, 166, 251, 255, 262, 337
    satellite, via 255
broadcasting
    digital, move to 186
    legislation 79
    ownership of licences 175
    regulation 78–9
    spectrum 78, 106, 126
    state involvement in 106
Broker iPad app 340
Bruns, Axel 61
'bullet theory' 70
Business Spectator 95
Buttrose, Ita 204, 205

Campion, Jane 162–3
Canberra Times 39, 101, 105
capitalism 17, 51
cash for comment 141, 143, 218
CCTV 241, 310, 311, 312
celebrity
    career path, as 304
    concept of 305
    culture 303–4
    industry producing 304
    magazine stories 304
    mass production 307
    parasocial interaction 304
    privacy 310, 311
    production of 305–7
    reality TV 306
    representation 305
    what is 305
censorship 335 *see also* classification

community standards test 335, 336
Centre for Contemporary Cultural Studies 19
Centre for Independent Studies 76
change, velocity of 6–9
Channel 11 240
The Chaser's War on Everything 183
chat programs 261
children
    'corporate paedophilia' 66
    sexualisation of 66–7, 70
China Mobile 342
CHOICE 75
Chomp 342, 344
Christchurch earthquake 352, 353
Christian, Michael 345
Christian radio 148
cinemas
    Australian 152, 154
    discourses of 159–64
    early Australian 159–60
civil participation 62
classification 335–6
    censorship and 335
    community attitudes to regulation 336–7
    community standards test 335–6
    future 336–8
    legislation 336
    principles 335–6
    purpose 335
    restriction of access 335
    review 334
    state and Commonwealth differences 336
Cleo 205
climate change 323–4
cloud computing 259
co-regulation 77
Code of Ethics 346
Cole, Jeffrey 96
commercial radio 142–4
Commercial Radio Australia 84

Commonwealth powers 77
Commonwealth Scientific and
  Industrial Organisation
  (CSIRO) 255
Communication Research 23
Communications Alliance 83
communications services
  119–21
Community Broadcasting
  Association of Australia
  (CBAA) 84, 147
community media
  interventions 301–2
community radio 147–8, 238
competition
  convergence and 4–6
  laws 78
  telecommunications 80–1
computer games *see* electronic
  games
Comscore 285
conflicts of interest 5
Consolidated Media 88–9,
  181, 186
consumer associations 75
Consumers'
  Telecommunications
  Network (CTN) 84
contempt laws 77, 348
content convergence 5
convergence 1, 4–6
  challenge of 89–90
  competition and 4–6
  content 5
  culture 62
  horizontal layers 89
  industry 4
  policy challenge 333–5
  technological 4
  television 186
  vertically integrated
    industry 'silos' 89
Convergence Review 2011–12
  76, 90–1, 334, 338, 348
cooking shows 44
copyright
  Copyright Tribunal 242
  popular music 230, 234–7
  review of laws 335

'corporate paedophilia' 66
Cosmopolitan 196, 201, 202,
  203, 204, 205
cosmopolitan
  multiculturalism 300
Courier-Mail 103
Crawford Productions 175,
  176
Creative Industries National
  Mapping Project 340
Cricket LIVE 189
Crikey 184, 258
crisis communication
  crowdsourcing 352–3
  emergency services
    strategies 354
  local communities 352–3
  media role 352
  natural disasters 351–2,
    354–5
  social media 352, 353–4
  strategies 355
critical theory 17
Cronulla riot 298
cross-media ownership 3, 86
crowdsource funding 158–9,
  231
CSL 116
'cultivation theory' 69
cultural clusters 240
cultural diversity 10, 178,
  184–5, 298, 300, 302
cultural imperialism 20
Cultural Ministers Council
  80, 240
cultural policy studies 74–5
Cultural Research Network 24
cultural studies 23–4
  analysis 33–4
  Marxist concerns 33–4
Cunningham, Stuart 28
CVC Asia Pacific 186
cyberbullying 351

Daily Mail 102
Daily Mirror 102
Daily Telegraph 38, 99, 100, 104
data-gathering 31–2
de Certeau, Michel 163

de Saussure, Ferdinand 19
defamation laws 77, 348
democracy and the press 106,
  107–8
Department of Broadband,
  Communications and the
  Digital Economy (DBCDE)
  77
de-regulation 77
DiG 149
digital distribution models 7
Digital Economy Goals 77, 81
digital radio 149
digital technologies 1
Dirani, Firass 298
direct regulation 77
disabilities, persons with
  253–4
Discovr Music 341
disenfranchisement 33–4
Dix Report 177
domain name services 256
dot.com bubble 254
downloading 7
  data 123
  illegal 8
  media industry
    participation 3
drinking, social 51–2
Dropbox 259
The Drum 36
Duchess of Cambridge 345
DVB-T 186
DVD 167–9 *see also* film
  content delivery 152, 168
  industry data 168, 169
  rental 168, 169
  rental kiosks 168
  role 167–8
  sales 167–8

electronic games
  actor network theory
    (ANT) 277
  affordances approach 277
  apps 343
  arcade games 273
  birth of gaming 272–5
  console games 273

convergence 270–1
convergent formats 270
developers 270
domestication approach
    277–8
generations of 273–4
growth of industry 270
hackers 272
histories 271–5
interactivity 275
location-based service
    (LBS) games 278–80
ludology 275–8
massively multiplayer
    online role-playing
    games (MMORPGs) 273
mobile gaming devices 270,
    273, 274
mobile phones 274
narratology 271, 275–8
Nintendo 260, 273
online gaming 273
player participation 271
popular culture
simulation 275
social constructivism 276–7
social technologies 275–8
Sony Playstation 270
Space Invaders 273
US military funding 272–3
user-created content 271
uses 269
video game crash 273–4
Wii 270, 273
Xbox 270
Electronic Program Guides
    (EPGs)
email 119–20, 252, 256–7
emergency media 352
Emerson, Craig 76
end-user licence agreements
    (EULAs) 288
environment
    bypass of mainstream
        media 324–5
    complexity of issues 323
    conflicts 325–6
    environmental movements
        324–5

Gibson's tree 321–2
ideological debate 323
internet 324–5
power of images 322, 324
reporting 322–4
role of media 323, 324, 325
ethics 345–9
education 349
inquiries and reviews 347–8
journalists 346–7
legal regulation 348–9
online/social media
    responses to events
    348–9
phone-hacking 6, 74, 310,
    347
policing 346
radio stunts 345–6
regulation 349
self-regulation 347
theory and practice 346
ethno-multiculturalism 300
ethnographic approach 24, 71
Experimental Film and
    Television Fund (EFTF)
    152–3

Facebook 62, 120, 223, 251,
    255, 259, 263, 264, 285,
    286, 287, 288, 289, 292,
    304, 309, 349, 352
    privacy 313
Facebook Places 259
Factiva 37
Fairfax 74, 95, 196, 199,
    204–5
    press ownership 100, 101
    redundancies 7, 95
    shift to digital products 95
    tabloid format 95
    television ownership 175
Fairfax Digital 257
Fame Attack 307
fanfiction 61
Fango 189
fans and fandom 69
Federation of Australian
    Commercial Television
    Stations (FACTS) 84

feminism
    representation of women
        49–50
Fetch TV 337
film 169–70
    anachronistic term 151
    Australian-international
        productions 162
    box office receipts 166–7
    cinema, predicted death of
        151–2
    content regulation 158
    crowdsource funding
        158–9
    digital distribution 165–6
    distribution 165–7
    DVDs 167–9
    exhibition 165–7
    foreign production 154–5
    fourth industry model
        163–4
    funding 152, 156, 157
    globalisation 156
    government role 152–3,
        154–8
    history of Australian
        cinema 159–64
    industry 160–4
    industry data 154, 155
    international projects
        155–7
    international shifts 157
    offset incentives 157
    production 163–4
    regulation of industry
        79–80
    structural issues 2010s
        156–7
    tax concessions 153, 157–8
    third industry model
        162–3, 164
    two-industry model 160–2
Film Australia 153
Film Finance Corporation
    (FFC) 153
Filter Squad 341, 344
Finkelstein Independent
    Media Inquiry 6, 334, 337,
    347

Fiske, John 69
flash mob events 293
Flickr 259, 262, 289
food magazines 205–6
foreign ownership 3, 86
Foucault, Michel 21, 28
Four Corners 184
4G 'Long Term Evolution' (LTE) technology 122
Foursquare 259, 266, 270, 278, 294, 295
Fox Sports 95–6
Foxtel 95, 115, 181, 343
    IQ2 337
    magazine 194
Frankfurt School 17, 19, 22
Fraser government 177
Free TV Australia 84
Freeview 186
French structuralism 19–20
Frontier Online 329
Fruit Ninja 340–1
Future Fund 117

Game of Thrones 60–1
games *see* electronic games
The Games 329–30
gang rapes 300
Garrett, Peter 240
gender roles 31
genre of texts 36
Gerbner, George 69
Gibson, Miranda 321–2
Gillard, Julia 34, 36, 38–9, 144
Gillespie, Marie 71–2, 298
Global Financial Crisis 96
Global Positioning System (GPS) 266, 278
globalisation 3, 15, 21, 27, 248
    advertising 213
    media, of 1
Go! 187
Good Universities Guide 11
Google 3, 7, 120, 122, 259, 334
Google Maps 279
Google Play 122
Google Street View 311, 313
Google's Project Glass 343
Gordon & Gotch 199

government
    audiences, interests in 65–7
    broadcasting, involvement in 106
    film production 152–4
    press, involvement in 106
    regulation 77–8
Gramsci's hegemony concept 18, 19, 53
Grazia 196, 203, 206
Greig, Mel 345
Griffen-Foley, Bridget 63
Griffith School 28
Gruden 342
The Gruen Transfer 224
Grundy Organisation 176
The Guardian 102, 108
Gyngell, Bruce 177

Habermas, Jürgen 62
hactivism 272–5
haka viral video 293
Hall, Stuart 19, 53, 71
Hawke, Bob 105
Hawke government 101
health and fitness magazines 200
hegemonic capitalism 8
Herald and Weekly Times 100
Herald Sun 38–9
Herzog, Herta 70–1
Hesmondhalgh, David 21
Hill, David 177
Hitler's Nazism 17
The Hobart Mercury 38
Hoggart, Richard 19
Homicide 175
homosexuality 176
Howard government
    ABC budget cuts 182
    copyright 230, 235
    foreign and cross-media ownership 186
    privatisation of Telstra 113, 116–17
Howard, John 39, 66, 143, 182, 329–30
Hulu 189
Hutchison 119

hybrid fibre/coaxial cable (HFC) 115, 124, 255
'hypodermic needle' conception 70
Hywood, Greg 95

iiNet 114, 115, 237, 255
Independent Media Inquiry 6, 334, 337, 347
IndieGoGo 158
Indigenous people
    apology to 329–30
    community radio 147–8
    internet usage 253
    Michaels' analysis of television and culture 28
    music 228–9
    radio 146, 147–8
    representations in media 297, 299
individualism 291
industry associations 83–4
    internet 254
industry convergence 4
information-based systems of delivery 1, 3
Inquiry into the Sexualisation of Children in the Contemporary Media Environment 50, 67, 69
Instagram 259, 262, 288–9
instant messaging 251, 252, 261
Institute of Public Affairs 76
intellectual property
    laws 235, 243–4, 288
    music piracy 235
INTELSAT 113
international telecommunications 112–13
internet 122–4
    access and use 252–4
    advertising 198, 259
    age of users 252–3
    blogs 262–3
    broadband 123
    chat programs 261
    cloud computing 259

commerce ban, lifting of 250
commercial structures 254–60
compulsory filters 80
concepts underlying 250
consumption 260–4
converged medium 62
cultures of use 260–4
dial-up 123, 250, 251, 255
disability and access 253–4
diversity 108
domain name services 256
email 119–20, 252, 256–7
environmental movements 324–5
globalisation 248–9
impact 247–8
Indigenous users 253
industry associations 254
informational content, source of 108
infrastructure 255–6
instant messaging 251, 252
launch of 249
nature of 248, 250
new technologies 250
online and interactive services 260
photo-sharing websites 251, 260, 261–2
policy 80–1
press and 107–8
p2p applications 163, 188, 250, 261–2
role 249–50
search engines 258–9
subscribers 122–3, 251
understanding 249–51
usage 248
users 251–4
video-sharing websites 261–2
VOIP technology 251, 252
web industry 257–8
wikis 262–3
wireless technologies 264–6
Internet Corporation for Assigned Names and Numbers (ICANN) 256

Internet Industry Association (IIA) 83–4, 254, 256
Internet Protocol television (IPTV) 337, 338
internet relay chat (IRC) 251, 261
Internet service providers (ISPs) 5, 255–6
iOS 342
iView 189–90, 337

Jacka, Elizabeth 24
Jamster 232
Jarvis, Gail 182
Jenkins, Henry 62, 69
Jiepang 278
Jones, Alan 143, 144, 298
Journal of Communication 23
journalism 62, 106–7
environmental reporting 323–4
quality 97, 107
styles 102
journalists
ethics 346–7
job losses 101
public scepticism 99

Kath and Kim 183
Kazaa 235
Keating, Paul 101
Kickstarter 158
Kohler, Alan 107
Kony Solutions 342

Labor Party 74
Lacan, Jacques 19
Laga'aia, Jay 297
language 52–4
Lasswell, Harold 22
Laws, John 141, 143
Lazarsfeld, Paul 23
legislation 77
Leveson Inquiry 6, 347
Levi-Strauss, Claude 19
Levin, Jordan 12
LG 122, 343
Liberal Party 74
lifestyle programs 179

LinkedIn 259, 263
Linux 122
Live Music Accord 241
location-based service (LBS) 269, 270, 271
disclosure concerns 294–5
electronic games 278–80
privacy policies 294–5
locative media 265–6
The Loop 240
Lucy, Judith 239

McChesney, Robert W. 21
McGuire, Eddie 186
McHugh, Michael 207
McQueen, Humphrey 26
Magazine Publishers of Australia (MPA) 194
magazines
advertising 194, 197–8
audit of sales 193, 196
categories 200, 202–3
celebrity gossip 206, 304 *see also* celebrity
changes in content 205–6
children's 201
circulation 193–4, 195–7
component of media companies 194
cover price 197
demographics 202–4
desktop publishing 205
digital sales 207
distribution 199
economics 197–8
editorial content 197, 204
fashion 196, 203
food magazines 205–6
gender and 199–200, 201–2
health 206
income sources 197–8
'lads' mags' 200
links to other media 198–9
market segmentation 199–202
men's 200, 201
microzines 205
new titles 196, 204–5

newspaper-inserted (NIMs)
    199
online threat, response to
    207–8
parenting 206
readership 196–7
special interest 208
supermarket sales 199
television versions 198–9
women's 199–200, 202–5
Magic Kingdom 341
Mansfield Review 182
Marie Claire 196, 201, 202
marketing and public relation
    strategies 2
Marxism 16–18
mass culture 19
massive multi-player online
    games (MMOGs) 3, 270, 274
massively multiplayer online
    role-playing games
    (MMORPGs) 273
Master Chef 187
Masthead Metric 207
Mayer, Henry 27–8
Meagher, Jill 348–9
Meagher, Tom 349
media and communications
    Australian 10–12
    campuses offering 11
    change, velocity of 6–9
    competition 4–6
    convergence 1, 4–6
    downloading as 3
    established 2
    history 2
    'new' 2, 6–8
    'old' forms 2, 6–8
    study of 10–12
    systems of delivery 2–3
    theoretical approaches 15–29
    traditional distinctions 1
    what are 1–4
    whose 3–4
media and communications
    policy *see* policy
media and communications
    theory
    Althusser 18, 28

American 16–17, 22–3
audience research 24
Australian cultural studies
    23–4
Australian quirkiness 27–9
Australian traditions 23–9
Birmingham School 19
Bonney and Wilson 26
British cultural studies
    18–19
content analysis 22
critical theory 17
cultural industries 21
dominant ideology thesis
    17
Edgar's *Children and Screen
    Violence* 25
empiricism 16–17
ethnographic method 24
European 16–17
Foucault, Michel 21, 28
Frankfurt School 17, 19, 22
French structuralism 19–20
functionalism 17
Gramsci's hegemony
    concept 18, 19, 53
Griffith School 28
Hall, Stuart 19
ideological critique 17–18
Jacka, Elizabeth 24
Lazarsfeld, Paul 23
linguistic turn 25–6
McQueen, Humphrey 26
Marxist 16–18
Mayer, Henry 27–8
media power 21
Michaels, Eric 28
policy studies 9 *see also*
    policy
political economy 20–2,
    26–7
positivism 16, 22
propaganda 22
relative autonomy 18
semiology 19–20
Smythe, Dallas 20, 28
social science model 24–6
socio-political 16
structuralism 24

Turner's *National Fictions*
    24
'uses and gratifications' 70
Western Marxism 17–18
Williams, Raymond 19
media audience *see* audience
media classification *see*
    classification
Media Council of Australia
    217
Media, Entertainment and
    Arts Alliance (MEAA) 75,
    78, 84, 346
media 'gatekeepers' 334
Media Information Australia 27
*Media International Australia
    (MIA)* 28
media literacy 45
mergers, regulation of 78
messaging, instant 251, 252,
    261
Meyer, Philip 96
Michaels, Eric 28
Microsoft 96, 273, 334
Mindfood 207
mobile enterprise application
    platform (MEAP) 342
Mobile Lifestyle 265
mobile media 264–6
    everyday uses of technology
    294
mobile phones
    apps 342
    growth of 112, 121
    handsets 121
    internet subscribers 122
    MMS 264–5
    mobile broadband 126
    mobile television trials 265
    ring tones 229
    SMS 121, 264–5, 352
    third-generation (3G)
        phones 119, 121–2, 274,
        322
    uses 265
    Wireless Access Protocol
        (WAP) 264
mobile television 265
MOG 115

monopolies 78
  newspapers 100, 103
moral panic 299
Morley, David 71
Morris, Graham 182
Morrison Media 203
Mott, David 187
MP3 technology 4, 148, 232, 277
MSN messenger 261
multiculturalism 177, 297–8, 299–300
  paradoxes of media and 298–9
multimedia messaging services (MMS) 264–5
multi-user dungeons (MUDs) 251, 261
  MUDs object-oriented (MOOs) 251
Mulvey, Laura 19, 49
Murdoch, James 328
Murdoch, Keith 100, 212
Murdoch, Rupert 74, 100, 102, 107, 328, 347
music *see also* popular music
  downloading 7
  subscription streaming service 115
Muslim Australians 299, 300–2
Mutter, Alan 96
MySpace 223, 251, 254, 264, 285

Napster 235
National Broadband Network (NBN) 77, 81, 87, 117, 124, 126–8, 130, 131, 166, 251, 255, 262, 337
National Classification Code 335–6
National Classification Scheme 336, 338
national competition policy 81
National Cultural Policy 335
National Ethnic and Multicultural Broadcasters' Council 148

National Indigenous Radio Service (NIRS) 147
National Library 37
National Reform Agenda 76
National Research and Education Network (NREN) 255
National Rugby League 181, 317
natural disasters 351–2
  media role 352
Nazism 17
Neighbourhood Cable 255
neoliberalism 21
Netcast platform 343
Network Services 199
New Idea 195, 196, 198
New York Review of Books 104
New York Times 108
news agencies 104
news and current affairs
  ABC 142, 144, 176, 182, 184
  public service broadcasting 327, 328
  quality 6, 84, 142, 182
  racist representations 299, 301
  radio 143, 144
  television 304
  websites 108
News Digital Media 257
News Ltd 73, 88–9, 95, 115, 194, 199, 347%
  Murdoch's approach 102–3
  newspaper cutbacks 96
  newspaper ownership 100, 101
News Media Council 347
NewsLifeMedia 194
newspapers
  advertising 96, 99, 104–5, 107–8
  Australia, in 97–8
  business of 104–7
  circulation decline 7, 96–8
  closures 98, 105
  competition 102
  costs 105

cross-media laws 100–1
cutbacks 95–6
distribution, slowness of 99
importance in 20th century 97
Indigenous representation in 41
international comparisons 96, 102–3
internet and 99–100, 107–8
magazines in (NIMs) 199
marginalisation of role 98–9
market niche 105
market research, use of 107
nature 105
new 105–6
numbers in Australia 100–1
oligopolistic structure 106
online titles 105
ownership and control 87–8, 100–1, 103
pessimism 96
population growth and 97–8, 106
profit maximisation 106
public appreciation 99
public transport, decline in 99
rankings 99
reasons for decline 99
reduction in number 96–7
self-regulation 347
shift to digital products 95–6
state involvement 106
structure of Australian press 101–4
textual analysis 38–41
titles closing 97–8
total market size 104
Nine Network 175, 178, 179, 186–7, 239, 318
Nintendo 260, 273
Nokia 122, 274

Obama, President Barack 62, 108
objectification 49–50

obscenity laws 77, 78
One 187
online delivery 152, 168–9
OpenSignal 343
Optus 3, 113, 114, 115,
   117–18, 121, 122, 124, 126,
   128, 131, 181, 232, 255, 256
Organization for Economic
   Cooperation and
   Development (OECD) 112
Overland Telegraph Line 111
Overseas Telecommunications
   Commission (OTC) 113
ownership and control 85–9
   changes in 3, 86–8
   cross-media rules 86, 101
   debate about policy 85–6
   deregulation 85
   diversity 85–6
   foreign ownership 3, 86
   influence on policy 74
   newspapers 87–8, 100–1
   print media 87–8
   radio 88
   television 86–7

Pacific Magazines 194, 202
'Pacific Solution' 300
Packer, Frank 100
Packer, James 74, 95, 186
Packer, Kerry 74, 186, 205,
   318
   Consolidated Press
      Holdings 175
   death of 74
   Nine Network 178
paedophilia, corporate 66
parallel importing 230
pay TV
   anti-siphoning legislation
      181, 318
   commencement 180–1
   content sharing agreement
      181
   Foxtel 181
   Point Piper Accord 181
   restructuring 181
   take-up rates 181
   Telstra involvement 181

peer-to-peer (p2p) networks
   163, 188, 250, 261–2
Peirce, Charles 71
phone-hacking 6, 74, 310,
   347
Phonographic Performance
   Company of Australia
   (PPCA) 242–3
photo-sharing 261–2
Pinterest 287
piracy 60, 188, 235, 288
Please Rob Me 294
policy 73–91
   advocacy groups 75
   arts 77–8, 80
   Australia, in 77–84
   broadcasting 78–9
   competition and social
      principles, balancing 76
   convergence, challenge of
      89–90, 333–5
   cyber file sharing 235
   decentralisation 4
   deregulatory standpoint 76
   film and video 79–80
   government regulation
      77–8
   input/output distinction
      77–8
   internet 80–1
   'media mates' approach 74
   neo-classical economic
      approach 76
   normative approach 74, 76
   over-regulation 76
   ownership and control see
      ownership and control
   participation in formation
      75
   players 81–4
   political economy
      approach 74
   politics and 75
   print media 78
   public participation 75
   regulation approaches 76,
      337–8
   reviews 334–5
   stages 4

telecommunications 80–1
think-tanks 76
political economy 20–22,
   26–7, 74
politics
   representation in media
      33–4
Pong 272, 273
Popper, Sir Karl 17
popular multiculturalism 300
popular music
   Australian music business
      233
   Australian rock 227–8
   broadcasting 237–40
   CD prices/sales 230
   commercial radio 238–9
   convergence 229, 232
   copyright 234–7
   crowdfunding 231–2
   dance music cultures 242–3
   definition 227
   digital consumption 243–4
   digital sales 233
   distribution 229, 232
   festivals 242, 243
   file sharing 235
   globalisation 229
   government policy 240
   hip hop 241
   income from 241
   Indigenous music 228–9
   international 228
   live performance 240–2
   local labels 229–32
   mashups 233
   MP3 technology 232
   open source remixing 234
   participation by fans 234
   profits 231
   protection of local industry
      230–1
   regulation of broadcasting
      237–8
   remixing songs 233
   role 240
   royalties 233, 238
   schools, in 241
   software 233–4

streaming services 232–3
television 239–40
postmodern public spheres 62
Pozible 158–9
the press *see* newspapers
Prices and Surveillance
  Authority (PSA)
  inquiry into sound
  recordings 230
print media 78 *see also*
  magazines; newspapers
  ownership 87–8
privacy 309–10
  celebrity right to 310, 311
  data collection 312–13
  image blurring technology
    311–12
  legislation 312–13
  limited privilege 310
  location disclosure and
    294
  nature of 309–11
  public interest test 312
  social privacy 310–11
  viral media events 311
Productivity Commission 148
'Produser' 61
public-interest advocacy
  groups 75
Public Relations Institute of
  Australia 84
public service broadcasting
  (PSB) 327–31
  ABC *see* ABC
  arguments against 328
  commercial arrangements
    329
  digital archives 327–8
  future of 328
  globalisation, adaption to
    327
  innovation 329–30
  institutional strength 328
  local content 328
  multi-platform products
    329–31
  news and current affairs
    327, 328
  one-to-many platforms 331

predictions and debate
  327–8
role 327–8
satire 329–30
SBS *see* SBS
public sphere 62, 254, 292
  postmodern 62

Queensland floods 352, 353,
  354
Queensland University of
  Technology 28
Quickflix 120, 168

racism
  media, in 298–9, 300–1
radio
  advertising 212
  cash for comment 141, 143,
    218
  Christian radio 148
  commercial 142–4
  community radio 147–8,
    238
  daytime radio serials 70–1
  deregulation 139–40
  development 138–9
  digital transmission
    148–50
  dual system 134
  expansion 136–8
  history 134–40
  Indigenous 147
  local content 135
  music broadcasting 135–6
  ownership 88
  structure 141–8
  stunts 345–6
  talkback 135–6
  television and 135–6
  types of services 139
Rage 240
ratings 6, 64, 65, 210–11
reality TV 3, 44, 63–4, 179–80,
  306
Redfern Now 331
reflexive modernity 291
regulation *see also*
  classification; policy

media ethics 346, 348
Reid, Campbell 107
representation 6, 19, 24
  analysing 43–4, 54–6
  Arab Australians 300–1
  capitalism and 51
  concept of 43–5
  effect 46
  environment 322
  feminist theory 49–50
  Gramsci's hegemony
    concept 18, 19, 53
  ideology 51–2
  Indigenous Australians 297
  judging 45–6
  language 52–4
  meaning 44–5
  multiculturalism 297–8,
    302
  Muslim Australians 300–1
  objectification 46, 49–50
  other countries/cultures,
    from 46–7
  reality, relationship to
    44–5
  research strategies 55
  semiotics 52–4
  sexualisation 49–50
  shared cultural resource
    298–9
  social judgments, forming
    46–8
  stereotyping 50–1
  textual analysis and 34
  theoretical approaches
    48–9
  value-driven practice 47–8
  women 45–6, 49–50
resale price maintenance 105
Reuters 104
Rinehart, Gina 74
rock music *see* popular music
Roku 343
Rosen, Jay 59–60
Roy Morgan Research 99, 196
Rudd government 66, 127,
  251
Rudd, Kevin 39, 66, 143, 264
Ruddock, Andy 68

Salam Cafe 301
Samsung 122
Sandilands, Kyle 143, 346
Save Live Australian Music
  241
SBS
  budget cuts 182
  demographic 185
  documentaries 185
  establishment 177–8
  function 177, 184
  legislation 79
  multiculturalism 177–8,
    184–5, 299–300
  1990s and 2000s, in 184
  radio 146
  regulation 79
  studies 133
Scott, C.P. 108
Scott, Mark 145, 184
Screen 19
Screen Australia 82, 153, 157
Screensound 37
ScreenWest 159
SDK 343
search engines 258–9
Second Life 261
Sega 273
Seiter, Ellen 32
self-identity 291
self-presentation 292
self-regulation 77, 82–3, 347
semiosphere 36–7
semiotics 19–20, 52–4
Seven Network 179, 186–8
sexism in Australia 31–4, 41
  definition of sexism 34
  representations of women
    45–6
sexualisation 49–50
  children, of 66–7, 70
Singtel 3, 117
Sky Technologies 342
Skype 5, 120, 252, 343
smartphones 122, 232–3, 342
SmartTrans 342
SMS 121, 264–5, 352
social capital 173–4
social inclusion 241, 253–4

social media 120, 144, 189,
  251, 259, 285–6
  apps 287–8
  business of 287–8
  convergence 286–7
  emergence of 286–7
  governance 288–9
  platforms 286–7
  privacy 288–9
  regulation 288–9
  role in emergencies 352,
    353–5
social networking 263–4,
  291–2
  advertising use of 223
  celebrity material 303–4
  communication and
    networking 292
  cultural affiliation 293–4
  information disclosure to
    third parties 294–5
  interactions 293
  location disclosure 294–5
    see also location-based
    service (LBS)
  mobile media technology
    use 294
  privacy concerns 294
  using 292–3
social sciences 24–6
Sony Ericsson 122
Sony Playstation 270
Sony Walkman 232
South Park 185
Southern Cross Media 142–3
Spacewar 272
Special Broadcasting Service
  see SBS
spectrum 126
sport
  anti-siphoning regime 318
  commercialisation 317
  conflicts of interest 5
  cultural citizenship 318–19
  gender and 316–17
  ideological uses 316–17
  'live' 189, 317, 318
  media coverage 5, 315–16
  mediatisation of 315–16

popularity 316, 317
rights-sharing deals 181,
  189
stereotypes 316–17
subscription television 318
television resources 317–18
Spotify 232
Star Trek 69
stereotyping 50–1
structuralism 19–20
Summer Heights High 183
Sun 102, 13
Sydney Morning Herald 38, 103

Tabula iPad app 340
Tanner, Lindsay 76
technological convergence 4
telecommunications
  Asia-Pacific telcos 118
  Australian market 121
  conduct regulation 81
  consolidation of providers
    114–15
  Constitution 112
  consumer regulation
    129–30
  deregulation 180
  economy and 111–12
  growth of industry 112
  history 111–13
  information society
    component 2
  international 112–13, 125
  Internet *see* internet
  market share of providers
    116
  misleading advertising
    129–30
  mobile phones *see* mobile
    phones
  policy 80–1
  private partners 114
  public ownership 114
  second-tier companies
    114–15
  service providers 114–19
  services 119–25
  society and 111–12
  structural regulation 81

subscriber numbers 123
Telstra *see* Telstra
universal service
    obligations 129
Telecommunications
    Industry Ombudsman
    (TIO) 82, 256
telemarketing 218
tele-participation 63–4
telephony
    fixed line voice 124–5
    music streaming services
    232–3
television
    ABC *see* ABC
    advertising 176
    apps 343
    breakfast 187
    digital broadcasting 186
    drama series 179
    entrepreneurial 178
    establishment 174–6
    free-to-air 178–80
    future directions 188–90
    historical development
        174–8
    history and analysis 2
    influence and power 173
    lifestyle programs 179
    local content 175–6
    magazines, TV versions of
        198–9
    multi-channels 186–8
    1970s and 1980s 176–8
    number of channels 106
    overseas programs 175
    ownership 86–7, 178
    pay TV *see* pay TV
    pervasiveness, effect 173–4
    popular culture, influence
        on 176
    popularity 173–4
    reality TV 179–80
    representation on *see*
        representation
    SBS *see* SBS
    social media and 189
    studies 174
    youth television 178

Telstra 4, 80, 81, 89, 255
    NextG 122, 130
    privatisation 113, 116–17
    Sensis 116, 259
Ten Network 74, 175, 178,
    186–8
terms of service agreements
    (TOS) 288
text genre 36
textual analysis 31–42
    academic and popular
        research 35
    analysis of audience
        interpretations 38–9
    content analysis 41
    data-gathering methods
        31–2
    how to do 33–41
    media research drawbacks
        32
    own interpretations
        39–40
    purpose 32–3, 40–1
    qualitative research 40–1
    questions 33–5
    relevant intertexts 35–6
    report on results 40–1
    representation 34
    semiosphere 36–7
    summary 41–2
    text gathering 37
    text types 35
theoretical traditions 15–29
theory, meaning of 48
think-tanks 76
TiVo 337, 343
Torrentfreak 60
trade practices
    Act 35
    competition *see*
        competition
    prohibitions 78
TransACT 255
Tumblr 60, 263, 286, 287
Turner, Graeme 24
Twitter 3, 60, 120, 189, 259,
    263, 285, 286, 287, 288,
    289, 292, 294, 295, 343,
    348, 352, 353

Underbelly 187
United Press International
    103
United States
    newspapers 96–7, 103
United States Free Trade
    Agreement 3, 155, 158
Universal Magazines 199
University of Southern
    California, Annenberg
    Center for the Digital
    Future 96
user-created content 89, 271,
    286, 289, 334, 337–8
Ushahidi Maps 353

Verizon Wireless 119
video *see also* film
    content delivery 152
    games *see* electronic games
    regulation 79–80
    video-sharing websites
        261–2
Vincent Committee 175
Virgin Mobile 118
virtual worlds 261
Vodafone 113, 114, 115, 119,
    121–2, 125, 126, 131, 232,
    256
The Voice 239
VOIP technology 251, 252

war on terror 300
Warlpiri people 28
Washington Post 96
Web 2.0 2, 8, 62, 250, 259, 274,
    286, 287
Webkit 343
websites 257–8
    online news 257–8
West Australian 100, 101
Westpac Group 340
Westpac iPad app 340
White House home page 62
Whitlam government 177, 335
Who magazine 87, 199, 206, 306
Whrrl 295
Wi-Fi 264, 344
Wii 270, 273

Wikipedia 263
wikis 262–3
Williams, Kim 95
Williams, Raymond 19, 277
Wireless Access Protocol
 (WAP) 264
wireless technologies 264–6
Woman's Day 198
women
 daytime radio serials 70–1

representation of 45–6,
 49–50
World Association of
 Newspapers 99
Wright Mills, C. 23
Writers Guild in Hollywood 8

Xbox 270

Yahoo! 87, 251, 257, 259, 262

Yellow Social Media Report 288
Yelp 286
YouTube 8, 62, 120, 169, 223,
 251, 259, 262, 263, 265,
 286, 287, 292, 295, 303,
 309, 311–12, 343
 viral circulation 293

Zeebox 189